ORGANIZATION THEORY

A Behavioral Analysis for Management

THE IRWIN SERIES IN MANAGEMENT

CONSULTING EDITOR   JOHN F. MEE   *Indiana University*

ORGANIZATION THEORY

A Behavioral Analysis
for Management

WILLIAM G. SCOTT, D.B.A.

Professor of Management and Organization
School of Business Administration
University of Washington

1967
RICHARD D. IRWIN, INC.
Homewood, Illinois

First Printing, March, 1967
Second Printing, September, 1967
Third Printing, May, 1968
Fourth Printing, December, 1968
Fifth Printing, June, 1969
Sixth Printing, October, 1969
Seventh Printing, August, 1970
Eighth Printing, January, 1971

Library of Congress Catalog Card No. 67–15843

PRINTED IN THE UNITED STATES OF AMERICA

Preface

THIS BOOK is an outgrowth of my previous volume. About eighteen months ago, I began to revise *Human Relations in Management*. I knew then a simple revision was not possible. Such a book could not begin to capture the magnitude of change in administration during the last five years in research, values, philosophy, and issues. In the early stages of my work, I had not planned a new book. However, the final manuscript was so different from the original in content and orientation that it could hardly stand as a revision. Even though I carried over material, I decided a new book would represent more precisely my interpretation of organization theory and the behavioral sciences as they relate to administration.

In structuring this book, I thought a prologue was in order where epistemological questions are raised. We assume the value of science to managers for understanding and dealing with human behavior. But we do not stop often to consider the presuppositions of science in terms of explanation and action. These are important matters, especially if management intends to use the behavioral sciences as bases of policy for molding the administrative climate of the organization.

Beyond blind faith in the power of science, managers should know something of its nature and limits—particularly the behavioral sciences. The prologue was written with this in mind. It is offered in the nature of unfinished business—not a complete epistemology—for administration.

The two chapters in Part I treat the history and values of management in the spheres of human motivation and organization. I think that since 1962 a new management movement has emerged, and has become sufficiently coherent to be a distinct ideology. I label this movement industrial humanism. Its influence is considerable. If we are to interpret correctly such developments as laboratory training and planned change, it is essential to know their values and their relationship to earlier movements like human relations and scientific management. I try to create these perspectives in Part I.

Parts II and III contain most of the substantive material pertaining to organization theory developed in this book. Part II maps the human territory of administration. It approaches the subject of organization on four levels: personality organization, small group organization, the formal organization, and finally the complex organization, or system theory, which attempts to weld the various subsystems into a conceptual framework.

Selected processes that perform strategic functions within the social territory are examined in Part III. These processes, or linking functions, include status and role, social influence, communication, decision making, and balance.

Problems and issues in the human territory of management are the focus of Part IV. The crucial issues posed by bureaucracy, organizational modification, modes of influence, and the problems of management are top-priority subjects in this part. Even though we encounter the conceptual foundations of industrial humanism frequently earlier in the book, it is not until we reach Part IV that the dimensions of this new ideological wave are fully unfolded.

Finally, the epilogue is presented much in the same spirit as the prologue—as unfinished business. The proposition that organizations are governments is readily assented to but not often explored. For the most part sovereignty, law, due process, and constitutionalization are alien ideas in the various tangents administrative thought has taken. The reason probably is that not many political scientists are found in the ranks of the behavioralists who enter the world of management art and science. Yet administrative organizations act like political entities, and their managers are concerned with problems which are governmental in nature. Indeed, how can we talk about democracy or autocracy in administration without some reference to the issue of organization government?

It was pointed out to me that my first book, *Human Relations in Management,* is not a human relations book. I accept this as a fair criticism. My interests have generally been in organization theory, and my commitment to this subject has grown stronger over the years. However, I am also deeply involved in questions of philosophy which shape management thought and practice in organizations. This book, like my first, is value-laden.

Someone told me I am too young to try to be a philosopher. I graciously acknowledge this left-handed compliment with a Gertrude Berg-type shrug. I believe recent events have borne out my preoccupation. Industrial humanists clearly agree on the idea that the change agent and the social consultant bring not only science, but values as well to the so-called "target system." It is essential to know about these values, their implications, and possible alternatives to them for enlightened administrative action.

In summary the main theme of this book is organization theory. The central concepts are developed in Parts II and III. It is here that a conceptual scheme following a "systems model" is elaborated. Hopefully, the model is broad enough to include all organizations in the range of administrative relevancy. The chapters in Parts I and IV are written more specifically with business organizations in mind. Nevertheless many of the topics, that refer to value concepts and issues in organizational change and human influence, are broad enough to pertain to other types of organizations as well. It is only when we come to the last three chapters that our focus narrows to specific issues peculiar to the administrative core of business organizations.

Early in the thinking stages of this volume, Professor Warren G. Bennis, of the Massachusetts Institute of Technology, gave me valuable suggestions for staging this work. His review of *Human Relations in Management* was most helpful and influential in setting a new direction and substance for this book.

Professor Wilmar F. Bernthal, University of Colorado, read the manuscript and recommended reorganization of chapters and subsections. The changes he suggested, I incorporated wholesale.

Professor John F. Mee, of Indiana University, also reviewed the manuscript and pointed out avenues of improvement for special interest to management teachers and scholars. He, as well, provided strong motivation for "closure" when it seemed as if I never would finish.

I appreciate the resources provided me by De Paul University and the University of Washington. Without this help my work on this book would have dragged on interminably.

Finally, thanks are due to Mrs. Gloria Theobald who labored diligently in preparing the book for publication.

W.G.S.

Seattle, Washington
January, 1967

Table of Contents

PART III: PROCESS CONCEPTS IN SOCIAL TERRITORY

PART IV

EPILOGUE

INDEXES

PROLOGUE TO THE ANALYSIS

Management and the Behavioral Sciences: Explanation and Action

WHEN an administrator asks, "why B?" he wants either a *causal* explanation, "because of A," or a teleological explanation, "in order that C." If question "B" is about individual, social, or organizational behavior then he may find "A" or "C" in the behavioral sciences.

We assume that the administrator is more interested in explanations of the "C" type than the "A" type. This is because administrators are *action* oriented. Therefore, while "C" type explanations rest on "A" types, the value of the behavioral sciences to management is in the applied sense of determining the direction of change and its implementation.

Our interest in this Prologue, and for that matter in this book, is with the sciences like sociology, psychology, and anthropology which produce information and generalizations about human behavior. These fields are called the behavioral sciences. To some extent they are "interdisciplinary." But the point of view taken here is that there is not a BEHAVIORAL SCIENCE APPROACH which is defined as a master science combining in a *Gestalt* fashion all the subsidiary sciences of human behavior.

So ours is not an interdisciplinary orientation in the sense that there is an integrated science of behavior. We agree with Roethlisberger's statement that ". . . the behavioral sciences are not yet one."[1] This view is reinforced by a content examination of Berelson's and Steiner's book *Human Behavior: An Inventory of Scientific Findings*.[2] There is little here to cause one to suppose that the findings presented are interdisciplinary in character. Indeed, the sources chosen by the authors as representative of "hard data" leads one to the conclusion that psychology dominates

---

[1] Fritz J. Roethlisberger, "Contributions of the Behavioral Sciences to a General Theory of Management," in Harold Koontz (ed.), *Toward a Unified Theory of Management* (New York: McGraw-Hill Book Co., Inc., 1964), p. 41.

[2] Bernard Berelson and Gary A. Steiner, *Human Behavior: An Inventory of Scientific Findings* (New York: Harcourt, Brace & World, Inc., 1964).

the other behavioral sciences in the production of valid and reliable scientific findings.[3]

Forsaking an interdisciplinary commitment is not a great loss. The fatal assumption of the human relations movement is that the interdisciplinary approach produces a problem-solving configuration which is greater than the sum of the disciplines going into it. Rather, what happens is that the interdisciplinary approach becomes an "OK label" but, (1) the field itself is dominated by one science which has developed far beyond the others, or (2) the level of explanation about behavioral phenomenon sinks to the weakest science in the lot, or (3) there may be local combinations like social-psychology which are productive of much explanatory good but are still a long way from the interdisciplinary vision. Our encounter with the behavioral sciences in this book will be in terms of concepts and findings, their action implications for management, and some of the issues they raise.

The behavioral sciences have values for management on at least three levels. First, they formulate abstract concepts and explanations about human behavior in open systems of interdependency. This is the *conceptual* contribution to management. Second, they provide a way of gathering data and thinking about these relationships. This is the *methodological* contribution. Third, they contribute to administrative policy decisions with respect to change. This is the *action* contribution.

One of the allures of the behavioral sciences to managers is the word science itself. Science has produced wonderments in our understanding and control of nature. Why not in the sphere of human behavior as well? It is useful to look at certain scientific presuppositions and relate the behavioral sciences to them as far as possible in a short section. We will concern ourselves next with what is science, what it proposes to do, and what is meant by scientific explanation.

THE SCIENTIFIC APPROACH

Braithwaite says that science seeks to establish ". . . general laws covering the behavior of empirical events or objects with which the science in question is concerned, and thereby enable us to connect together our knowledge of the separately known events, and to make reliable predictions of events yet unknown."[4] Science attempts to simplify into general laws the processes which govern the external objects of sense perception. Ideally no scientist is satisfied with a situational explanation of events. What he seeks is a general law which covers the same event in many situations. This is why, for example, the situational approach to leader-

---

[3] Of the journals cited in their bibliographical index, over 60 percent of the total were psychological.

[4] Richard Bevan Braithwaite, *Scientific Explanation* (London: Cambridge University Press, 1953), p. 1.

ship, while widely accepted, has not been fully satisfying as an explanation of the leadership phenomenon. It is also why the individual person is discomforting to scientists. He is a structure of physiological and psychological processes which defy submission to universal laws.

Science may be divided into three parts. The first is the *field* or that part of the external world with which the science is concerned. Psychology, for instance, aims at providing explanations of individual behavior, sociology of group behavior, and cultural anthropology of the effect of social value and norms on individual and group behavior. The second part of science is the *method* by which the world of the science is studied. There probably is not such a thing as THE SCIENTIFIC METHOD—that is, the various sciences have different methods for acquiring data, testing hypotheses, and formulating laws.[5]

Most scientists, however, would agree to certain methodological presuppositions. Specifically, concepts are based upon sense impressions,[6] and theories are the result of an inductive process.[7] The tests of hypotheses, theories, and laws are instrumental, mathematical, and conditional, respectively. This means that in testing hypotheses *public* data must be employed utilizing experiments which can be *replicated*.[8]

The theories which emerge from the inductive process have to be consistent. That is, their internal constructs hang together by rules of correspondence which are expressible rigorously. This is one of the major shortcomings encountered by the behavioral sciences. The theory of the formal organization has a great deal of internal consistency but the relationships which exist among its components has yet to be expressed in mathematical form. It may be, however, that the paucity of mathematical applications to the behavioral sciences is a symptom of a deeper difficulty. After all mathematics is a shorthand. It could be that there is such a lack

---

[5] Howard Becker, "Science, Culture, and Society," *Philosophy of Science*, October, 1952, pp. 273–87.

[6] The problem encountered here is that of perception or how one goes from private experience of one's own sensations to public knowledge. Benjamin wryly observes, "But the inductive problem of how we *get* the laws is, according to the recent point of view, unimportant and belongs, in fact, to psychology. Whether the problem belongs to psychology because it is unimportant, or it is unimportant because it belongs to psychology, is not always made clear." A. Cornelius Benjamin, "Is the Philosophy of Science Scientific?" *Philosophy of Science*, October, 1960, p. 356.

[7] Induction "[is] . . . the type of nondemonstrative reasoning consisting in the generalization of propositions whether singular or general, on the basis of the examination of cases." Mario Bunge, "The Place of Induction in Science," *Philosophy of Science*, July, 1960, p. 262.

[8] The physical and biological sciences use only public data open to observation by all, but the behavioral sciences may also use private data of immediate experience. Braithwaite does not see this as an insurmountable methodological difficulty which would disqualify the behavioral sciences from the ranks of the "pure" sciences as long as they can produce empirically testable hypotheses. However, the use of private data does pose value problems when we consider the role played by the *applied* behavioral sciences in policy decisions. See Braithwaite, *op. cit.* pp. 8–9.

of verified theoretical relationships in the behavioral sciences that the expression of rules of correspondence verbally or mathematically is a rather unrewarding endeavor. Indeed, the work of the system or theory builders is currently out of fashion among empirically oriented behavioral scientists.

A final methodological presupposition is that the laws of science are *conditional*. This means that science must always be prepared to accept change. It is usually possible for reason to go beyond experience by the process of *deduction*. But reason must be ready to re-examine its deductively derived laws in the light of new experience.

The third part of science is the production of *laws* or generalizations about events. But the mere generation of laws is not sufficient in the eyes of science. The new law must be established in a higher level deductive system. At a high stage of scientific development, laws form a hierarchy with many special laws derived from a few very general laws of considerable universality. Sciences in early stages of development have so-called classificatory laws. For the most part the behavioral sciences have not moved far beyond the stage of taxonomy.

To the scientist, the field becomes the *knowable*, the method becomes the process of *knowing*, and laws become *knowledge*. Feibleman[9] has an excellent summary of the assumptions which the scientist makes about the knowable and knowledge. Let us look at the "knowable" first.

1. The external world is independent of the scientist. The researcher does not investigate his own sense impressions.

2. The uniformities of the external world are knowable. The assumption here is that the world of behavior does have stable properties; it is not entirely random. Further these properties can be uncovered by various methodological techniques.

3. The nonuniformities constitute inferences in method. This assumption is that the behavioral world possesses vast potential for change. Indeed, this potential is so great that the widespread use of statistical inference (probability theory) in the behavioral sciences is evidence of attempts by scientists to extract the last modicum of uniformity from nonuniformity.

4. The mind and the external world are similar. Reason and nature share common properties.

5. As knowledge increases the knowable recedes from the investigator. The advancement of instrumentation removes the object of study increasingly further away from the observer. This is most revealing in the behavioral sciences since the accumulation of data relies almost entirely on direct investigator participation in interviews, observations, or written surveys.[10]

6. The order of discovery differs from the order of nature. Logic is not history. This is probably the main reason why the cyclical theories of social

---

[9] James K. Feibleman, "The Scientific Philosophy," *Philosophy of Science*, July, 1961, pp. 250–57.

[10] For an excellent discussion of the "methods of inquiry" in the behavioral sciences see Berelson and Steiner, *op. cit.*, chap. 2.

change are not favored greatly today. There is no reason to suppose that history intrinsically organizes human events.

7. Sensations can be planned. This assumption is the essence of scientific experimentation. It is also an important assumption for those who plan and implement behavioral changes in organizations.

8. Lastly, experimental results are capable of being fitted into abstract structures or theories.

These eight assumptions or conditions are the predispositions which the scientist carries into the field of study. We have already looked at method rather closely so now let us ask what assumptions underlie knowledge itself. The first assumption is that the knowledge of relations increases faster than the knowledge of qualities. A perfect example of this is the span of control concept in management. We have a fairly intricate understanding of the relationships which exist in superior-subordinate systems. But we are not able to qualify these relationships successfully in the sense of making policy prescriptions about ideal spans.

Second, knowledge is limited by the techniques employed in obtaining it. This assumption involves us in the problem of indeterminancy or the extent to which the instruments used in collecting information interfere with the subjects observed.[11] This matter is dealt with at length in another chapter. But its relevancy is evident for the behavioral sciences where the experimenter often becomes part of the system he is studying.

The third assumption is that language is never completely adequate to represent the world. Jargon has become one of the crucial shortcomings in the behavioral sciences. Often a word becomes a scientific fact, rather than the other way around. As Gross says, "Independent groups of men strive to order their experiences by inventing languages. . . ." These languages generate internal criteria of consistency that are largely unrelated to concrete reality. The objectivity of a science may be reduced to playing a game with standardized word projections, uniformly and consistently, but not necessarily more empirically.[12] The problems created for the behavioral sciences by language games have led Roethlisberger to remark:

When things get tough and our findings seem paradoxical or contradictory, let us stop trying to seek for explanations by means of new words, lables, and concepts that are more logically consistent, psychologically appealing, or culturally attractive.

Instead let us concentrate upon the findings that our conceptual schemes have helped us to obtain. Let us keep looking at these findings for the simple uniformities which they may reveal in the form of "x varies with y." These

---

[11] For an interesting discussion see Norbert Wiener, "The Role of the Observer," *Philosophy of Science,* July, 1936, pp. 307–19.

[12] Llewellyn Gross, "An Epistemological View of Sociological Theory," *American Journal of Sociology,* March, 1960, pp. 442–43.

simple empirical propositions are our most enduring possessions. With them explanation begins, without them there is nothing to be explained.[13]

Beyond the need for a specialized, less-ambiguous language to express behavioral concepts, theories, and laws, the other obvious conclusion of Roethlisberger's position is that the behavioral sciences should stay with grass roots empiricism until more basic facts and relationships are uncovered. Hence, the quest for knowledge through the accumulation of scientific facts ought to be the paramount objective in the behavioral sciences. This form of enumerative empiricism is reminiscent of Bacon's concept of induction. He recommended for science the collection of facts like the gathering of "countless grapes, ripe and in season.[14]

As Popper says, "this legendary method . . . still inspires some of the newer sciences which try to practice it because of the prevalent belief that it is the method of experimental physics."[15] If this is what we must wait for then it is likely to be a long time before the behavioral sciences will do administrators much good. Fortunately the delay is not necessary. Even though they are primitive in their explanatory potential compared to the natural sciences, the behavioral sciences are useful to men of affairs. They have an explanatory power which is necessary to look at rather closely.

EXPLANATION

Scientific theory lays down a difference between what needs to be explained and what does not, and *how to* make the explanation or account for the difference. Scientific theory needs a set of uniformly behaving entities in terms of which those deviating need explaining. Thus, the role of science is to provide explanations. But, in fact, explanation is a philosophic concept with several meanings. And the meaning which the behavioral scientist might have to settle for would not be at all acceptable to a natural scientist. But this is getting a bit ahead.

P. W. Bridgman, the exponent of operational analysis says, ". . . the essence of an explanation consists in reducing a situation to elements with which we are so familiar that we accept them as a matter of course and our curiosity rests."[16] There is, according to Bridgman, no end to the process of explanation. But in the operational sense, any attempt to explain beyond the limits of an experiment is meaningless. This is because every concept is equivalent to a corresponding set of operations. No operations, no meaningful concepts!

However, every experiment, every finite experience, is surrounded by

---

[13] Roethlisberger, *op. cit.*, p. 65.

[14] Francis Bacon, *Novum Organum*, I, p. 123.

[15] Karl R. Popper, *The Logic of Scientific Discovery* (New York: Basic Books, Inc., 1959), p. 279.

[16] P. W. Bridgman, *The Logic of Modern Physics* (New York: The Macmillan Company, 1927), p. 37.

what Bridgman calls a "penumbra of uncertainty." As the limits or outer edges of an experiment are reached, the final stages become hazy and the elements of experimentation less familiar requiring us to admit new possibilities for explanation. But until new operations are devised for the new elements of experience to be investigated the questions raised about them are meaningless.

Without pushing operational analysis to the extreme, it does raise important questions for the behavioral sciences. We might ask if our concept of the informal organization is bounded by the operations of sociometry? Or if we have five different methods of observing and measuring small group relationships, do we in effect have five different concepts of the informal organization? The same questions can be posed for other important behavioral concepts, such as role conflict. One of the causes of no end of argument and disagreement in the behavioral sciences stems from operationally defined concepts where two research studies ostensibly investigating the same phenomenon have just one thing in common—the name of the object under investigation.[17]

Explanation, in other spheres of opinion, is more than simply data drawn from a set of operations creating a psychological cessation of curiosity. Data are not explanations, but inferences obtained from data tend to be. Now, logically there may be just as many inferences, some diametrically opposed, as there are operations measuring the same object of experience. However, according to Youlton, explanation exists only when a fact or law is related to the system to which it belongs.[18] This implies that we have sufficient knowledge of the system to perform this relationship. The new law or fact must be shown to be coherent with the whole.

This is suggestive of why the concept of the formal theory of organization, bureaucratic theory, if you wish, dies so slowly. Even though much behavioral data has been unearthed which points to the disutility of the formal theory of organization, this information has not been framed in an alternative conceptual scheme which rivals the classical model for completeness, consistency, and, indeed, serviceability in the world of practical application.

---

[17] An excellent example comes to mind. It pertains to two studies of organizational growth, one conducted by Mason Haire and the other by F. Stuart Chapin. Both studies sought to establish, using different operations, a generalized explanation of organizational growth configurations. Haire in his research found that organization growth corresponds to the square-cube law, which produces a linear pattern, whereas Chapin found in his study that organizational growth corresponds to a spiral configuration. See Mason Haire, "Biological Models and Empirical Histories of the Growth of Organization," in Mason Haire (ed.), *Modern Organization Theory* (New York: John Wiley & Sons, 1960), pp. 277–83 and F. Stuart Chapin, "The Optimum Size of Institutions: A Theory of the Large Group," *American Journal of Sociology,* March, 1957, pp. 449–60.

[18] John W. Youlton, "Explanation," *British Journal of the Philosophy of Science,* November, 1959, p. 205.

It might seem terribly narrow to say, but it takes more than facts to overturn an established system of thought and behavior. Indeed, a competing system must be offered which in time demonstrates that it has greater factual resolving power, and hence, greater practical utility than the older system. Curiously enough it may be only from the arena of applied arts that the value of different approaches to organization are proven.

In the same vein, but somewhat more generally, Youlton points out that there are two sets of criteria which prove out any explanatory system.[19] The basic set includes understanding and intelligibility; the specific set are testability and deducibility. In these respects explanation demands:

1. Definite information and grasping of preliminary concepts.
2. Independence from particular minds.
3. Statements of antecedent conditions of the phenomenon to be explained.
4. Statements of general laws under which the phenomenon to be explained is subsumed.
5. Internal consistency of the logical system.
6. Empirical content of both that which is to be explained and that which explains.

The behavioral sciences aspire to both the general and the specific requirements of explanation. But these criteria demand a rigor which is not yet available within these sciences at least on the level of human behavior. Does this mean that we must abandon all hope of explanation from these sciences? Some scholars would say so, yet there are others who feel explanation has levels or degrees. In this latter sense the behavioral sciences explain behavioral phenomenon but not with the same degree of reliability or generality that natural sciences show in their areas of competence.

What the Behavioral Sciences Explain

True explanation occurs when an event is successfully predicted and systematically related to a general prediction system.[20] That some aspects of the work in the behavioral sciences fulfill this requirement cannot be argued. But for the most part such laws as those which have been discovered refer to animal behavior. When it comes to human behavior and social phenomena, the explanatory character of the behavioral sciences is less impressive. This is due, of course, to the complexity of social facts coupled with (1) their less repeatable nature, (2) their less-direct observability, (3) their greater variability, and (4) the greater difficulty of isolating experimental factors from unwanted influences.[21]

---

[19] *Ibid.*, pp. 196–97.

[20] Becker, *op. cit.*, p. 277.

[21] Morris R. Cohen, "Reason in Social Science," in Herbert Feigl and May Brodbeck (eds.), *Readings in the Philosophy of Science* (New York: Appleton-Century-Crofts, Inc., 1953), pp. 663–64.

Those who follow a hard empiricist line feel that the only creditable explanations of an event are those which are made in reference to a general law following the acceptable methods of knowledge of initial condition, confirmation using public data, repeatability of tests, and so on. But there are some in both the behavioral and even the natural sciences who feel that explanation also exists in the process of *verstehen.*

Verstehen means understanding but a peculiar type of understanding which is applicable to human behavior. Its proponents, such as Riesman,[22] see it as a method for explaining human behavior. *Verstehen* gives the certainty that a particular interpretation of an event is possible because we (the investigators) have had the same feeling or experience ourselves. Thus, we give an empathetic interpretation or confirmation to the observation.[23]

Critics of this position indicate that *verstehen* may generate hypotheses, insights, programs, and policies for research. But the subjectiveness of the process disqualifies it as an alternative to the accepted methods of explanation which we have already discussed.[24] The argument seems partially to reduce to the issue of whether or not explanation is possible in the absence of public data and tests which are able to be replicated.[25] As we have said, Braithwaite seems to think so, if the "illuminations" are capable of test. If not, these empathetic behavioral understandings may still serve for policy decisions, but they do not have the standing of a true scientific explanation.

In conclusion, Figure A shows three levels of explanation in science. The first level, the theoretic, is the one most often associated with the more advanced natural sciences, such as physics. They have a high degree of confirmation, but what is more they have the ability to relate predictions and laws to more general theories and broad deductive systems.

The second level is where a large amount of empirical work in the behavioral sciences is found. While impressive correlational values are

---

[22] "One must be willing to take seriously theories which are not established, and even theories which are, in some formal sense, 'refuted,' when they offer a real illumination and insight, which will undoubtedly turn out to be a partial illumination." David Riesman, "Some Observations on Social Science Research," in *Individualism Reconsidered and Other Essays* (Glencoe: The Free Press, 1954), p. 473.

[23] Theodore Abel, "The Operation Called *Verstehen*," in Herbert Feigl and May Brodbeck (eds.), *Readings in the Philosophy of Science* (New York: Appleton-Century-Crofts, Inc., 1953), p. 679.

[24] Arthur C. Danto, "On Explanations in History," *Philosophy of Science* January, 1956, p. 18.

[25] The problem of replication causes the behavioral scientist particular difficulty in bridging the gap between his theoretical language and his operational language. Any theory of causality requires a theory of how the other variables besides those being measured behave as well as how they link up in an explanatory system. A satisfactory theory must contain measuring operations of a high degree of face validity, but measurement language often becomes entangled in theoretical language such that it is difficult to separate the two. See H. M. Blalock, Jr., "Theory, Measurement, and Replication in the Social Sciences," *The American Journal of Sociology*, January, 1961, pp. 343–45.

FIGURE A
Levels of Explanation

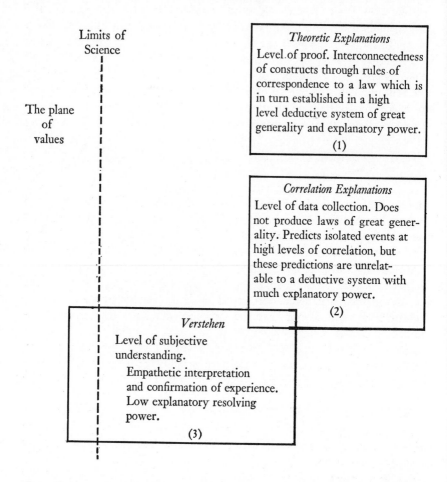

Limits of
Science

The plane
of
values

Theoretic Explanations
Level of proof. Interconnectedness
of constructs through rules of
correspondence to a law which is
in turn established in a high
level deductive system of great
generality and explanatory power.
(1)

Correlation Explanations
Level of data collection. Does
not produce laws of great generality. Predicts isolated events at
high levels of correlation, but
these predictions are unrelat-
able to a deductive system with
much explanatory power.
(2)

Verstehen
Level of subjective
understanding.
Empathetic interpretation
and confirmation of experience.
Low explanatory resolving
power.
(3)

often discovered, the predictions based on them are not related to more
general deductive systems, to the degree they most certainly are in the
natural sciences. This level of explanation often produces negative predictions, as such and such will not occur, or such and such will not occur
together. The values of these kinds of predictions rests largely in protecting us from striving for incompatible goals. As Hayek points out, "The
service of a theory which does not tell us what particular events to expect
at a definite moment, but only what kinds of events we are to expect within
a certain range, or on complexes of a certain type, would be better described by the term orientation than by speaking of prediction."[26] It is in
part because of this idea of orientation that we show correlational explanation overlapping *verstehen*. High and significant correlations may suggest

---

[26] F. A. Hayek, "Degrees of Explanation," *British Journal of the Philosophy of
Science,* November, 1955, p. 255.

policy orientations useful for shaping long-range programs, although they cannot provide short-range predictions of specific outcomes.

Verstehen is the third level of explanation. Because of the subjective and individualized character of this process, much of it lies outside the limits of science in the plane of values. We also observe, in Figure A, that it shares somewhat in the correlational level of explanation. This indicates that *verstehen* à la Riesman, may rely on empirical data as well as subjective judgments for its own peculiar form of illumination and insight. It is probably out of this level where most policy and action recommendations come from behavioral science consultants to administrators.

BEHAVIORAL SCIENCES AND ACTION PROGRAMS

The preceding sections stated the philosophical ground rules of science and explanation. This section investigates how these assumptions, carried forward in the behavioral sciences, relate to requirements of administrative action. We said on page 3 that, ". . . the value of the behavioral sciences to management is in the applied sense of determining the direction of change and its implementation." This point must be reemphasized because it is the applied aspects of the behavioral sciences which are instrumental in forecasting and generating change in administrative organizations. We do not intend to ignore in the following chapters the conceptual and the methodological values of these sciences. Much of the material to come deals with concepts. We simply wish to stress here that the true worth of the behavioral sciences to management is their contribution to policy decisions and programs of action.

Pure and Applied Sciences

Pure and applied sciences depend on similar assumptions about the knowable, knowing, knowledge, and explanation. But despite this common philosophical dependency, the division between pure science and applied sciences has carried the connotation that the applied sciences are somehow tainted. The popular image of science is that applied sciences use and adapt the abstractions, laws, and generalizations of the pure sciences to solve concrete problems. While this may be true in the case of engineering and physics, and this is not altogether certain, it is not applicable to the behavioral sciences. As Gouldner says, "Any metaphor which conceives of applied social science as the offspring, and of the basic disciplines as parents, is misleading. It obscures the point that the applied sciences often contribute as much to pure science as they receive from it.[27] Indeed, if the applied branches of the behavioral sciences stood in dependent and subsidiary relation to pure science, administration would derive little of value from them. The reason rests in the tradition of positivism and its effect on the behavioral sciences.

---

[27] Alvin W. Gouldner, "Explorations in Applied Social Science," *Social Problems*, January, 1956, p. 19.

Positivism. Since the time of Auguste Comte the behavioral sciences in America and England, have been strongly influenced by positivism. Positivism, which Allport equates with operationalism, "holds that the devices employed in experimentation or measurement shall be specified in the definition of every concept."[28] As we have seen, unless this requirement is met all other concepts are meaningless. Positivism, however, is much more.

First, it is a form of empiricism which focuses on minute phenomena; in psychology there is strong belief in the equivalence of species. That is a basic feature of human behavior, such as learning, can be studied in lower forms of life without loss of meaning in generalizing to a similar process in higher forms of life. So while some psychological experimentation, or sociological for that matter, might seem trivial, it is in keeping with the positivistic heritage of the study of microphenomena rather than macro.

Second, positivism imposes on the behavioral sciences a posture of ethical neutrality. The necessity of nonideological involvement has long been held in the natural sciences. So partly in their efforts to emulate, the behavioral sciences assume that they cannot formulate and specify *ends* for their clients.

For our purposes, the significance of these observations is that the nature of positivism is deeply *conservative.* "For the positivist, measurement and formalization have been the ideal and almost the sole criteria of scientific knowledge since . . . 1830."[29] The conservative-positivistic syndrome has imposed a nonchange orientation on the behavioral sciences. There are theories of change but few theories of changing. This is because positivism holds that only the established order can be studied scientifically. All else is speculation, intuition, nonscience, etc.[30]

Since one cannot scientifically go beyond the content of observed events, then the sociological positivistic principle is that custom makes anything right or wrong. And to the positivist, custom changes only in three ways:[31]

1. Because of change in life condition.
2. Because of imperfect cultural transmission.
3. Because of internal strains (contradictions) in the culture.

One needs little imagination to see how this tradition imposes an antichange flavoring to sociological research. Sociologist Wilbert E.

---

[28] Gordon W. Allport, *Becoming* (New Haven: Yale University Press, 1955), p. 11.

[29] Frank E. Hartung, "The Social Function of Positivism," *Philosophy of Science,* April, 1945, p. 123.

[30] Arthur K. Davis, "Social Theory and Social Problems," *Philosophy and Philosophical Review,* December, 1957, p. 203.

[31] Hartung, *op. cit.,* p. 131.

Moore has said, "The mention of 'theory of social change' will make most social scientists appear defensive, furtive, guilt-ridden, or frightened."[32]

But sociology is not alone in this situation. Allport observes that in the area of cognitive processes, which deal with perception, learning, and concept formation, psychologists are far more at home with static constructs of maps and sets.[33] Thus an area which is closely related to personality development—the dynamics of personality change—has been approached by scientists out of a "being" rather than a "becoming" framework.

Gouldner, summarizing the relationship between pure and applied sciences, makes four points.[34]

1. Applied social scientists are more likely to use the concepts than the generalized propositions of their basic discipline.

2. Not all concepts or theoretical models of pure social science are equally useful to applied social scientists.

3. Applied social scientists will more likely borrow from their basic disciplines those concepts and theoretical models which aid them in understanding or producing changes.

4. When the basic discipline does not provide theoretical systems or concepts aiding the applied social scientist to deal with change, the latter will develop these himself.

From this we must admit that if the primary role of applied science is to predict and produce change it finds little of a generalized nature in the reservoir of behavioral research to aid it in its task. Indeed, not only is this difficulty obvious, but also is the negative tone of the pure branches of the behavioral sciences toward change itself. Such is the problem confronting those who feel that organizations must be redirected to extract greater effectiveness, participation, and allegiance from their members. The positivistic tradition of the behavioral sciences has little room for this sort of endeavor for two reasons at least.

1. Any change of this magnitude introduces elements which cannot be made explicit experimentally—operationally. This is so because the area of application is macro in scope; i.e., a change in the leadership climate of an organization.

2. Changes of the kind visualized by the applied behavioral sciences imply value judgments about outcomes which cannot be wholly corroborated objectively. While the notions that a democratic, participative leadership climate produces a more effective work environment has empirical support, it is as well an article of faith among many applied behavioral scientists.

[32] Wilbert E. Moore, "A Reconsideration of Theories of Social Change," *American Sociological Review*, 1960, p. 810.

[33] Allport, *op. cit.*, p. 14.

[34] Gouldner, *op. cit.*, p. 172.

This returns us to the idea that whatever use the applied behavioral sciences are in administrative planning and programming of change it is likely that their greatest contribution will come as *verstehen* where the values of the scientist will have a substantial role in framing recommendations to clients. It probably will not be in the rigorous positivistic, scientific tradition except to the extent that some experimentally verified operation has specific value to management; for example, the measuring of IQ's for personnel selection.

Now let there be no doubt that this type of activity and others of this genera are very important. They consume the time and energy of many scientists and administrators. The work in industrial psychology has been instrumental in developing numerous programs of rational personnel management some of which are indispensable for handling many essential functions such as selection, interviewing, training, promotion, and counseling. But our interest is in the larger impact of the behavioral sciences in shaping and achieving policy goals. It is precisely at this point where all the pure scientists and most of the applied scientists drop off from the few who are attempting to apply the concepts and the methods of the behavioral sciences to the large-scale problem of changing human organizations.

Levels of Scientific Participation in Policy Formulation

Alderson said that the pragmatic test of truth does not appeal to the man of action. He has little patience with the proposition that a statement is true because it works. Not only must data work, but a program of action must be framed with the data in mind. The program is aimed at the objective transformation of the situation. "Facts alone, or facts and generalizations together cannot dictate the shape of action or relieve the executive of his ultimate responsibility for the commitment of resources to action."[35] Thus, as we have already stated, programs, not data, ought to be both the administrative and scientific focus of attention.

Traditionally behavioral scientists have been employed on the level of collecting facts for decision purposes.[36] They are often destined to serve in "intelligence staff function," generating data sought by policymakers on concrete situations. This function is partially what Baritz[37] has in mind when he speaks of behavioral scientists as "servants of power."

Another level of scientific employment is "dynamic applied research" where more than data magnitudes are reported but an analysis is given of underlying causal relationships which produce the data presented. The

---

[35] Wroe Alderson, "A Systematics for Problems of Action," *Philosophy of Science*, January, 1951, p. 18.

[36] The levels of policy participation are adapted from E. A. Shills, "Social Science and Social Policy," *Philosophy of Science*, July, 1949, p. 223–27. See also Robert K. Merton, "The Role of Applied Social Science in the Formation of Policy: a Research Memorandum," *Philosophy of Science*, July, 1949, pp. 161–81.

[37] See Loren Baritz, *The Servants of Power* (Middletown, Conn.: Wesleyan University Press, 1960).

emphasis here is still on *what* happened rather than *why* it happened, and most importantly *what to do about it*. However, some appraisal of causal relationships is an explanatory step which is necessary in developing a program of change.

The third level of policy participation is the use of behavioral scientists as advisers to policymakers. Here, situational research is not primarily intended. But rather the knowledge and wisdom of the adviser is sought. Obviously, the extent of participation is fixed by the level of scientific knowledge which is relevant to particular policy decisions and the value judgments of the adviser.

The last level of participation is the "therapeutically oriented research" through which the behavioral scientists simultaneously discover causal factors and recommend programs to alter the environment. This function combines data collection, analysis, recommendations, and policy execution. It fulfills most completely the requirements Alderson sets for action programs.

This level of participation reflects what numerous behavioral scientists and administrative theorists view as the proper role of the behavioral sciences in the policy function. It incorporates the clinical notions of applied research. More recently this point of view has been restated by Gouldner as the Clinical Model.[38] And to bring it right up-to-date, it is a precise term covering the action role suggested for the behavioral sciences by the "planned change" school, about which we have more to say in Chapter 13.

The Use of Science and Scientists in Action Environments

A good deal of what we have said so far in this section is negative. But it is important to account for why the behavioral sciences run into difficulties in action surroundings. The real status of the behavioral sciences lies somewhere between wholehearted integration into the policy-making environment and complete detachment from it. The applied behavioral sciences are enjoying more influence in administrative setting than ever before. There are at least four reasons why.[39]

First, the behavioral sciences are an integral part of our culture. Perhaps, a reason for this is because they hold the promise of solving some of the important social issues of the time—issues which are incapable of even discussion within the parameters of the natural sciences.

Allport observes on the point of cultural acceptance that, "No one who attempts to depict the spirit of the age in which we live can possibly overlook the importance of psychological science in the culture of today.

[38] Gouldner, *op. cit.*, pp. 178–80.

[39] Warren G. Bennis, "Theory and Method in Applying Behavioral Science to Planned Organizational Change," presented as keynote address to the International Operational Research Association (Cambridge, England: September 14, 1964), (mimeographed), pp. 26–31.

It is gradually assuming a commanding influence upon the thought forms of Western man."[40] Probably the same can be said for the lesser behavioral sciences as well. In any event, even the most casual observer of administrative behavior could hardly miss the influence of these sciences upon managers. Their cumulative effect is yet to appear, but most likely it will in successive generations of executives.

Second, because of the cultural acceptance of the behavioral sciences, their applied branches are regarded less as stepchildren today.

Third, since the end of World War II the accomplishments of applied research cannot be ignored. Because of the acceleration of research projects, data, reports, and analyses we know more about human behavior than we ever have.

Fourth, there is presently a feeling among scientists, administrative theorists, and many executives, that something is wrong with the way we define and organize work. It is hoped that the applied behavioral sciences, besides data, will offer programs for direction and orientation of policy which will create more effective structures of work relationships.

---

[40] Allport, *op. cit.*, p. 1.

PART I

Perspectives in the Analysis

IT WAS ONCE SAID that those who forget history are destined to relive it. With this warning in mind, the chapters in this part are aimed at giving the reader a "feel" for the background of the modern administrative attitude toward the human elements in administration. Beyond this we wish to underscore in the following pages the determinants which changed administrative practice and philosophy.

Traditionally beginning with the work of Charles Babbage and Andrew Ure in the 1830's we see broadly in the flow of events a gradual movement away from the harsh autocratic and paternalistic spirit governing management's relationships with the "hands." In its place has arisen the more benign influence of democracy and the recognition of the dignity of each person regardless of his organizational function.

In the course of changing management attitudes, specific manifestations called programs appear. Those with the greatest impact and the more enduring appeal are scientific management and human relations. But there are reasons to believe that these movements are waning and another is on the rise. It is industrial humanism—the latest outgrowth of the social ethic.

But beyond these programs or movements, which are merely localized adaptations to the task-oriented organization, are sweeping social and cultural changes. Who can deny that the popularity of some aspects of scientific management was largely the result of the fact that they vibrated sympathetically with notions of individualism dominating economic and managerial philosophy around the turn of the century? In the same way, the current ascendancy of industrial humanism must be the result of contemporary acceptance of the notions of democratic liberalism and the rights of man. To appreciate the present texture of management thought it is essential to get the perspective of what went before and the wider circle of events surrounding the notable landmarks on the managerial continuum.

The mission of the next two chapters is to give this perspective. The reader will see, for example, that in the earlier stages of management thought the application of motivational philosophy and techniques was restricted mainly to business organizations—except the work of Morris L. Cooke who applied scientific management concepts to public administration.

These limited perspectives persisted up to a fairly recent date. But with the expanding influence of the behavioral sciences, and with the natural desire to widen managerial science to higher degrees of generality, organization theory emerged. With it the concepts of human motivation, small group behavior, social influence, leadership, decision making, participation, executive development, and so on were generalized as meaningful ideas for managers in all kinds of organizations. Instead of business firms, it is more fashionable, and indeed more pertinent, to talk about "Organizations" which include many varieties and types with differing goals under this heading. So then the tools of organizational analysis and influence are as relevant for sheltered workshops, government agencies, and military formations as they are for business firms. These developments can do nothing but lend vitality to the field.

CHAPTER 1

Management Approach to Human Motivation: A Historical Overview

INDUSTRIALIZATION creates special human problems which require for solution a distinctive philosophy and combination of techniques. Management's decisions on the choice of philosophies and techniques, out of a wide range of alternatives, depend on assumptions about the nature of human behavior and human motivation. The question underlying the formulation of such assumptions is: what sort of job situation best affords employees work satisfaction but also stimulates them to act so as to accomplish objectives?

There is a scarcity of a management point of view concerning human motivation in pre-20th-century literature. However, a few early commentators on the industrial scene were attracted to problems which can be considered motivational. The early views of motivation can hardly be called the humanistic approach familiar to modern management. Yet the background that follows provides perspective to the advances introduced into management thought.

EARLY CONTRIBUTIONS

The contributions of Andrew Ure and Charles Babbage to management thought appeared in the early to middle 1830's.[1] The imprint of Adam Smith and his *Wealth of Nations* is indelibly impressed on the philosophy in these works. While Ure and Babbage quibbled with Smith on some minor issues they accepted the economist's doctrine on major points. But for their purposes Babbage and Ure interpreted Smith as saying:

1. The greatest social good will result from each person operating in his own intelligent self-interest.

---

[1] Andrew Ure, *The Philosophy of Manufacturers* (London: Charles Knight, 1835); and Charles Babbage, *On the Economy of Machinery and Manufacturers* (3d ed.; London: Charles Knight, 1833).

2. Wages are the primary motivating force behind employee action.

3. The profits of employers and the wages of employees are geared to productivity.

The synthesis of these three assumptions is best expressed by the term *mutuality of interests.* This concept means that the well-being of the worker and of the employer is inextricably allied. For example, it is in the best interest of the employee to work hard because higher productivity means more money, and money is the main source of his satisfaction and happiness. At the same time, of course, the employer profits from increased productivity. Babbage, it appears, was the first to note the significance of this theory for manufacturers.[2] He observed that workers should be more concerned with producing for the mutual benefit of themselves and their employers rather than combining in unions against their employers. A union of operatives, Babbage felt, would not further the objectives of either the employees or the employers.

Ure also accepted the money-and-motivation equation and the mutuality-of-interests concept. He went beyond Babbage, however, in describing other benefits of industrial employment not directly associated with wages.

Ure discussed the salutary moral, health, and educational influences of industrial employment upon operative employees. These "fringe benefits" of factory employment, plus high wages, were to Ure important motivational features. His account of the "salubrious" conditions in factories seems overdrawn and naïve in the face of evidence concerning the life of an industrial worker in early 19th-century England.[3] But Ure's purpose in writing his book was in part to contrast factory life with the expiring cottage system of production. Perhaps from this point of view life in a factory was preferable.

Ure's and Babbage's attitudes toward human motivation and happiness in manufacturing were simple and optimistic. Labor was deemed a commodity which responds to immutable economic laws. Money and motivation were synonymous. The economic man was paramount. The individualistic ethic was a source of inspiration; if people were left free to seek their own interests the maximum in material and nonmaterial benefits would accrue to the individual and also to the community.

Not much of particular interest for management appeared between the time of Babbage and Ure and the first contributions of the scientific management writers. This period was roughly 50 years; it was ended by papers before the American Society of Mechanical Engineers. These

---

[2] As he states, "A most erroneous and unfortunate opinion prevails amongst workmen in many manufacturing countries, that their own interest and that of their employers are at variance." Babbage, *op. cit.,* p. 250.

[3] Book the Third entitled the "Moral Economy of the Factory System" in Ure's *Philosophy of Manufacturers* contains his interesting descriptions of the life of factory "inmates." See Ure, *op. cit.,* pp. 277–429.

papers were reproduced in the *Transactions* of the society. The beginning of the scientific management movement was an address by Henry R. Towne, "The Engineer as Economist," in 1886.[4] After Towne's plea to the engineers to build a management literature of "science and practice" several other contributions were made by W. E. Partridge, Towne himself, and F. A. Halsey.[5] Frederick W. Taylor's paper delivered in 1895 was significant because it anticipated his later work in scientific management.[6]

These writers reduced the problem of human motivation and satisfaction in industry to money. Interestingly enough, the fundamental philosophy of these writers was not essentially different from the philosophy expressed by Babbage and Ure. They endorsed the concept of mutuality of interests. High wages, high productivity, and greater human happiness were viewed as interconnected elements in the philosophic framework of industrial efficiency.

The central problem which concerned these writers was elevating wage systems to a scientific plane. The older forms of piece-work wage plans were criticized by the writers because they did not result in the desired motivational outcomes. Taylor commented, "The ordinary piece-work system involves a permanent antagonism between employer and men . . . even the best workmen are forced continually to act the part of hypocrites to hold their own in the struggle against the encroachments of their employers."[7] Taylor claimed exactly the opposite results for his system, the differential piecework system, which ". . . makes each workman's interests the same as that of his employer."[8]

Taylor's plan to induce proper worker motivation was a revolutionary form of piecework payment; Towne and Halsey proposed programs of premium wage payments. These latter plans were designed to give workers monetary rewards directly in relation to time saved in the performance of jobs. Although these plans were *not* suggested as substitutes for older forms of piecework pay methods they did attempt to introduce another economic incentive into a wage-payment structure. One of the members of the society, a Professor Denton, commented that Towne's "gain-sharing" plan answers the question of: "How can we at once get the

---

[4] Henry R. Towne, "The Engineer as Economist," *Transactions*, American Society of Mechanical Engineers, Vol. 7 (1886), pp. 428–32. All subsequent references in this chapter to the transactions of this society will be identified by the initials ASME. The page numbers include the major paper, and discussions of the paper where appropriate.

[5] W. E. Partridge, "Capital's Need for High-Priced Labor," *Transactions*, ASME, Vol. 8 (1886–87), pp. 269–94; Henry R. Towne, "Gain Sharing," *Transactions*, ASME, Vol. 10 (1889), pp. 600–26; and F. A. Halsey, "Premium Plan of Paying for Labor," *Transactions*, ASME, Vol. 12 (1891), pp. 755–80.

[6] Frederick W. Taylor, "A Piece-Rate System," *Transactions*, ASME, Vol. 16 (1895), pp. 856–903.

[7] *Ibid.*, p. 856.

[8] *Ibid.*, pp. 856–57.

workman to squeeze a little more out of himself and at the same time be good-natured in doing it?"[9]

These early wage-system proposals were efforts to objectify the remuneration of the "economic man." The major assumption—that man was primarily motivated by and received work satisfaction from economic gain—was not questioned. Given this premise the next logical and scientific step was to quantify, as far as possible, the economic contribution of a man to the firm and the firm's reward for the contribution.

Money was the 19th-century answer to the "motivation-satisfaction" question posed at the start of this chapter. This attitude was amplified to some extent by introducing systems to determine "fair" wages and techniques to promote "mutuality of interests." But management's understanding of human motivation did not progress very far in this century. Economic man was still rattling his coins. Contrasted with the lean years of the 19th century, management literature proliferated during the 20th century. Management thought also grew more sophisticated.

THE SCIENTIFIC MANAGEMENT MOVEMENT

The social and technological changes underway in America in the late 19th century accelerated in the 20th century. The result was that management needed new values consistent with the proximate and dependent condition of people in an industrial society, and it also needed better methods to cope with complex technology and business organization.

The scientific management pioneers[10] sought answers to this twofold problem. They realized a new approach was required to accomplish two tightly knit goals: (1) higher industrial efficiency through improved management practice and (2) greater collaboration among those working in industry. The pioneers hoped to achieve this second goal through the promotion of a true mutuality of interests.

Testifying before a congressional committee, Taylor had the following to say about scientific management:

> Scientific management is not an efficiency device . . . not a system of figuring costs . . . not a piecework system . . . not a bonus system . . . not a premium system . . . it is not holding a stop watch on a man and writing things down about him . . . it is not time study, it is not motion study . . . it is not any of the devices which the average man calls to mind when scientific management is spoken of. . . .
>
> . . . In its essence scientific management involves a complete mental revolution on the part of the workingmen . . . and it involves an equally complete mental revolution on the part of those on the management's side. . . .

---

[9] Towne, *op. cit.*, p. 616.

[10] Frederick W. Taylor, Frank and Lillian Gilbreth, Morris L. Cooke, Henry L. Gantt, and Harrington Emerson.

The great revolution that takes place in the mental attitude of the two parties under scientific management is that both sides take their eyes off of the division of the surplus as the all-important matter, and together turn their attention toward increasing the size of the surplus until this surplus becomes so large . . . that there is ample room for a large increase in wages for the workmen and an equally large increase in profits for the manufacturer.[11]

Taylor's testimony revealed that scientific management was more than techniques; it was a way of thought. The early advocates of this movement felt it was truly a revolution in management values—a revolution through which the pioneers saw a way to obtain a mutuality of interests among those dependent on business for a living. The immediate objectives of a mutuality of interests were visualized as human collaboration in the organization effort and ever-increasing productivity accompanied by a wider, more equitable distribution of an economic surplus.

The pioneers felt that if these proximate objectives could be realized the ultimate objectives of industrial harmony and human work satisfactions would be forthcoming. Looked at in this way, scientific management was a philosophy reflecting the social ethic. It attempted to reconcile the paradox of the need for cooperation among people in industry with the philosophy of individualism.[12]

Taylor made it clear that the philosophy of scientific management should not be confused with its mechanisms. In the following sections, the major areas of scientific management which have broad human implications are discussed. The mechanisms, such as specific wage plans, or motion and time study, which fall into these areas are avoided so that just the major issues are developed. No one area constitutes the total philosophy of scientific management. They are all part of an inclusive format designed to solve the problem of human collaboration by mutuality of interests and greater productivity.

Work and Wages

Taylor, his disciple Gantt, and the Gilbreths labored extensively with the analysis of work and the setting of the "right" wage. Taylor's approach to work was a significant step in the science of management.

---

[11] "Special House Committee to Investigate the Taylor and Other Systems of Shop Management," reprinted in Frederick W. Taylor, *Scientific Management* (New York: Harper and Bros., 1947), pp. 26, 27, 29–30. These quotes were presented in this form by Reinhard Bendix, *Work and Authority in Industry* (New York: John Wiley & Sons, Inc., 1956), p. 276.

[12] Taylor characterizes scientific management by four elements: (1) science, not rule of thumb; (2) harmony, not discord; (3) cooperation, not individualism; (4) maximum output, not restricted output. Frederick W. Taylor, *Principles of Scientific Management* (New York: Harper and Bros., 1919), p. 140. Taylor's third characteristic might appear contrary to the individualistic ethic. This point is cleared up when he says, ". . . All great things will be done by that type of cooperation in which each man performs the function for which he is best suited, each man preserves his own individuality and is supreme in his particular function, and each man at the same time loses none of his originality and proper personal initiative."

Work was taken for granted for thousands of years. No one attempted to deal with the elements involved in the performance of a task. Taylor tackled this problem.

The right wage was an explosive issue that grew out of an industrialized economy. Taylor felt the wage paid must be related in some way to the work done. To find the relation, he formulated time-study experiments to measure work. Taylor's work was refined and expanded by the Gilbreths' method analysis and Gantt's task and bonus system.

It is apparent that these writers considered the analysis of work and the payment of wages crucial elements of industrial harmony. In essence, their theory ran that given a fair wage, scientifically set in relation to a fair amount of work, an employee would be induced to see his objectives for higher wages as mutually compatible with the employer's objectives for profit. Thus, the reasons for unions to protect workers from exploitation would be eliminated and organized labor would have no reason to exist.[13]

This theory of work and wages makes a good deal of sense, given the unwavering nature of the motives of economic man. An honorable worker, according to Taylor, will soldier (loaf) only if he feels he is not going to be properly rewarded for work. But if his efforts are honestly evaluated and fairly paid the worker will be only too happy to produce more to get greater rewards.

The Standardized Man

Standardization, to the pioneers, went beyond the standardization of parts, equipment, and methods. Standardization was applicable to all the personnel in the organization. The "quest for the one best way" led the Gilbreths to the systemization of personnel practices, notably selection and training. The theory is that a standardized system of personnel techniques will produce a standardized man. The standardized man is an integral part of the theory since by studying him the most reliable motion and time data are obtained.[14] And these data are basic to process engineering, work simplification, and wage payment.

Standardization was applied to employee levels above the operative. Functional foremanship was Taylor's unconventional view of organizing personnel in the most effective way. Without running the course of Taylor's arguments, it should be enough to say that work was to be divided so that men with certain abilities (specializations) could be placed where their talents would be best utilized. Taylor felt that under the military-type organization a foreman was required to have too many specialized tasks to supervise. Functional foremanship allowed concentration on a few special-

---

[13] Hoxie, one of the first major critics of scientific management, did not see it this way. While he felt the theory of scientific management was acceptable, he thought many abuses would appear in practice. See Robert Franklin Hoxie, *Scientific Management and Labor* (New York: D. Appleton and Co., 1915).

[14] L. M. Gilbreth, *The Psychology of Management* (New York: Sturgis and Walton Co., 1914), p. 152.

izations within a job toward which each foreman had some individual bent. Of course, the concept of functional foremanship could be applied to higher levels of management as well. The result would be a high degree of standardization and specialization in all managerial positions.

Gantt, Emerson, and Cooke saw from several points of view the benefits resulting from standardization. Gantt was interested in standardization for establishing "habits of industry." Habits of industry meant conditioning workers for industrial life. It included management planning, training of workmen, and noting the influence of the informal organization on job behavior. Emerson assigned a major role to standardization in his efficiency principles which he visualized as guides for management. Cooke applied the concept of standardization to public administration.[15]

Standardization was a necessary part of scientific management. From the human standpoint it is interesting to observe that the pioneers did not feel that standardization would result in less incentive or greater feelings of anonymity for employees. Indeed, their attitude was that standardization increased employee happiness and self-realization.[16]

Prosperity and Productivity

The prosperity and productivity ideals of the scientific management pioneers were closely related to their notions of work and wages just discussed. Gantt noted that the utilization of resources is more effective through scientific management. As a result, greater wealth would be created, contributing to national social and economic well-being.[17]

Taylor was convinced an individual's prosperity can only be maximized when national prosperity is maximized, in the long run of course. In this respect, as noted before, the interests of workers and employers would be allied. If workers produced as much as possible, and managers managed scientifically, relatively higher degrees of prosperity would be enjoyed by all. "Relative degrees" is an important modification. Taylor believed that many factors contributing to prosperity were outside the control of the scientific manager. However, he insisted that firms run

---

[15] For representative examples of these three authors' viewpoints see H. L. Gantt, "Training Workmen in the Habits of Industry and Cooperation," *Transactions*, ASME, Vol. 30 (1908), pp. 1037–63; Harrington Emerson, *The Twelve Principles of Efficiency* (New York: The Engineering Magazine Co., 1913); and Morris L. Cooke, *Our Cities Awake* (New York: Doubleday, Doran and Co., 1918).

[16] For example, see Gilbreth, *op. cit.*, chap. VI. Mrs. Gilbreth used the same reasoning as the eminent sociologist Émile Durkheim in justifying standardization in humanitarian terms. Durkheim felt that the division of labor with its subsequent specialization and standardization was a source of solidarity. He said, "The division of labor presumes that the worker, far from being hemmed in by his task, does not lose sight of his collaborators, that he acts upon them, and reacts to them." Émile Durkheim, *On the Division of Labor in Society* (Glencoe: The Free Press, 1947), p. 373. (The date of the original work was 1893.)

[17] H. L. Gantt, "Efficiency and Democracy," *Transactions*, ASME, Vol. 40 (1918), pp. 799–808.

scientifically would fare better than others, even in periods of economic decline.

The immediate goal of scientific management was increased productivity closely tied to the profit and service objectives of business. But the pioneers had faith that scientific management could accomplish other aims as well. These other objectives were the broader considerations of social welfare. Again, this is the mutuality-of-interest idea applied on a much wider scale; that is, the goals of society, industrial employees, consumers, and owners of businesses are mutual and can be realized by the same device—scientific management.

Scientific Management and Welfare

Frank and Lillian Gilbreth working as a team made important contributions to scientific management. Lillian Gilbreth is a psychologist by training, and one of her early books dealt with the scientific application of psychology to management. One section of this book reveals what scientific management can do to improve the welfare of employees. In short, Mrs. Gilbreth said scientific management provides for:

1. Physical improvement of workers (increased health, better color and general appearance).
2. Mental development (wider interest, deeper interest, increased mental capabilities).
3. Moral development (personal responsibility, responsibility for others, appreciation of standing, self-control, "squareness").
4. Contentment, brotherhood, and the "will to do." (These developments are natural consequences of item three—moral development.)[18]

These effects of scientific management, predicted by Mrs. Gilbreth, are somewhat reminiscent of the "salubrious" benefits industrial employment had on factory "inmates" observed by Ure almost 80 years before.

Gantt and Emerson also forecast welfare consequences of scientific management, but they made their predictions on an international scale.[19] They considered the efficiencies resulting from scientific management as the cornerstones of national strength. The nations most proficient in industrial efficiency would rise to international supremacy. Gantt pointed out that in a successful industrial nation the industrial leaders will move into positions of national power. He understood the necessity for American business leaders to develop an attitude of social consciousness not only in dealing with employees but also in supplying services to the community. Only in this way, Gantt felt, could the menace of socialism be overcome.

---

[18] Gilbreth, *op. cit.*, chap. 10.

[19] H. L. Gantt, *Work, Wages, and Profits* (New York: The Engineering Magazine Co., 1911), esp. chap. 9; and Emerson, *op. cit.*, chap. 1, 2.

The Implication of Scientific Management

The scientific management movement laid the foundation for the professionalization of management. While the pioneers may have recognized this point, they did not exploit it. The key idea, however, was presented in 1913 by Edward D. Jones as a result of a historical study of famous administrators of the past. Jones observed that, ". . . The dominant problem now is one of originating and formulating a science of administration."[20]

Jones singled out for special emphasis:

1. The trusteeship role of management, occasioned by the separation of ownership from control.
2. The duality of administrative skills: human skills and process skills.
3. The development of a "whole new race of executives."

Jones concluded that scientific management was just a tool for professional managers. This "new breed" of management by necessity would have to look beyond the simple dictums of profit making and economic man in order to make decisions which would enhance industrial social solidarity. The "new manager" had to be a leader of men.[21] An understanding of the complex interrelationships of people, groups, methods, firms, and industries had to come within the scope of executive decision making.

Jones was ahead of his time. His work makes an excellent transition into the next periods because he anticipated much of what was to happen. Up until 1920, the history of management thought was dominated by scientific management. This movement provided a new set of management values.

CHANGES IN THE 1920's

The bulk of the pioneers' contributions to scientific management was made before World War I. After the war these contributions were expanded. The expansions in depth appeared in the form of more analytical approaches to the mechanisms of scientific management. Many refinements in motion and time study, cost analysis, and wage measurements were offered. The expansions in breadth included the introduction and use of psychology in management practice.

The economic work motive stressed by the pioneers began to decline in popularity. Money and motivation, it was recognized, were not synony-

---

[20] Edward D. Jones, *Industrial Leadership and Executive Ability* (New York: The Engineering Magazine Co., 1920), p. 5. (First edition appeared in 1913.)

[21] Gantt was very much aware of Jones's work, and agreed with his views. See H. L. Gantt, *Industrial Leadership* (New Haven: Yale University Press, 1916), chap. 1.

mous. Psychology offered suggestions for the satisfaction of work motives which were essentially noneconomic in nature. Personnel policies were designed to meet such employee needs as recognition, participation, accomplishment, and security.[22]

It must also be recognized that the 1920's were the period of the "open shop" or "American plan" movement. This movement was geared to defeat organized labor by giving workers directly what they had to get indirectly through the union and the process of collective bargaining. Better wages figured into the American plan, but this program also included many fringe benefits and organized worker activities. The success of the American plan was demonstrated by the decline in union membership during the twenties. However, the movement collapsed in 1929 for obvious reasons.

The mutuality-of-interests objective as the source of human collaboration was not changed, although the content of scientific management was broadened to include both material and nonmaterial motives for work. But probably of greater significance was the beginning of experiments in human relations at the Hawthorne plant of Western Electric in the 1920's. The findings of this research did not have much effect on management philosophy until the 1930's, so it will be discussed in the next section.

DEVELOPMENTS IN THE 1930's

It is odd that the general disenchantment with business resulting from the depression in the 1930's did not prevent this period from being one of the most fruitful in the production of management ideas. Several strands of thought solidified in this decade and the direction of future thought in management was established. A full appreciation of this period involves the discussion of a number of related developments. These developments are treated in this order:

1. The professionalization of management.
2. The business plan.
3. The organization.
4. The human relations movement.

---

[22] The 1920's were heydays for industrial psychologists. It was popular to think that people naturally do not like to work and that more and more money will not yield more and more happiness. A flood of literature during this time showed the "broader" applications of industrial psychology. The following are some books of the period with indicative titles: Cecil D. Burns, *Industry and Civilization* (New York: The Macmillan Co., 1925); Stuart Chase, *Men and Machines* (New York: The Macmillan Co., 1929); L. Frankel and Alexander Fleisher, *The Human Factor in Industry* (New York: The Macmillan Co., 1920); J. D. Houser, *What the Employer Thinks* (Cambridge: Harvard University Press, 1927); W. D. Scott, *Science and Common Sense in Working with Men* (New York: Ronald Press, Co., 1921); John H. Van Deventer, *More Work per Man: Tested and Selected Methods of Managing Men* (New York: Engineering Magazine Co., 1921); W. Eugene, *Human Engineering* (New York: Appleton and Co., 1921).

The Professionalization of Management

Ownership and Control. The separation of business ownership from control and the numerical increase of people in managerial functions contributed to the management professionalization trend. Berle's and Means's masterly analysis, *The Modern Corporation and Private Property*,[23] was like a manifesto for the professionalization of management. It was the contention of Berle and Means that the modern corporation upset the traditional theory of property in which ownership and control of property were inseparable qualities. In many companies the stockholders, while legal owners, were for all practical purposes deprived of the privilege of control over their property.

This peculiar by-product of the corporation device placed management in a stewardship position. Stewardship can be visualized as management running a corporation to achieve the objectives of the owners. Basically, management acts as an intermediary between the corporation on one hand and the owners of the corporation on the other hand. This concept of stewardship resembles a "pure theory." The corporate structure allows management to operate fairly independently of the controls traditionally associated with the ownership of property. This situation often places management in a good position to exploit an organization's resources for ends not necessarily owner oriented.[24] The idea of exploitation also applies in cases where management's inside knowledge of a special situation allows it to profit although no damage is done to the corporation. These exploitive opportunities might overstate the case somewhat; the ethics of the management of every corporation must be judged on the merits of the situation. The realistic point of view is that professional managers, in the modern, complex world, are often better able to handle an owner's property than is the owner himself.

Organizational Size. Another phenomenon contributing to the professionalization of management was expansion in organizational size accompanied by a rapid increase in administrative personnel. The problem of size and bureaucracy had started to unfold early in this century and by 1930 was in urgent need of analysis. Measurements of bureaucratic growth indicated that the numbers of administrative personnel in business organizations were expanding at a faster rate than were the so-called production employees.[25] The ratio of administrative employees to production employees in 1937 stood at 17.7 percent, while this same ratio in 1899 was 7.7 percent.[26]

---

[23] Adolf A. Berle, Jr., and Gardiner C. Means, *The Modern Corporation and Private Property* (New York: The Macmillan Co., 1932).

[24] *Ibid.*, p. 354. Berle's and Means's observations on this point anticipated a more extensive analysis of managerial exploitation by Burnham. See James Burnham, *The Managerial Revolution* (New York: The John Day Co., 1941).

[25] Bendix, *op. cit.*, chap. 4. This chapter gives an excellent account of the bureaucratization process.

[26] *Ibid.*, p. 214.

Thus, more managers were appearing with specialized functions. The division of labor in management required consideration of internal coordination. The framework of business organization was becoming exceedingly complicated and needed explanation.

In summary, the impetus to management professionalization was provided by:

1. An accelerated use by business of the corporation device which in turn, created a climate that made the stewardship concept very significant.[27]

2. The rapid growth in organizational size, accompanied by the appearance of more and more employees in management jobs.

The embryonic management profession did not have a particularly inclusive or sophisticated body of thought with which to approach the technical and human problems created by these changes in the business institution. There were, to be sure, the philosophy and the techniques inherited from the scientific management pioneers. But these contributions did not meet professional needs. The philosophical aspects of early scientific management had almost utopian overtones. But when the pioneers considered specifics, the application was generally to the operative levels of the organization.

A professional approach needed a rather high level of abstraction, plus universality and practicality in explaining what management does and how an organization works. Two routes were followed to meet this need for a professional philosophy: process and the human routes.

The Business Plan

Ralph C. Davis' *Industrial Organization and Management* is probably one of the most enduring and representative examples of the process route to a modern management philosophy.[28] The quality of this work is in its comprehensiveness. Davis deals with the universality of business elements. Starting with a philosophy, he derives business objectives, ethics, policies, and the role of leadership in business. From here he moves to the business functions of creation, distribution, and finance, and then to an analysis of the management functions of planning, organizing and controlling. All these elements are woven into a business plan.

Davis was not the first to write about industrial management but he was the first to generalize the management process. Although he discusses specifics such as quality control, maintenance, supply, and the like, these find direction in the fundamentals laid out at the beginning. This work, coming as it did in the 1930's, filled a definite need for management since it was professionally oriented.

---

[27] The reader should not interpret this to mean that the corporation device was peculiar to the 1920's and the 1930's. The rush to incorporate was begun by businesses in the late 19th century.

[28] See Ralph C. Davis, *Industrial Organization and Management* (New York: Harper and Bros., 1939).

The Organization

Another aspect of the process route to a management philosophy was the study of organization. And to organize is to establish a cooperative system.[29]

This statement has dual implications. The first is a notion of action —*organizing;* the second is the result of organizing action—*organization.* This duality created difficulties for a theory of organization. Organizing, as a management function, can be dehumanized. That is, the relationships among work, the work place, and the people who do the work can be established without reference to personality. However, the product of the organizing activity—organization—cannot be managed without considering the people involved.

Many of the attempts to explain the organizing process and organization were fuzzily handled because of the duality problem. Both Dennison[30] and Dutton[31] offered thoughts on the organization question early in the 1930's. They began with the premise that the organization was a system and then they interpreted the effect the system has on the individual.

Henry Dennison, in particular, was concerned with the human side of organization. Such matters as social environment, leadership, teamwork, coordination, and mutuality of interests are found in his book. Both Dennison and Dutton devoted much space to showing how the individual can be adjusted to the demands of the organization system by managements' use of fairly conventional personnel techniques like training, job analysis, and placement. Neither of these works, however, possessed an integrated picture of organization, nor did they put forth a clear exposition of the process of organizing as connected to the functions of management in an organization.

The outstanding work which solved the duality problem by ignoring it was *Onward Industry* by Mooney and Reiley.[32] Mooney's and Reiley's main hypothesis was the distinction between organizing as a depersonalized process and the day-to-day personalized administration of an organization. Organizing activities, in the authors' views, takes place before administration of the organization. Thus, organizing is placed on the level of a science whereas administration they consider an art.

Mooney and Reiley were not concerned with techniques. They devel-

---

[29] This concept of the organizing process is based upon the work of Barnard. See Chester I. Barnard, *The Functions of the Executive* (Cambridge: Harvard University Press, 1938), esp. chaps. 6, 7.

[30] Henry Dennison, *Organization Engineering* (New York: McGraw-Hill Book Co., Inc., 1931).

[31] Henry P. Dutton, *Principles of Organization* (New York: McGraw-Hill Book Co., Inc., 1931).

[32] James D. Mooney and Alan C. Reiley, *Onward Industry* (New York: Harper and Bros., 1931). Later revised by Mooney and published under the title *The Principles of Organization* (New York: Harper and Bros., 1947). All subsequent references to this book will be made to the later edition.

oped a sequential arrangement of principles to demonstrate the meaning and logic behind functional relationships in formal organizations. The first of these principles is the coordinative principle. Defined, this principle means an "orderly arrangement of group effort, to provide unity of action in the pursuit of a common purpose."[33] Essential to this principle are doctrine, discipline, and mutual service. Later, Barnard made much the same point in describing the foundations of the formal organization as communication, willingness to contribute action, and common purpose.[34]

The second principle is the scalar principle, which is the grading of duties according to the degree of authority and corresponding responsibility. The functional principle is the third; it involves the differentiation of duties performed in the organization.

Mooney and Reiley did not have much to say about running the organization once organizing activities were completed. The task of solving the problems of day-to-day management of people was left to Elton Mayo and his group.[35] The Hawthorne studies caused revolutionary changes to occur in management philosophy and practice. We turn briefly to the human relations movement because of its importance in the historical continuum of management thought.

The Human Relations Movement

The Hawthorne Studies. The Western Electric experiments at its Hawthorne plant began as a straightforward attempt to determine the relationships between work environment and productivity. The results of the experiments conducted at the Hawthorne plant led the researchers to conclude that they were dealing with classes of sociological and psychological phenomena which could not be adequately explained with the tools of analysis developed up to this time. The formal organization was shown to be merely a "blueprint" of structure. The Hawthorne studies exposed many management misconceptions. An organization is more than a formal arrangement of functions. *It is a social system.* The organization is a system of cliques, grapevines, informal status systems, and rituals; it is also a mixture of logical and nonlogical behavior. The Hawthorne experiments demonstrated that the people in the organization want to participate and to be recognized. They are not rabble but individuals with psychological drives and social yearnings.[36]

The Hawthorne studies created an alternative explanation of human behavior at work. It gave management, through the human relations movement, a new set of assumptions and decision criteria for motivation.

---

[33] *Ibid.,* p. 5.

[34] Chester I. Barnard, *The Functions of the Executive* (Cambridge: Harvard University Press, 1938), chap. 7.

[35] Elton Mayo, F. J. Roethlisberger, William J. Dickson, T. N. Whitehead, and L. J. Henderson.

[36] A complete report of the Hawthorne studies may be found in F. J. Roethlisberger and William J. Dickson, *Management and the Worker* (11th printing; Cambridge: Harvard University Press, 1956).

These assumptions came from the behavioral sciences, whereas the traditional assumptions were essentially economic. Figure 1–1 is given for the convenience of comparing the two classes of behavioral assumptions. It is important to note in concluding this section that the Hawthorne researchers were in their turn indebted to a famous sociologist for their theoretical constructs and models. The parallels between Vilfredo Pareto's concepts and those of the Hawthorne human relationists are shown in Appendix 1.

FIGURE 1–1

Traditional versus Human Relations Assumptions Concerning Human Behavior

Traditional Assumptions	*Human Relations Assumptions*
	1. *From psychology* *a*) Man is diversely motivated. *b*) Man is not always rational; he often behaves nonlogically in terms of the rewards he seeks from work. *c*) Man is interdependent, and individual behavior frequently must be explained in terms of the social setting at work. *d*) An executive can be trained in "good" human relations practice.
1. People try to satisfy one class of need at work—*the economic need.* 2. There is an automatic sharing of goals in an organization; that is, no conflict exists between individual and organizational objectives—*mutuality of interests.* 3. People try to maximize rewards—*rationality.*	2. *From sociology* *a*) The social environment on the job affects and is affected by those in the situation and not only by management. *b*) The clique or informal organization is a reality, and it affects and is affected by the formal organization. *c*) Job roles are more complex than job descriptions suggest because of personal and social factors inherent in job functions. They are usually excluded in job analysis techniques, however. *d*) The organization must be realistically viewed as a social system composed of numerous interacting parts. 3. *From social psychology* *a*) People are not always anxious to see their objectives in the light of organizational objectives. People have to be influenced. *b*) Communication channels carry information relating both to the logical-economic functioning of the organization *and* to the feelings and sentiments of the people who work in the oganization. *c*) Participation in the decision-making process has a positive effect on morale and productivity. *d*) Teamwork is essential for cooperation and sound technical decisions.

Adapted from Leavitt's comments on organization theory in Harold J. Leavitt, *Managerial Psychology* (Chicago: The University of Chicago Press, 1958), pp. 291–303.

The Administrator

The professionalization of management followed two routes to arrive at a modern philosophy which met the tests of universality and practicality. Davis, Mooney and Reiley made basic contributions to a technical philosophy of management; the Harvard human relationists contributed the human aspects of a management philosophy. The concept of the administrator evolved from a merger of these routes.

Two sets of skills are needed by an administrator. The first is composed of those skills which enable him to practice competently such functions as planning, organizing, and controlling. These functions include the human element, of course. But people in the light of these functions are only one of a number of productive factors which must be coordinated for the administrator to be effective in achieving the organization's objectives.

The second set includes those skills uncovered by the findings of the human relations experiments at the Hawthorne plant. The conclusions of these experiments focused on the administrator as a motivator of people. To be adequate in this capacity the administrator needs to be equipped with more than the "logical" skills inherent in the functions of planning, organizing, and controlling. Additionally, the administrator has to view the organization as a system of relationships. He has to approach, concretely and with a clinical attitude, such matters as the small group, communication, status, social and psychological needs of employees, and social roles and personality. *In short, the administrator has to be an expert in understanding and handling the variety of technical and human relationships in an organization's social system.*

The ultimate pre-World War II expression of the concept of the administrator was given by Chester I. Barnard in his book *The Functions of the Executive.*[37] In this book he discusses two executive imperatives—achieving in organizations technical effectiveness and human efficiency. Effectiveness refers to the technical capacities of management to accomplish organizational goals through planning, organizing, and controlling. Efficiency pertains to motivating or to shaping and securing of participant needs. In short, effectiveness is impersonal, efficiency is personal. In Barnard's scheme, both are necessary to secure a cooperative system. Barnard attempted in this way to synthesize the process and human branches into which management thought divided in the 1930s.

A LOOK BACK

This chapter has reviewed over 100 years of history—roughly, from 1832 to 1940 (see Figure 1–2). It is a history of a search for philosophy, values, and techniques to be used by management in governing its rela-

---

[37] Chester I. Barnard, *op. cit.*, pp. 19–20, 50–55.

tions with employees. It is also a history of an evolution in management thought regarding human motivation. There is quite a contrast between Babbage's and Ure's approach to motivation and the findings of the Hawthorne researchers.

FIGURE 1–2
Landmarks in Management Thought

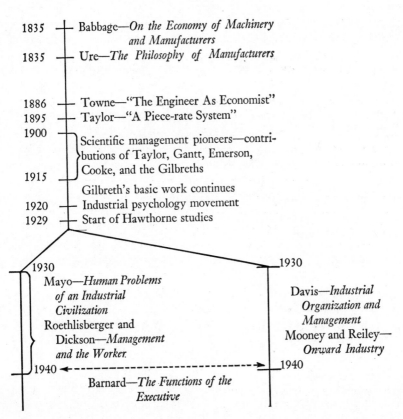

1835 —— Babbage—*On the Economy of Machinery and Manufacturers*
1835 —— Ure—*The Philosophy of Manufacturers*

1886 —— Towne—"The Engineer As Economist"
1895 —— Taylor—"A Piece-rate System"
1900 ——
       Scientific management pioneers—contributions of Taylor, Gantt, Emerson, Cooke, and the Gilbreths
1915 ——
       Gilbreth's basic work continues
1920 —— Industrial psychology movement
1929 —— Start of Hawthorne studies

1930
Mayo—*Human Problems of an Industrial Civilization*
Roethlisberger and Dickson—*Management and the Worker.*
1940
Barnard—*The Functions of the Executive*

1930
Davis—*Industrial Organization and Management*
Mooney and Reiley— *Onward Industry*
1940

Building on the scientific management movement, Jones's prediction of the professionalization of management began to materialize in the 1930's. Along with the professionalization trend came management philosophies oriented toward the social ethic. The concept of the administrator and his human skills amply demonstrates the impact of the social ethic on management thought. The administrative notion was in large part a product of a search for values to offset the collision effect, in the same way as scientific management was an early approach to this same problem. Such terms as plans, coordination, leadership, the human factor, teamwork, collaboration, social system, equilibrium, and efficiency are symbolic of a philosophy reflecting an ethic rooted in a social value system.

The ascendancy of the professional manager was an unparalleled event.

In the face of growing technical and human problems he had to prove himself not only from the standpoint of his organization but also to society in general. The new manager had to emphasize peace and harmony in the industrial system. Only in this way would organizations make a positive contribution to a society characterized by proximity and dependency. The next chapter deals with those forces which changed management practice by redirecting organizational values.

APPENDIX: Pareto and the Human Relationists

THROUGH the research, writing, and evangelical zeal of the human relationists, the importance of human skills in dealing with human situations was hammered home to management. The results of the Hawthorne experiments provided a fountainhead of philosophy which influenced contemporary management attitudes.

Yet the theoretical edifice built by the Harvard human relationists was not new. Knox points out, "Pareto's treatise on general sociology provided the major theoretical framework for the Western Electric research."[38] Thus Pareto, one of the last great sociological system builders, contributed a steppingstone toward a modern philosophy of administration.

Following Knox, it appears that Pareto's theories found in his *The Mind and Society*[39] were introduced informally to Mayo, Roethlisberger, and their associates by Lawrence J. Henderson, a physiologist on the Hawthorne research team. Knox's case is that, aside from Henderson, the Hawthorne researchers were not aware of the extent to which they were influenced by Pareto.[40]

A comparative analysis of Pareto's general sociology and the major works of the Hawthorne human relationists reveals striking similarities in the theoretical systems. Figure 1–3 presents the central ideas flowing from the Hawthorne experiments. This figure also shows some of the most evident parallels found in Pareto's work and in the work of the human relationists. The concepts of the social system, logical and nonlogical behavior, equilibrium, the functions of language, and the circulation of the elite are the essential features of the theoretical scheme of Pareto and the human relationists.

[38] John B. Knox, "Sociological Theory and Industrial Sociology," *Social Forces*, March, 1955, p. 242.

[39] Vilfredo Pareto, *The Mind and Society*, trans. and ed. Arthur Livingston (New York: Harcourt, Brace and Co., 1935).

[40] Henderson's study of Pareto is demonstrated by his essay. See Lawrence J. Henderson, *Pareto's General Sociology* (Cambridge: Harvard University Press, 1935).

From the experiments and the theoretical explanation of the findings of the experiments, the Hawthorne researchers dramatically showed the fallacy of early management attitudes regarding the motivation of people. The atomistic, self-seeking economic man was effectively dispatched. A new era and a new philosophy focusing on the human skills of management were introduced.

FIGURE 1–3

Parallelisms: Pareto and the Hawthorne Human Relationists*

Pareto†	The Human Relationists‡
1. The social system	**1. The social system**
Pareto's definition of a system is mutually dependent variations of variables. Society is a cluster of interdependence, but variable, units. The concept of interdependence of the units in a social system is a key part of Pareto's theoretical framework (see pars. 2060–66; 2079–104).	"By 'system' is meant something which must be considered as a whole because each part bears a relation of interdependence to every other part" (ref. *A*, p. 551).
	The concept of the social system plays an essential part in the philosophical orientation of the Hawthorne researchers. The significance of the interdependence of the social and physical components of the work environment is noted also in ref. *B*, Chap. X, esp. pp. 184–87, and in ref. *C*, p. 256.
	Roethlisberger and Dickson note their indebtedness to Pareto for the concept of the social system in ref. *A*, p. 272.
2. Logical and nonlogical behavior	**2. Logical and nonlogical behavior**
a) By logical behavior Pareto means logical actions that conjoin means to ends not only from the standpoint of the subject performing them but from the standpoint of other persons who have more extensive knowledge (par. 150).	*a)* In trying to separate fact from sentiment in human actions (or verbalizations of such actions), the human relationists defined a fact as ". . . a statement from experience involving sensory processes and physical and logical operations, such that if the statement is challenged there exist certain generally accepted procedures by means of which the statement can be tested. . . ." The connection between this approach and Pareto's definition of logical behavior is evident when tied in with human conduct (ref. *A*, chap. XII).
b) Nonlogical behavior was dealt with by Pareto under the term "residues," or sentiments (par. 145–248). At times Pareto treats sentiments as manifestations of residues; at other times he uses the terms "residues" and "sentiments" interchangeably. Rationalizations of nonlogical behavior were termed "derivations" by Pareto (pars. 249–367).	*b)* Nonlogical behavior and the concept of sentiments are a basic aspect of the human relationists' analysis.
Nonlogical conduct originates in definite psychic states, sentiments, subconscious feelings, inclinations, preconceptions, and so on. These residues or sentiments are essential to the equilibrium of the social system.	Sentiments mean the same thing to the human relationists as residues mean to Pareto (ref. *B*, chap. II, and ref. *C*, chap. 15).
Nonlogical conduct is contrary to logical behavior in that the objective ends of nonlogical actions differ from the subjective purpose of such actions. Residues or sentiments change slowly; they tend to persist. Derivations or rationalizations change rapidly. (For further references see pars. 1397–686).	Whitehead analyzes some experimental results of the Hawthorne study in terms of certain of Pareto's classes of residues—for example, persistence of aggregates and instinct for combination (ref. *C*, pp. 226, 232).
	Relative to Pareto's concept for derivations, Roethlisberger observes: "One of the most time-consuming pastimes of the human mind is to rationalize sentiments and to disguise sentiments as logic" (ref. *B*, p. 91).

3. Equilibrium

Pareto defines equilibrium in the following way: "... the state of X is such a state that if it is artificially subjected to some modifications different from the modification it undergoes normally, a reaction at once takes place tending to restore it to its real, its normal, state" (par. 2068).

The social system, residues, and equilibrium are integrally connected in Pareto's general sociology. Equilibrium is a logical and operative necessity of a system as Pareto conceives it. Residues function to maintain social equilibrium by acting to resolve social forces. (For further reference see pars. 2067–78, 2203–2236.)

4. The functions of language

Language to Pareto is simply a vehicle for expressing (reflecting) logical and nonlogical actions in terms of words. (See Index-Summary of the Theorems, pp. 1927–30.)

5. The circulation of the elite

The elite is defined by Pareto as the ruling class in society. The circulation of the elite is a process whereby the quality of this class is maintained. The function of the elite class is to provide imaginative leadership. (See pars. 2477–85).

3. Equilibrium

The human relationists treat equilibrium in much the same way as Pareto handles it. Roethlisberger and Dickson, following Henderson (who in turn follows Pareto), define social equilibrium as "... an interaction of sentiments and interests in a relation of mutual dependence, resulting in a state of equilibrium such that if that state is altered, forces tending to reestablish it come into play" (ref. *A*, p. 365; for further reference on this point see ref. *C*, pp. 225, 257, ref. *B*, chap. X).

Equilibrium has a value connotation to the human relationists in that the administrator functions to maintain equilibrium and thereby preserve social values of the cooperative system (ref. *B*, p. 193).

4. The functions of language

The human relationists talk of language as functioning in logicoexperimental, emotive, and daydreaming capacities. Logicoexperimental language is associated with logical forms of behavior; emotive language is connected with nonlogical behavior (ref. *B*, pp. 88–92).

5. The circulation of the elite

Mayo made much of this concept. He considered the function of the elite as maintaining equilibrium through successfully dealing with problems associated with gaining greater human collaboration. Mayo considered the elite of his time (1933) as the "elite of yesterday." To handle modern problems, he felt, the present elite must circulate and be replaced by those more capable of administering human situations (ref. *D*, chap. VIII).

* The references noted in discussing the five parallels should be taken as suggestive, not exhaustive. Space does not permit cross references among the human relationists themselves or elaborate cross references between the human relationists and Pareto.

† Unless noted in the text of Figure 1–3, all references to Pareto are made in terms of his paragraph numbers. The source used is the American edition translated and edited by Arthur Livingston. See Vilfredo Pareto, *The Mind and Society* (New York: Harcourt, Brace and Co., 1935).

‡ The key for references to the human relationists is as follows:
Ref. *A*: F. J. Roethlisberger and William J. Dickson, *Management and the Worker* (Cambridge: Harvard University Press, 1939; 7th printing, 1956).
Ref. *B*: F. J. Roethlisberger, *Management and Morale* (Cambridge: Harvard University Press, 1941, 12th printing, 1956).
Ref. *C*: T. N. Whitehead, *The Industrial Worker* (Cambridge: Harvard University Press, 1938), Vol. I.
Ref. *D*: Elton Mayo, *The Human Problems of an Industrial Civilization* (2nd ed.; Boston: Graduate School of Business Administration, Harvard University, 1946).

CHAPTER **2**

A Philosophy of Human Behavior
at Work

ARISTOTLE said, "He who is unable to live in society or who has no need because he is sufficient for himself, must be either a beast or a god. . . ."[1] He certainly could not be a man! Because, in Aristotle's opinion, one of the hallmarks of individuals in the human species is the need for social relationships. Aristotle tells us in this way that man's nature has two aspects, the individualistic and the collective. Too much emphasis of one at the expense of the other creates a distorted understanding of human behavior. This dual nature concept has caused doctrinal disputes among the learned for centuries. Considering the grand nature of some of these controversies, it may be a bit impetuous to note that management thought has been infected as well. We see how it has in the next two sections.

Man's need for human association stems from a variety of want-satisfying activities such as family life, recreation, education, government, and plain companionship. This book deals with one form of human association—work. People's behavior on their jobs, their motives for employment, and the satisfactions or dissatisfactions they experience in work have long been topics of speculation. However, study of man's behavior in his work environment through the use of the behavioral sciences is of recent origin.

New avenues of thought and investigation were opened as the behavioral sciences matured and behavioral scientists became interested in work and man's relation to it as a legitimate field of study. Since work is, indeed, a way of life in our civilization, the study of individual and organizational behavioral patterns yields useful information to students of society. But more important, at least for the purposes of this book, the behavioral sciences offer to *management* relevant concepts and data about the processes of individual and group behavior in the work setting. A major aim of this book is to show the contributions of behavioral theory and research to management. Our hope, however, is to give more than a catalog of research findings. We also present a point of view on management

[1] Aristotle, *Politics*, Book I, chap. 2.

42

philosophy, history, and issues in which the behavioral sciences play a role or raise problems.

INDUSTRIAL HUMANISM

Frederick W. Taylor did not intend that it should, but scientific management became associated with a system of "technicist" methods which represented to the popular mind the ultimate of dehumanization in industry. Scientific management appeared to be the final touch in degrading workers. To many in America, and particularly to Europeans, Taylorism, rationalization, and scientism were bound up in an ideological package which fit neatly in the bundle of early 20th-century individualism.

Industrial humanism is a reaction to those forms of task organization and management which not only deprive workers of job satisfaction but, what is worse, violate human dignity. Basic to the philosophy of industrial humanism is the design of the work environment to provide for the restoration of man's dignity. Industrial humanism has taken numerous forms. It is currently expounded by well-known writers such as Douglas McGregor, Chris Argyris, and Rensis Likert. The proposals these people make involve concepts and practices as Theory Y, job enlargement, T-group and sensitivity training, and democratic and participative leadership.

We consider all these aspects in this book at one place or another. For now it merely should be observed that industrial humanism has both a philosophy and an assortment of practices with which it proposes to change the conventional structure of work relationships and the content of work itself. Most important of all, the industrial humanists' program includes changing management's mind as to what is good administration of people. Needless to say the proponents of industrial humanism feel that these changes will more accord with man's nature producing greater freedom and satisfactions at work. Of course, the organization stands to gain from modifications in structure, work content, and management attitude by more effective accomplishment of its goals.

Industrial humanism embraces all movements which are liberal in spirit and which seek to bring to man at work freedom from oppression and an opportunity for self-determination. More is said about this in subsequent chapters. In the following section our attention is directed to the revolution in social climate which made for the ideological prospering of a humanistic-democratic philosophy in administration. Professor Dwight Waldo has observed that administration has undergone a mellowing from harsh paternalism in the years since the turn of the century. While Waldo feels that the change stems from less than altruistic management motives, he says:

. . . even if we discount entirely any democratic motives on the part of private administration, the movements toward an enlightened paternalism may nevertheless have created conditions out of which democratic administration can grow—can grow more easily, at least, than it could have grown a generation ago.[2]

Some of the dynamics which have caused changes in management values are treated next.

MANAGEMENT VALUES AND HUMAN RESOURCES

Professor Harold Koontz and Col. Lyndall Urwick are disturbed by the management theory jungle.[3] They feel that because there is such a hodgepodge of conflicting theories and research data nothing of much use will come of it for practicing managers. No small part of the confusion is a result of the influence behavioral theory and research has had on administration. But if this is the whole story the maze would not be quite so complicated. Mixed in with objective research findings of scientists are infusions of values so that often the most sophisticated reader has trouble separating the two. To get some perspective on the subject of management values we will review in this section the ethical systems which have molded management thought. Later in the chapter we will relate such movements as industrial humanism and human relations to them.

Two Ethical Systems which Influence Management Thought: A Description

Frequently, "management philosophy" is used synonymously with "value systems" to denote the base upon which the objectives and policies of an organization are built. Ethics in turn provide operational values for the management of the organization. As a result of this view of ethics, it is appropriate to ask what system of values management embraces. The answer is most probably that management values are not fundamentally different from the values of society. Broader social values, however, are modified and adapted in specific forms by management to fit into an operating philosophy consistent with the purposes of the organization.

The *individualistic ethic* and the *social ethic* are two broad value systems which have a profound effect on management thought. These ethics are like "super value systems" for management. They supply the ethical points of departure from which management formulates its own specific systems of values, such as scientific management, human relations, and industrial humanism.

Value systems constructed on an ethic of individualism or on a social ethic are not new in our society. They have been discussed since people first began theorizing about the nature of man. These philosophical arguments are often concerned with whether or not man's nature is essentially

---

[2] Dwight Waldo, "Development of Theory of Democratic Administration," *The American Political Science Review*, March, 1952, p. 84.

[3] L. F. Urwick, "The Tactics of Jungle Warfare," *Journal of the Academy of Management*, Vol. 6, No. 4 (December, 1963), pp. 316–29; H. Koontz, "The Management Theory Jungle," *Journal of the Academy of Management*, Vol. 4, No. 3, December, 1961), pp. 177–88.

individualistic or collectivistic. Modern value systems based on either the social ethic or the individualistic ethic can be traced through the historical traditions of such philosophic speculations. Yet even today there is no consensus on what view should be taken by management in regard to this basic problem.[4]

The Individualistic Ethic. The individualistic ethic, from the standpoint of its place in management thought, springs from the ideals of economic freedom. These ideals, in turn, are rooted in liberalism,[5] the Protestant ethic,[6] and the American frontier.[7] Liberalism (sometimes referred to as the doctrine of natural liberty) and the Protestant ethic were European in origin. The frontier in America was a phenomenon which deeply influenced national and, hence, management thought during the history of this country. The frontier gave an American twist to the doctrines of human freedom inherited from Europe.

A precise definition of the individualistic ethic is useless because the result would be a history, not a definition. At best, it can be said that *the individualistic ethic is a conglomeration of ideas pertaining to personal freedom and the preeminence of individual action.* The European intellectual foundations of individualism were framed in an American context because of the frontier. The ability to "go West" if the press of civilization in the East became too great was part of the meaning of the frontier in America.

The Social Ethic. The social ethic is as solidly founded in the history of ideas as is the individualistic ethic.[8] In the largest sense, the social ethic centers on the *collectivity* and the corporate well-being of society. This

---

[4] For a wide expression of views on this point see "A Faith for Modern Management," *The Atlanta Economic Review*, September, 1958, pp. 1–7.

[5] Liberalism as a concept of economic freedom is founded in the notion on "natural liberty." Within this philosophy personal liberty, private property, and freedom of contract are of central importance. Versions of this doctrine run from "man has a right to do what he will with his own" to "every man is free to do that which he wills, provided he infringes not on the equal freedom of any other man." For an analysis of the natural-liberty question see Henry M. Oliver, Jr., *A Critique of Socioeconomic Goals* (Bloomington: Indiana University Press, 1954), chap. 1.

[6] Of all the works dealing with the idea of religious approbation of business behavior, Max Weber's *The Protestant Ethic and the Spirit of Capitalism* (New York: Charles Scribner's Sons, 1930) is the best known and the most influential. The thesis of this essay is that Protestantism formed an ethical base for capitalism. From this base, profit making, and the accumulation of material goods found approval in the sight of God. In this sense, worldly possessions were evidence of divine favor and eventual salvation. Most significant, however, is that economic individualism flourished as an outgrowth of the Protestant reformation.

[7] There have been a number of ideas pertaining to the significance of the frontier as a shaper of American attitude and philosophy. One of the best known is the "safety-valve doctrine." This theory is stated in Frederick Jackson Turner, *The Frontier in American History* (New York: Henry Holt and Co., 1920), p. 259. Turner's work is a classic, revealing how the presence of a frontier affected life, thought, and economic development in America.

[8] For a short history of the backgrounds to the contemporary social ethic see Harry Elmer Barnes (ed.), *An Introduction to the History of Sociology* (Chicago: The University of Chicago Press, 1948), chap. 1–2, esp. pp. 71–76.

ethic emphasizes the value of harmony and solidarity in interpersonal and intergroup relationships. The social ethic has grown as a dominant current in social thought during the 20th century because of increased human interdependency.

The urbanization and industrialization of America must be underscored in this respect. With the changing economic and social aspect of America came a civilization of specialized, urbanized, dependent employees.[9] This change began shortly after the Civil War but proceeded at a much more rapid pace in this century.

The magnitude of this change cannot be dismissed lightly. Old values no longer seemed particularly appropriate when management was faced with the problems that resulted from the American Industrial Revolution. The fact of human proximity and dependency required a new base of interpretation and ethical rationalization. The modern forms of social organization and, of course, business organizations needed justification for the tendency toward collectivism and control characteristic of 20th century civilization.

The social ethic provided a source of justification. Indeed, when people are dependent on each other for employment, the necessities of life, and even the discharge of their job functions, the collectivistic aspect of human nature is forced to the forefront of ethical consideration. Interdependency requires a social philosophy directed toward collaboration and solidarity rather than competition and conflict.

In the social sense management philosophy is composed of a polyglot of ideas that give points of departure for solving social problems caused by industrialization. The behavioral sciences are called upon to answer such questions as: what do people want from their jobs? How can people be made happy in their work? How can people be motivated to meet organizational objectives but remain content and derive job satisfaction at the same time? Presumably, the individualistic ethic had answers for these questions. However, the answers were incomplete. Psychology, sociology, and the newer disciplines like social-psychology, organization theory, and decision theory had to be consulted for more comprehensive answers to the problem of human motivation and satisfaction in an industrial civilization.

To summarize, the reference point of the social ethic is the collective nature of man. The social ethic affirms the value of human collaboration and social solidarity. The individual is, of course, not neglected. But individual satisfactions are seen as resulting from participation in a social environment characterized by oneness and harmony.[10] Berrien comments that the prerequisite for individual self-realization comes from ". . . the

---

[9] The problem and implications of dependency in employment are discussed in Peter Drucker, "The Employee Society," *American Journal of Sociology*, January, 1953, pp. 358–63.

[10] Sigmund Diamond has an interesting sidelight on this point with respect to obituaries of major businessmen. In the early 19th century greater stress was placed

development of close relationships which anchor the individual securely in some stable, continuing group."[11]

In contrast, the individualistic ethic starts with the person as the ultimate source of individual and social values. The "atomistic" person acting intelligently in pursuit of his own self-interest will eventually contribute the most to the good of the group.

The social ethic has not supplanted the individualistic ethic in management philosophy. These two ethics are found side by side today. In fact, some writers feel that management is torn in its allegiance between these ethics. They argue that lip service has to be given to the symbols of individualism while collectivism is the practical and acceptable form of management practice.[12]

It is, however, presumptuous to make an "either-or" case for the natures of man supposedly reflected in these two "super value systems." Man is neither purely individualistic nor purely collectivistic. As Demant points out, "The community and the individualist propensities are part of man's *natura* in dialectical interplay. . . ."[13]

In Demant's sense, man has both social and individualistic tendencies, and the dominance of either tendency results from man's environment, or, more generally, man's "web of culture." Thus it appears that adjustment to the dilemma created by these ethics is a personal thing. Maybe some managers develop a split personality by attempting dual allegiance to these ethics. But if man's nature is really a complex of individualistic *and* collectivistic propensities it would appear that management can roll quite satisfactorily with the transition to the social ethic.

In conclusion, the conditions existing in pre–20th-century America caused an ethic of individualism to make sense for management. Equally, the changed conditions in 20th-century America created a climate in which the social ethic has progressively enlarged its role in management philosophy. The events which caused this shift in value emphasis are investigated next.

Two Forces behind Social Change

The process of social change is enormously complicated. In order to simplify the analysis only two major forces at work in American history

---

on the personal, unique qualities of the individual businessman. More recently Diamond finds the values expressed in the obituaries place greater reliance upon the "system" and on the nonbusiness characteristics of the businessman, emphasizing not what set him apart but rather the qualities he had in common with all persons. See Sigmund Diamond, *The Reputation of the American Businessman* (Cambridge: Harvard University Press, 1955), pp. 178–82.

[11] F. K. Berrien, *Comments and Cases on Human Relations* (New York: Harper and Bros., 1951), p. 236.

[12] For example see William H. Whyte, Jr., *The Organization Man* (New York: Simon and Schuster, 1956).

[13] V. A. Demant, *Religion and the Decline of Capitalism* (New York: Scribner's Sons, 1952), p. 139.

have been selected for application. These forces are called the expansion factor and the collision effect.

The Expansion Factor.   The expansion factor is intimately connected to the geographical frontier which existed until around 1900. The meaning of the frontier has been clouded by symbolic usages such as educational frontiers, the frontiers of science, and religious frontiers. The part played by a physical, geographic frontier, however, has particular significance in American social thought.

The frontier meant expansion into a new land and an opportunity for relatively unhampered individualistic expression. The expansion factor placed a premium on individualism. In addition, with room to expand, the competitive social and economic environment in the highly populated part of the country was diluted. It was possible for an individual to get away if his life became unbearable.[14] An illusion of competition without brutality was present when the expansion factor was operative.

The effect the expansion factor had on the attitude of the American people was even more important. Anything seemed possible as long as the individual had enough tenacity to endure hardships. Success was measured by the individual's ability to tap the material wealth abounding in expanding frontiers.[15]

This optimistic spirit was not limited to those who sought opportunity on the frontier. The halo of optimism covered even those in the more densely populated regions. The glamour of a golden horizon conditioned the individualistic philosophy of the nation. As a result, management almost unequivocally accepted the individualistic ethic in the 19th century.

The Collision Effect.   The collision effect is characterized by conflict. The collision effect results from environmental conditions which draw people into inescapable *proximity* and *dependency* on one another. The frontier was not infinite; its closing, coupled with *technological* and *population dynamics,* contributed to an intensifying collision effect. These two dynamics are explored further.

1. *Technological Dynamics.*

a) Industrialization.   The causes underlying American industrializa-

---

[14] It is noted by Krooss that the frontier did not necessarily provide a "safety valve" for oppressed urban populations and that booms on the frontier took place during periods of prosperity instead of during periods of depression. Herman E. Krooss, *American Economic Development* (Englewood Cliffs, N.J.: Prentice-Hall, Inc., 1955), pp. 108–12. As explained further on in this section, the "safety valve" is as much a psychological doctrine contributing to national optimism in individualism as it is an explanation of the economic forces which were active in the growth of the American economy.

[15] For some interesting comments on the West as related to the expansion factor see Merle Curti, *The Growth of American Thought* (New York: Harper and Bros., 1943), chaps. 11, 19. For a study of the influence of the frontier on American economic development and foreign policy see William Appleman Williams, *The Contours of American History* (New York: The World Publishing Co., 1961).

tion are many-faceted. Industrialization required new power sources, a program of mechanization, the growth of capital-goods industries (machine tools and precision instruments), financial sources, and an innovative spirit behind the development of processes, materials, and methods. The economic history of the United States records how these factors and others combined to change America from a handicraft and rural economy to a major industrial nation in the twentieth century.

b) Standardization. One key feature of industrialization is standardization. Uniformity in performance is necessary for complex, large-scale business enterprise to exist. The necessity for uniformity applies to policy matters throughout the company as well as to interchangeability of parts and equipment. Thus, the concept of standardization applies equally well to administrative activities as to the physical uniformity of parts and equipment required by mass-production techniques.

c) Division of Labor and Job Specialization. The division of labor is the breaking down of work into smaller elements or parts so that an employee may "specialize" in a simplified task rather than "generalize" in a fairly complicated job. The division of labor process has often been called the rationalization of work.

The division of labor is, in one sense, an extension of the idea of standardization to job performance. Control over many aspects of the production process is simplified when jobs are reduced to their most basic elements—made routine.

Job specialization and the division of labor often refer to operative jobs at the point of production. However, the treatment can be easily extended to apply to executive functions. The vertical growth of an organization through the subdivision of management jobs is a case of specialization in the line functions. The horizontal growth of an organization by the addition of staff is an example of specialization through advisory and facilitative services for the line organization.

It follows that no matter where the division of labor occurs—at the operative or administrative levels of the organization—all the subdivided functions are closely interrelated in terms of the total operation of the system. The result is that coordination of the parts is a paramount need. Further, the processes of industrialization, standardization, division of labor, and specialization are linked inseparably; and in this combination they contribute greatly to the proximity and dependency features of the collision effect. Specifically, the increase in the number of functions to be performed requires more people and thus contributes to proximity; and the increase in the interrelation of these functions contributes to dependency.

d) Improved Communication and Transportation. Adam Smith observed that the division of labor was limited by the extent of the market; that is, the degree to which industry can be rationalized is limited by the available market outlets for the goods produced.

Market extension was, of course, facilitated by the dramatic growth of the transportation and communication networks. Besides enlarging the market for industrial output, the effect of this development in American industrial growth was to tie people even closer—and thus aggravate the collision effect.

 2. *Population Dynamics.*

a) Population Growth Trends.   Population growth added to the intensification of the collision effect.

Population increase is shown in the census figures in Figure 2–1. It is

FIGURE 2–1
The Growth of American Population
1790–1960

Year	Population	Year	Population
1790..........	3,929,214	1880.........	50,155,783
1800..........	5,308,483	1890.........	62,947,714
1810..........	7,239,881	1900.........	75,994,575
1820..........	9,638,453	1910.........	91,972,266
1830..........	12,866,020	1920.........	105,710,620
1840..........	17,069,453	1930.........	122,775,045
1850..........	23,191,876	1940.........	131,669,275
1860..........	31,443,321	1950.........	150,697,361
1870..........	38,558,371	1960.........	179,323,175

Source: Bureau of the Census.

interesting to observe that before 1890—the date the Bureau of the Census declared the frontier officially closed—the population was around 59 million. Since that time it has increased by 120 million.

Up until recently, space (or population density) has not been a matter of very great concern. However, because of the rapid increase in population, note is being taken now of the mounting competition for available space, particularly in urban areas. The raw data on American population trends serve to reinforce the validity of the proximity aspect of the collision effect.

b) Urbanization Trends.   Significant also to population dynamics is the location of people. According to the 1960 census of population:

In 1790, 1 out of every 20 of the 3,929,214 inhabitants of the United States was living in urban territory. In every decade thereafter, with the exception of that from 1810 to 1820, the rate of growth of the urban population exceeded that of the rural population. By 1860, 1 out of 5 persons was included in the urban population. The process of urbanization continued in the following decades, and by 1920 the urban population had exceeded the rural population. In 1960 about 5 out of every 8 persons were living in urban territory.[16]

---

[16] Bureau of the Census, *Census of Population: 1960* (Washington, D.C.: U.S. Government Printing Office, 1961), Vol. I, p. xiv. These comparisons are based on the definition of "urban territory" used prior to the 1950 census.

The relationship of rural to urban population is illustrated in Figure 2–2.

Most urban dwellers are aware of the closeness of their neighbors and of their dependence on others for the supply of essential goods and services. Urbanization coupled with population increase has accentuated

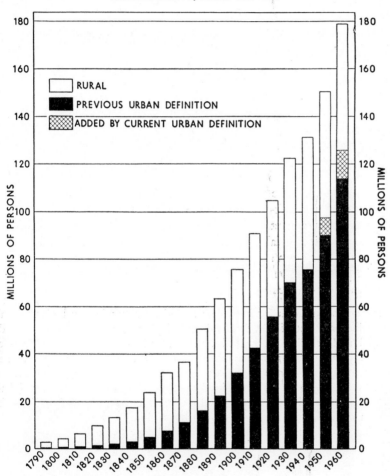

FIGURE 2–2
Urban and Rural Population: 1790–1960

Source: Department of Commerce, Bureau of the Census.

the problems arising from the proximity and dependency of people. Additionally, no end seems to be in sight to expanding urban populations. Hence, on the score of population dynamics plus contributions to proximity and dependency made by technological dynamics, the collision effect would appear to be an intensifying rather than an abating process.

3. *The Significance of Technological and Population Dynamics.*
The key social and technological developments in our society during

this century are those which have tended to make people more dependent upon and proximate to each other. These ingredients make the collision effect thrive.

The collision effect, *if left unharnessed,* would breed brutal competition, then conflict, to end in the degeneration of society. However, this cycle did not occur as the collision effect matured. Simultaneously with the growth of the collision effect a change in values began which was necessitated for survival reasons. This is another way of stating the sociological process of competition, conflict, and accommodation.

The American Industrial Revolution spawned the collision effect; and in turn the collision effect generated its own countervailing ethical force—the social ethic. The "pure" principles of the individualistic ethic lost realism with the diminishing expansion factor. The individualistic industrial buccaneer in the expansion period could not be the hero of the new order.

The values which shored him up, indeed even glorified him, were becoming obsolete at the beginning of this century. The industrial individualist was replaced, slowly at first, by the professional managerial "relationship expert." The competitive struggle as a vital force *within* an organization was soft-pedaled. Group solidarity as a goal began to be substituted for competition with the expectation that a social philosophy would lead to industrial harmony and human satisfaction.

The novel is often a good reflection of prevailing sentiments. Regarding the purpose of business, in 1905 Upton Sinclair wrote the following about the meat-packers:

> Here was Durham's, for instance, owned by a man who was trying to make as much money out of it as he could, and did not care in the least how he did it; and underneath him, ranged in ranks and grades like an army, were managers and superintendents and foremen, each one driving the man next below him and trying to squeeze out of him as much work as possible. And all the men of the same rank were pitted against each other; the accounts of each were kept separately, and every man lived in terror of losing his job, if another made a better record than he. So from top to bottom the place was simply a seething caldron of jealousies and hatreds; there was no loyalty or decency anywhere about; there was no place where a man counted for anything against a dollar.[17]

Mirroring the modern change in attitude about the purpose of a business, Bernard Lester, in 1956, says:

> First of all the objective of a business should be to attain abiding satisfaction for all those persons who are a part of it irrespective of position of relative responsibility. . . .
> With this objective for the superstructure, the foundations are men. They

---

[17] Upton Sinclair, *The Jungle* (New York: The Viking Press, 1946), pp. 59–60. Used with permission.

FIGURE 2–3
Management Thought in a Changing Culture

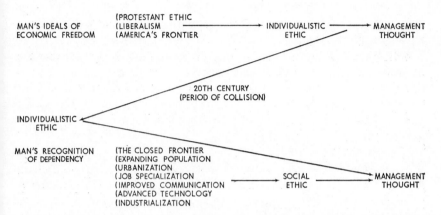

support everything. . . . Two families exist in the industrial world today. They are the home-family with its duties and relaxations, and the company- or factory-family with its responsibilities to be gladly and cogently performed. We can't measure accomplishments with a yardstick but each act in each family must give life meaning and reality. . . .

The best equipped plant will drag in production or even periodically come to absolute rest simply because men don't continue to work harmoniously together. . . . Industrial leaders . . . have emphasized competition, and a ruthless approach to that. . . . This approach to efficiency is misleading; the false gods deceive, for the efficiency of men can never be plotted on a curve when they have been robbed of the personal satisfaction of their work. . . .[18]

These quotations suggest the changed philosophy in management thought. Sinclair speaks of competitive individualism; Lester extoles the values of human satisfaction and company harmony.

Two Models of Management Thought: A Summary

Four rather involved points have been covered in this discussion. Figure 2–3 illustrates the connections among the individualistic ethic, the social ethic, the expansion factor, and the collision effect. This figure also shows how these forces and ethics, in combination, have significantly influenced management thought. Figure 2–3 may be interpreted as follows:

1. The expansion factor operating in the 19th century—in part because of the frontier—established the necessary setting for the flowering of the ideals of

---

[18] Bernard Lester, *Weatherby Crisis* (New York: Twayne Publishers, 1956), pp. 220–21. Used with permission.

economic freedom. These ideals were based on the Protestant ethic and the doctrine of liberalism.

2. As a result, the philosophy which emerged was the individualistic ethic since it provided the justification for a form of behavior demanded by circumstances in pre–20th-century America. Individualism consequently had its impact on management thought.

3. The character of society began to change around 1870. By 1900, the new face of society was clearly one of human dependency and proximity. The older order of the preeminence of individual action—or, in its pathological form, individualism without a conscience—was becoming outdated.

4. The developing conditions of proximity and dependency, and thus the collision effect, were accelerated by the closing frontier, advancement in all forms of technology, and the movement to the city of large segments of the rural population and waves of immigrants.

5. The escape valve provided by the frontier was no longer available. Competition could turn into conflict. The alternatives resulting from this situation were two—social degeneration or accommodation.

6. Accommodation requires a change in values to offset the effects of conflict. A change of values did occur with a shift toward the social ethic to counter the collision effect. Management, in its own way, has been and is increasingly susceptible to the point of view of the social ethic.

The serious shortcoming of a descriptive model is the difficulty of introducing a dynamic quality into it. This failure might be overlooked when certain historical processes that are over and done with are being described. The lack of a dynamic attribute, however, becomes downright misleading when an explanation of contemporary events is needed. The collision effect is still going on. And, consequently, greater refinements in the concrete applications of the social ethic are being sought.

THE HUMAN RELATIONS MOVEMENT

Human relations is an outgrowth of the social ethic. It is the label applied to a particular point of view which dominated management thought for a number of years.

We need to understand the historical significance of the human relations movement as an answer to the collision effect. Beginning with the Hawthorne studies in the 1920s and 1930s, this movement had a double impact on management thought. First, Elton Mayo articulated a philosophy which influenced the development of industrial humanism. Second, by the empirical work done at the research site, the role of the behavioral sciences in solving management's "people problems" was unfolded.

Its Perspective

Human relations is a specific modification of the social ethic used by management to understand and to influence a certain form of human association which is peculiarly sensitive to the collision effect. This form of association is of people at work. Human relations is a way of looking at and affecting the conflict-biased sociological and psychological processes in any organizational undertaking.

The general assumption of human relations upon which it rested its claim for scientific legitimacy is the interdisciplinary approach to the behavioral sciences. Most of the substantive content of human relations is drawn from sociology, psychology, cultural anthropology, and social-psychology. Synthesizing the contributions of these fields could help management solve problems of human conflict more adequately. The most important aspect of this assumption, however, is that human relations is uniquely greater than the sum of the disciplines which make it up.[19]

The whole being greater than the sum of its parts is a *Gestalt* or configurationist method of analysis. The study of a painting serves as an example of the meaning of this theory. When one looks at an oil painting from a distance, say of one foot, all that is seen is a mass of paint blobs and a certain texture. But as the viewer moves back the painting assumes a structure, a form, a contour. The configuration which emerges as the subject of the canvas is, indeed, more than the sum of the blobs of paint which make it up. Paint and canvas are only the media through which art is expressed.

The configurationist approach is the central feature of the general assumption of human relations stated above. Human relations amalgamates behavioral science disciplines and focuses their theories, data, methods, and findings *in combination* on human problems. The problem-solving virtue of human relations may be expressed as "two plus two equals five." The extra "one" in the formula comes from the special twist that human relations problem solving gets by using the interdisciplinary method. Human relations, as a result, claims different and singularly useful insights into human problems. Human relations attempts to overcome the short-sightedness of specialists working independently on a problem.[20]

Its Clinical Nature

Management is supposed to find in human relations a *clinical* instrument for settling problems of conflict and human satisfaction at work. Administrative action through human relations consists of applying behavioral science data and principles to promote human collaboration and solidarity within the social system of the organization. The technical skills of administrators have to be backed by human skills so the cooperative

---

[19] In fact Friedmann thinks the human relations movement sought its doctrinal foundations in *Gestalt* theory. See Georges Friedmann, *Industrial Society* (Glencoe: The Free Press, 1955), pp. 368–69. This might be so operationally. Philosophically, the foundations of the human relations movement are in the social ethic.

[20] A statement and criticism of the interdisciplinary assumptions may be found in William H. Knowles, *Personnel Management*, (New York: America Book Co., 1955), pp. 102–6.

action and solidarity will be created without loss of individual identity. This is a large order but those who stress the clinical aspects of human relations feel it will produce these desirable outcomes.

In a classic statement of the clinical approach, F. J. Roethlisberger outlines two sets of questions for managers. They are:

1. A Useful Way of Thinking about Individuals in a Business Organization
   a) What is the individual bringing to the work situation?
   b) What is the work situation demanding of the individual?
   c) What is the resulting equilibrium?
2. A Useful Way of Thinking about the Interactions of Individuals in a Business Organization
   a) What are the formal patterns of behavior in a group?
   b) What are the informal patterns of behavior in a group?
   c) What are the major schemes in terms of which individuals are being evaluated?
   d) What is the resulting equilibrium?[21]

If the above questions are to be answered honestly the manager is forced to view human interactions in the system concretely and specifically. The manager has to accept the fact that problems of human behavior are not purely individual matters but often involve the individual plus the group, plus job requirements, plus formal and informal criteria against which the behavior of the individual is measured. *The manager must look at his organization as a social system.*

Through the clinical approach the manager takes a hard look at the human situation in which he is involved and then acts in this situation following experience, intuition, and behavioral science data and principles as guides. To summarize, the clinical approach to human relations is using human tools and data to solve concrete human problems in the situation where they occur. This approach is supposed to result in a minimization of conflict, the encouragement of collaboration, and the solidarity of the social system.

Its Action Orientation

With its clinical emphasis it is not surprising that the human relations movement has a set of action-designed propositions which point the way to effective management practice. The eight action propositions which follow represent a consensus among human relations writers on measures to improve and promote successful human relations practice.

1. *Good human relations practice is the product of the manager using experience, intuition, and interdisciplinary generalizations to guide him in the action he takes.*[22] This assumption is the essence of the clinical nature

---

[21] F. J. Roethlisberger, *Management and Morale* (Cambridge: Harvard University Press, 1941), pp. 118–24.

[22] Roethlisberger, *op. cit.*, pp. 138–41.

of human relations. It is the most inclusive; the remaining assumptions are more or less corollaries or tools for implementing good human relations practice.

2. Employee *participation* is often essential to higher productivity and greater human satisfaction. Employees will be happier if they have something to say in affairs that affect their destinies on the job. Organizations have applied this assumption in the forms of allowing operative employees a chance to engage in the decision-making process on their jobs,[23] and in development schemes which promote more "involvement" of managers in the problems of their company.

Another aspect of the participation assumption is the leadership climate which elicits participation. *Democratic leadership*, where leader seeks out group advice, is considered essential for establishing a "permissive" environment in which participation can flourish.[24] For purposes of contrast, democratic leadership can be compared with authoritarian leadership characterized by unilateral decisions on the part of the manager.

3. The *role* proposition stems from the variety of demands an individual faces at work. Two general categories of roles are identifiable: the "job-oriented role" and the "informal group-oriented role." In a sociological sense roles are institutionally determined—for example, the role of the company president, the role of the staff specialist, the role of the foreman, and the role of the operative employee. Social psychologists approach the subject of role in terms of the individual's niche and function in small groups.

From the standpoint of the executive the operating aspect of the role concept is linked to his understanding of an individual's behavior as a product of the demands made on him from the different directions in an organization. These demands can be called expectation forces. Thus an individual's behavior is partially a result of the expectations of the job and the organization and also the expectations of those with whom the individual associates at work. The first group of expectations may be termed *formal;* the second group is frequently *informal,* which means the expectations are social and not necessarily part of the demands of the job itself.

4. *Communication* has often been referred to as the nervous system of the organization. Anything which impairs the functioning of the communication system will limit organizational effectiveness in terms of the accomplishment of objectives. The "good communication" assumption is not entirely in the province of human relations. It may, in some cases, be a technical or engineering matter relatively immune from human manip-

---

[23] Lester Coch and John R. P. French, Jr., "Overcoming Resistance to Change," *Human Relations,* 1948, pp. 512–32.

[24] A. Bavelas, cited in N. R. F. Maier, *Psychology in Industry* (Boston: Houghton Mifflin Co., 1946), pp. 264–66.

ulation. However, communication is largely a human problem, subject to human foibles. Therefore, good communication has become the main point of attention for theories and practices designed to unclog communication channels.

5. The next assumption is that *teamwork* is an indispensable element of management practice for organizational survival. The substance of teamwork is put formally by Simon as follows: ". . . in a cooperative pattern both participants prefer the same set of consequences; hence if each anticipates the other correctly, they will both act so as to secure these consequences. In a competitive pattern, the optimum outcome for the first participant is not the optimum for the second. Hence the realization by the first participant of the consequence he prefers will frustrate the other participant. . . ."[25]

Thus, teamwork is a matter of mutual anticipation and agreement on goals. Teamwork and cooperation go hand in hand; one stimulates the other in a situation where people are striving to obtain the same set of desired outcomes.

6. Man is *diversely motivated;* he has a hierarchy of needs which are quite changeable. This assumption is the opposite of the money-and-motivation, economic-incentive notion. Work satisfaction, according to this assumption, is not entirely money-directed.[26] People derive work satisfactions from job accomplishment, recognition, participation, and the like. Frequently morale and contentment are based not on the paycheck but on the social and psychological conditions of employment. This assumption questions the core of the traditional theory of human behavior, which assumes economic rationality and the maximization of monetary rewards by people at work.

7. The seventh assumption is that the organization is a *social system.* Viewing the work situation as a network of variable and interrelated elements is a major feature of human relations practice for the executive.[27] The executive must be a relationship expert to maintain the balance (equilibrium) of the social system in which he is involved.

8. The capstone assumption states that *executive skills in human relations practice can be developed.* This assumption means that the executive's clinical ability can be improved so that he will be equipped to handle concrete human problems successfully. The executive can be trained to be aware, sensitive, and competent to cope with the human problems of the organization.

---

[25] Herbert Simon, *Administrative Behavior* (New York: The Macmillan Co., 1954), p. 72. Another approach to teamwork may be found in Peter Drucker, *The Practice of Management* (New York: Harper and Bros., 1954), pp. 170–78.

[26] For descriptive illustrations of the point see William F. Whyte, *Money and Motivation* (New York: Harper and Bros., 1955).

[27] The basic character of the assumption was noted by the researchers in the Hawthorne experiments. F. J. Roethlisberger and William J. Dickson, *Management and the Worker* (Cambridge: Harvard University Press, 1939), chap. 24.

Its Present Status

The decade of the 1950's was the era of greatest prestige for the human relations movement.[28] But even by the late 1950's there was evidence that human relations was waning as a significant force in management thought and practice. Today the name "human relations" strikes a sour note with some managers and most behavioral scientists. For many the field represents at best a pedestrian effort in research and scholarship or at worst a cynical attempt to manipulate people.

Despite its failures in the past and its present diminished stature, human relations has historical significance in management thought. It represents in its philosophical and behavioral premises a transition from an old order of managerial ideology to a new. Therefore we refer frequently to human relations in this book.

Because human relations is not dead, conventional mores prevent us from performing a premature autopsy. But as observed before the signs clearly indicate that human relations is declining. What caused this dwindling influence can just be hinted at here. It may have been that human relations promised too much as a paliative for management's difficulties in "handling people." Who knows! One thing is certain however, it is that the field has been by-passed by advances in such areas as decision theory and organization theory. Most devastating of all, is that those who have been active either in advancing the cause of industrial humanism or doing research in the behavioral sciences have abandoned the banners of human relations. In other words, the important things that are happening in management are not occurring in the human relations movement.

CONCLUSIONS

Human relations is the first systematic attempt to introduce the behavioral sciences into management practice within the framework of a humanistic philosophy toward the role of man in organizations. This is why we pay particular attention to the movement in this chapter. Today most of the action-oriented propositions of the human relations movement have meaning. Indeed, they provide industrial humanists and behavioral scientists with points of departure. Democracy and participation are every bit as essential to industrial humanism as to human relations. Communication, role, management development, and the rest have given behavioral scientists endless opportunities for research. No doubt the roots of organization theory and decision theory can be found in the early empirical work of human relations.

---

[28] At the height of its prestige human relations was not without its critics. See Harold L. Sheppard, "Approaches to Conflict in American Industrial Sociology," *British Journal of Sociology*, December, 1954, pp. 324–41.

But management thought has taken new directions. These directions have introduced many foreign ideas and much disturbing data into the jungle of theory. This is, however, a sign of health rather than decadence. Because there is a common denominator in the jungle. It is of attitude. Specifically, this attitude is shown by practicing managers wishing to know more in depth about human behavior. It is demonstrated by educators in business schools as a desire to lead students into areas which will challenge their potentials to conceptualize problems of human behavior in the business setting. And finally it is indicated by many scientists from the behavioral disciplines through their research in organizational behavior.

The new direction in management thought requires treatment of human motivation and organizational behavior on higher conceptual levels. It necessitates more extensive consideration of research and generalizations in the behavioral sciences. It also points to a need for a realistic appraisal of the ethical aspects of administrative practices. We have it seems moved away from human relations as a vehicle for providing for the satisfaction of these needs.

Management is in a critical position in our society. It must respond sensitively and correctly to social, economic, political, and technological changes. Further it must be concerned with the wants of the participants in organizations. Administrators should create an environment structured to prevent destructive forms of conflict and to promote the personal development of those in the organization. This administrative imperative becomes more evident yearly as the occupational character of the work force changes toward more emphasis on higher skills. Our intention in this book is to give the reader an accurate reflection of the present character of administrative philosophy, theory, practice, and issues in the sphere of interpersonal relationships.

CHAPTER 3

Personality Dynamics and Motivation

THE BASIC UNIT of satisfaction in a social territory is the individual. He is, as well, the focal point of motivation and productivity. Therefore, it is logical to begin this part of the book with a chapter dealing with personality. Embarking on this venture takes us through one of the stormiest passages in modern psychology.

We have seen in the prologue that the behavioral sciences, dominated by psychology, have been strongly affected in their research posture by positivism and operationalism. This influence generated research which is basically microcosmic in character. That is, psychological studies largely attend to narrow elements of behavior rigidly defined in terms of the parameters of the experimental design and the measuring instruments used in it. Molecularization occurs. We have bits and pieces of information about behavior ranging from rats, through the higher primates, to man. But it has not been within the main stream of psychological science to expend much energy and resources to study the integrated whole of human personality in its normal modes. Of course, notable exceptions to this tradition exist and it is our intention to examine them here.

THE CONCEPT OF PERSONALITY

The Matter of Uniqueness

That the individual possesses bodily sensations, perceptions, drives, attitudes, motives, values, and goals is undeniable. In fact these elements which comprise human behavior have been widely studied. So in one sense we know a great deal about behavior. Nevertheless something is lacking in this superabundance of scientific research on behavior. There is a deficiency in our understanding of the process which integrates into an acting whole the many facets, both physiological and psychological, which comprise the individual. This integrating process has been called by some the self, by others personality. But in any case it is conceived of as an organizing element beyond the parts which in total comprise the individual. Because of the almost limitless possibilities for variety and combination of these parts, uniqueness, as a product of personality organizing, is a commonplace observation.

The notions of personality and uniqueness pose difficulties for science in general and psychology in particular. On the one hand, science seeks generality. The particularization which the study of personality forces on science is hard to reconcile. Indeed, because of this difficulty some psychologists claim that it is impossible to study personality scientifically. They say if we are to know anything about this process we will learn through art or literature which involves purely subjective insights.

On the other hand, certain psychologists (or school of psychology as the behaviorists) have denied that such a thing as personality exists at all. Behavior, they say, can be explained according to stimulus-response and conditioning principles. They would go further noting that the admission of an intrinsic organizing force which produces uniqueness in man is not only unscientific, but borders on the unpardonable crime of a metaphysical interpretation of behavior.

Be this as it may, Allport observes that in recent years, after decades of obscurity, the concept of self or some similar label, has been resurrected and given currency as an integrating, organizing process in human personality.[1] The fact that this can and has been done without trespassing on the mystical regions of metaphysics is necessary to recognize. This change in attitude is important to administration and its use of the behavioral sciences. Anticipating a bit, those theories of behavior which have found acceptance in administration, such as Maslow's hierarchy of needs and Argyris' notion of psychological development, have rested largely on a holistic interpretation of personality.[2] A policy framework for executive action in motivation and organizational design requires an integrated conceptualization of personality.

Following Alderson's position noted in the prologue, administrators need more than facts on such discrete subjects as perception, learning, and drives. A *program* of motivation requires the assumption that it is the "whole man" who seeks satisfaction in the organizational setting. Dissecting man in terms of IQ or attitudinal profiles might serve limited personnel objectives for selection, placement, or promotion. But it is not useful when it comes to modifying the organizational climate in order to secure higher levels of motivation and satisfaction. It is only by:

1. Recognizing the uniqueness of personality (the principle of individual differences),

2. But appreciating that there are certain uniformities in personality which can be studied scientifically, and

3. Knowing that each personality is anchored in a social matrix that a meaningful program of change in the environmental milieu can be evolved.

---

[1] Gordon W. Allport, *Becoming* (New Haven: Yale University Press, 1955), pp. 36 ff.

[2] See A. H. Maslow, *Motivation and Personality* (New York: Harper and Bros., 1954), chap. 3.

What Is Personality?

Personality is a process of change. More specifically it is the instrumentality of human psychological growth and development. Within the context of change and development, Bonner gives six propositions intended to clarify the nature of personality.[3] It is useful to review these propositions and to show their relevance to administrative practice before going on to the more segmented concepts of attitudes, motives, values, and motivation.

1. *Human behavior consists of acts.* In any complex behavioral form such as play or participation in an organization the whole individual acts. In seeking goals the individual acts totally. While such discrete processes as learning, perception, or cognition may be important aspects of acts they are merely a part of it. Hence a view of personality must focus on the pattern of the total act rather than isolated psychological or physiological aspects of it. One might say that personality itself is the equivalent of this conceptualization of the total act. This proposition is the most generalized and it ties in with what we said in the previous section about the need in administrative theory and practice for a unified conception of behavior.

2. *Personality conceived as a whole actualizes itself in a determinant environment.* This proposition indicates that the individual cannot be understood apart from his environment. In fact person-environment forms a syndrome, two or more mutually dependent interacting parts, creating a fairly stable structure of relationships which possesses an inherent potential of predictability, as long as one is sufficiently sensitized to it.

The importance of this proposition has not been lost on students of administration. The interactional nature of the individual, the small group, and the formal work situation has been a source of emphasis since the Hawthorne experiments. Recently, as a result of changes in the applied behavioral sciences, efforts have been made through training to sensitize executives to the interactional climate so that they can act in it and on it with greater effectiveness. More is said about this in Chapter 16 on management development.

3. *Personality is characterized by self-consistency.* The normal personality is in a state of dynamic equilibrium. It preserves its identity, yet is able to change. It is flexible, but it maintains a consistent character. This proposition and the next are closely related.

4. *Personality is goal-directed behavior.* In a real sense it is the choice among goals that distinguishes one personality from another. The individual, through his personality strives for more than self-consistency. He tries to obtain ends. Granted those ends he seeks and those he avoids are in part determined by their contribution to the maintenance of self-stability.

---

[3] Hubert Bonner, *Psychology of Personality* (New York: Ronald Press Co., 1961), pp. 38–40.

But at the same time, the power to select and strive for goals imparts a dynamic quality to personality as well as lending unity to it.

A great deal of the literature draws management's attention to the unity and individuality of each personality on the one hand, coupled with a person's striving for the satisfaction of motive on the other. Motives and goal-directed behavior are discussed at greater length in the following sections of this chapter. For now it should be noted that of all the qualities of personality, these have the most extensive treatment in the literature of administration.

5. *Personality is a time-integrating structure.* Personality embodies the past and anticipates the future. From the standpoint of explaining behavior, the behaviorists and the psychoanalytic schools emphasize the past. Man is a product of conditioned responses, habits learned in the past; or man in adulthood reenacts in new styles the archaic solutions to conflicts which he faced in childhood. While much is true in these explanations of behavior they are inadequate. They do not work out well in terms of man's anticipation of the future.

Man is future oriented. Nowhere is this more evident than in administration which counts planning first among the executive functions.[4] It is just recently in the area of decision-theory that any serious attention has been given to the forward-lookingness quality of personality which plays a key role in policy, production, and participation decisions throughout the organization. More is said of this in Chapter 10.

6. *Personality is a process of becoming.* Bonner states this last proposition in these terms. ". . . personality is an organization of potentialities striving to actualize themselves."[5] One might use this statement as a rallying slogan for the value system of industrial humanism. Indeed, the organizational changes and modifications suggested by those movements claiming allegiance to the social ethics in American management thought have foremost in mind an environment which will allow for the actualization of the individual's personality. We see this in detail in this chapter's discussion of Maslow's and Argyris' theories.

Determinants of Personality

The interplay of three major determinants affect the formation and development of personality. They are the individual's physiological inheritance, the groups with which he is affiliated, and the culture in which he participates.

Physiological Determinants. Heredity supplies the individual with the basic equipment for survival and growth. This includes such constitutional factors as body type, muscular and nervous systems, and the glandular apparatus. Also heredity equips the person with a basic intellectual

---

[4] Not just first sequentially but first in order of importance since organizational design and systems of control are based upon plans.

[5] Bonner, *op. cit.*, p. 40.

capacity. But the ways in which intelligence manifests itself in later life are more a function of environment.

Other physiological determinants of personality include reduction of organic drives such as hunger, thirst, and sex. These drives and others like them, while basic to the species, may be satisfied in many ways which are determined more by the culture than by the primitive urge itself.

The Group. The family and the school are the most influential institutions in shaping the emerging personality. Later in life so-called anchorage groups or primary affiliations at work or in social or recreational activities mold the personality. These associations are labeled anchorage groups because they give the individual points of reference; they define the role played by the individual along with his position in a social matrix. We deal with this in greater detail in the following chapters in this Part.

The Culture. This determinant is closely associated with the anchorage groups above. The individual is a participant in a generalized or prevailing culture which defines social roles and sanctions their performance. The individual has acting on him certain broad cultural expectations with respect to major roles, like that of parent, husband, clergyman, or teacher. Also because he is a member of many anchorage groups within a society, he participates in a number of subcultures which modify his behavior.

Perception and Cognition

The attitudes, motives, and behavior which ultimately become the hallmarks of each individual's personality rest upon the process of perception, and upon it, the process of cognition. The senses do not deceive. Perception imparts to the brain through the senses what is "seen" in the world outside the person. But sensing is not perceiving. As Berelson and Steiner put it, ". . . sensory information does not correspond simply to the perception that it underlies. The fundamental reason for the difference between sensory data and perception is that sensory impulses do not act on an empty organism; they interact with certain predispositions and states already there. . . ."[6]

Thus, the processes of perception and thought provide us with true and verifiable information. However, these processes are more than a reflection of the outside world. They are *selective* in terms of what is seen and how it is thought about. Therefore perception has two aspects. The first includes the "verifiable" information which keeps the individual in touch with reality. The second involves personal or selective perceptions where, through the mediation of personality, certain sensations are admitted and others omitted to cognitive activities.

Similar perceptions do not mean the same thing to people. This is

---

[6] Bernard Berelson and Gary A. Steiner, *Human Behavior: An Inventory of Scientific Findings* (New York: Harcourt, Brace & World, Inc., 1964), pp. 99–100; see also James J. Gibson, "The Useful Dimensions of Sensitivity," *American Psychologist*, January, 1963, pp. 1–15.

here cognition enters because environmental cues evoke different sets in each individual. A fisherman hires a guide hopefully to lead him to fish and to get him in and out of difficult country. A tree, rock, or promontory may look like another to the sportsman in unfamiliar country. But to the guide they are cues which produce behavior based upon learning and experience of where the fish are and how to get back and forth to camp with a minimum of danger.

Various stimuli (cues) in the environment trigger sets which cause us to behave in characteristic fashion. Personality comprises extended sets, or as McClelland calls them, "associative net works or clusters."[7] These clusters have also been labeled traits, attitudes, predispositions, and sentiments. As we see in the next section the concept of sets is important in the administrative approach to motivation.

ATTITUDES

Because of long-accepted usage in administrative literature, the concept which is meant to be conveyed by the terms extended sets and associative clusters is called attitudes here. Roethlisberger, in discussing the Hawthorne studies, frequently refers to the researchers' interpretation of attitudes. When the studies began, a simple, direct connection was assumed between a given change on the one hand and a predictable response on the other hand. As experimentation progressed the stimulus-response relationship was found to be neither direct nor predictable. People did not respond to a certain stimulus as it was predicted they would. The often-cited illumination experiments at the Hawthorne plant are an example.

The purpose of this experiment was to determine how productivity would vary under different light-intensity conditions. The design of the experiment was fairly simple—change the brightness of the light and measure the amount of output at different intensities.

Intuitively, it might be thought that there would be a certain optimum or "normal" range of light intensity which would correlate significantly with higher levels of productivity. As the light intensity approached, then went beyond the upper and lower limits of the optimum range, productivity would start to drop.

This bit of a priori prediction sounds quite reasonable, but the experiments did not have these results. Summarizing the third illumination experiment, it was said:

> After the level of illumination in the test group enclosure changed to a lower value, the efficiencies of both the test and control groups increased slowly but steadily. When the level of the illumination for the test group finally reached three foot-candles, the operatives protested, saying that they

---

[7] David C. McClelland, "Toward a Theory of Motive Acquisition," *American Psychologist,* May, 1965, pp. 321–34.

were hardly able to see what they were doing, and the production rate decreased. The operatives could and did maintain their efficiency to this point in spite of the discomfort and handicap of insufficient illumination.[8]

The moral of this story (and of other Hawthorne experiments) is that people did not do what they were supposed to do according to the simple stimulus-response postulate. The researchers hypothesized that some unaccounted for, purely human factors must be acting as intermediaries between the stimulus and response. They were called attitudes or sentiments.

Roethlisberger developed his "X" chart, shown in Figure 3–1, to portray the relationship of attitudes to behavior.

FIGURE 3–1
The "X" Chart

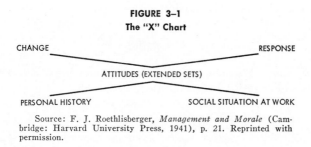

Source: F. J. Roethlisberger, *Management and Morale* (Cambridge: Harvard University Press, 1941), p. 21. Reprinted with permission.

The chart is interpreted as follows:

So that a response to a change may be understood, much less predicted, the attitudes of the individual involved must be known. Attitudes are in themselves products of a person's background (personal history) and the total work environment (the social situation at work).

It is easy to see how an enormous variety of responses could be found among individuals in similar stimulus situations. Recognition of this fact has led psychologists to formulate the Principle of Individual Differences. This principle is another way of labeling the phenomenon noted by Roethlisberger. People act differently—if you will, unpredictably—because of different environmental experiences. These differences, in turn, cause each person to view the work situation in a manner not quite like his fellow employees.

Human differences, in the psychological order, are crystallized in attitudes. The sort of response which results from an environmental change is largely dependent on the individual's attitudes regarding the total situation in which the change takes place.

Psychologists have given much attention to the subject of attitudes, and a number of formal definitions are readily available in the literature. Cattell and Baggaley define attitudes as ". . . a readiness to respond with a defined course of action, in relation to an object, in a given stimulus

---

[8] F. J. Roethlisberger and William J. Dickson, *Management and the Worker* (Cambridge: Harvard University Press, 1939), pp. 16–17.

situation."[9] Or attitudes are ". . . an enduring organization of motivational, emotional, perceptual, and cognitive processes with respect to some
aspect of the individual's world."[10]

Attitudes precede activity. As Viteles puts it, attitudes are ". . . a
fundamental state of readiness for motive arousal or a reaction in a
characteristic way to certain stimuli or stimulus situations."[11] So attitudes
are intimately associated with motives which are the basic edifice of
goal-directed behavior. Motive arousal depends on what mental sets, what
prejudices, predilictions, or predispositions are set off in the environment.
That we cannot be sure of the set triggered is amply demonstrated by the
"Hawthorne effect."

Yet this view and the structure of administrative theory which followed
the Hawthorne studies is too restricted. As we have seen personality is
not just a passive respondant to environment cues, even though a response
can be very complex. The person is capable of acting upon and changing
the environment. Consequently attitudes are crucial in directing the individual's passive reaction to and active modification of the external world.
The relation of attitudes to behavior is shown in Figure 3–2.

FIGURE 3–2
The Relation of Attitudes to Behavior

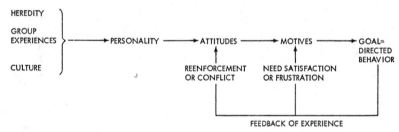

Like all schematics, Figure 3–2 is an oversimplification of a complex
process. Motives are unsatisfied needs and immediately influence the direction of behavior. However, what is a motive to a person depends upon
his attitudinal configuration, which, in turn, is part of his personality. In
his efforts to satisfy needs, the individual will experience varying degrees
of success or failure. Experience may be fruitfully thought of as feedback
which can be perceived as satisfaction or frustration of a motive and
attitudinal reinforcement or incongruency. Because of feedback from
experience in the environment, an individual may modify his attitudinal

[9] Raymond B. Cattell and Andrew R. Baggaley, "The Objective Measurement of
Attitude Motivation: Development and Evaluation of Principles and Devices,"
Journal of Personality, 1955–56, p. 421.

[10] D. Krech and R. S. Crutchfield, *Theory and Problems of Social Psychology*
(New York: McGraw-Hill Book Company, Inc., 1948), p. 152.

[11] Morris S. Viteles, *Motivation and Morale in Industry* (New York: W. W.
Norton and Co., 1953), p. 74.

and motivational structure. We must recognize, however, that mainly adjustments of attitudes and motives are accomplished in a way which is consistent with the total personality pattern of the individual.[12] Later we consider such concepts as conflict, frustration, and aspirational levels which this discussion foreshadows.

Personality is unique. And as it is, it is rich and varied. Even though the individual tends to act consistently and to hold attitudes which preserve the stability of his personality, the opportunity within his framework is enormous for flexibility and variety of behavior. The line between attitudes and behavior is not straight. It is usually jagged and discontinuous because of the search process which the individual undertakes to find the means to satisfy his motives.

Attitudes and Values

Attitudes are thought to fall into two general classifications—logical and nonlogical. This method of classification was proposed by Elton Mayo and associates who were involved in the Hawthorne studies. But even before these studies were conducted, Pareto had suggested a similar classification of attitudes.

Logical Attitudes. Logical behavior is prompted by logical attitudes. Logical behavior is such that means are united directly with ends in the ultimate pursuit of a goal. Logical behavior, according to Pareto, must meet the test of outside, objective criticism from someone, besides the acting subject, who knows more about the objective situation. A chemistry professor, for example, is in the position of an outside observer who can evaluate the degree of logic in a student's behavior when the student is performing an experiment.

Thus, when one acts logically the means and subordinate ends are welded to one another for both the objective and subjective purposes of achieving a goal. To illustrate:

Nonlogical Attitudes. Not much of human behavior can be neatly specified as logical. Nonlogical conduct is more characteristic of "typical" behavior. It arises from the opinions, beliefs, and values held by people with respect to the events surrounding them. A dish of porridge may be perceived as too hot, too cold, or just right. Values will differ with regard to major issues over civil rights, a change in the steel contract, or the commitment of American troops to combat in support of foreign policy. Between these extremes are a wide range of events which involve values. For example, a worker might ask himself should I or should I not restrict

---

[12] Functionally induced changes in personality as a result of psychoses and neuroses are not treated in this book. Efforts to change personality through programs of indoctrination are treated in Chapter 16.

output on this job? What if everybody else is doing it? How important is the extra money to me? Is it worth being given the cold shoulder over? No "objective outside observer" exists who can give an answer to these questions, not at least in the sense of our chemistry professor. There are people to give opinions, to judge "right or wrong" conduct out of their frame of reference. But there is not in the strict sense of the word a logical answer or judgment which can be expressed in this situation.

One interesting aspect of nonlogical behavior is the tendency for people often to give logical reasons for their conduct. A man may quit his job, and give inadequate pay for the reason. This may be considered by many as quite logical. In reality, however, the man might actually have left because of a nonacceptance by fellow employees, or dissatisfaction with supervision, or lack of recognition for accomplishment, and so on. This type of behavior may be illustrated as follows:

FIGURE 3-3

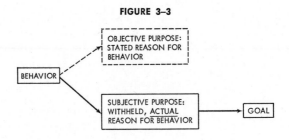

Management and Attitudes

The management implications in the above discussion of attitudes are threefold. First, very little of human conduct is logical. Most human conduct, says Pareto, is nonlogical and originates in psychic states, inclinations, preconceptions, and subconscious feelings. Thus, management must be aware that people are not logic machines, rationally conjoining means with ends in the relentless pursuit of some goal.

Second, the most usual form of behavior is a nonlogical one based on feelings and prejudices. The attitudes underlying nonlogical behavior have been long established and are brought by the employees to the organization. Additionally, other attitudes in this sense are socially produced in the work situation. Nonlogical attitudes are subtle and varied, but they are no less a reality than logical attitudes.

Third, it is often a purely relative matter whether attitudes are logical or nonlogical. It is not enough to consider our attitudes as logical and the other fellow's as nonlogical—a bias which management frequently has. If an individual fails to respond to an incentive system, management might consider him as acting completely at variance with a perfectly logical method of wage payment. But, the individual might think of his actions as quite logical, feeling that it is management's lack of insight into his motives for work which causes him to behave as he does.

MOTIVES

We saw in the last section that motives are states of tension (unsatisfied needs) which trigger behavior aimed at achieving some goal which reduces the tension (or satisfies the need). Thus motives are the impelling force behind goal-directed behavior. An individual perceives a need and responds with a form of behavior appropriate to its satisfaction.

FIGURE 3–4
Basic and Derived Work Motives

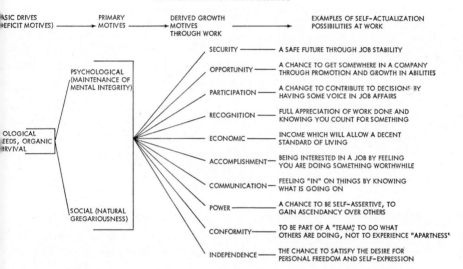

There are different classes of motives influencing an individual's behavior. And just as there are endless numbers of motives, psychologists have endless systems of classification for them. One useful system for our purposes has been suggested by Maslow. He divides motives into deficit and growth types. In the deficit class are those basic motives which are geared to the organic survival of the individual. They include hunger, thirst, nurture, safety, and sexual needs. This list is not exhaustive since these so-called basic drives can be reduced to more refined categories.

The growth motives are derived in the sense that they are learned in the cultural environment and they differ from person to person. These motives provide the opportunity for "higher" forms of satisfactions which lend richness to life. They are, indeed, the instruments of human self-actualization. Figure 3–4 sets out a topology of these classes of motives, both deficit and growth. Much of what is said in the section on motivation rests on it.

Basic Drives

The biological drive, already mentioned, requires the satisfaction of those basic needs essential to maintain physiological integrity—organic survival. The nature of satisfaction for this drive is specifiable. The need for food, water, rest, air, and elimination is necessary for the survival of the human organism, even though the level of satisfaction of these biological requirements differs from person to person.

Primary Motives

There are two primary motives—psychological and social. The psychological motive results in a quest by an individual to maintain his mental integrity or balance. The social motive stems from the natural gregariousness of man, and his need to associate with his fellowman.

Derived Motives

This last category provides the richest source of motives underlying human behavior. The ten derived motives are only a few of many possible reasons why people work. These motives are derived from the basic social and psychological motives. But they are not connected in a specific way to one or the other basic motives. Who can say with any degree of certainty that the recognition motive is social or psychological in origin? The only possible way to find out is by studying an individual, not by generalizing to a whole population.

Derived work motives have the interesting characteristic of being highly dynamic in nature. In this regard, (1) each person at a point in time has a certain hierarchy, a special ordering of importance of the derived motives; and (2) when the motive which is first on his "list" is satisfied, it slips in urgency and another motive takes its place.

Thus when research studies in worker motives turn up the "discovery" that money is not at the top of the list of motives for a group of employees, the correct conclusion is *not* that money is no longer important. Money is still vital but it is not the only reason for working. Once the basic income requirement is satisfied, other motives supersede it on the list of motives, for a time at least.

Functional Autonomy

This note on the concept of functional autonomy is a link between motives and the theories of motivation. As we have observed, American psychology has been a coping, adapting, pragmatic psychology instead of a doing or action psychology. Therefore, it has been more receptive to the so-called "unchanging" theories of motives, rather than "changing" theories.

We have met the unchanging schools before in our discussion of personality. Their general line holds similarly for motives. While it may be a little repetitious, it is instructive to see how their theories work out with respect to motives.

One approach is the concept of reduction which is closely associated with behaviorism. This view holds that adult behavior is merely an habitual response of learned ways of satisfying deficit motives first encountered in childhood. For example, we never rid ourselves of the drive for food. But we learn how to satisfy the hunger need in ways which are both culturally acceptable and pleasure yielding to the individual.

The psychoanalytic school claims that an adult motive is a recapitulation or transference of a childhood conflict or desire. This is reminiscent of the film *Citizen Kane* in which Kane was motivated in his quest for power and fortune by his deprivations in childhood. The symbol of these deprivations was a sled called Rosebud. Both these theories view adult motives as functionally dependent upon the events of childhood.

The concept of functional autonomy, of which Allport is the leading proponent, ". . . regards adult motives as varied, and as self-sustaining, contemporary systems, growing out of antecedent systems, but functionally independent of them."[13] Motives which start as subgoals of drives in childhood may become ends in their own right in adulthood. In this respect functional autonomy emphasizes changes in motives and the factors which cause them.

Thus functional autonomy stresses the importance of social motives such as the need for approval, power, and recognition. But as man is not born with a desire to make money any more than he is born with a love of liberty and justice, functional autonomy makes much of the role of *learning* in the transmutation of goals. Additionally, functionally autonomous motives are not susceptible to extinction. That is, once satisfied they do not disappear, indeed, they may intensify. Once an avid gun collector acquires a rare specimen, his desire is not satiated. Rather he will be motivated to search even harder for difficult to find items.

The importance of this concept is that it frees, conceptually, the individual from slavery to his childhood. The concept is dynamic. It is change oriented. As such this concept occupies a significant position in theories of motivation which have been most widely accepted in the literature of administration.

MOTIVATION

Motivation, in a more traditional sense among management writers, means a process of stimulating people to action to accomplish desired goals. Although many words are substituted for motivation (such as actuating

---

[13] Gordon W. Allport, *Pattern and Growth in Personality* (Holt, Rinehart and Winston, 1961), p. 227. For an appraisal of the status of functional autonomy see John P. Seward, "The Structure of Functional Autonomy," *American Psychologist,* 18 (1963), pp. 703–10.

and directing), the meaning of the process is reasonably clear. Motivation is a function which a manager performs in order to get his subordinates to achieve job objectives.

There is another side to the coin of motivation. It is profitable to look at the motivated state of the individual himself. We need to be concerned with those inner forces which energize and move the individual into avenues of behavior directed toward accomplishing goals.

A theory of motivation implies a theory of personality growth. Motivated states can be researched and reported in static contexts, but when we wish a framework for motivation theory we cannot avoid introducing the dynamic notions of development. As we have said before two theories have been proposed which achieved wide acceptance in administration. They are discussed next.

Two Theories of Motivation

The motivational theories treated in this section are suggested by Maslow[14] and Argyris.[15] These theories should not be considered in any sense as opposed. They are in fact complimentary.

Maslow's Theory. The familiarity of the hierarchial concept of human needs must be attributed to the excellent interpretation given it by Maslow. His well-known approach is based on the idea of *prepotency* of needs.[16] Maslow scales human needs; the most prepotent are lowest on the scale. The physiological needs are first (lowest), then safety needs, love, esteem, and finally the needs for self-actualization. Once the more specific physiological needs are satisfied, *they cease to be motivators of behavior*. The individual then turns to the satisfaction of successively higher levels of needs which are, in order of prepotency:

1. *Safety.* Freedom from fear of external threats such as criminal assaults and climatic extremes.

2. *Love.* The desire for affectionate relationships among family and friends. It is the need to belong to warm supportive associations of other people.

3. *Esteem.* The wish for a high valuation of one's personal worth by oneself and the need for the esteem of others. This need manifests itself in two ways. First, a person requires self-knowledge of competence and mastery in some aspect of the world's endeavors. Second, a person needs the recognition of these achievements by others.

4. *Self-Actualization.* The need to actualize one's intrinsic potentials. The satisfaction of the preceding needs does not produce contentment in the individual. Rather he will be restless unless he can find fulfillment in doing

---

[14] Maslow, *op. cit.*, chap. 5.

[15] Chris Argyris, *Personality and Organization* (New York: Harper and Bros., 1957), chap. 2.

[16] Prepotency means urgency of satisfaction. A thirsty man will devote all his energies to finding water; his thoughts will be dominated by water; all his personal resources will be organized to find satisfaction of this need. Once the need is satisfied, needs at the next level will be activated and the cycle of satisfaction begun again.

what he is fitted to do. As Maslow puts it, "this need might be phrased as the desire to become more and more what one is, to become everything that one is capable of becoming."[17]

There are several refinements of Maslow's theory which must be made explicit. First, this hierarchy refers to the motivational scale of normal, healthy people living in a relatively highly developed society.[18] That is, a society which provides with reasonable reliability for the satisfaction of physiological and safety needs.

Second, if we are interested in what actually motivates behavior, not in what has or will motivate it, we have to say that a satisfied need is not a motivator.

Third, for any normal adult the physiological, safety, and love needs are not motivators. It is only in sick people in our society, those abnormally deprived by one circumstance or another, that these lower needs dominate behavior. It is true among those who have not experienced warm affiliative relationships, or even the esteem of others, that these needs become dominant motivators. The withdrawal of satisfaction of these needs from those who have experienced such satisfactions in the past does not cause these people to begin immediately to search for reaffirmation of love and recognition.

Therefore, and this is crucial from the standpoint of policy conclusions, it is really only the quest for self-actualization that is the motivating force, organizing and directing the behavior, of a normal adult person.

Argyris' Theory. Argyris is less concerned with the hierarchy of needs than he is with tracing in broad terms the normal course of human psychological development. In this respect Argyris points out that from childhood to adulthood personality change is characterized by a movement from passivity and dependency to activity and independency. Thus as a person matures he becomes progressively less reliant on others for the satisfaction of his needs. The emerging force of psychological growth and development is the tendency toward personal freedom—self-actualization.

While this is the key dimension of the theory, there are other supporting elements. For example:

1. As an individual grows he successively differentiates his attention. That is, the adult classifies and categorizes his environment to a far greater extent than the child. He makes finer distinctions among events. This in turn causes the adult's emotional responses to be more varied than the child's.

2. The adult develops lasting and deep interests as opposed to the child's fleeting and shallow concerns.

3. Maturity means increasing control over and awareness of self. The

---

[17] Maslow, *op. cit.*, p. 92.

[18] Maslow carefully observes how a reversal in the hierarchy of needs can occur. The reversal in particular circumstances is not evidence of a pathological condition. See Maslow, *op. cit.*, pp. 98–100.

activity and independence of adulthood is realized only by awareness of it. The individual has to understand its significance and contain it so as not to interfere with the activity and independence of others.

What These Theories Mean in Administration. The compatibility of Maslow's and Argyris' theories has been recognized. But to be a bit more explicit, a child is initially dependent upon his parent for the satisfaction of physiological and safety needs. Later, the need for love and belongingness develops. At the onset of maturity the needs of esteem and self-actualization appear. Thus, the emergence of needs in Maslow's hierarchy is correlated with the physiological maturation of the individual. This illuminates Maslow's point, when he observes that an adult in our society is psychologically unhealthy if his behavior is motivated by the satisfaction of lower needs.

The literature of industrial humanism has echoed one theme consistently. *Design the organization to increase the opportunities for its participants to achieve self-actualization.* There is little doubt that the inspiration of this administrative policy recommendation is directly traceable to the Maslow-Argyris approach.

If the natural course of man's psychological growth is in the direction of self-actualization; and if his mental health depends on the satisfaction of higher needs; then it is obvious that artificial obstacles to higher levels of satisfaction must be removed. This is certainly the *psychological* interpretation one might give to social legislation. For instance, discrimination is an artificial barrier preventing a large number of citizens from achieving self-actualization because of their unnatural concern for the satisfaction of lower needs. Civil rights legislation was formulated to eliminate some of the more flagrant economic, social, and cultural deprivations.

The formal organization and authoritarianism are viewed, in the work setting, as barriers to individual self-actualization. So it has been suggested for the good of its participants, and its own good, *that the organization be redesigned in order to achieve a congruency with the psychological growth needs of its healthy members.*

This, also, is a fundamental aim of industrial humanism. And we see the psychological premise upon which it rests. This aim is so far-reaching that it touches on every facet of organization and the management of people. Several chapters which follow in Part IV consider many of the proposals pertaining to the modification of the formal structure of the organization and the traditional methods of management.

Motivational Frictions

Motivational friction may be defined as either a barrier which prevents an individual from satisfying needs or an incongruity within or between goals sought. These frictions are discussed by psychologists in terms of frustration and conflict. They take many forms and are, of course, a function of what the individual perceives to be a barrier or a conflict. A source of frustration to one person may be a strong incentive to positive action to another. Our treatment must be general and restricted to the organizational setting.

Frustration. Frustration may occur when the organization, or the formal system of authority, implants barriers between the individual and the satisfaction of what he sees to be his needs. Most people react to frustration by adaptive forms of behavior.[19] They may change their goals or reorient their methods of achieving them. There can be degrees of frustration which depend in part on the importance of the goal sought and in part on the strength of the barrier. A weak barrier, considered as the punishment expected by the individual if a course of action is or is not pursued, will not produce a high degree of frustration. The converse is also true. A more basic kind of frustration, noted by Argyris, is when the individual is blocked by the organization in his search for self-actualization.

Conflict. Psychological conflict occurs when the individual is confronted with the need for choice between goals. Conflict in this sense assumes three forms.

1. *Approach–Approach Conflict.*—Choice between mutually exclusive positive goals. For example a person who is being transferred by his company is given the option of relocating in one of two desirable spots.

2. *Approach–Avoidance Conflict.*—Ambivalence toward a goal with both positive and negative outcomes. The problem an individual faces in output restriction often has these elements. By restricting output in accordance to group norms the individual sacrifices money but gains the acceptance of the group. Whyte shows in his study of output restrictors how most subjects had ambivalent attitudes. Sometimes they restricted output, other times they did not. In any case they did not commit themselves to one form of behavior or the other.[20]

3. *Avoidance–Avoidance Conflict.*—Dilemma between two threats. This conflict may be represented by the person who is confronted with the decision to submit to the tyrannical authority of his boss or leave his job. As the individual approaches quitting he retreats because of the fear of economic insecurity. As the individual tries to accept the role he must play to please his boss, he retreats from the point of complete submission to retain some vestige of independence and self-esteem. This kind of conflict tends to go unresolved. Obviously the constant oscillation between unacceptable goals creates discontent and impairs job performance.

Motivational Strength

An individual is propelled toward the accomplishment of goals with varying degrees of motivational strength. This is so whether or not he

---

[19] The mechanisms by which people deal with frustration would constitute a chapter in itself. They include rationalization, projection, and repression of the blocked motive. For further discussion see Berelson and Steiner, *op. cit.,* pp. 282–86.

[20] See William F. Whyte, *Money and Motivation* (New York: Harper and Bros., 1955), esp. chap. 6.

operates out of a framework of goal conflict or an uncomplicated, straightforward effort to satisfy some need. A good deal of research has been done on motivational strength. The model developed by Atkinson provides a valuable orientation to the subject.[21] Motivational strength, according to Atkinson, is a function of three variables which is expressed as follows:[22]

$$\text{Motivation} = f \text{ (Motive} \times \text{Expectancy} \times \text{Incentive)}$$

The terms of the equation mean:

1. *Motive* refers to the general disposition of the individual to strive for the satsfaction of the need. It represents the urgency of the need for fulfillment.

2. *Expectancy* is the subjective calculation of the probability that a given act will succeed in satisfying the need (achieve the goal).

3. *Incentive* is the subjective calculation of the value of the reward hoped for by obtaining the goal.

The Atkinson model has been tested in a number of experimental situations.[23] The model has been applied often to the measure of the achievement need or *n* (achievement). The terms of the equation may be expressed both positively and negatively. Motivation to achieve success and the motivation to avoid failure. Both motives, M_s and M_{af} are aroused in cases where performance is evaluated in terms of standards of excellence. In terms of approach and avoidance tendencies which we discussed in the last section, it may be assumed that the strength of approach is equal to $M \times E \times I$; whereas the strength of avoidance is a negative value of these variables.

These ideas can be extended to embrace the concept of *level of aspiration*. It has been shown that when an individual has had a successful experience achieving a goal his motivational (approach) strength intensifies and he raises his level of aspiration. The opposite result—failure to achieve—is likely to cause an individual to lower his level of aspiration.[24]

Berelson and Steiner point out that people in many situations set their

---

[21] John W. Atkinson, "Motivational Determinants of Risk Taking Behavior," *Psychological Review*, November, 1957, pp. 359–72.

[22] In an earlier study, Kahn and Morse pointed out that motivational strength was dependent upon (1) the strength of the need served by the behavior, (2) availability of alternative behaviors to meet the need, (3) the extent to which behavior sets up opposing tensions to interfere with the satisfaction of other needs, and (4) the ratio of need satisfaction to required energy input–pleasure-pain. R. L. Kahn and N. C. Morse, "The Relationship of Morale to Productivity," *Journal of Social Issues*, 1951, p. 12.

[23] See for example, Charles P. Smith, "Achievement-related Motives and Goal Setting under Different Conditions," *Journal of Personality*, 31 (1963), pp. 124–39.

[24] One researcher reports on a typical situation where success causes a lowering in the level of aspiration while failure causes increases in the level of aspiration. See Robert W. Moulton, "Effects of Success and Failure on Level of Aspiration as Related to Achievement Motives," *Journal of Personality and Social Psychology*, May, 1965, pp. 399–406.

level of aspiration where the tendencies to approach a goal cross the tendencies to avoid the goal for fear of failure.[25] This can be shown diagramatically as follows.

FIGURE 3–5

Aspirational Levels and Approach-Avoidance Tendencies

Adapted from Neal E. Miller, "Experimental Studies of Conflict," in *Personality and the Behavior Disorders,* J. McV. Hunt. Copyright 1944, The Ronald Press Company, New York.

Success or failure affect the position of the gradients. For example success ordinarily raises (strengthens) the approach gradient and lowers (weakens) the avoidance gradient. This causes the intersection at higher goal levels of the approach-avoidance tendencies.

CONCLUSION

McClelland's book *The Achieving Society* and his article "Business Drive and National Achievement"[26] have given immediacy and direct significance to the concepts of personality, motivation, and n (achievement) developed in this chapter. His imaginative hypotheses underscore the importance of the motivating potential of the need to achieve, a trait peculiar in American businessmen, in the emergence of a national character. This need has assumed cultural overtones in which Americans participate to some extent.

Our discussion in this chapter dwelt upon personality and motivation. One of the major points in this analysis is the social context in which personality growth and motivation takes place. With this in mind we turn to the small group.

---

[25] Berelson and Steiner, *op. cit.,* p. 275.

[26] David C. McClelland, *The Achieving Society* (New York: D. Van Nostrand Co., 1962), and "Business Drive and National Achievement," *Harvard Business Review,* July–August, 1962, pp. 99–112.

CHAPTER **4**

The Small Group

SOME CONCEPTUAL HANDLES as structure, communication, function, and goals, are equally applicable to several classes of organization. But the processes to which they refer and the behavioral dynamics which flows from these processes are quite different on the level of the small group vis-à-vis the large organization. Therefore it is important that we make a careful distinction among organizational types.

The small group is composed of a restricted number of people, usually fewer than seven, who enjoy personal interaction over a fairly long span of time. People in this relationship show a degree of commonality of interest often expressed as a goal upon which there is mutual agreement. To facilitate the actual process of goal accomplishment, a differentiation of role and function exists in the small group. Additionally, the group itself has some amount of self-sufficiency to enable it to adapt to changing conditions in its environment.[1] This discussion gives us some clues to the variables which we must consider in this chapter. They are:

1. Solidarity.
2. Continuity and duration of association.
3. Size.
4. Role and the nature of group tasks.
5. Goals and group output.
6. Autonomy and interorganizational accommodation.

These variables are treated, not necessarily in this order, in the following three sections on group formation determinates, group characteristics, and group output.

GROUP FORMATION DETERMINATES

In order for a group to exist there must be *interpersonal consensus*.[2] Group members need a common ground of agreement on goals and to a

---

[1] Bernard Berelson and Gary A. Steiner, *Human Behavior: An Inventory of Scientific Findings* (New York: Harcourt, Brace & World, Inc., 1964), p. 326.

[2] Theodore M. Newcomb, "The Study of Consensus," in Robert K. Merton *et al.* (eds.), *Sociology Today: Problems and Prospects* (New York: Basic Books, Inc., 1959), pp. 227–29.

lesser extent perhaps, a common orientation on ways to achieve goals. From consensus, comes what sociologists call "we feeling" or group solidarity. Given appropriate conditions, consensus forms naturally as it were. Even starting with a group of strangers, subgroups appear based upon mutual acceptance of each other by people who perceive they hold similar attitudes and values.

Granting the fundamental character of consensus, there are still other determinates which precede it and support it. One such determinate is interaction.

Interaction

At the root of consensus is the psychological basis for social interaction. That is, a human need exists to interact with others to solve problems, to obtain goals, to facilitate coordination, to reduce tension, and to achieve a balance in human relationships. An extreme example of what happens when people are unable to achieve these basic social quanta is nicely illustrated in Vladimir Nabokov's novel *The Defense.*

This story is about how a man's monolithic devotion to chess prevented any meaningful, sustaining relationship to develop with any other human being including his wife. The hero's interpretation of the structure of his interaction with his wife and her family and friends was in terms of a chess game which required moves and countermoves on his part. He communicated with no one. He was almost nonverbal. He was unable to achieve consensus with others even in the simplest of human situations. In the end, his sole defense against the encroachments he thought were being made on his abstract world of chess was suicide.

While the hero probably was insane, the basis of his insanity was failure to establish any sensible pattern of interaction with others. This vacuum was filled for years by his passion for chess. But because of circumstances in his later life he was engulfed in the "real" human situation of marriage. This was his undoing, because his chess art could not be substituted for effective interpersonal relationships.

In the absence of pathological barriers, face-to-face contact among people usually produces consensus or withdrawal from interaction. Homans, in his classic work, has shown that, "the more frequently persons interact with one another, the more alike in some respects both their activities and their sentiments tend to become. Moreover, the more a person's activities and sentiments resemble those of others, the more likely it is that interaction between him and these others will increase."[3]

Thus, frequent interaction reinforces consensus. The point is made by Newcomb who shows that the "psychological need" for consensus will generate a circular tendency magnifying a perceived consensus with another person or several persons.[4]

---

[3] George C. Homans, *The Human Group* (New York: Harcourt, Brace and Company, 1950), p. 120.

[4] Newcomb, *op. cit.,* pp. 289–90.

People will tend to move into groups where they share values and norms with others. Such a situation is supportive and comfortable for the individual. When interests are held in common, consensus is more easily achieved. However, the perception of common interest and shared values is possible only when the parties communicate. Hence, communication becomes another crucial determinate in group formation.

Communication

Generally speaking, consensus is rewarding to group participants. Since this is so, interaction and communication as means to consensus are also rewarding. We speak in a later chapter of the psychological basis of communication as the reduction of tension between or among individuals with regard to resolving the nature of goals or ambiguity in the social situation. We may draw on this idea now and say that if in the process of interaction A and B find they are in disagreement over some other object or individual C, a state of imbalance exists in their relationship. This imbalance is accompanied by tension or strain, which in turn motivates communication. The ensuing communication between the parties may lead to a positive resolution of the source of imbalance thus creating a consensus or a balanced state between the individuals. Of course, it is possible that communication may clarify the issue such that the parties may see that consensus is impossible. In this case two alternatives emerge. One, the individuals may withdraw[5] from the field of interaction. Two, if withdrawal is out of the question conflict may result.

Communication Patterns in Small Groups. Numerous experiments have tested the behavioral and performance outcomes of various small group communication patterns. Perhaps the best known are those conducted by Bavelas[6] whose findings have generally been supported in subsequent studies by other researchers.[7] Four types of networks were used by Bavelas, the circle, chain, "Y," and wheel (see Figure 4–1). Communication between individuals was permitted just along those channels prescribed by the pattern. The communicators were experimentally "insulated" from cross talk.

Three experimental results with respect to these networks need comment.

1. Centrality of position in sending and receiving messages produces

---

[5] Withdrawal can either be physical or psychological. In either case, interaction is terminated. While withdrawal may produce a kind of balance in interpersonal relations, it could in the larger sense be detrimental in the accomplishment of organizational goals particularly if the interaction occurs in a work-oriented formal organization.

[6] Alex Bavelas, "Communication Patterns in Task-Oriented Groups," *Journal of the Acoustical Society of America,* 22 (1950), pp. 725–30.

[7] For example see, Harold Guetzkow and Herbert A. Simon, "The Impact of Certain Communication Nets upon Organization and Performance in Task-Oriented Groups," *Management Science,* 1 (1955), pp. 233–50.

group leaders. The leaders, identified in the networks by a black dot, are strategically positioned to relay the information to other group members which is necessary for task performance.

2. From the standpoint of efficiency in organizing for task perform- ance, the wheel is the fastest, followed by the "Y," the chain, and the circle. The reader should observe that this is a descending order of centrality. In the wheel, the leader may communicate with each other member with equal facility. Communication becomes increasingly dif- ficult for the leader in each of the other networks.

3. The researchers found a differential effect in solving problems. For simple problems which require a minimum of interaction the wheel is the fastest. Group members are content to send all information to the central source to be acted upon and coordinated. For more difficult problems,

FIGURE 4–1
Small Group Communication Patterns

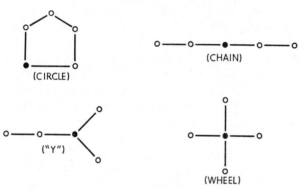

requiring interaction the circle is fastest. In another set of experiments, Shaw[8] found an all-channel network with free communication to be the fastest among all other types in handling complex problems.

4. While these experiments artificially establish various communication patterns, the conclusions drawn from them about speed of organization, efficiency, problem solving, and leadership are useful in understanding group behavior in natural settings. In this respect, we observe that the studies considered above on communication networks tend not to be con- cerned directly with the satisfaction variable. There is research, however, on small group communication in real organizational settings such as gov- ernment, business, and military. Frequently noticed in these situations is the fact that people derive far more satisfaction and are usually more productive under conditions which allow open communication among all group members.[9]

---

[8] Marvin E. Shaw, "Some Effects of Problem Complexity upon Problem Solution Efficiency in Different Communication Nets," *Journal of Experimental Psychology,* 48 (1954), pp. 211–17.

[9] Robert C. Ziller, "Communication Restraints, Group Flexibility, and Group Confidence," *Journal of Applied Psychology,* 42 (1958), pp. 346–52.

We must be careful to point out that there is a difference between inter- and intragroup communication. Usually the problem of communication flexibility arises in individual, small group, and formal organizational relationships. Here, there is considerable evidence that a permissive formal climate which encourages free communication draws upon the strength of small groups (work teams) to accomplish organizational goals. But within the small group itself there is a great deal of communicative freedom and exchange. Whether or not small group transactions and goals are consistent with or antagonistic toward formal organizational interests is not the issue at present.

Returning to the theme of this section, we propose that operationally defined a small group is composed of those who have reached a consensus as the result of free exchange of information. In this sense, we define the group in terms of the *communication network* which evolves to handle interactional transactions. Given this point, other determinates arise to facilitate exchange. They are location, common interests, and group size.

Location

One of the most obvious truisms in the analysis of small group behavior is that people must be proximate to each other for an extended period of time in order to interact, communicate, and form a consensus. A group cannot exist unless interpersonal relationships are maintained on a continuous basis for some duration. This requires frequent face-to-face contact which can result only from geographical proximity. Georg Simmel, the sociologist, made this point many years ago.[10] The same phenomenon was reported by Festinger in a study of sociometric choice of friends based upon their location in a housing project. He says:

> . . . the greatest number of choices were made to people living closest to the person choosing and the choices decreased continuously as distance from the home of the chooser increased. The actual measured distances involved were quite small, in no case being larger than 180 feet.[11]

Location alone certainly is not the sole determinate of small group composition, but it is an indispensable prerequisite to group formation. Location is significant in analyzing small groups in large organizations. In the course of daily work routines, location, distinct from functionalization, determines who will see whom. In one mail-order company, for example, two almost identical functions are performed in units located at either end of a building one block long. Although the functions are similar, the geographic barrier prevents the employees in these units from forming a lasting informal association.

---

[10] Georg Simmel, *The Web of Group-Affiliations*, trans. Reinhard Bendix (New York: The Free Press of Glencoe, 1955), pp. 128–30.

[11] See Leon Festinger, Stanley Schachter, and Kurt Back, *Social Pressures in Informal Groups* (New York: Harper and Bros., 1950), pp. 153–63.

But because of functionalization and departmentation, those who are in similar occupations tend to be grouped in the same location. Factory workers, secretaries, technicians, engineers, and scientists usually have to look no further than their job station, bench, desk, or laboratory table to see someone else doing a similar job. Occupational groupings which go hand in hand with physical location provide a natural setting for the formation of group affiliations. Indeed, initial groupings of total strangers may be based on little more than several people doing something similar in adjacent physical space. Occupations, additionally, provide people with a basis for forming status differentials which are used in marking off the boundaries of one small group from others.

For example, visualize a large room in a business office where 25 girls are performing clerical jobs. Suppose the work is broken down thusly:

1. File clerks—8.
2. Comptometer operators—6.
3. Typists—7.
4. Stenographers—4.

In this case location does not pose a barrier to group affiliation because though the room is big, people can circulate freely enough to have frequent contact with others if the desire is there. Since geography is not a problem, then the next basis for group affiliation is occupation. That is, stenographers associate with stenographers, typists with typists, and so on.

The occupational determinate of affiliation will be potentially operational if the people in the office *perceive status differentials* in their jobs. Comptometer operators will maintain exclusiveness in their small group if they perceive file clerks and typists below them statuswise. In turn the comptometer operators will not be admitted to the inner circle of stenographers if these latter see themselves at the peak of the occupational status pyramid in the office. If no status differences in occupation are perceived, or if they are but are not considered relevant, then small groups will form without occupational bias. In this instance, the determinate of group composition is mutual perception of shared values and common interest.

Common Interest

We see, therefore, people will form in small groups with membership that crosses occupational lines if they find others who share the same values. Among them an individual can enjoy comfortable relationships and at the same time gain support. The group reinforces the individual in his search for "correct" standards of behavior. This is especially important in situations which tend to be externally threatening or ambiguous. The group gives the individual confidence.

Output restriction is a classic example of this behavior.[12] Researchers

---

[12] See William F. Whyte, *Money and Motivation* (New York: Harper and Bros., 1955).

identify it as a group rather than an individual phenomenon. Output restriction is a response to an external threat. Either a group of workers fear that an easy job on which standard output can be made without much effort will be restudied and the standards changed or they are protesting against a job on which standard output is exceedingly difficult to achieve. In either case the threat comes from the formal structure of authority in general, and the time and motion study experts in particular. Now the protest-protection behavior would be too hazardous for an individual to engage in alone. But being backed up by a group of like-minded people on the job lends the individual courage.

The life of modern man, particularly in urbanized and industrialized areas, is so complicated that the above constructions about the determinates which underlie the formation of discrete groups obscures the role of group relationships in the whole of an individual's life. Indeed, a person has numerous connections with different groups which are basic such as the family, social groups, work-oriented groups, and service groups. Simmel's concept of the *web* of group affiliation expresses it well from the individual's standpoint.

A person is a member of several small groups which overlap in his life. Frequently he is caught between groups with conflicting values. When values conflict, the individual will move toward the group which has the most influence over him, that is, the most relevance to him. If family ties are loose, gang loyalties and values will prevail in a child's life. If a company does not have an employee's confidence that it will administer work standards fairly, then the individual seeks appropriate defensive support in a group, or a union, or both. People, too, drift in and out of groups seeking those with values and interests complementary to and reinforcing their own. They are motivated by the "need for consensus" in the quest.

The perception of common interest is a motivating force joining a particular combination of individual personalities in a small group. Once people are gathered in physical proximity, sometimes functionally differentiated, sometimes not, the existence of shared values acts to refine, to sift down into small subgroups, those who make up the larger assemblage. These arrangements facilitate intragroup communication, leading to effective interaction, and finally consensus, thus filling a basic human need for social interaction.

Group Size

One of the more intriguing questions connected with group formation is what size group contributes most to effective interaction and stability. Certainly we have no difficulty establishing lower limits to group size. The dyad, or two-person group, is minimum in terms of social interaction. The maximum number presents more of a problem. We know that as group size increases beyond seven communication and interaction rigidifies.[13] For example, the high status person in the group becomes the focus of interactional attention. Lower status persons tend to interact less among themselves. At the same time, the high status individual personifies the group in his communication downward and deals less with individuals as personalities in the group.

These transformations in intragroup behavior probably are the embryonic stages of formalization. Concomitant with increased size, to the point where personal interaction is reduced substantially, is a fragmentation of the larger group into smaller subgroups where freer exchange among members can occur. This is not to say that the larger organization goes out of existence. It may or may not. Often the larger group preserves its identity as a more or less formalized structure with purposes distinct from subgroups.

It should be clear that certain kinds of tasks require more human resources than others. Thus, while size may limit the freedom for personal interaction, it may be absolutely necessary to add people for the performance of tasks which require from them greater inputs of skill and information. All this is simply to say that the task demands, which cause an organization to increase in size, are of a different order from the interactional needs.

The Dyad. The two-person group has been widely studied in both natural and experimental settings.[14] This group is most interesting because it is the only size where task performance is definitely thwarted by the withdrawal of one of the parties. Also it is impossible in this relationship for either party to form a coalition with another against one of the members. Therefore, those in a two-person group are forced, as it were, to establish a working relationship if they intend to accomplish anything through their mutual efforts. This situation gives rise to some unique behavioral responses.

The pressure to cooperate tends to produce high rates of tension between parties manifested as a conscious attempt to avoid disagreement and antagonism. Hence, each must be responsive to the cues sent by the other. So in any successful dyad there is an intense degree of information exchange and feedback.

The balance of power in such a group is fragile because both parties are aware that disagreement or withdrawal could result in the failure of the relationship. Thus the tendency is present to set permissible limits to the interactional range. For example, husbands and wives will avoid matters which one perceives to be distasteful to the other. If they did not the total

---

[13] Robert F. Bales, "Some Uniformities of Behavior in Small Social Systems," in Guy E. Swanson, Theodore M. Newcomb, and Eugene L. Hartley (eds.), *Readings in Social Psychology* (New York: Henry Holt and Co., 1952), p. 155.

[14] This discussion is based on Robert F. Bales, A. Paul Hare, and Edgar F. Borgatta, "Structure and Dynamics of Small Groups: A Review of Four Variables," in Joseph B. Gittler (ed.), *Review of Sociology* (New York: John Wiley and Sons, 1957), pp. 399–400.

relationship might possibly be wrecked, destroying the opportunity for obtaining other advantages which married life offers.

Even though power arrangements in dyads are finely balanced, there is a differentiation of roles. One role is of initiative and overt power. The other is a passive role in which the party holds a veto over action. Depending on the situation these roles may be exchanged between the parties.

What happens if a third person is added to an established dyad? It has been postulated that if the original partners view each other negatively, one of them (if not both) will look upon the new member in a favorable light. In other words an inverse relationship between existing partners' attitudes toward each other, and their attitudes toward a newcomer is thought to exist.

While evidence is scarce, this hypothesis does not seem to hold. Heiss's study[15] on newcomers' acceptance shows that partners with positive attitudes toward each other will also have positive attitudes toward the third person who newly arrives on their group field. This in part can be explained by the fact that if two people enjoy a pleasurable relationship, they have no reason to expect that the experience will change with the addition of another. As Heiss puts it, ". . . a satisfying relationship with the partner leads to a pleasant interaction, and the pleasantness of the interaction colors [favorably] the perception of the newcomer."[16] This conveniently moves us into the analysis of behavior in established three-person groups.

The Triad. Of keen interest in three-person groups is their tendency to form coalitions. Because of the group size, one of the number may be isolated in the interaction process. The power of the majority of two has to be considerable over the minority of one when a decision must be reached. Thus deadlock is not as great a threat to group integrity in the three-person group as it is in the two. However, there is the danger that if the role of a minority person is continuously thrust upon the same person the group will dissolve into a dyad because the isolated individual will withdraw from interaction. Therefore, it has been observed in this size group that the minority person switches so that the same person is not always the focal point of majority power.

Freilich[17] presents an interesting special case of triads in formal organizations. He points out that natural triads form among persons playing roles differentiated by function and status. The pattern of the triad includes:

---

[15] Jerold S. Heiss, "The Dyad Views the Newcomer," *Human Relations*, August, 1963, pp. 241–48.

[16] *Ibid.*, p. 248.

[17] Morris Freilich, "The Natural Triad in Kinship and Complex Systems," *American Sociological Review*, August, 1964, pp. 529–39.

1. A high status authority.
2. A high status friend.
3. A low status subordinate.

They are arranged as shown in Figure 4-2.

In a business organization the HSA might be a department manager and the LSS a young management trainee. HSA-LSS form a typical formal authority relationship. In this case, let us assume that HSF represents another executive in the company who is interested in LSS's career but has no formal authority over him. LSS looks to HSF for guidance, he feels a degree of warmth toward him that he cannot have for HSA who relates to him out of a position of formal authority and power. The interesting

FIGURE 4-2.
The Formal Organizational Setting of a Triad

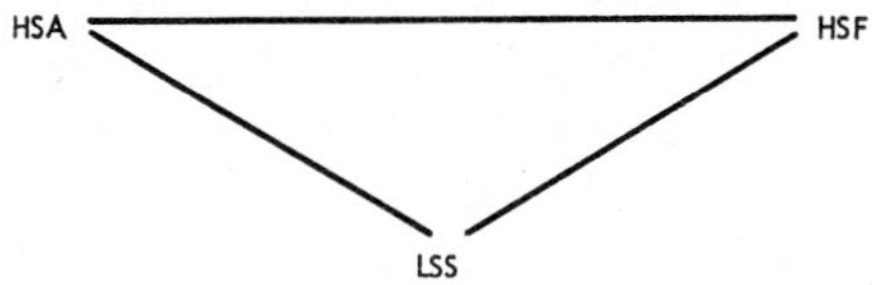

aspect of the relationship LSS bears to HSA and HSF is that while they differ in content they are both nonreciprocal. That is, HSA initiates action for LSS. LSS seeks advice from and cries on the shoulder of HSF, but never the other way around.

Out of this interaction is the inevitable coalition which we have seen is peculiar to triads. However, in this relationship in a formal setting the coalition always includes LSS as one member usually joined by HSF as the other. This leaves HSA in the permanent role of "minority" member. However, the relationship does not, in fact cannot, collapse into a dyad. The formal authority and power of the position which HSA holds ensures the continuity of the three-way relationship. What actually happens is that the friendship coalition between HSF-LSS creates a balance offset to the formal position of HSA thus producing a stable triad.

Well, one might ask, what happens to all the LSSs who do not have friends in high places? Of course there are lots of these sorts, and what seems to occur in many organizations, particularly large ones, is for the role of HSF to be institutionalized in some function supported by the organization. In the military services an obvious example is the chaplain. Less obvious in these organizations, serving a similar function, is the Inspector General. The personnel department often operates as a high-status friend in business organizations. One could interpret these activities, and the support given them by the top policymakers, as an effort to promote organizational stability through triads which pose some offset to the formal power possessed by officials.

The Four-Person Group. The research which has been done on this size group indicates high incidence of disagreement and antagonism among group members.[18] There are strong tendencies to deadlock over decisions resulting in the collapse of the group into a pair of dyads. The pressure for agreement in order to preserve group identity is less apparent in the four person than in the dyad. This is because in the four-person group, coalitions of two find mutual support in opposition to the other two in the group.

The Five-Person Group. Some evidence exists[19] indicating that this size group is the most satisfying to participants. It is small enough to allow easy interaction among members. At the same time, there are sufficient people pooling information resources to provide mutual stimulation in problem solving and decision situations. In the case of disagreement, individuals may find support (in the event of a 3–2 split).

Summing up, odd number groups tend to show greater stability and produce more satisfying relationships for group members than even numbered ones. An exception is in the case of the three-person group which does not have shifting coalitions, thus forcing one person constantly to play the role of minority member. Even numbered groups tend to have higher rates of tension as in the case of the dyad. In larger groups of four or six, deadlock, disagreement, and antagonism often arise instead of constructive interaction toward consensus.

However, before we stray too far from the main theme, groups of any size between two and seven maximize the potential for interaction in spite of their internal peculiarities which make for ease or difficulty in achieving consensus. Beyond seven, interaction is reduced, communication tends to be directed toward a focal member, and splintering among the larger group's members into groups of smaller size occurs. Thus, size, as we said before, is a basic determinate of small group formation, stability, and continuity.

Concluding Remarks on Group Formation

In this section we reviewed six determinates which are crucial in forming and sustaining small groups. Of these consensus is probably the most fundamental. But leading to it are the other determinates which make consensus possible: interaction, communication, common interests, location, and size.

These determinates should not be considered as arranged in some sort of sequence leading eventually to consensus. It is obvious that communi-

---

[18] See Robert F. Bales and Edgar F. Borgatta, "A Study of Group Size: Size of Group as a Factor in the Interaction Profile," in A. Paul Hare, Edgar F. Borgatta, and Robert F. Bales (eds.), *Small Groups: Studies in Social Interaction* (New York: Alfred A. Knopf, Inc., 1955), pp. 396–414.

[19] Robert F. Bales, "In Conference," *Harvard Business Review,* 32 (1954), pp. 44–50.

cation, interaction, and perceptions of common interest go on together in the early stages of group formation. The parts played by communication and interaction in sustaining group life are practically indistinguishable. The location and size determinates are qualitatively distinct from the others. They either facilitate or impede small group processes. They are not actually behavioral components of the processes themselves. With these ideas established, we turn next to the characteristics of small groups.

CHARACTERISTICS OF SMALL GROUPS

Once formed small groups develop structure, control member's behavior, tend to resist change, and produce leaders. These characteristics occupy our attention in this section.

Structural Relationships

Because small groups are based on a sociopsychological logic, their structure appears less symmetrical than the "idealized" structure of formal organizations which is depicted as neat, straight lines connecting functions and levels of command in a hierarchy. Sociometric analysis provides an instrument to find and plot the pattern of interaction in small groups.

The organization shown in Figure 4–3 is one sort of chart which sociometric analysis can produce. Note that there are three status categories: the primary group, a fringe status, and an out status. The primary group, which corresponds to the concept of "small group" as we have been using it, is the focal point of this organization's orbit. It is made up of people who have reached consensus. The primary group establishes and maintains a value system comprising behavioral norms.

The individuals in it cluster about a key person designated "A." This individual is the informal leader.

FIGURE 4–3
The Orbit of Small Group Relationships

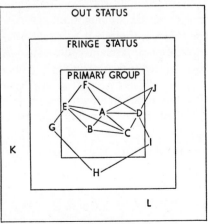

The fringe status position ordinarily is dynamic. Individuals occupying it remain for a short time. They are new to the orbit of the small group. For example in a company they may be newly hired, or transferred from another department, or promoted. Because they are recently on the scene, they are evaluating and are being evaluated by the primary group. Eventually, either they will be accepted by the group or they will move into the out status position.

Those who are "out" have neither close ties among themselves nor with others in the system. They are referred to as *isolates*. An out status may or may not be a personal catastrophe. If an individual is not interested in

FIGURE 4–4
Nonprescribed Work Relationships in
Formal Organizations

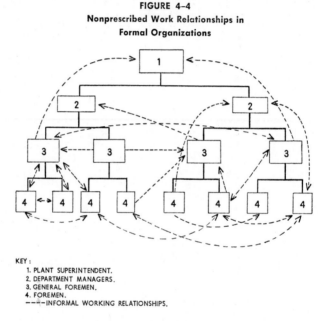

KEY:
1. PLANT SUPERINTENDENT.
2. DEPARTMENT MANAGERS.
3. GENERAL FOREMEN.
4. FOREMEN.
−−−−INFORMAL WORKING RELATIONSHIPS.

ascribing to group values for one reason or another, he may not mind this status. But if the individual seeks companionship and is not accepted, his ostracism could be a personal disaster.

Sometimes an individual's decision not to accept the norms of the group may be interpreted by the primary group as a threat to its existence. For example, a rate-buster is a threat to those practicing output restriction. Group retaliation for the threats posed by the isolate can range from a "cold-shoulder" treatment to a blob of grease in the lunch bucket.

Another use of sociometric technique lies in analysis of working relationships which exist in the formal organization. One method is to show a conventional diagram of the formal organization, and then superimpose on it dotted lines showing working relationships. This technique, illustrated in Figure 4–4 depicts work relationships among people on the same functional level and up and down the chain of command. The results indicate work patterns considerably different from the structural relations prescribed by the formal organization.[20]

Social Control

Small groups exert social influence. Like most organizations, the group provides rewards, but it also makes behavioral demands on its members. Each group has a culture with standards of conduct to which individuals must conform if they expect to derive advantages of group association. Some of the advantages are:

1. Relief from monotony, boredom, and fatigue.
2. Opportunities for status through belonging to prestige groups and associating with those in power positions.
3. Increased flow of emotional responses where the group offers a chance for self-expression to the individual.
4. Increased security by support and reinforcement of the individual, providing him assurance of the "correctness" of his behavior with respect to others in and out of the group.[21]

The degree to which a group can influence its members, of course, can vary. In general, it is said that the greater the relevance to achieving his own goals an individual sees in group participation, the greater the influence the group has over him. Other variables also exist.

1. The amount of cohesiveness and stability of the group determines the extent of its influence. Thus, ambiguity in the group regarding its own values and objectives cause reduced control over members.
2. But, if the environment about the group is ambiguous or threatening, the more able the group is to influence participants. This is because members look to it for support and reassurance in situations with high degrees of uncertainty.

However, even in cases where group membership was not highly relevant for achieving individual goals, and where the situation was not threatening, Asch,[22] in a series of classical experiments, demonstrated the profound effect group pressure has on individual judgment. Asch rigged an experimental situation in which a group was preinstructed to state wrong judgments publicly when asked to match the length of a given line with one of three unequal lines. In a substantial number of cases, an uninstructed subject, who perceived the correct relationship between the lines denied the evidence of his sense when subjected to group pressure.

---

[20] This method is demonstrated by Ralph M. Stogdill, "The Sociometry of Working Relationships in Formal Organizations," *Sociometry*, November, 1949, pp. 276–86.

[21] Eugene V. Schneider, *Industrial Sociology* (New York: McGraw-Hill Book Co., Inc., 1957), pp. 193–203.

[22] S. E. Asch, "Effects of Group Pressure upon the Modification and Distortion of Judgment," in Dorwin Cartwright and Alvin Zander, *Group Dynamics* (Evanston: Row, Peterson and Company, 1960), pp. 189–200.

The independent subject did not know he was being plotted against. Furthermore he was so placed in the group that he was the last to state his judgment.

Resistance to Change and Preservation of Culture

Group tendency to resist change is frequently observed. But to state this phenomenon more precisely, a group tends to resist those changes which are perceived as threatening to its survival. Certainly groups do not resist all changes.

As we have stated before, groups develop a culture with standards of behavior and a value structure. These groups have utility for their members. Therefore, any force outside the group which is perceived as a threat to its integrity, such as changes in supervision, work content, or work relationships, will cause resistance. The classic study of resistance to change was conducted by Coch and French.[23] They found that resistance to change was manifested in several ways. The overt demonstrations were reduction of productivity and turnover. But there were also the more subtle reactions of frustration and then aggression toward the supervisor, the time study man, and higher levels of management.

Group culture is quite durable largely because of the wariness its members have toward potentially disrupting influences originating in its surroundings. Even turnover in group membership seems not to alter greatly the content of a group's culture. Suppose we are observing a hypothetical group of six members in a formal organization. This group is closely integrated and has clear consensus of its values and goals. However, due to changes initiated by the formal organization, a different member of the group leaves every six to eight months and is replaced by a new person. For simplicity, we assume the new man is accepted and becomes a member of the group. At the end of three to three and one-half years the entire membership of the group has changed from our arbitrary starting point. But if we examine the content of the culture of this group on a before and after basis, we find very little change in it.[24] The group preserves its culture through the process of transmitting it from the older members to the new. Thus, staggered succession over a period of time is less disruptive to group members and group culture than wholesale replacement of group members in a single unit of time.[25]

---

[23] Lester Coch and John R. P. French, Jr., "Overcoming Resistance to Change," in Schuyler Dean Hoslett (ed.), *Human Factors in Management* (New York: Harper and Bros., 1951), pp. 242–68.

[24] The implicit assumption in this discussion is that the structural, technological, and social climate surrounding the group does not change substantially over this period. If conditions external to the group do not remain fairly constant, the group may have to change its values, norms, and goals to adapt in order to survive.

[25] See Donald B. Trow, "Membership Succession and Team Performance," *Human Relations*, 13 (1960), pp. 259–68. Another interesting discussion of cultural preservation in units of a housing development is given by William H. Whyte, Jr., *The Organization Man* (New York: Simon and Schuster, 1956), chap. 25.

Group Leadership

The leader is more or less elected to this position by his associates. It is difficult to say just what criteria are used to determine who the leader will be. Work skills, sympathetic personality, age are all possible criteria. However, it appears to be generally true that group leaders possess two broad characteristics.

1. *Ability to Communicate.* The leader is both a transmitter and receiver of information. He is a sort of clearinghouse of information for the informal organization. He is "in on the know." And, probably more important, he is willing to transmit all information to his followers in the informal organization.

2. *Ability to Embody the Values of the Primary Group.* This characteristic is somewhat more elusive than the first. The leader is a kind of living representation of the things the group stands for. He is able to perceive the values of the group, crystallize them into a coherent ideology, and verbalize them to others outside the group. This is what is meant when the informal leader is referred to as the spokesman of the group.

As long as the values of the primary group remain stable, as long as the informal leader continues to embody and communicate these values, and as long as the membership and environment of the primary group remain relatively stable, the informal leader is likely to retain his position. But, as the provisos indicate, stability of values, membership, and environment seem to be critical conditions for his continued leadership. Each provision should be examined in a little more detail.

The composition of group membership and the stability of its values are of course important to the designation of a particular leader. As observed above, a moderate turnover of group membership over a relatively long period of time will not result in a radical change in the values of the group. Under circumstances such as these it is likely that a leader will continue in his function. However, a rapid and large turnover of group membership—not including the leader himself—may introduce new ideas and values into the group which are not adequately represented by the old leader. In this case the old leader may be displaced and his position assumed by an individual selected from the newer employees.

It almost goes without saying that a leader will be replaced if he no longer embodies and communicates the values of the group. This provision explains cases where the leader no longer acts in a leadership capacity for his old group when he is promoted to a higher level in the formal organization. For example, a leader might be promoted to foreman. This change in status requires him to reorient his values. More often than not he is forced to relinquish his former leadership role in the group.

Finally, if the environment changes, the leader may also be changed. For example, one individual may serve as a leader under stable, slowly changing conditions, but if an emergency situation arises a different individual might emerge to take leadership.

Much of what we say in Chapter 9 on "Social Influence" about leadership functions, determinates, and the duality of leadership roles bears on this discussion. The reader is referred to this chapter if he wishes to go more deeply into this matter right away.

GROUP OUTPUT

Broadly conceived, group output is conceptualized as two interdependent variables: (1) effectiveness of the group in accomplishing goals and (2) the satisfaction of group members. Satisfaction of members is increased when they perceive congruency between their personal objectives and those of the group. If group members perceive a mutuality of interest between what they are seeking and group goals, then working toward one's own goals will facilitate the achievement of group goals. The opposite is true as well. That is, conflict between member goals and group goals lower levels of satisfaction and group output.

In their analysis of the extensive literature on the subject, Heslin and Dunphy have isolated three dimensions of member satisfaction in groups which if fulfilled will increase group effectiveness.[26]

Dimension 1—Status consensus. Group agreement on relative status of all group members yields uniformity and reinforcement of group norms which, in turn, produces higher levels of satisfaction.

Dimension 2—Goal achievement. Member perception that the group is progressing satisfactorily in achieving its ends contributes to member satisfaction. When the group fails consistently to achieve goals, or is frustrated by achievement below anticipated levels, membership satisfaction declines.

Dimension 3—Participation. Satisfaction and output depend on perceived freedom by persons to participate in decision-making and communication activities. Free communication seems to produce higher levels of satisfaction. Increased participation raises member satisfaction as well.

These observations lead to the conclusion that in general more democratic, less-constrained environments are associated with both high satisfaction and output within small groups. The relationship of participation and communication to the output-satisfaction variables in formal task-oriented organizations is discussed at greater length in Chapters 7 and 13.

AUTONOMY AND ORGANIZATIONAL INTEGRATION

As we see in Chapter 6, there are various levels of systems. In fact a system is an arbitrary thing. It is what we define it to be. Hence, one system could be an individual person, another the small group, a third, the formal organization, and finally the fourth, the "complex" organization which encompasses conceptually the other three. If we take the latter as

---

[26] Richard Heslin and Dexter Dunphy, "Three Dimensions of Member Satisfaction in Small Groups," *Human Relations,* May, 1964, pp. 99–112.

our "system" point of departure, as many do who study the bureaucratic phenomenon, then we must allow that the other subsystems (the individual, the group, the formal structure) are interdependent. But beyond their interdependency they have varying degrees of self-sufficiency. In this context, the self-sufficiency of subsystems in complex organizations is synonymous with autonomy.

One obvious truth often ignored or misconstrued by traditional theorists is that small groups have some independence within complex formal organizations to evolve patterns of behavioral influence which are quite apart from those imposed by the larger structure. This autonomy has been viewed by numerous writers as the origin of mischievous, hostile combinations of people who work against the purposes of the formal organization. Output restriction is an example often cited.

However, autonomy permits organizational members to work out within their small groups various forms of accommodations with other systems which contact it, such as the formal organization. This function has been pointed to by both Selznick[27] and Gouldner[28] as an important source of adaption. Through autonomy, individuals and groups are informally delegated the chance to work out various adaptive modes to cope with environmental change.[29] This process is really a structural characteristic of complex organizations which facilitates the maintenance function.

[27] Philip Selznick, "Foundations of the Theory of Organization," *American Sociological Review*, February, 1948, pp. 25–35.

[28] Alvin W. Gouldner, "Reciprocity and Autonomy in Functional Theory," in Llewellyn Gross (ed.), *Symposium in Social Theory* (Evanston: Row, Peterson, 1959), pp. 241–70.

[29] Fred E. Katz, "Explaining Informal Work Groups in Complex Organizations: The Case for Autonomy in Structure," *Administrative Science Quarterly*, September, 1965, p. 222.

CHAPTER 5

The Formal Organization:
Classical and Neoclassical Views

FROM THE STRUCTURE of interpersonal and small group behavior we turn now to analyze another facet of social territory—the formal organization. Organization has long been a subject of much interest. Some of the first comprehensive treatises on organization are found in military and political literature. In the latter part of the last century, and particularly in this century the study of organization expanded to produce the familiar analyses on bureaucracy. Now organization and organizing activities are considered essential functions of administrators. Since organization theory has blossomed into a discipline of study standing on its own merits, it is important to develop some of its major points as they pertain to the formal organization and to system theory.

Modern man is intent on drawing himself into a web of collectivized patterns. He ". . . has learned to accommodate himself to a world increasingly organized. The trend toward ever more explicit and consciously drawn relationships is profound and sweeping; it is marked by depth no less than by extension."[1] This comment by Seidenberg nicely states the pervasive influence of organization in all forms of human activity, including work.

Some of the reasons for the extension and depth of organizational activity are found in the fundamental transitions which revolutionized our society. These transitions have already been discussed in Chapter 2. To repeat, they changed our country from a rural-agricultural civilization to one based on technology, industry, and the city. These changes resulted in the intensification of the collision effect stemming from the proximity and dependency of people on each other. In turn, proximity and dependency, as conditions of social life, harbor the threats of human conflict, capricious antisocial behavior, instability of human relationships, and uncertainty about the nature of the social structure and its concomitant roles.

Of course, these threats are present to some degree in all societies from the primitive to the modern. But these threats become dangerous when

---

[1] Roderick Seidenberg, *Post-Historic Man* (Boston: Beacon Press, 1951), p. 1.

the harmonious functioning of a society rests on the maintenance of a highly intricate, delicately balanced form of human collaboration. The civilization we have created depends on the preservation of a precarious equilibrium. Hence, disrupting forces impinging on this shaky form of collaboration must be minimized or eliminated.

Traditionally, organization is viewed as a vehicle for accomplishing goals and objectives. While this view is probably true enough, it tends to obscure the inner workings and internal purposes of organization itself. For example, the automobile is a form of organization designed to accomplish transportation objectives, and so are trains and airplanes. This bland statement, however, tells nothing of their internal organizational arrangements. And further, it says nothing of the behavioral forms people adopt when riding in a car versus riding in a plane. This analogy can be applied to human organizations. Both the so-called formal and informal organizations are vehicles for accomplishing objectives. But their internal arrangements and purposes are different, and so the behavioral patterns of people in them are often different.

Another and more fruitful way of treating organization is as a mechanism having the ultimate purpose of offsetting those forces which undermine human collaboration. In this sense, an intensification of the organization trend can be thought of as a product of an intensifying collision effect. Organization tends to minimize conflict and to lessen the significance of that individual behavior which deviates from values the organization has established as worthwhile. Further, organization increases stability in human relationships by reducing uncertainty regarding the nature of the system's structure and the human roles inherent in it. As a corollary to this point, organization enhances the predictability of human action because it limits the number of behavioral alternatives available to an individual. As Presthus points out, "Organization is defined as a system of structural interpersonal relations . . . individuals are differentiated in terms of authority, status, and role with the result that personal interaction is prescribed. . . . Anticipated reactions tend to occur, while ambiguity and spontaneity are decreased."[2]

In addition, organization has built-in safeguards. Besides prescribing acceptable behavior forms for those who elect to submit to it, organization is also able to offset the influence of human action which transcends its established patterns.[3]

---

[2] Robert V. Presthus, "Toward a Theory of Organizational Behavior," *Administrative Science Quarterly*, June, 1958, p. 50. Regulation and predictability of human behavior are matters of degree varying with different types of organizations in something of a continuum. At one extreme are bureaucratic-type organizations with tight bonds of regulation. At the other extreme are informal organizations, with relatively loose bonds of regulation.

[3] This point has an interesting sidelight. A bureaucracy with tight controls and a high degree of predictability appears to be unable to distinguish between destructive and creative deviations from established values. Thus, it seems that the only thing safeguarded is the status quo.

Few segments of society have engaged in organizing more intensively than business.[4] The reason is clear. Business depends on what organization offers. Business needs a system of relationships among functions; it needs stability and predictability in terms of the internal and external activities in which it engages. Business also appears to need harmonious relationships among the people and processes which make it up. Put another way, a business organization has to be relatively free from the destructive tendencies that may result from divergent internal interests.

Various theories of organization have been, and are being, evolved to meet these needs. This chapter and Chapter 6 take up three theories of organization which have considerable influence on management thought and practice. They are the classical, neoclassical, and modern. Each of these theories is fairly distinct, but at the same time they are not unrelated. These theories are on-going, being actively promoted by several schools of management thought.

THE CLASSICAL THEORY

The classical theory of organization deals almost exclusively with the anatomy of the formal organization. It has a rich heritage including such famous scholars as Weber, Fayol, Mooney and Reiley, Gulick and Urwick, and Barnard.[5] Today, just about every textbook on management, on the introductory level, contains a treatment of organization following the lead set by these people and others who pioneered the development of formal theory.

Defining the Formal Organization

Finding a definition of the formal organization is not a difficult job. Four elements of a definition reappear consistently in management literature. Briefly explained, they are:

1. *A system of coordinated activities.* This element underscores the fact that all organizations are composed of parts and relationships. The "parts" of the organization refer to activities or functions performed. The formal system appears when these activities are geared into a logical relationship.

2. *A group of people.* Although an organization can be charted on paper

---

[4] The monolithic institutions of the military and the government are other cases of organizational preoccupation.

[5] For reference see Max Weber, "The Essentials of Bureaucratic Organization: An Ideal-Type Construction," in Robert K. Merton *et al.* (eds.), *A Reader in Bureaucracy* (New York: The Free Press of Glencoe, 1952), pp. 18–27; Henri Fayol, *General and Industrial Management,* trans. Constance Storrs (London: Sir Issac Pitman and Sons, 1949); James D. Mooney and Alan C. Reiley, *Onward Industry* (New York: Harper and Bros., 1931); Luther Gulick and Lyndall Urwick, *Papers on the Science of Administration* (New York: Institute of Public Administration, 1937); and Chester I. Barnard, *The Functions of the Executive* (Cambridge: Harvard University Press, 1938).

it needs people to bring it to life. Personnel are required to implement the activities.

3. *Cooperation toward a goal.* Cooperation is strictly a human phenomenon. In normal behavior cooperation is always purposeful. Therefore, organizations must have objectives to lend purpose to the actions of people performing functions.

4. *Authority and leadership.* Organizations are structured on superior-subordinate relationships. As the result, authority is a universal element in all formal organizations. Leadership, however, is an executive's personal quality which prompts willing collaborative effort toward a goal.

A comprehensive operative definition is obtained by combining these elements. *A formal organization is a system of coordinated activities of a group of people working cooperatively toward a common goal under authority and leadership.*

A definition does little to illuminate the rationale of formal organizations. For this reason we examine the classical foundations and pillars of the theory.

The Foundations of Classical Theory

Following Barnard, the foundations of the theory are common purpose, communication, and willingness to serve.[6]

Common Purpose. The purpose of every organization is found in its goals and objectives. They provide the aims toward which coordinated activities of administrators are directed.

Communication. Communication is a "linking process" that supplies information to and from the working parts of the organization, both human and nonhuman, which are responsible for pursuing the primary and subgoals of the organization.

Willingness to Serve. This foundation refers to the motivational framework out of which attitudes of positive cooperation are evoked from the human elements of the organization for the accomplishment of organizational goals. We alluded to this framework at the end of Chapter 1 when we spoke of the "Barnard synthesis" employing efficiency and effectiveness in administration to achieve a cooperative system.

Built upon these foundations are four instrumental processes peculiar to formal organizations. We call these processes *pillars.* They are the division of labor, scalar and functional processes, structure, and span of control. Of these pillars, which are closely related conceptually, the division of labor is the most basic.

Pillars of the Formal Organization Theory

1. *Division of labor* is without doubt the cornerstone of the four pillars of classical organization theory. Division of labor has been mentioned in

---

[6] Barnard, *op. cit.*, pp. 83–91.

previous chapters as constituting one of the technological dynamics underlying the collision effect.

As a human organization grows work must be divided, otherwise one job would be so inclusive that its performance would be impossible. So work is broken down, usually along lines as natural as possible, to provide clear areas of specialization. The reason for dividing work is to improve the technical performance of the organization.

Division of labor, or specialization, is not restricted to production-line jobs but extends to all the functions at the highest levels in the organization. Figure 5–1 illustrates the growth of managerial specialization in a business organization.

Stage I in this figure represents a one-man operation in which the owner is performing all three organic business functions. As business gets better the boss hires another employee to perform the function of production, as shown in Stage II. Stage III represents a phase in growth where all three organic business functions are performed by specialists, with the boss acting as coordinator. Finally, Stage IV demonstrates a further division of labor within the organic functions themselves.

This demonstration of organizational growth is a classical treatment, showing how a business will expand by specializing the organic business functions of creation, distribution, and finance. This approach to the division of labor in classic organization theory is frequently treated under such topical headings as departmentation, or functional evolution and devolution.[7]

The division of labor is so basic to classic organization theory that the other three pillars derive from it as corollaries. For example, vertical and horizontal growth, through the scalar and functional processes, requires specialization and departmentalization of functions. Organization structure is dependent on the direction which specialization of activities travels during company development. Finally, span of control problems results from the number of specialized functions, and specialists, under the jurisdiction of an administrator.

2. The *scalar and functional processes* deal with the organization's vertical and horizontal growth respectively.[8] The scalar process refers to the growth of the chain of command which results in levels added to the organizational structure. The scalar process is accomplished through the *delegation* of authority and responsibility. Figure 5–2 demonstrates this process.

Assume that "A" starts out with specific job responsibilities 1, 2, 3, 4, and 5 in Stage I. In Stage II, "A" delegates to "B" responsibilities 1 and 2,

---

[7] For an excellent discussion of the division of work and related topics see Joseph A. Litterer, *The Analysis of Organizations* (New York: John Wiley and Sons, Inc., 1965), chap. 8–11.

[8] These processes are discussed at length in Ralph Currier Davis, *The Fundamentals of Top Management* (New York: Harper and Bros., 1951), chap. 7.

FIGURE 5–1
The Growth of Managerial
Specialization

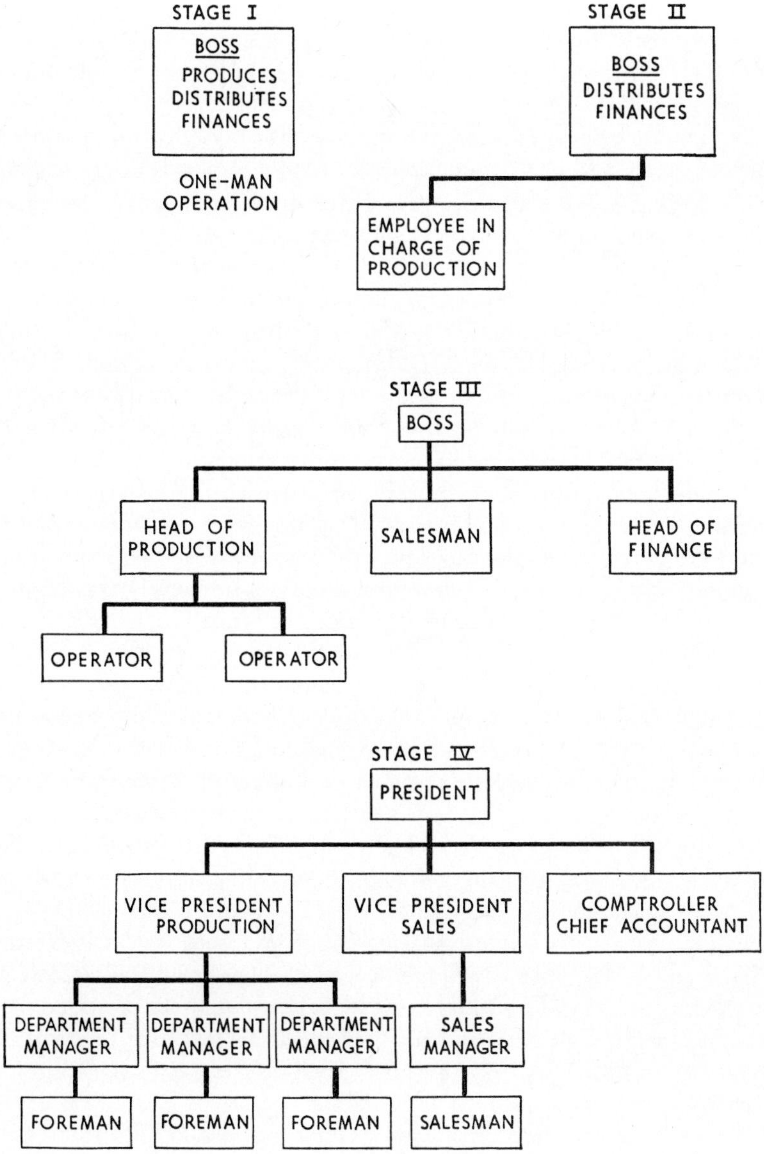

STAGE I

```
┌──────────────┐
│     BOSS     │
│   PRODUCES   │
│  DISTRIBUTES │
│   FINANCES   │
└──────────────┘
   ONE-MAN
  OPERATION
```

STAGE II

```
┌──────────────┐
│     BOSS     │
│  DISTRIBUTES │
│   FINANCES   │
└──────────────┘
        │
┌──────────────┐
│ EMPLOYEE IN  │
│  CHARGE OF   │
│  PRODUCTION  │
└──────────────┘
```

STAGE III

```
              ┌──────┐
              │ BOSS │
              └──────┘
    ┌────────────┼────────────┐
┌──────────┐ ┌─────────┐ ┌──────────┐
│ HEAD OF  │ │SALESMAN │ │ HEAD OF  │
│PRODUCTION│ │         │ │ FINANCE  │
└──────────┘ └─────────┘ └──────────┘
   ┌───┴───┐
┌────────┐ ┌────────┐
│OPERATOR│ │OPERATOR│
└────────┘ └────────┘
```

STAGE IV

```
              ┌───────────┐
              │ PRESIDENT │
              └───────────┘
    ┌───────────────┼───────────────┐
┌──────────────┐ ┌──────────────┐ ┌──────────────┐
│VICE PRESIDENT│ │VICE PRESIDENT│ │ COMPTROLLER  │
│  PRODUCTION  │ │    SALES     │ │CHIEF ACCOUNTANT│
└──────────────┘ └──────────────┘ └──────────────┘
  ┌───────┼───────┐          │
┌────────┐┌────────┐┌────────┐┌────────┐
│DEPARTMENT││DEPARTMENT││DEPARTMENT││ SALES  │
│MANAGER  ││MANAGER  ││MANAGER  ││MANAGER │
└────────┘└────────┘└────────┘└────────┘
┌────────┐┌────────┐┌────────┐┌────────┐
│FOREMAN ││FOREMAN ││FOREMAN ││SALESMAN│
└────────┘└────────┘└────────┘└────────┘
```

and to "C" responsibilities 3, 4, and 5. "C" in Stage III delegates to "D" job responsibilities 4 and 5. The shaded areas indicate ultimate authority and responsibility which cannot be delegated. Thus, while at Stages II and III, "A" does not have the *specific* job responsibilities he had formerly, he still is accountable to a higher authority for the performance of those to

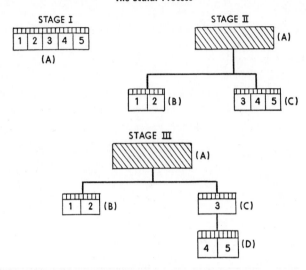

FIGURE 5–2

The Scalar Process

whom he has delegated these tasks. Through the scalar process, then, the organization has grown vertically from one to three levels.

The functional process is the method by which the organization grows horizontally. This process is illustrated in Figure 5–3.

In Stage I, "A" is supervising "B" who has job responsibilities 1, 2, 3, and 4. On the authority of "A" in Stage II, three of the jobs formerly performed by "B" are split off into separate functional jurisdictions *on the same level* under "C," "D," and "E." Thus, the second level in this

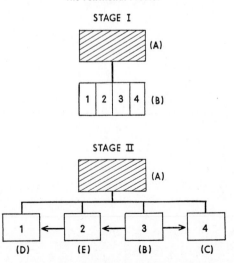

FIGURE 5–3

The Functional Process

diagram has moved from one position in Stage I to four positions in Stage II via the division of labor along functional lines.

The basic processes of organizational growth described here are applicable to the line as well as to the emergence of the staff functions in an organization.

3. *Structure* is a term which is applied to the relationships that exist among the various activities performed in an organization. The purpose of structure is to provide an orderly arrangement among functions so that the objectives of the organization can be accomplished effectively. Structure implies system and pattern.

Classical organization theory usually works with two basic structures: the line and the staff. The line organization refers to the primary chain of command which devolves directly from organic functions—creation, finance, and distribution of a good or service. The staff organization is frequently treated as advisory and facilitative functions for the line. Also, such activities as committees and liaison functions fall quite readily into the purview of structural considerations.

The functional structure also falls within the scope of our deliberations. It certainly is "classical" since Frederick W. Taylor introduced the concept about 60 years ago. However, we postpone considering it until later in the chapter because of the special problem of analysis it poses.

4. The *span-of-control* concept relates to the number of subordinates a manager can effectively supervise. Graicunas has been credited with first elaborating the point that there are numerical limitations to the subordinates one man can control.[9] In a more recent statement on this subject, Brech points out that "span" refers to ". . . the number of persons, themselves carrying managerial and supervisory responsibilities, for whom the senior manager retains his over-embracing responsibility of direction and planning, co-ordination, motivation and control."[10]

Regardless of interpretation, the span concept directs attention to the complexity of human and functional interrelationships in an organization. The number of interrelationships among individuals grows at a rapid pace when people are added to a department. Further, span of control has

---

[9] V. A. Graicunas, "Relationships in Organization," *Papers on the Science of Administration* (New York: Columbia University, 1937).

[10] E. F. L. Brech, *Organization* (London: Longmans Green and Co., 1957), p. 78. Udy talks of the span of control in terms of technological processes to formal organization structure. He suggests that size alone does not explain span. Span is related to technological process and the span of attention. Span of attention is equal to the total number of tasks, plus the maximum number of specialized operations ever performed at once, plus a factor "C" which is 1 or 0 depending on whether combined effort is ever present (1) or always absent (0) in the entire process. If the span of attention is greater than five than any technological process will tend to be performed on three or more levels of authority. If the span of attention is equal to or less than five then technological processes will tend to be performed on fewer than three levels. Stanley H. Udy, Jr., "The Structure of Authority in Non-Industrial Production Organizations," *American Journal of Sociology*, May, 1959, pp. 582–84.

significance also in terms of the shape of the organization that evolves through growth. Wide span yields a flat structure; short span results in a tall structure (see Figure 5–4).

FIGURE 5–4
Span of Control and Organizational Structure

Tall Structure	Flat Structure
X X X X X X X XX XX XX XX	X X X X X X X X X X X
Levels...4 Span.....2	Levels...2 Span....10

The Classical Principles of Organization

The pillars of classical organization theory have certain logical counterparts which may be expressed as principles. The principles most often cited, and which have some relevant behavioral content, are (*a*) the coordinative principle, (*b*) the scalar principle, and (*c*) the functional principle. The coordinative principle is best stated as *unity of action* for obtaining goals. It encompasses *all* the necessary measures needed to achieve unity. This is the mother principle. The others are derived from it.

In the classical scheme, the scalar principle prescribes a determinate hierarchy and unity of command. The purpose of the scalar principle is completely revealed in the functional principle. This principle requires the differentiation and grouping of like duties for the sake of the effective performance of work. The classical position is that the diverse organizational activities resulting from the division of labor are coordinated best by a structure which fulfills the scalar principle's precepts of *unity of command*.

These principles have two dimensions which are so obvious that they are frequently overlooked. Knowing them, however, is crucial to understanding the nature of classical theory. The first dimension involves the precise meaning of coordination, and the second the hierarchial character of the principles themselves.

As we said, the purpose of coordination is to provide unity of action in the pursuit of goals. This is the end of coordination. But the means prescribed by classical theory to accomplish this end *are not contained as a logical component of the coordinative principle*. Presumably, from the standpoint of coordination alone, *any* means will do as long as unity of action is achieved.

The scalar principle, which is subordinated to the coordinative principle, does prescribe a means to achieve unity of action with a formal organization—the means is unity of command—or the structuring of organizational relationships so that each subordinate has one and only one superior to whom he is responsible. This thoughtway is more a product of traditionalistic commentary on the theory than it is a logical necessity of classical theory itself. In any event, this interpretation has straightjacketed classical theory by thinking of unity of action and unity of command in roughly equivalent terms. They are not at all alike, and may be mutually exclusive at times. That is, it might be possible that the best way to achieve unity of action is to ignore unity of command. We say more of this in the next section.

March and Simon have two indictments of the classical theory of organization. "First, in general there is a tendency to view the employee as an inert instrument performing the tasks assigned to him. Second, there is a tendency to view personnel as a given rather than as a variable in the system."[11] Because of its focus on the mechanics of organization, the classical school overlooks the significance of the impact of people on the anatomy of the formal structure.

It would not be fair to say that the classical school is unaware of the human problems which affect organization. They simply do not treat in any systematic way the interplay of individual personality, informal groups, intraorganizational conflict, and the decision process in their conception of the formal structure. Additionally, the classical school has failed to incorporate in its theory the contributions of the behavioral sciences as part of a comprehensive explanation of human behavior in the organization.

Classical theory, however, has relevant insights into the nature of organization which should not be discounted. But the value of this theory is limited by its narrow concentration on the formal anatomy of organization.

THE NEOCLASSICAL CRITIQUE

The neoclassical school has been associated in the past with the human relations movement. Recently, it has identified more broadly with those movements which recognize and attempt to compensate for deficiencies in classical doctrine. The best estimate of the neoclassical school's contribution to management thought is that in its "middle of the road" form, it attempts to save classical theory by introducing behavioral modifications to the formal system.

An excellent example of this approach, which has indeed become "classic" in itself, is Pfiffner's and Sherwood's concept of *organizational*

---

[11] James G. March and Herbert A. Simon, *Organizations* (New York: John Wiley and Sons, Inc., 1958), p. 29.

overlays.[12] *Building upon* the anatomical structure of classical formal theory, Pfiffner and Sherwood add the various modifications which result from such behavioral overlays as small (informal) groups, decision and power systems not synonymous with formal authority systems, informal communication channels circumventing prescribed channels, and so on.

The neoclassicist school does not have a bona fide theory as do the classicists. Rather, the neoclassical school includes all those who protest against the inadequacies of the classical model of organizational behavior, but are not willing to divorce themselves completely from its structural frame. This book represents one kind of a neoclassical commitment, so we should not pretend that this section comprehends more than merely a savoring of what is going on in this school. We restrict ourselves to the neoclassical critique of the pillars of classical theory.

The Division of Labor

Since the division of labor is such a basic construct in the structural field of organization theory, it is not surprising to find that it has elicited a vast amount of comment. Around the turn of the century Émile Durkheim had this to say about the division of labor in industrial organizations:

The division of labor presumes that the worker, far from being hemmed in by his task, does not lose sight of his collaborators, that he acts upon them, and reacts to them. He is, then, not a machine who repeats his movements without knowing their meaning, but he knows that they tend, in some way, towards an end that he conceives more or less distinctly. He feels he is serving something. For that, he need not embrace vast portions of the social horizon; it is sufficient that he perceive enough of it to understand that his actions have an aim beyond themselves.[13]

This is a strange statement of support for the division of labor. It comes from a man whose work on suicide produced the concept of *anomie* which seems appropriate for the analysis of the behavioral consequences of the division of labor.

Anomie is a French word translated as "lack of rules." However, its implications go far beyond this literal rendering. *Anomie* means a lack of self-discipline resulting from an individual's inability to identify with the rule-ladened activities which surround him or in which he is a direct participant. *Anomie* also means an "aloneness among many." While the division of labor causes great functional interdependency among work activities, it also depersonalizes these activities so that the individual finds little meaning in them much less meaning in the complex organizational system which is created to sustain advanced forms of specialization.

---

[12] John M. Pfiffner and Frank P. Sherwood, *Administrative Organization* (Englewood Cliffs, N.J.: Prentice-Hall, Inc., 1960).

[13] Émile Durkheim, *The Division of Labor in Society* (New York: The Free Press of Glencoe, 1947), p. 373.

While Durkheim did not see *anomie* applying to the division of labor others have, and it has provided an endless source of research and speculation. Long before organization theory as such absorbed the interest of behavioral scientists, early studies were made of accidents, fatigue, monotony, and boredom which were caused by specialization.[14] Later, the research emphasis shifted from the physiological consequences of the division of labor to the problems of psychological alienation which resulted from workers' inability to find satisfaction in their jobs. Thus, one dimension of neoclassical criticism has been directed against the depersonalization of work *at the operative level* which has been shown to have dysfunctional outcomes for the organization.

Another dimension of neoclassical comment on the division of labor concerns the problems of interdependency. The division of labor intensifies employee interdependency. Each segment of a production line is intimately connected by the functions which come before and after it. Similarly, executives at high levels in an organization are dependent on the activities and decisions of other executives.

The conditions of interdependency generated by the division of labor create strains and tensions. Whyte, in his study, *Human Relations in the Restaurant Business*, lucidly describes the stresses which result from the interrelations of cooks, countermen, waitresses, and kitchen runners.[15] Nor are these tensions restricted to operative-level employees. The division of labor which results in the emergence of staff organizations creates its own special frictions with the line executives.

Because the division of labor gives rise to many different, and often quite narrow, areas of specialization, the need for managerial coordination becomes paramount. Frequently coordination, or the meshing together of parts, requires a higher order of motivational ability to get people to work cooperatively. This is not a particularly easy assignment. At the operative level, for example, it is extremely difficult to convince an assembly-line worker that his function is contributing significantly to the final product. The routine and boring nature of the job stifles enthusiasm and inhibits any latent desire this employee might have to see "the big picture" and the relation of his job to it.

Specialization breeds a somewhat different problem at executive levels. The division of labor tends to segment the organization into enclaves of authority and influence. Often executives come to regard these domains as their own special empires which have first call on their attention and abilities. Efforts to weld areas of executive specialization into a consistent, synchronized part of the overall organization are frequently resisted by managers as an undue infringement on their jurisdictions. Thus, specializa-

---

[14] Hugo Munsterberg, *Psychology and Industrial Efficiency* (Boston: Houghton Mifflin Co., 1913).

[15] William F. Whyte, *Human Relations in the Restaurant Business* (New York: McGraw-Hill Book Co., Inc., 1948).

tion brings about jealously guarded functional segments in the organization.

These few comments about the effects of the division of labor should be contrasted with the classical idea that the reason for specialization is efficiency. It cannot be doubted that mass-production techniques have brought about a high order of industrial output. But at the same time, the ultimate of efficiency hoped for from the division of labor has been denied because of the human problems it has created.

In order to overcome these problems, a number of recommendations have been made by the neoclassical school. Participation in the decision-making process has been offered to get the operative employee "involved" in his job and interested in the company. Participation allows the employee to have some say in his destiny in an often all-too-impersonal environment.

Job enlargement is another approach which has gained currency as an offset to the ill effects of the division of labor. Job enlargement proposes to reverse the specialization pattern. Organizations, particularly manufacturing companies, are advised to reintegrate highly specialized tasks into larger job blocks requiring greater skills of the employees and presumably providing them with greater satisfactions. This subject is discussed further in Chapter 13, "Modifying the Organization."

For the younger executive, bottom-up management, or the establishment of junior boards, is another management device. Bottom-up management gives the junior executive a chance to participate in top-management decisions. This technique allows the younger man to see the company from a top-level perspective and acts as a counterbalance to specialization in one activity.[16]

The Scalar and Functional Processes

This pillar causes a class of problems associated with the delegation of authority and responsibility. The implicit assumption of classical theory regarding the delegation process is that the *capacity* (ability) of the individual is equated to the *authority* (command and task) of the function. We might call this the perfection assumption. It is not altogether as unrealistic as it seems at first. The classic theory has a "classic" solution for cases where individual capacities are greater than their authority and less than their authority.

Case 1. Capacity Exceeds Authority. The obvious solution is promotion or transfer to functions with responsibilities commensurate with the ability of the individual.

Case 2. Capacity less than Authority. There are several alternatives in this case which include demotion, or discharge in extreme circumstances. Also, in

---

[16] For further discussion of this subject see William B. Given, *Bottom-Up Management* (New York: Harper and Bros., 1949).

some situations deficiencies in individual capacities may be overcome by training.

Thus, we conclude classic theory assumes that authority tends to equal the capacity of people actually performing organizational functions. And the catalyst which promotes this tendency is a *rational program of personnel administration.*

This position is based upon sufficiency assumptions regarding administrative information of the content of organizational functions and of individual capacities so that adjustments toward the "ideal" can be made. This information has to be available, not only for the present organizational state, but for future states as well so that changes in functional content and personnel can be made with as little friction as possible.

Neoclassicists reject the classical position on delegation on two levels. First, they feel it is not instrumentally possible to gain a real feel for individual capacity to the degree that an adequate match can be made of individual ability and motivation to lines of organizational career opportunities. Beyond this, neoclassicists would severely criticize the state of personnel appraisal methods which often determine the degree of success a person will achieve in an organization.

At the same level of criticism, neoclassicists point out that future projections of functional change are largely in the realm of fantasy. Organization planning still is so primitive that the prospect of frictionless personnel adjustments based on these plans is illusory.

The classicist counters these points by arguing that while the present "state of instrumental arts" is crude, administrators are improving selection, placement, promotion, and planning techniques. In other words, there is nothing *in principle* which precludes establishing and maintaining long-run equalized relationships between capacity-authority variables. If the issue is merely one of instrumentation, it can be improved to whatever arbitary level of perfection administrators choose.

This brings us to the second level of criticism. The neoclassicists maintain that it is not possible in principle to establish the sought for relations between capacity and authority. This is because the logic of formal relationships is not the only logic prevailing in human organizations.

Systems of power, influence, and decision are present in organizations which operate according to a logic of their own and thereby do not correspond to those systems prescribed by the formal structure. They may be capable, therefore, of perpetuating imbalances between capacity and authority. This is a small example of what Pfiffner and Sherwood are talking about when they analyze the organizational modifications resulting from power and decision overlays. Capacity and authority imbalances cannot be compensated for either instrumentally or in principle within the structure of the classic logic of the formal organization. This discussion could be prolonged indefinitely. In the interest of preserving chapters of manageable size, we defer further discussion of power and decision over-lays to Chapters 9 and 10.

Structure

Structure provides endless avenues of analysis for the neoclassical theory of organization. The general theme is that human behavior disrupts the best laid organizational plans and thwarts the cleanness of the logical relationships founded in the structure. The neoclassical analysis of struc-ture centers on frictions which appear internal to the organization among people performing different functions.

Line and staff relations constitute a problem much discussed in this respect. Many organizations have difficulty keeping the line and staff working together harmoniously. Line-staff frictions have numerous causes. Dalton, in a study of line-staff relationships, isolated five which he feels to be most important.[17]

First, the basic differences in duties carried on by line and staff execu-tives can be a cause for friction among them. The staff executive usually lives in a technical world and speaks a technical language. The line executive is more of a "generalist"; that is, while he has specific job duties to perform he also is occupied by problems of leadership and motivation.

In a very real sense, there is a language barrier thwarting effective communication between the line and the staff. The staff man speaks the language of his technical specialty, which is often misunderstood by the line official. The breakdown in communication resulting from functional differences is a basic cause of line-staff conflict.

Second, Dalton found marked distinctions between the line and the staff executives on the counts of age and education. Overall the staff executive was younger and, as might be expected, better educated than the line executive. A distrust of youth and an anti-intellectual bias on the part of line managers could make for conflict situations. In addition to these differentials, Dalton also found differences between the line and the staff in terms of dress, recreational interests, and social backgrounds.

Third, as a matter of attitude, staff personnel constantly felt they had to justify their existence. This sentiment could stem from the insecurity staff personnel might feel in terms of the importance of their jobs relative to the jobs performed by the line.

Fourth, the line executives felt the staff was trying to undermine its authority by expansion into areas thought by line managers to be properly in their jurisdiction.

And fifth, the staff had a feeling it was "under the thumb" of the line organization in the sense that promotion could come only through the approval of influential line managers.

Dalton does not wish to generalize these findings to all industrial

---

[17] Melville Dalton, "Conflicts between Staff and Line Managerial Officers," *Amer-ican Sociological Review*, June, 1950, pp. 342–51.

situations. However, they certainly contain some universal ingredients of conflict. In many ways the staff executive is not prepared for what he meets in day-to-day organizational operations. He is trained to enter a world of logical relationships and to carry out precise functions. Instead, his freedom to act logically is limited by the sentiments of the people with whom he must work. It appears the most successful staff men are those who side with the informally powerful line officers.

Further, traditional management thinking points out clear-cut divisions in line and staff roles. Theoretically, line work ends in a finished product or service which is distributed to consumers. Staff work ends in paper. In some companies, however, it is difficult to see a black-and-white distinction between line and staff work. Under such circumstances, a member of a staff organization feels his contribution is an integral part of the finished product. He may be wrong, according to management theory, but it is hard to make him believe otherwise.

Also, it seems that the logic of structure is against the staff man. Typically, the staff organization is a flat type of structure while the line is tall. Some meditation on this point leads inevitably to the conclusion that no matter how good the staff man happens to be there are fewer places for him to be promoted in the staff as compared to the line. The plusher, more lucrative jobs are more plentiful in the tall-type line organization. But, again, the emphasis for line management is balanced more toward administrative, generalist skills rather than technical specialties. This perhaps is a partial explanation for the rather large numbers of engineers, accountants, and the like, who, after taking their first degree in a specialty, are back in graduate school working for an M.B.A. in "management." They found they could progress just so far in their specialty. Advancement, as many of them see it, rests on being equipped to assume broader administrative responsibilities.

The structural difficulties raised by line-staff relationships brings us to the broader problems subsumed by Pfiffner and Sherwood under the functional overlay. We observed earlier that the concept of the functional organization was introduced by Frederick W. Taylor. He proposed it as a way of making more intensive use of foreman specialization.

Taylor observed that many foremen had abilities and specialties which were not used to their fullest extent. His solution to this waste of supervisory talent was to employ the foreman as overseer of those who were working in his area of specialty as well as overseer of those who fell within the administrative scope of his department. Thus, under functional foremanship the foreman would have dual responsibilities. He had functional responsibility for a certain specialized activity of operatives in another department; and he had general administrative responsibility for all the operatives in his own department regardless of the specialized jobs they performed.

To illustrate, let us imagine a furniture manufacturing company making four lines—traditional, modern, French provincial, and colonial. Let us suppose that in producing each line four activities (similar in each line) are performed—cutting, shaping, assembling, and finishing. Lastly, assume that the foreman in charge of the traditional line is a cutting specialist; the foreman over modern is a shaping expert; the French provincial foreman is an assembly expert; and the colonial foreman is a specialist in finishing. To meet the objectives of the functional organization, a system of relationships as shown in Figure 5–5 is required.

FIGURE 5–5
The Functional Organization

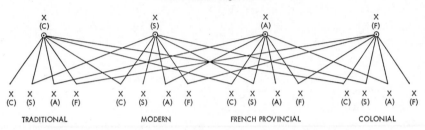

This cumbersome arrangement was not accepted by industry in the form Taylor recommended. But functional foremanship was the genesis of the concept of *functional staff authority*. A technical staff organization is delegated functional authority within a limited area of jurisdiction over a specialized area of line operations. For example, the foreman must be concerned with quality. However, in order to ensure the maintenance of quality many manufacturers established quality-control staff departments with authority over this functional area. In a very real sense the staff can exercise line authority over the foreman to guarantee his department is run in conformity to the quality standards the staff sets up and administers. The example of the quality-control staff applies equally well to other technical staff jurisdictions in a large manufacturing company.

The obvious difficulty created by the functional concept is that it violates one of the most sacred classic principles—the unity of command. But no amount of rationalization on the part of classicists regarding the line origins of functional authority ever will circumvent the fact that where it exists a set of behavioral transactions are introduced among administrators which are not encompassed in the classical model.

Span of Control

Neoclassicists react in two directions against classic span of control presuppositions. The first line of criticism is aimed at the notion that there is a *determinate* supervisory-subordinate ratio which can be generalized to most administrative situations. Thus, we read about such "ideal" ratios, although less frequently now, as 15 to 25 subordinates for first level supervision and 5 to 8 subordinates in executive spans.

Critics are quick to point out that merely the mathematically possible relationships among people are the least significant determinate of span. Rather, more importantly, the effectiveness of supervision is determined by four other factors which in combination situationally create "satisfactory or unsatisfactory" spans of control.[18]

1. Individual differences in managerial ability.
2. Effectiveness of organizational communication.
3. Effectiveness of formal control exercised over operations.
4. Organizational philosophy on centralization versus decentralization of authority.

The second direction of neoclassical criticism is more telling than the first. It is against the "close supervision bias" in classic theory. Most classic statements of "ideal" spans imply close supervisory control of subordinates. Five to eight executive subordinates is ideal because it enables their boss to supervise them closely. The same can be said about the ratios recommended for first level supervision.

As we have shown in Figure 5–4, the extent of span determines the shape of the organization. A wide span with a significant delegation of authority generates a flat organization. A narrow span with authority retained centrally results in a tall structure. Now in line with current thinking, backed by a considerable amount of research on the differential effectiveness of leadership styles, neoclassicists stress that ideal spans are those which reduce tight control through delegation of authority creating a decentralized structure. Their argument is for a general or democratic leadership climate reflected by a wide span of control. It has been demonstrated, they claim, that this approach is more productive of human satisfaction and organizational goals, contrasted with the classic centralized authoritarian structure inherent in narrow spans of tight supervision. So as the classic bias is toward close supervision, the neoclassicists favor loose supervision.

The Trouble with the Principles

Previously we stated that classical theory is rigidified by insistence that unity of command is the royal road to coordination. In truth what occurred was for a secondary principle of organization, the scalar principle, to dominate the primary organizational imperative—coordination. How did this happen?

To answer this question, we have to appreciate the character of organi-

---

[18] These four factors were drawn from the following sources: John M. Pfiffner, "The 'Third Dimension' of Organization," *Personnel*, March, 1952, pp. 391–99; Waino W. Suojonen, "The Span of Control—Fact or Fable?" *Advanced Management*, November, 1955; and Walter B. Schaffir, "Current Trends in Organization," *Management Review*, March, 1954, pp. 145–46. For a discussion of an attempt to establish a rational basis for span of control see Harold Stieglitz, "Optimizing Span of Control," *Management Record*, September, 1962, pp. 25–29.

zation which provided the "foot in reality" for the main formulators of the classical model. In general terms, this organization was big, but not gigantic; it had considerable interrelatedness among functions due to specialization, but it was not enormously complex as a consequence of advanced technology and products; finally, the bulk of the people employed needed a low order of skills, and comparatively few highly trained specialists, engineers, and scientists were necessary.

It is fair to say that these characteristics were evident in the organizations with which the greats of the classical school had direct experience. James Mooney was a vice president of General Motors prior to its postwar expansion. Max Weber's orientation was toward the Prussian governmental bureaucracy. And Gulick and Urwick were industrial consultants and students of government administration in England. When the works of Henri Fayol became generally available (they were not translated for many years after their writing), it was found that he too observed similar formal organization phenomena and had evolved similar principles of organization. But here again Fayol's experience was with French organizations much alike in size and character as those which provided the reality orientation for the mainstream of German-English-American theory.[19]

The significance of this is simply that certain presuppositions of classical theory have to be suspended for the sake of coordination if, empirically, a particular organization falls outside the conceptual limits of the classical model. That is, an organization may be tiny and simple or gigantic and complex. There are numerous examples of how giantism and technological advancement have in concrete circumstances made a mockery of unity of command, idealized line-staff relationships, and close supervision.

This is to say, that within the limits of the model unity of command, separation of line and staff activities, and close supervision might make some sense, especially since classic orientation was toward work which required a relatively low order of skills. Remember the heavy production-clerical nature of archetypical classic organization! But to impose the same conceptual constraints upon organizations which do not have these characteristics, or are at least not dominated by them, involves costs in coordination breakdown which are not compensated for by the dubious values which unity of command, unrealistic separation of line and staff work, and close supervision might yield. We continue this discussion in the next chapter where we take up the system approach to organization.

In her excellent book, *Industrial Organization: Theory and Practice,*

---

[19] While Barnard was president of New Jersey Bell Telephone Company, which had organizational characteristics in common with those providing experience for the classicists, he broke with many of the conceptual patterns they evolved and formulated new ones of his own.

Joan Woodward[20] has research evidence for essentially the same observations. The thrust of her work is that organization structure is related to technologies of various kinds of manufacturing roughly classified as job order, intermittent, and continuous. The technologies associated with the manufacturing types influence the development of the scalar chain, the span of control, line-staff relationships, and the rigidity or informality of role relationships within organizations. Since the founders of classical theory experienced primarily intermittent manufacturing undertakings, it is not surprising to find that traditional theory is reflective of this type. And, as Woodward observes, it is quite serviceable in this technological context.

But she goes on to make the point that organization theory should *not* be as prescriptive as classical theory is inclined to be. For some technically advanced organizations, in firms with process (continuous) kinds of manufacturing, coordination is designed into the production system. In these situations, organization, "serves primarily social ends, its function being to define roles and relationships within a social system."[21] The conclusion is obvious—the planner should develop an organization which best facilitates the interaction of the people in it. This holds even if it means a departure from such revered constructs of classic organization theory as prescriptive spans, determinate hierarchy with unambiguous roles and definite channels of communication, unity of command, and clear distinctions between line and staff authority and responsibility.

----

[20] Joan Woodward, *Industrial Organization: Theory and Practice* (London: Oxford University Press, 1965).

[21] *Ibid.*, p. 123.

CHAPTER 6

The System Concept

IF A KEY EXISTS which will unlock the mysteries of human behavior in organizations, it will be in the form of a theory of systems. Lawrence J. Henderson has pointed out that, "The interdependence of the variables in a system is one of the widest inductions from experience that we possess; or we may alternatively regard it as the definition of a system."[1] System and the interdependency of parts are interchangeable ideas. It is really quite impossible to understand individual behavior or the activities of informal organizations apart from the social system in which they interact. A human organization is a social system; the various discrete segments and functions in it do not behave as isolated elements. All parts affect all other parts. Every action has repercussions throughout the organization because all units, human and nonhuman, are linked.

Henderson has a diagram, shown in Figure 6–1, which by analogy explains the concept of the interdependence of variables in a system. He says, in explanation of this diagram:

The four rigid bodies A, B, C, and D are fastened to a framework a, b, c, d by the elastic bands 1, 2, 3, 4, and 5. A, B, C, and D are joined one to another by the elastic bands 6, 7, 8, 9, and 10. Here the conditions of statical equilibrium can be worked out mathematically, or determined empirically by introducing spring-balances into the bonds 1, 2, . . . 10, and reading the balances.

Now imagine the point of attachment of 5 on the frame to be moving toward b, all other points of attachment remaining unchanged. What will happen? Consider A. There will be action on A by the path 5, 9, by the path 5, 8, 10, and by the path 5, 8, 7, 6. But in each case these actions do not cease at A, just as they do not previously cease at D. The first, for example, continues along the path 10, 8, and so back to 5. If we try to think of all this as cause and effect we must inevitably reach a state of confusion.[2]

The complicated interdependence problems brought out by Henderson in Figure 6–1 are magnified in a far more complex human system. Human systems contain a huge number of variables which defy the most sophisti-

---

[1] Lawrence J. Henderson, *Pareto's General Sociology* (Cambridge: Harvard University Press, 1935), p. 86.

[2] *Ibid.*, pp. 13–14.

FIGURE 6–1
The Interdependence of Parts in a System

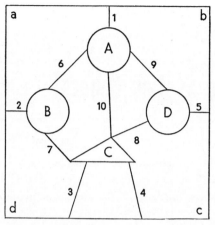

Source: Lawrence J. Henderson, *Pareto's General Sociology* (Cambridge: Harvard University Press, 1935), p. 14. Used with permission.

cated equations to solve. Yet in spite of the complexity of human organizations, studying them as systems provides a fruitful tool of analysis.

GENERAL SYSTEM THEORY

General system theory is a fairly recent development in organization analysis which is devoted to discovering organizational universals. The aim of general system theory is the creation of a science of organizational universals—or, if you will, a universal science—using the elements and processes common to all systems as a starting point.[3] Needless to say that this synthesis, if accomplished, and it has yet to be, will be at a very high level of abstraction. Even though general system theory is still in a tentative phase there is much to be learned from it.

There are several levels of system which eventually should be integrated as the general system theorists speculate into an inclusive theory. Boulding presents a convenient classification of these levels.[4]

1. The static structure—level of framework, the anatomy of a system.
2. The simple dynamic system—level of clockworks that involve necessary predetermined motions.
3. The cybernetic system—level of the thermostat, simple feedback and control circuit designed to enable a system to maintain a given equilibrium.

---

[3] This approach has some strong advocates among biologists. For example see Ludwig von Bertalanffy, *Problems of Life* (London: Watts and Co., 1952).

[4] Kenneth E. Boulding, "General System Theory—The Skeleton of a Science," *Management Science*, April, 1956, pp. 202–5.

4. The open system—level of self-maintaining systems that exhibit the ability of rejuvenation, growth, and reproduction. This level moves toward and includes living organisms.
5. The genetic-societal system—level of cell society, characterized by a division of labor among cells.
6. Animal systems—level of mobility, evidence of goal-directed behavior
7. Human systems—level of symbol interpretation and idea communication.
8. Social system—level of human organization.
9. Transcendental systems—level of ultimates and absolutes that exhibit systematic structures but are unknowable in essence.

By finding universals common to all levels of organization, this approach to the study of systems has intriguing possibilities for the science of administration. For example, a good deal of light could be thrown on social systems if structurally analogous elements could be found in simpler systems. It is usually easier to study the less complex and generalize to the more complex. Cybernetic systems, as a case in point, have characteristics which seem to be similar to the feedback, regulation, and control phenomena in human organizations. Thus certain facets of cybernetic models may be generalized to human organizations.

Considerable danger, however, lies in poorly founded analogies. Superficial similarities between the simpler systems and social systems are apparent everywhere. But instinctually based ant societies, for example, do not yield particularly valuable information for understanding rationally conceived human organizations. Care should be taken that analogies used to bridge system levels are not mere devices for literary enrichment. For systems to be analogous, *they must exhibit inherent structural similarities or implicitly identical operational principles.*[5]

Organization theorists in administration cannot afford to overlook the contributions of general system theory. It leads us directly to modern organization theory.

MODERN ORGANIZATION THEORY

The distinctive qualities of modern organization theory are its conceptual-analytical base, its reliance on empirical research data, and, above all, its synthesizing, integrating nature. These qualities are framed in a philos-

---

[5] Roderick Seidenberg, *Post-Historic Man* (Boston: Beacon Press, 1951), p. 136. The fruitful use of the type of analogies spoken of by Seidenberg is evident in the application of thermodynamic principles, particularly the entropy concept, to communication theory. See Claude E. Shannon and Warren Weaver, *The Mathematical Theory of Communication* (Urbana: The University of Illinois Press, 1949). Additionally, the existence of a complete analogy between the operational behavior of thermodynamic systems, electrical communication systems, and biological systems has been noted by U.S. Touloukian, *The Concept of Entropy in Communication, Living Organisms, and Thermodynamics* (Purdue Engineering Experiment Station, Research Bulletin 130 n.d.).

ophy which accepts the premise that the only meaningful way to study organization is as a system.

System analysis has its own peculiar point of view. Modern organization theory accepts system analysis as a starting point. It asks a range of interrelated questions which are not seriously considered by the classical and neoclassical theories of organization. Key among these questions are:

1. What are the strategic parts of the system?
2. What is the nature of their mutual interdependency?
3. What are the main processes in the system which link the parts and facilitate their adjustment to each other?
4. What are the goals sought by the system?

Modern organization theory is in no way a homogeneous body of thought. Each writer and researcher has his special emphasis when he considers the system. Perhaps the most evident unifying strand in modern organization theory is the effort made to look at human systems in their totality. Wolf, for instance, stresses the need to view organization as a "system of causality, which determines an organization's character."[6] He emphasizes the necessity of studying organizations as a whole and not just parts of the organization in isolation.

Wolf's position is similar to that of other writers in the area of modern organization theory. Much of the literary output has been in scholarly journals, but two books that are representative in this field are March and Simon's *Organizations*[7] and Haire's anthology *Modern Organization Theory.*[8] More recently Johnson, Kast, and Rosenzweig have made an excellent contribution in their book, *The Theory and Management of Systems.*[9]

The work in modern organization theory is pioneering—which makes its appraisal difficult and its direction obscure. While its future is not clear, one thing is patently certain. The questions being asked about human behavior within the structure of organizations cannot be adequately answered by classical and neoclassical doctrine. Understanding human organization requires a creative synthesis of massive amounts of empirical data, a high order of deductive reasoning, and an intuitive appreciation of individual and social values. Accomplishing all these objectives and including them in the framework of the concept of the system appears to be the goal of modern organization theory.

---

[6] William B. Wolf, "Organizational Constructs: An Approach ot Understanding Organization," *Journal of the Academy of Management,* April, 1959, p. 7. See also W. W. Haynes, "Toward a General Approach to Organization Theory," *Journal of the Academy of Management,* August, 1959, pp. 75–88.

[7] James G. March and Herbert A. Simon, *Organizations* (New York: John Wiley and Sons, Inc., 1958).

[8] Mason Haire (ed.), *Modern Organization Theory* (New York: John Wiley and Sons, Inc., 1959).

[9] R. A. Johnson, F. E. Kast, and J. E. Rosenzweig, *The Theory and Management of Systems* (New York: McGraw-Hill Book Company, Inc., 1963).

Organization Theory in a System Framework

All the concepts we discuss in Part III of this book are used in the systems framework for human organizations. It is useful to present an overall model of what is involved in system analysis. Figure 6–2 adapts Henderson's frame to the topics of interest here. The large box represents the total system or, if you will, the organization. The circles stand for the parts in the system, keyed as follows:

(A) Individuals.
(B) The formal organization.
(C) The informal organizations.
(D) The structure of status and role-expectancy systems.
(E) The physical environment of the work situation.

The lines both dotted and solid indicate linking processes. The linking processes are:

1. Communication.
2. Balance.
3. Decisions.

The dotted lines simply signify intrapart links—that is, linking individuals to individuals, jobs to jobs within the formal organization, and so on.

FIGURE 6–2
The Framework of System Analysis

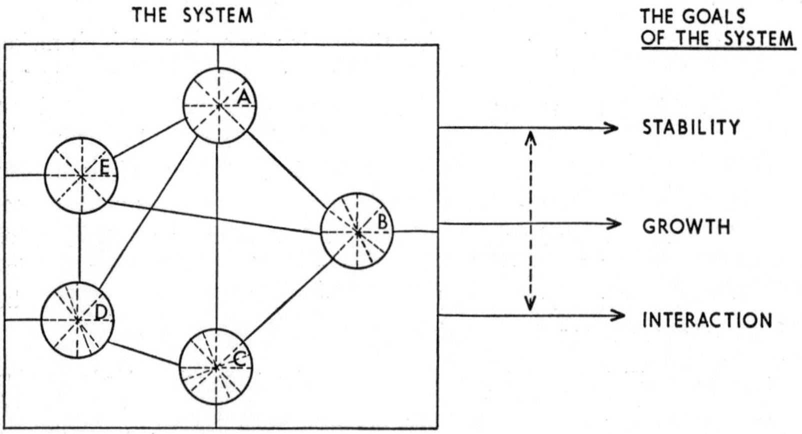

Key:
    1. Circles represent parts of the system.
    2. Dotted lines represent intrapart interactions, i.e., individuals with other individuals.
    3. Solid lines represent interpart interaction.
    4. Both the solid and dotted lines are links which tie the parts of the system together.

The solid lines represent interpart links—that is, individuals to the informal organization, the formal organization to the systems of status and roles, and so on.

Finally, the system as a whole strives to achieve certain goals. They are:

1. Stability.
2. Growth.
3. Interaction.

The system can seek any one of these goals, or any combination of them.

With this framework in mind, a discussion of the system's respective parts and processes follows.

The Parts of the System. The first basic part of the system is the individual and the personality structure he brings to the organization. Elementary to an individual's personality are his motives and attitudes which condition the range of the personal expectancies he hopes to satisfy by participating in the system.

The second part of the system is the formal arrangement of functions, usually called the *formal organization*. The formal organization is an interrelated pattern of jobs which provides the structure for the economic and efficiency pursuits of the organization.

The third part in the system is the *informal organization*. The nature of this organization has been explained in a previous chapter. The fourth part of the system is the *status and role* arrangements which exist in the organization. It is obvious that in any formal organization, statuses and roles are internally linked by hierarchical ordering. At the same time, there are also informal orderings of statuses and roles in terms of prestige groups and occupations.

The fifth part of the system is the *physical setting* in which the job is performed, plus the technical-engineering-efficiency considerations which link the various jobs together.

1. *Intrapart Interactions.* Within each of these parts, interactions exist among the units which comprise them. Obviously individuals interact with individuals, and informal groups with other informal groups; status systems and roles by their relative nature are dependent on each other for meaning, different jobs are interdependent on other jobs for the satisfactory performance of the total organization, and so on.

The fundamental cause for intrapart interactions is the division of labor. Dependency of units within the parts of the system arises from specialization. Now, since the parts are internally interdependent, they have to be bound together by processes. As mentioned before, these processes are communication, balance, and decisions.

2. *Interpart Interactions.* Just as the units in the parts of the system have interactional patterns, so also do the parts interact with each other.

The individual has expectancies regarding the job he is to perform; and, conversely, the job makes demands (or has expectancies) relating to the performance of the individual. Considerable attention has been given by writers in modern organization theory to incongruencies resulting from the interaction of organizational and individual demands. Argyris, for example, sees a conflict resulting from the demands made by the job and the nature of the normal, mature personality. The formal structure of the job does not meet the demands of the mature individual, hence he is forced to find outlets for his demands in informal organizations.[10]

The interactions which exist between the informal organization and the individual can be conveniently discussed as the mutual modification of expectancies. The informal organization has demands which it makes on members in terms of anticipated forms of behavior, and the individual has expectancies of satisfaction he hopes to derive from association with people on the job.[11] Both sets of expectancies interact, resulting in the individual modifying his behavior to accord with the demands of the group, and the group—perhaps—modifying what it expects from an individual because of the impact of his personality on group norms.[12]

In the physical surroundings of work, interactions are present in complex man-machine systems. The human "engineer" cannot approach the problems posed by such interrelationships in a purely technical fashion. As Haire says, these problems are in the domain of the social theorists.[13] Attention must be centered on the human responses stemming from a logically ordered production function. From this standpoint, work cannot be effectively organized unless the psychological, social, and physiological characteristics of people participating in the work environment are considered. Machines and processes should be designed to fit certain generally observed psychological, physiological, and social properties of men, rather than men being hired to fit machines and technical processes.

The interactional pattern among jobs, the informal organization, and the individual may be considered within the framework of E. Wight Bakke's *fusion process*. The fusion process is largely concerned with the modification of role expectancies relative to both role demands made by the formal and informal organizations and role perceptions peculiar to the individual. Organizational expectancies and individual perception of the

---

[10] Chris Argyris, *Personality and Organization* (New York: Harper and Bros., 1957), esp. chaps. 2, 3, 7.

[11] Conditions determining whether or not individual expectancies are satisfied are discussed by Alvin Zander, "Group Membership and Individual Security," *Human Relations*, 11 (1958), pp. 99–111.

[12] For a larger treatment of modification of expectancies see George C. Homans, *The Human Group* (New York: Harcourt, Brace and Co., 1950), chap. 5.

[13] Mason Haire, "Psychology and the Study of Business: Joint Behavioral Sciences," in *Social Science Research on Business: Product and Potential* (New York: Columbia University Press, 1959), pp. 53–59. See also George F. Weinwurm, "Computer Management Control Systems through the Looking Glass," *Management Science*, July, 1961, pp. 411–19.

expectancies modify each other. This process is basic to the continuity and stability of the organization.

Let us summarize what has been said so far about systems. First, systems are made up of parts which are interdependent. Additionally, the parts themselves are composed of units which also are interdependent, and the intrapart and interpart interdependencies have been discussed. The parts are woven into a configuration called the organizational system. The processes which link the parts together, which contribute to the maintenance of the configuration, are taken up next.

The Linking Processes. We encounter these processes in more detail in subsequent chapters. They are communication, balance, and decisions. It is through them that basic interactions are carried out which sustain the life of the organization. As Deutsch points out, communication allows the parts of the organization to "talk" with each other; it brings in information from the outside world, and it provides the means for storing and retrieving information within the system.[14]

Communication and decision function within a structure of networks. These networks bear little semblance to the idealized formal structure of organizations. Indeed, communication may travel along routes to decision centers which bypass or override formally established communication channels. Decisions may be made at centers in the organization which have small relation to the formal authority "officially" designated to the holder of a specific position in a center. Keyed to this complex system of transactions and network interrelationships is the process of administrative balance, which attempts to maintain stability among the parts of the organization.

To view the linking processes in a network concept is not to admit anarchy or to introduce chaos to organizations. It merely acknowledges that large organizations have many more dimensions than those recognized by classic theory. From these dimensions, these organizational overlays, come the dynamics of organizations. If communication *had* to follow formally established channels at all times, little of organizational importance would get done. If decisions were always made by the people who had the authority to make them, then we would have to deny the existence of power systems which correspond to nothing else but the formal structure of authority. But yet power systems do exist in organizations which are superimposed on the prescribed system of formal authority. It is through these links, formally specified or not, that the parts of the system are vitalized and moved toward the accomplishment of goals.

The Goals of the System. Organizations have three goals which may be interrelated, as is usually the case in complex systems, or independent ends in themselves. These goals are growth, stability, and interaction. The last goal refers to systems which provide a medium for association of members

---

[14] Karl W. Deutsch, "On Communication Models in the Social Sciences," *Public Opinion Quarterly*, 16 (1952), pp. 356–80.

from which they gain satisfaction. Human organizations are, of course, an example. We could interpret this more broadly, however, and say that any system which is dependent on the proper functioning of interrelated parts, like a clock, seeks the interaction goal.

Returning to Boulding's classification, we see that the first three systems—the static structure, the simple dynamic system, and the cybernetic system (homeostatic system is a preferred designation of this goal for reasons which we discuss later) are single ended in the sense that they seek the stability goal. If you like the broader meaning of "interaction" then for the more complex of these systems, we can say they have dual objectives with stability and interaction being mutually reinforcing. The important point, however, is that growth is a property of open, living systems, or of aggregations of living structures.

Growth Means Change.   And for open systems it means change along two vectors—development and structural evolution. Development pertains to the unfolding of an organism from the embryonic stage to the stage of maturity. Of course, there is negative development in which life energies are dissipated and death results. Evolution refers to a structural change in an organism (or species) stemming from its adaptation to new environmental conditions.

These growth vectors apply to human organizations. But the problem we encounter is distinguishing between what appears to be "natural" organizational development, that is, normal change over time from infancy to maturity, and evolution, or structural modifications resulting from environmental adaptation.[15] Maybe in the case of human organizations, the biological dichotomy of ontogenesis and phylogenesis is not particularly meaningful. Anyway we take a closer look at the problem of organizational growth theory in the appendix to this chapter.

In living organisms and human organizations we find the best examples of the interdependent character of goals. These kinds of organizations must change or die. But they must do so as stable interacting systems. Integrity of the system in growth is assured by balanced, integration of parts and processes.

Modern organization theory is on the periphery of general system theory. Both these theories study:

1. The parts (individuals) in aggregates, and the movement of individuals into and out of the system.

2. The interaction of individuals with the environment of the system. Haire's comments on the interrelation of the individual with the physical surroundings of work is apropos to this facet of system study.

3. The interactions among individuals in the system. Role theory and the theory of the informal organization are two cases of system study applying here.

4. General growth and stability problems of systems.

---

[15] There is simply insufficient empirical data to establish what is a "normal" course of organizational development.

Some Extensions of Modern Organization Theory

Whether or not you accept the foregoing framework of parts, processes, and goals as a way of understanding systems is a matter of taste. We hope, however, we have made one point clear. Modern organization theory is an offspring of the system concept and all it implies. Growing out of this contemporary approach to organizations are two concepts which are relevant to the overall theme of this part of the book on social territory. One is the concept of cybernetics, the other is the matrix organization.

Cybernetics. While this subject has been mentioned before in connection with communication, it is well to emphasize that the essence of cybernetics is found in the function of control.

Cybernetics is a most fruitful concept because it integrates the linking processes and generalizes them to a wide variety of systems. Decisions, information (communication), and control (balance or regulation) are indispensable elements of complex systems. This is true regardless of whether we are speaking of human, mechanical, or electrical systems. The flip-flop of an electronic relay acting upon the information fed it through a communication channel in a computer is as much a decision center as a handsome, iron-maned marketing executive pondering alternative promotion programs for a new product. Stafford Beer notes that ". . . decisions are the events that go on in the network, and they are describable . . . in terms of the information in the system, and the structuring of communication."[16]

In this sense, then, decisions and information cannot be understood apart from the system's communication pattern, and this pattern in turn is a reflection of the decisions required and the information necessary upon which to base them. Now, balance, the third linking process, is introduced in the form of control or regulation.[17] Here we come to the heart of cybernetic processes. *Regulation of the system network by the information produced in it is the core of cybernetics.*

The key phrase in the above sentence is regulation ". . . by the information produced . . ." in the system. This means that some of the energy (output, information) created by a system is tapped to provide a means of control through feedback. There is no need to go over the *mechanics* of feedback. This concept is elaborated in Chapters 7 and 11 on "Communication" and "Balance."

We need to note, however, that *one* of the requirements of a cybernetic system is self-regulation. There are many systems which exhibit stability, like the solar system, but not self-regulation. A self-

---

[16] Stafford Beer, *Cybernetics and Management* (New York: John Wiley and Sons, Inc., 1959), p. 11.

[17] The basic reference on cybernetics and its wider implications is Norbert Wiener, *The Human Use of Human Beings* (New York: Doubleday Anchor Books, 1950; rev. ed., 1954).

regulated system is one which utilizes some of its internal energy to preserve its level of behavior around some preestablished norm. A room thermostat is a common example; statistical quality control in a factory is another.

Now, while self-regulation is a necessary condition for a cybernetic system, it is not a sufficient condition. A steam engine with a governor is self-regulating but not cybernetic. Nor are other more complex systems exhibiting self-regulatory properties of equal interest to cyberneticians. An advanced computer capable of reading out or adjusting for input errors is not properly a cybernetic system. Beer presents an interesting method of classifying systems to pinpoint cybernetic areas. Figure 6–3 shows his approach.

FIGURE 6–3
Classification of Systems

Degree of Complexity	Type of System	
	Deterministic	Probabilistic
Simple	Adding machine Shotgun Machine-shop layout	Coin tossing Jellyfish movements Statistical quality control
Complex	Electronic digital computer Radar-controlled antiaircraft battery Automated factory	Stock market speculation Conditioned reflexes Allocation of sales promotion dollars in a multiproduct company
Exceedingly complex	None	The economic system The human brain The human organization

Source: Stafford Beer, *Cybernetics and Management* (New York: John Wiley and Sons, 1959), p. 18. Used with permission. The classification method is shown as presented by the author. Minor changes in the system examples are made.

Deterministic systems do what they are told to do. For all practical purposes their outcomes are predictable even though their internal workings may be complicated. They offer no variety in outcomes other than what their "programs" allow and these outcomes are uniquely forecastable for each system.

Probabilistic systems do not have uniquely determined outcomes. They have varying degrees of variety which for prediction purposes may be described in chance terms. As we move from simple systems, through complex, to exceedingly complex, we find that our application of statistical probability techniques becomes less productive of meaningful predictions about the behavior of the system. In the extremely complex category, systems are capable of such a wide variety of behavior that probability analysis is of little value for forecasting. Now, according to Beer, it is precisely at this level that cybernetics focuses.

Cyberneticians are interested in problems of regulation and control in exceedingly complex, probabilistic, self-maintaining (open) systems. The economy, the human brain, and human organization are systems which fit the description. Because of the insensitivity of these systems to conventional forms of analysis, cybernetics is necessarily interdisciplinary. That is cyberneticians, must look for answers in many fields like biology, physics, information theory, semantics, highly imaginative mathematics as that involved in game theory. It is from synthesis of data and generalizations from these areas that analytic resources will come for investigation of control problems.

The Matrix Organization. The matrix organization, sometimes called project organization, is an advanced form of Taylor's functional concept. It has not been widely used, except when an organization is unusually large and engaged in some complex technical undertaking like the development and manufacturing of guided missiles. Figure 6–4 depicts a matrix organization in just such a hypothetical company.

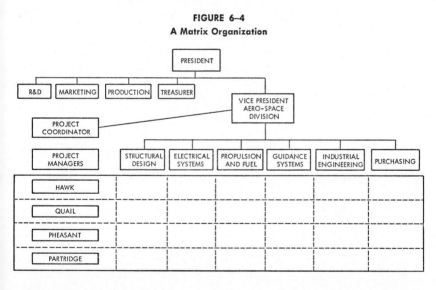

FIGURE 6–4
A Matrix Organization

Note that the left side of the chart shows the production, marketing, and support divisions involved in the conventional aircraft business. This segment of the company follows a typical line-staff structure. The right side of the chart depicts the organization of the Aero-Space division. Horizontally shown are the line departments where engineers, scientists, and technicians are "housed" for administrative purposes. Thus we see a structural design department, an electrical systems department, and so on.

To the left of these departments, vertically arranged, are the missile projects for which the company currently has contracts, i.e., Hawk, Quail, etc. Supervising each of these projects is a project manager. The personnel he needs to operationalize his project are drawn from specialists out of their respective administrative departments. Upon completion of a project these people may return to their administrative "pool" for reassignment.[18]

The similarity between the matrix organization and the functional organization is clear. For one thing, the unity of command principle is violated. Each engineer, scientist, and technician has two bosses—his administrative head and his project manager. Also the matrix organization violates the scalar principle because of an absence of a determinate hierarchy in one part of the structure. That is, project managers and department managers, while functionally distinct, do not stand in a scalar relationship. *Neither do they stand in a sort of relationship which can be meaningfully spoken of as line-staff*. It is not relevant to try to make such a distinction in this situation.

These activities are laterally related in a way that accentuates forms of behavioral accommodation which tends to be minimized in conventional organization structures. The scalar indeterminacy which exists between project managers and department managers gives rise to a transactional climate where bargaining and compromise are common in resolving conflicts over the allocation of personnel and performance appraisal. Even though these transactions might be considered as a price which must be paid, the improvements in coordination are worth it. Furthermore, if serious impasses arise at the project-department level, there are higher authorities such as the project coordinator and the vice president of the Aero-Space division who can intervene.

In summary, the matrix organization must be conceptualized as a total system which is constructed to achieve maximum coordination. Because of its reliance on networks of functions, communication, and decision making, it is peculiarly adaptable to such advanced planning and control techniques as PERT and CPM. These devices place great stress on coordination and synchronization of activities to achieve the optimum utilization of resources available in that part of the organization defined as the project system.

Directions and Trends in Organization Theory

Most sciences have a vision of the universe to which the science is applied. This universe is composed of parts. One purpose of the science is to synthesize the parts into an organized conception of its field of study. As a science matures its theorems about the configuration of its universe change. The direction of change in three sciences—physics, economics, and sociology—are noted below for comparison to the development of an administrative view of human organization.

---

[18] Of course, there are other reasons for reassignment. A project might be discontinued, or it might be running ahead of schedule so that some of its personnel can be transferred to other projects. Then, too, individuals might be promoted or request transfer from one activity to another. One important function of the administrative department head is to keep track of these changes as well as to anticipate the personnel requirements of the project managers.

The first comprehensive, and empirically verifiable, outlook of the physical universe was presented by Isaac Newton in his *Principia*. Classical physics, founded on the work of Newton, constituted a grand scheme in which a wide range of physical phenomena could be organized and predicted.

Newtonian physics may rightfully be regarded as "macro" in nature because its system of organization was concerned largely with gross events, of which the movement of celestial bodies is an example. For years classical physics was supreme. But as it became applied to smaller and smaller classes of phenomena in the physical universe physics eventually adopted the view that everything in its realm could be discovered simply by subdividing problems. At that point physics had moved into the "micro" order. In the 19th century, however, a revolution took place in physics largely because events in the physical universe were being noted which could not be explained adequately by the analytical equipment supplied by the classical school. The consequences of this revolution are described by Eddington:

> From the point of view of philosophy of science the conception associated with entropy must I think be ranked as the great contribution of the nineteenth century to scientific thought. It marked a reaction from the view that everything to which science need pay attention is discovered by microscopic dissection of objects. It provided an alternative standpoint in which the centre of interest is shifted from the entities reached by the customary analysis (atoms, electric potentials, etc.) to qualities possessed by the system as a whole, which cannot be split up and located—a little bit here, and a little bit there. . . .
>
> We often think that when we have completed our study of *one* we know all about *two*, because "two" is "one and one." We forget that we have still to make a study of "and." Secondary physics is the study of "and"—that is to say, of organization.[19]

Although modern physics deals in minute quantities and oscillations the conception of the physicist is on the "macro" scale. He is concerned with the "and"—that is, the organization of the world in which the events occur. This does not invalidate the usefulness of classical physics in explaining a certain range of phenomena. But classical physics is no longer the undisputed law of the universe. It is instead a special case.

Early economic theory—and Adam Smith's *Wealth of Nations* comes to mind—examined economic problems in the macro order. Fundamentally, *Wealth of Nations* is concerned with matters of national income and welfare. Later, the economics of the firm, "microeconomics," dominated the theoretical scene in this science. And, finally, with Keynes's *The General Theory of Employment, Interest and Money*, a systematic view of the economic universe was reintroduced on the macro level.

---

[19] Sir Arthur Eddington, *The Nature of the Physical World* (Ann Arbor: The University of Michigan Press, 1958), pp. 103–104.

The first era of the developing science of sociology was occupied by the great social "system builders." Comte, the so-called father of sociology, had the macro view of society in that his chief works are devoted to social reorganization. Comte was concerned with the interrelationships among social, political, religious, and educational institutions. But as sociology progressed the science of society compressed. Emphasis shifted from the macro approach of the pioneers to detailed, empirical study of small social units. The compression of sociological analysis was accompanied by study of social pathology, or disorganization.

In general, physics, economics, and sociology appear to have two things in common. First, they offered a macro point of view as their initial systematic comprehension of their areas of study. Second, as the science developed, attention fragmented into study of the parts of organization rather than the system as a whole. This is the "micro" phase.

In physics and economics, discontent was evidenced by some scientists at continual atomization of the universe. The reaction to the micro approach was a new theory or theories dealing with the total system on the macro level again. This third phase of scientific development seems to be more evident in physics and economics than in sociology.

The reason for this "macro-micro-macro" order of scientific progress lies in the hypothesis that usually the things which strike people first are of great magnitude. The scientist attempts to discover order in the vastness. But after "macro" laws or models of systems are postulated, variations appear which demand analysis, not so much in terms of the entire system but rather in the specific parts which make it up.

Intense study of the microcosm may result in new general laws replacing the old models of organization. Or, the old models and the new may stand together, each explaining a different class of phenomenon. Or, the old and new models of organization may be welded into a creative synthesis. In any event, microcosmic studies appear to be part of a cycle in science which leads to a reformulation of principles on higher levels of generality than had previously existed in the earlier macro phase.

Organization concepts seem to have gone through the same order of development as the three fields just mentioned. It is evident that the classical theory of organization, particularly as expressed in the work of Mooney and Reiley, is concerned with principles common to all organizations. It has a macro organizational view. The classical approach to organization, however, dealt with the gross anatomical parts and processes of the formal organization. Like classical physics, classical theory of organization is a special case. Neither can account for variations from the established framework.

Many variations in the classical administrative model of organization result from human behavior. The only way these variations could be understood was by a microscopic examination of particularized, situational forms of human behavior. The mission of the neoclassical school of organization is "micro" analysis.

Modern organization theory appears to be concerned in large measure with Eddington's "and." This school bases its operational hypotheses on a macro point of view, a study of the organization as a whole. Much of the data and methodology used by modern organization theory is gathered from studies conducted in the micro-order. But these studies are synthesized—creatively, it is hoped—into an overall view of organizational behavior.

It is questionable just how far modern organization theory can progress as a synthesizing effort primarily. Modern organization theory needs tools of analysis and a conceptual framework uniquely its own. It may be that the framework and perhaps some of the tools will come from general system theory. There is also promise of analytical and conceptual tools from relatively new areas of research in decision theory, information theory, and cybernetics. Modern organization theory lies on the frontier of research in the behavioral sciences. Its potential is great, because it offers the opportunity of uniting what is valuable in classical and neoclassical theory into a systematic and integrated conception of human organization.

Appendix: Organization Growth[20]

MAN LIVES in a world of dimensions, where the objects frequently encountered have familiar sizes and shapes. This circumstance allows man to determine his relationship to and plan his behavior in his environment. Under ordinary conditions of life, man moves conveniently among the inanimate and living objects which surround him. But other phenomena with which man is associated do not assume the same kind of dimensional characteristics exhibited by things in the physical universe. Human organization is one such phenomenon. Human organization is an abstraction, and it might be argued metaphysically that it has no dimensions whatsoever. What merit there might be to this consideration is not discussed here. *The basic assumption is that organizations do have magnitudes which can be spoken of as shape and size existing in a framework of time.*

It is almost axiomatic in organization theory that the size and shape of an organization is a function of the environment it is in and the problems it must solve to survive in this environment. But a crucial problem in organization theory, which has not yet received an acceptable answer, is the nature of the processes which cause an organization to assume a certain shape and reach a certain size. In short, these are the problems of *growth*.

---

[20] From W. G. Scott, "Organization Size: Some Theoretical Issues," *Management International* (5–6), 1961. Used with permission.

Biologists have a generalized answer to the matters of size and shape in living organisms. Their view is that adaptation is the mechanism whereby the organism is able to solve the riddle of survival in a hostile environment. Of course, in a vague way, the adaptation principle applies to human organizations also. But the key difference between the organization and the organism is that organizations solve the problem of adaptation by conscious, rational, and volitional processes; the organism does not.

This appendix is a critique of organizational growth theories and the research which has accompanied them. There is no one best way to study organizational size. It has numerous perspectives. A few ways the problem has been approached are listed below.

1. One approach to organization size is the *description of structure* found in various sizes and types of human associations. A segment of descriptive analysis is concerned with the small, informal group ranging in size from 2 to around 15 people. Another segment of descriptive analysis covers medium-size to large formal organizations. Descriptive analysis ends usually with the structure of the giant "super organization" such as church groups or political parties which contain a huge heterogeneous aggregate of people.

2. Another approach to organization size is the study of differential patterns of behavior of members and leaders in various sizes and types of organizations.

3. A third way to study size is to analyze organizational "behavior" as it adjusts its size and shape in response to changes in the environment during the process of pursuing goals. This problem is considered here under the subtitle of growth.

4. Next, size may be treated in its relationship to efficiency. Is there an optimum organization size and shape which makes for the most efficient accomplishment of goals? This research question is discussed in this appendix.

5. The last way of studying organization size poses the most elusive problems of all. These problems involve the mechanisms of organizational growth which create the form or shape of an organization as it matures.

Much has been said already in this part of the book about perspectives 1 and 2. Therefore, this appendix concentrates on the perspectives of growth and efficiency—items 3, 4, and 5. However, some analysis from perspectives 1 and 2 is woven throughout.

ORGANIZATION GROWTH

Bertalanffy observes that growth is one of the main problems of biology and is a central mystery of life.[21] Traditionally, biologists are concerned with the study of growth. Organization theorists have come to rely heavily on them for analogies. Currently a good deal of what passes

---

[21] Ludwig von Bertalanffy, *Problems of Life* (London: Watts and Co., 1952), p. 36.

for a *theory* of growth in human organization is based on facets of growth theory drawn from biology. Inherent in these analogies are pitfalls which are misleading unless recognized.

This appendix does not present a theory of organizational growth because the research and speculations which exist do not allow for the development of one. Rather its purpose is to examine some of the work which has been done and to make tentative observations about what might be useful, and what perhaps is detrimental, to the development of an organizational growth theory.

It may be said with assurance that a theory of growth, either in the framework of biology or human organization, deals with three fundamental variables—*size, shape, and age.*[22] From the standpoint of business organizations, size is often measured in terms of numbers of employees, domination of the market, invested capital, and so on. The age variable is simply measured on a time continuum. The shape of the organization is not so easily measurable. Organization shape is qualitative. It involves the relationship of parts to each other, arranged in such a way as to facilitate the accomplishment of organization goals. Large varieties of shapes are possible because all organizations do not have the same goals. Or, where goals for separate organizations are similar, decision makers perceive their accomplishment differently. In both cases, different arrangements of organizational parts, hence different organizational forms, emerge. Therefore, it is impossible to compare along a single scale the shape of the formal organization with the structural form of a small group. For example, to say the small group tends to be flatter than the production organization of a company makes little sense. Whereas, it is appropriate to say that the formal organization tends to be larger than the informal organization; and that the formal organization tends to persist over a longer period of time than the informal organization. These variables may be looked at another way in which time plays the role of common denominator.[23]

Changes in Size through Time

Most often in research on organization development the starting point of analysis is consideration of changes in size over time. A common procedure is to plot the number of *people employed* against points on a time continuum.[24] For periods in the life history of a firm, times of spurts

---

[22] P. B. Medawar, "Size, Shape, and Age" in W. E. Le Gros Clark and P. B. Medawar (eds.), *Essays on Growth and Form* (Oxford: Clarendon Press, 1945), p. 158.

[23] In biology, size and shape are functions of time. Time is the independent variable, whereas size and shape are dependent variables. In an organization theory of growth and development, the size and shape of an organization may vary independently of the time factor.

[24] See Mason Haire, "Biological Models and Empirical Histories of the Growth of Organization," in Mason Haire (ed.), *Modern Organization Theory* (New York: John Wiley and Sons, Inc., 1959), pp. 277-83.

and declines in the growth rate (employment rate) can be noted. The growth rate of any company at a point in time depends on such matters as the introduction of new technologies, adaptation to change, and external forces of demand and competition. Haire concludes that the general growth rate for a firm seems to fit a growth equation applied to populations in which each member of the population produces 1.5 second-generation offsprings.[25] Limitations on an unrestricted increase in size of the population are imposed by the environment.

Historical changes in size are an area of growth research which has been subjected to empirical investigation by behavioral scientists. Biologists also do considerable research in the size-time relationship. Their laws of growth provide the basis for tempting analogies to human organizations. More is said of this later under the topic of "Proverbs of Organization Growth."

One point of criticism may be raised now. How satisfactory is the measurement of organization size based on number of employees? Are there not other yardsticks which may be more relevant? The extent of market and amount of invested capital certainly are criteria which cannot be neglected. Under changing technologies it is conceivable that the total number of employees in a firm might be reduced. But is it realistic to say that its size has diminished when by innovation it has increased its invested capital and share of the market? The image of size and growth which a company reflects is composed of a number of factors of which *total employees is only one.*

Changes in Shape through Time

The famous biologist Sir D'Arcy Wentworth Thompson pointed out that ". . . the form of an object is a 'diagram of forces' . . . from it we can judge or deduce the forces that are acting or have acted upon it. . . ."[26] This observation led Haire to state that in business organizations ". . . modification of form as size increases may give us at least a clue to the strength of the force tending to destroy it. . . ."[27] Thus, the shape of the organization is in part a product of the forces which impinge on it from the environment. But the uniqueness in form of human organizations is due to other factors as well.

1. The environment within which organizations operate is not uniform. It would be unlikely therefore that business organizations assume the same forms as religious organizations.

2. Even where the environment is roughly the same, in the case of two comparable firms in an industry, the number of alternative arrangements for the parts of the respective companies is so great that it is highly

[25] *Ibid.*, pp. 277, 279.

[26] Sir D'Arcy Wentworth Thompson, *On Growth and Form* (2d ed.; Cambridge, England: Cambridge University Press, 1942), p. 16.

[27] Mason Haire, *op. cit.*, p. 276.

improbable that precisely the same forms of organization would result for both firms. Their structures may be similar, however.

3. The present form of an organization is partially a result of anticipation of the future. The management of similar companies may make different forecasts of the future. These forecasts would have a differential impact on the present structure of the company. Thus one firm might begin organizing and structuring for automation; the other firm might anticipate no change in its production techniques. The result, however, would be different organizational forms.

Shape refers to structure. And while no two organizations will have identical structures for the reasons noted above, certain classes of organizations have similarities in structure. Formal chain-of-command-type organizations constitute one such class. Some work has been done comparing organizational systems of this type.[28] But this research usually deals with structures at a given point in time and constitutes a static form of analysis.

Considering changes in shape over time is dynamic. The research question is: "Is there any uniformity in the transformation of organization shape along a time continuum?" In other words, as organizations mature, do they undergo predictable changes in shape at identifiable points in their development? As biological organisms develop they predictably change shape at definite stages. Can the same be said for human organizations? An answer to this intriguing question cannot be given one way or the other as far as research currently stands.

Change of form in a biological organism is largely predicated on survival. If the organism lives during the period of its maturation, it will change. Time and life are the important considerations, given a fairly favorable and reasonably constant environment. Time and survival, of course, are basic to change in form of a business organization. But the environmental forces operating on a company from the outside also shape its structure. Under normal circumstances the biological organism finds the sort of environment which is conducive to its survival, and the organism has reasonable assurance of environmental stability which precludes the necessity for numerous drastic adaptations. The business organization frequently is in an environment of intense change where its surroundings oscillate from favorable to unfavorable, from stability to frantic transition. These environmental changes often require changes in organizational shape. From this it can be concluded that to the extent to which changes in the environment of a business are unpredictable, so also are the transformations in its shape unpredictable.[29]

---

[28] See James D. Thompson (ed.), *Comparative Studies in Administration* (Pittsburgh: University of Pittsburgh Press, 1959).

[29] The larger the organization becomes the more capable it is of modifying its environment, whereas the ability of a biological species to control its environment is quite unfeasible. This is not altogether true in the case of man.

It is not of much value to report changes in organizational shape after the fact, if these data are used to project similar changes for comparable organizations. One must be assured that forces operating externally to the firm will maintain prescribed patterns. There is no proof, however, that this requirement can be fulfilled.

In addition to the external forces, internal forces also shape the structure of the firm. The decision makers in the firm react partially to external forces. They operate also within the internal frameworks of power and influence which change as personalities change. The degree to which power and influence affect structure is unknown in any quantifiable sense. Intuitively, it is felt that power and influence alliances do modify organization structure. Tentatively stated, changes in organization power arrangements will be reflected in structural transformations. But the precise time such changes will occur defies prediction; and so too, structural modifications resulting from these changes are difficult to predict. Thus, internal decisions which affect structure might pose a greater barrier to predicting points of structural transformation than external forces.

All in all, changes in organizational shape over time present extremely abstruse problems for analysis. The surface has hardly been scratched by research in this area. The values of such research are evident, however. Some guidelines formulated for predicting transformations in a firm's structure could facilitate management's planning and controlling functions enormously.

Changes in Size and Shape over Time

Up to this point shape and size are treated as discrete variables. They are not. Both size and shape are interrelated in such a way that a quantitative increase (or decrease) in size over time causes qualitative modifications in structure. And qualitative modifications may result in changes in the growth-rate factor of size. The analytical and conceptual difficulties which have been noted for the variables of size and shape treated independently are compounded when they are viewed as interdependent variables along a time continuum.

Some work of a modest nature has been undertaken on this problem. Writers have observed that as organizations grow (in terms of the number of people employed) a qualitative change in the composition of the work force occurs. From this change certain structural modifications are imputed.

Bendix, discussing bureaucratic indices, reports that industrial nations since 1900 have exhibited an increase in the numbers of people employed. And further, as more individuals are employed an occupational transition occurs which is reflected in what he calls the A/P ratio.

This ratio compares the growth in numbers of administrative employees to production workers. Over a period of roughly 50 years the numbers of administrative employees increased at a more rapid rate than production workers in five industrial nations. For example, in 1909 there were 750,000 administrative employees and 6,256,000 production workers in the United States, resulting in an A/P ratio of 12 percent. The ratio in 1947 was 21.6 percent with 2,578,000 administrative employees compared with 11,916,000 production workers. Upward trends in the A/P ratio hold for all the other industrial nations reported in the Bendix study.[30]

While Bendix discusses the A/P ratio from the standpoint of compositions of *national* work forces, Haire studies work-force compositions in transition for several firms. He reports a growth in both the clerical and staff functions which progresses more rapidly than the growth of the line. Staff and clerical functions are roughly comparable but not identical to Bendix's definition of administrative personnel.

Haire observed that the growth of the staff, relative to the line, occurs at a faster pace in the earlier stages of its introduction into the organization. The growth of the staff tends to level off as the organization matures. The growth of the clerical function for the firms studied was steady, but not runaway over time.

Haire concludes that the increased growth of staff members and clerical employees relative to line employees is caused by external forces and the internal necessity for communication through the passage of years.[31] Thus, changing technology; more complex relationships with other business, the government, and the community; and the imperatives of internal communication, coordination, and control have been factors causing administrative staff groups to grow faster than line groups. As organizations get bigger problems of coordination and communication appear causing the number of people in organizational units concerned with these activities to increase. Both staff and clerical bodies deal with matters of coordination, control, and dissemination of information.

Hence, it is demonstrable that through time the line maintains more or less a "normal" growth rate, while staff organizations and clerical functions increase personnel at a more rapid rate. Growth emphasis shifts from the line to supporting staff and clerical activities.[32] As a result, it is hypothesized that a growing firm changes shape from a symmetrical pyramid to a structure with a "bulge in the middle." The bulge encompasses the disproportionately large number of personnel engaging in activities in support of the line. Another modification of structure is the centralization of most administrative staff and clerical functions in support of

---

[30] Reinhard Bendix, *Work and Authority in Industry* (New York: John Wiley and Sons, Inc., 1956), pp. 211–26.

[31] Haire, *op. cit.*, pp. 287–302.

[32] Terrien and Mills make the following formulation: "The relationship between the size of an administrative component and the total size of its containing organization is such that the larger the size of the containing organization, the greater will be the proportion given over to its administrative component." See Frederic W. Terrien and Donald L. Mills, "The Effect of Changing Size upon the Internal Structure of Organization," *American Sociological Review*, February, 1955, p. 11.

decentralized production and sales functions. In very large organizations, these latter functions radiate from the "home office" which acts as a centralized coordination and communication source. Looking at past records, it is easy to determine that changes like these take place in histories of companies. However, from the "state of the arts" of prediction in the behavioral sciences today, a reliable forecast of when such changes will occur for a given company is impossible. A step in the direction of improved prediction must be the accumulation of huge amounts of research data revealing the crucial points in time when shape transformations take place in organizations. These transformations must then be related to the growth factor of size (using other criteria besides number of employees), plus the strategic changes which occur in the environment that also have an effect on the change of structure.

Proverbs of Organization Growth

Biologists do considerable work on the problems of growth and development in living organisms. Their conclusions have fallen on willing ears among organization theorists. As noted earlier, the behavioral scientists rely heavily on biological axioms for the formulations of their theories. These analogies may or may not be valid.

It seems that much of what is offered by biologists is accepted uncritically by behavioral scientists. The behavioral scientists who too willingly adopt biological analogies have at least one strike against them. Human organizations are not biological organisms. Evidence simply is not sufficient to support the claim that organizational processes correspond to biological processes. In addition to the lack of empirical substantiation, there are logical reasons for believing that biological analogies are on shaky ground. The stage is set for the "proverbs" by discussing next the laws of growth developed by biologists.

Biological Growth "Laws."[33]   There is a danger in calling anything a "law," because the best of laws can be disproved by changing the frame of reference. Nevertheless, the following points represent uniformities in observations of growth over time in biological organisms.

1. There is an average optimum size for all living organisms.

2. Organisms increase in size, or at least do not decrease in size, as they grow old.

3. In a constant environment, growth proceeds with uniform velocity. Under actual conditions, there is a progressive dissipation of growth energy. That is, the growth rate decreases as the organism gets older.

4. As a group (species) advances in biologic age, its individuals increase in size, but decrease in fertility. As a result, survival for the species and individuals in the species becomes more difficult.

---

[33] Most of the points below are adapted from Medawar, *op. cit.*, pp. 166–67 and E. R. N. Griggs, "Essay on a Fundamental Law of Life: The Time-Factor (Relativity) in Biological Phenomena," *Human Biology*, February, 1956, p. 15.

5. As an organism gets larger it uses up the more favorable parts of its environment, leaving the more hostile parts. Thus, growth is limited.

6. Growth and form are partially controlled by the inexorable workings of the mechanical forces in the organism's environment like gravity, or the surface tension of water, or the buoyant characteristic of water, or air.

Organizational Growth "Laws." The points that follow constitute the proverbs of organizational growth.[34] It is not coincidence that these "laws" parallel some of the biological axioms just outlined.

1. Each organization has an optimum size with an appropriate structure. Attempts to push beyond this optimum result in an organizational breakdown.

2. Size is limited by an increasingly unfavorable internal structure as an organization grows. Limits to growth arise from breakdowns in communication and coordination.

3. As an organization grows it uses up the more favorable parts of its environment. Life becomes harsher as the organization's surroundings grow more hostile.

These analogies are tempting. They do, however, involve difficulties. Some problems encountered when these "laws" are looked at critically are discussed next.

A Critique of Organizational Growth Proverbs. The "laws" listed above reveal that constraints on organizational growth are found in the limiting notions of optimum size, unfavorable internal conditions, and unfavorable environmental forces.

1. *The Problem of Optimum Size.* It is commonly observed in nature that each species of plant or animal has an average size. The individuals in the species do not deviate from this average by a very great amount. The first law of organization growth states that there is an optimum size for organizations from which tangible deviations result in lowered organizational effectiveness or complete collapse in extreme cases. How valid is this argument?[35]

Caplow has concluded that size affects organizational character, but that changes in size at certain points on a scale of expansion are more important than other points. He goes on to say that two-person groups have different properties than three-person groups. Doubling a group of

---

[34] In reality these "laws" are not growth laws at all in a dynamic sense. Actually they describe conditions which limit growth. The main source for these laws is Kenneth B. Boulding, *The Organizational Revolution* (New York: Harper and Bros., 1953), pp. 21–23. Other references include Mason Haire, *op. cit.,* and F. Stuart Chapin, "The Optimum Size of Institutions: A Theory of the Large Group," *American Journal of Sociology,* March, 1957, pp. 449–60.

[35] The average size of a species of plant or animal seems to be close to the optimum size for individuals in the species. This does not hold by analogy for firms in the same industry where the average size of firms is not necessarily the optimum for a particular firm.

15 is more likely to change patterns of interaction, structure, and activities of members than will doubling a work group of 200.[36]

The optimum size of an organization is defined as that size which allows it to accomplish goals more effectively. Therefore, the reason why small groups are small is because they can obtain their objectives most effectively when few people are involved. As Caplow indicates, changes in size of small groups have dramatic consequences on structure and the behavioral patterns of members. Thus, for any small group there appears to be an optimum size whereby the goals can be achieved most satisfactorily. Conversely, upward changes in size, without concomitant changes in goals, are likely to cause reduced group effectiveness or destruction of the group's existing structure.[37]

The same conclusion does not hold for large organizations, which possess the curious property to withstand great fluctuations in size without the need for making extreme modifications in structure. Indeed, not only are large organizations capable of absorbing considerable numbers of people, they also seem to be quite flexible in accepting changes in goals and policies without a great deal of internal restructuring. It may be concluded tentatively that so far as large organizations are concerned there seems to be no upper theoretical limit to their size.[38]

Formal organizations can effectively pursue goals within the framework of the same basic structure even though their membership expands enormously. Size is only important from the standpoint of diminishing returns, which may provide a practical limitation for a particular company at a specific time with a given "state of the arts." However, when favorable changes occur in technology, the market, or the competitive situation, this same firm can increase its number of employees quite conveniently.

The "law" of optimum size is unfortunate because it supposes that generalizations made about one type of organization can be carried over to other organizations. Actually, the large organization has means for absorbing membership, adapting to new goals, maintaining stability, and surviving that far surpass the small group.

---

[36] Theodore Caplow, "Organization Size," *Administrative Science Quarterly*, I (1950–1951), p. 484.

[37] The optimum size for an informal social group might be ten, because at this level the satisfaction of the participants is maximized. The structure of the group would be loose, allowing each member the greatest opportunity for self-expression and interaction with others. Suppose, however, because of a change in goals the group expanded to 50 members. The structure of the group would undoubtedly change also. Given a change in goals with an accompanying increase in size, the informal structure which previously existed might give way to a more formal structure which would be less fluid. Thus by introducing a new set of goals the former structure became obsolete.

[38] Although this point is made now and then in current literature of administration, it is interesting to note that the same observation was made some years ago in John J. Williams, "Is There an Optimum Size of Organization?" *Bulletin of the Taylor Society*, February, 1930, p. 22.

Again, the question of "optimum size" is only relevant when measured by the organization's effectiveness in achieving goals. Optimum size is an important issue in economic model building of rationalized profit-making machines. Here optimum size is determined by criteria derived from the law of diminishing returns. But when the goals lie outside profit rationality, diminishing returns fade into obscurity as a standard. A militant religious group does not stop recruiting members because someone determines they have already gone beyond the point of efficient utilization of the seats in church.

There are other criticisms of the optimum-size notion. However, they are more conveniently treated in the context of the next topic of "unfavorable internal structure," where additional support is also offered for the idea that there are no upper limits to the size of the large organization.

2. *The Problem of Increasingly Unfavorable Internal Structure.* As organizations get larger, increasing burdens are placed on communication systems and executive coordination. A point of size is reached where the communication network has difficulty in supporting organizational activities. In addition, executive coordination is taxed because of an extension of the span of control. Therefore, communication and coordination are thought to be effective limiting factors of organization size. First, what can be said about the nature of constraints imposed by communication?

Larger organizations seem to have denser networks of communication than smaller organizations. This is because as organizations grow the need for information increases at a disproportionate rate. There are two ways of handling increased communication bulk. First, the growing bulk can be transmitted more rapidly. Second, more people can be assigned to handle the bulk within the same time span.[39]

This is the same as saying that a given bulk of information can be transmitted in one half the time by doubling the speed of transmission or by doubling the capacity of the channel. With a given state of communication technology, such as the procedures for processing administrative communication, the usual way of handling increased bulk is to increase the *capacity* of the communication network. In practical circumstances this involves hiring more clerks and staff personnel who engage in creating, processing, transmitting, and assimilating information. Eventually this method of handling larger and larger bulks of information becomes quite cumbersome. Under these conditions, there is a point where additions to channel capacity are no longer feasible. This point represents a limit to the growth of the organization. This limit may be stated as follows: communication channels in a network will be added or the capacity of existing channels increased to the point where the incremental *cost* of such addi-

---

[39] Drawing from information theory, Haire states the case formally. He says, "If a message takes a channel of x frequencies to travel in y time, one can usually use $2x$ frequencies, and, by simultaneous transmission, achieve $\frac{1}{2}y$ time." See Haire, *op. cit.*, p. 302.

tional capacity expansions is equal to the *value* of the incremental addition to the bulk of information carried in the system.[40] When this point is encountered, a limiting factor to the size of the organization is reached.

Business organizations have usually dealt with increasing information bulk by simply expanding capacity; that is, by adding more people. But this is not the only alternative. Greater bulk can be handled by speeding up communication activities. This alternative requires, however, *new technologies* of information handling in business firms. Such technologies are on the horizon with "office automation." The constraints to organization growth created by the extension of capacity are overcome by reducing the time involved in communication dissemination and assimilation. Thus, the unfavorable barrier to further growth resulting from expanded communication needs can be reduced in significance by changing communication technology.[41] This line of analysis is explored at greater length in the appendix to Chapter 15.

Coordination is thought to be the second internal factor limiting organization growth. The proposition is that as organizations grow larger, the executive has greater difficulty timing and synchronizing activities. N. S. Ross sets forth, and then criticizes, a series of propositions which argue that managerial coordination is a limiting factor in the size of the firm. The propositions supporting this hypothesis are, according to Ross, the following.[42]

a) Co-ordination must be the act of a single center and, therefore, the division of labor cannot be applied to it.

b) The supply of co-ordinating talent available to the firm cannot be expanded as readily as other productive factors.

c) Co-ordinating centers must have detailed knowledge of problems—so the larger the field of co-ordination the greater the need for more knowledge.

d) Every increase in size must be, beyond a certain point, achieved by an extension of the scalar chain. This results in increasing co-ordinating cost which eventually will offset the economies of the division of labor.

e) The scalar chain cannot be extended indefinitely.

After considerable analysis, Ross offers these conclusions:[43]

a) The job of co-ordination is subject to the division of labor. It is naïve to assume that all co-ordinating work is solely the job of a single head.

b) By decentralization and control the firm may expand without increasing

---

[40] On the "cost of information" see Herbert A. Simon, "Theories of Decision Making in Economics and Behavioral Science," *American Economic Review*, June, 1959, p. 269–70.

[41] Another attack on the bulk problem is decentralization, by which the organization splits into self-contained administrative units. Decentralization does not constitute a new form of communication technology.

[42] N. S. Ross, "Management and the Size of the Firm," *Review of Economic Studies*, 19, (1951–52), p. 148.

[43] *Ibid.*, p. 154.

costs of co-ordination over a range sufficiently large to cover all possible cases within the limits imposed by scarcity of resources.

c) It is unlikely that the technical optimum size will outgrow the limits of managerial capacity, but there may be technical as distinct from managerial obstacles which place limits to growth.

Taking all his data into account, Ross concludes that ". . . the proposition 'that an optimum firm with an upper limit imposed by difficulties and costs of co-ordination is both a logically satisfactory and a necessary hypothesis to explain facts' is open to doubt."[44]

Fayol casts some light on an interesting aspect of this problem. By making modest assumptions regarding the span of control of executives, Fayol demonstrated that an organization of 12 levels of authority could encompass over 251 million workers, where each superior had 4 subordinates and each foreman had 15 workers under him.[45] Thus, writers who emphasize span of control and length of the scalar chain as limiting factors to size seem to underestimate the magnitude of the unit which can be administered effectively with relatively few authority levels.[46] Considering everything, limiting factors to the size of organizations must be looked for elsewhere; coordination alone apparently does not impose insurmountable barriers to the size of organizations within the range of practical experience.

3. *The Problem of an Increasingly Unfavorable External Environment.*
A biological species would increase in number at an explosive rate if it were not restrained by hostile forces in its environment. The proposition is thought to apply to human organizations as well, in the following sense. The larger the organization gets, the more difficult it becomes to grow more because it has used the favorable parts of its environment for previous growth. The parts of the environment left oppose extension. This might be analogous to a company gobbling up increasing shares of a market. A point is reached, everything else being equal, when the most favorable parts of the market are digested, leaving just lean pickings that are not profitable to take over. At this point, further growth is not tenable.

But in a dynamic setting, everything usually is not equal. By changing its marketing strategies, its products, technology, and by modifying its structure, an organization does not need to be bound to the environment of one market and one industry. Adaptation of human organizations to

---

[44] *Ibid.*, p. 154.

[45] Henri Fayol, *General and Industrial Management*, trans. Constance Storrs (London: New York: Pitman Publishing Corp., 1949), pp. 55–56.

[46] For example, the Internal Revenue Service employs in excess of 50,000 people, but the basic line organization comprises only 9 levels of authority extending from the commissioner in the national office to the group supervisor in district offices. It might interest the IRS to know that according to Fayol's calculations they can expand by roughly 3,880,160 people without adding more levels of authority.

change is a good deal more convenient and common than mutation of a biological species. Through change, the human organization reorients itself to exploit a new "environment" when the old seems played out. Of course there are limits to such reorientations. But these limitations, since they are imposed by the environment, are in the class of vague ultimates, and even these ultimates will differ from one type of organization to the next. For example, the environmental limits of the United Nations comprise the countries and population of the world.

In conclusion, the hypothesis of the increasingly hostile environment provides little by way of an operational notion of the limits to growth because of the facility of human organizations to redefine their environmental parameters. In terms of markets, products, policies, objectives, size, structure, capitalization, and research, the E. I. du Pont de Nemours & Co. of today is hardly the "same" company it was 50 years ago.

Much more could be said of organizational growth laws. The use of mathematical formulations for the purpose of generating a geometry of growth could be noted in detail.[47] The work in this area, however, is even more tentative than the research and analyses reported previously on growth.

The reader should be aware upon finishing this discussion that there is no "theory" of organizational growth. What passes for a theory are a few questionable proverbs based on biological analogies. It seems, however, that if a theory of growth is to emerge, it must be based on a study of the size, shape, and age variables. Several methodological and research difficulties which should be anticipated in such work have been noted.

---

[47] See Haire, *op. cit.*, pp. 284–87, and Chapin, *op. cit.*, pp. 449–60 for examples. Haire in his research found that organization growth corresponds to the square-cube law, which states a *linear* relationship between mass and surface areas of organisms influenced by the force of gavity. It might be noted parenthetically that if organizations were submerged in water, the law probably would not apply. For his part, Chapin observed in a study of church organizations that the growth configuration approximated a *spiral* which could be expressed in terms of Fibonacci proportions.

PART III

Process Concepts in Social Territory

IN THE LAST PART, social territory was the theme in which we observed the interlocking of autonomous subsystems in complex organizations. We gave a surface description of the nature of these systems and the factors which condition their behavior. This part opens up the territory to see how certain *strategic* processes contribute to the transformation and maintenance functions of organizations.

Most agree that human systems communicate, determine status and roles, exercise social influence, make decisions, and establish balance. These are processes which go on in all organizations. They are, indeed, the dynamics which underlie the internal life of an organization, in addition to being the regulators of relationships among organizations. These processes are the vital *linking* functions which we spoke of in Chapter 6.

There are many facets to a process. Decision making is a good example. We may talk about decision per se as choosing among alternatives, and the so-called rational criteria for making a choice; or we may focus on individual decisions to participate in and produce for an organization; or we can talk about organizational decisions in terms of routine and innovative activities. Beyond these facets are many others. The same can be said for communication, role behavior, and so on. A full treatment of just one process would be a book in itself.

We have tried in the analysis of processes to select for each a range of concepts which give a fair statement of the nature of the process, its relation to the social territory, and its relevance to management. This approach has built-in difficulties about which the reader should be warned. First, we tried to avoid giving a particular theory about a process. In discussing each process concepts and data relating to it, suggested by researchers and theoreticians working in the area, are developed. This approach reflects, but does not exhaust, the tremendous reservoir of information pertaining to these processes in the literature. But, it, as well, demonstrates the lack of consensus about the nature and relative importance of the processes' role in the social territory. Second, each chapter is rather like an essay on the subject covered by it. Therefore, one chapter does not follow the other for any particularly compelling reason. This again is indicative of the development of the field. There is hardly an integrated theory of human systems which forces on us a logical method for arranging this part. However, after all this is said, the topics treated constitute the crucial internal and interactional processes in organizational life.

CHAPTER 7

Communication Concepts

COMMUNICATION is the link between man and role. It also is the connector of role and function. Therefore communication embodies some of the most strategic concepts discussed in this part of the book.

Communication is the vehicle which executives use to establish policy and to obtain action. Administrators deal in language symbols. Their world is verbal. A number of studies have shown that most of an executive's time is spent in communication. A British researcher[1] analyzing executive behavior gives a detailed account of the activities of a group of managers. The results show that 80 percent of their time on the job is spent in conversation. Most of the remaining hours are devoted to reading or writing. In short, communicating is the core of executive activity.

An obvious question at this point is, why this managerial occupation with communication? Answers are many and complex, and it is the purpose of this chapter to delve into some of the reasons. In part, it could be said that organization demands communication. Information is the vital force upon which organization depends. Or it may be posited that a fundamental, distinguishing feature of man is his ability to transmit ideas. Thus, when man communicates he is acting in accordance with his nature.

In any case, communication is every bit as important in the life of the individual as it is in the life of the organization. It is the means by which the individual presents his inner-self to others; it is the link between personalities; and it is the process which ties personalities to the organization. This chapter presents a framework for understanding the process of communication. Communication is considered in social, psychological, and administrative terms. An appendix is provided to treat some of the technical

---

[1] Tom Burns, "The Directions of Activity and Communication in a Departmental Executive Group," *Human Relations*, 1954, pp. 73–97. Burns' study was of "middle managers." A study by Piersol found that supervisors—foremen—spent approximately 50 percent of their working time in oral communication, either as speakers or listeners. Of this time, 60 percent was with subordinates, 30 with superiors, and 10 percent among themselves. See D. T. Piersol, "Communication Practices of Supervisors in a Mid-Western Corporation," *Advanced Management*, February, 1958, pp. 20–21. See also George L. Hinds, "The Communicative Behavior of the Executive," *Journal of Communication*, Spring, 1957, pp. 29–34.

aspects of information theory. We do not deal with the "pathological" conditions which arise in communication practice. The discussion of communication breakdown is reserved for Chapter 15.

BASIC CONCEPTS IN COMMUNICATION

The term communication is fairly common. Most people have an idea of what the word means, associating it usually with the telephone, television, radio, newspapers, and the like. But as the concept of communication is examined in appropriate administrative contexts, it takes on far different connotations. In the broadest sense, the aim and outcome of communication is the resolution of uncertainty.[2] This general proposition pertains to interpersonal as well as intermachine communication.

Defining Communication

The reader could probably produce a satisfactory definition of communication by addressing himself to the question: what is involved when I want to express myself to others? To conserve mental energy, the answer is that you want to duplicate the ideas in your mind in the minds of other persons. This elementary consideration prompts Cartier and Harwood to say, "If you analyze any act of communication, you will always discover this same function: the replication of a memory or a complex of memories. Communications is a process for the replication of memories."[3]

This definition has sufficient generality to apply to communication functions in nonhuman situations as well as in human situations. For example, a simple thermostatic system exhibits the facility of memory and replication. The system "remembers" the information pertaining to the temperature it is to maintain. It then acts to replicate this information by comparing the temperature in the room with the desired temperature. Automatically controlled devices of higher levels of complexity have very intricate internal means of duplicating information stored in their "memories." Thus, even though this chapter is devoted to communication in human systems, the fact should not be overlooked that communication has a considerably broader range of application.

Definitions of communication for administration do not differ essentially from the general definition given above. Browne defines communication as ". . . the process of transmitting ideas or thoughts from one person to another, or within a single person, for the purpose of creating understanding in the thinking of the person receiving the communica-

---

[2] J. K. Pierce, *Symbols, Signals and Noise: The Nature and Process of Communication* (New York: Harper and Bros., 1961), p. 79.

[3] P. A. Cartier and K. A. Harwood, "On the Definition of Communication," *Journal of Communication*, November, 1953, p. 73. See also Dale D. Drum, "Change Meaning, and Information," *Journal of Communication*, Winter, 1957, p. 162.

tion."[4] According to Johnson, Kast, and Rosenzweig, "communication . . . is a system involving a sender and a receiver, with implications of feedback control."[5]

Important, either explicitly or implicitly in most administrative definitions of communication are two factors.

1. *Understanding. Recognized in most administrative concepts of communication is the need for a high order of understanding.* The reason is quite pragmatic. Organizations depend on human action to accomplish goals. Goal-directed behavior is evoked through communication. So, the greater the degree of understanding present in the communication process, the more likely it is that human action will proceed in the direction of accomplishing goals stated by management. Thus, the higher the degree of understanding, the lower the ambiguity on the part of the receiver regarding goals and the appropriate behavior necessary to achieve them. Viewed in this way, communication in organization is *utilitarian.* That is, management uses communication primarily to accomplish organizational goals.

2. *Closed-Loop Systems.* Most definitions of communication include the idea of feedback and control. Feedback assures the regulation of communication systems in accordance to preset objectives. It is necessary to promote both understanding and control. The concept is applicable in human, electrical-mechanical, and mixed systems of communication.

With these points in mind a definition of communication can be offered. *Administrative communication is a process which involves the transmission and accurate replication of ideas ensured by feedback for the purpose of eliciting actions which will accomplish organizational goals. Since administrative communication largely concerns people, the necessity for a high degree of understanding is implicit in the phrase "accurate replication of ideas."*

Factors in the Communication Process

Administrative communication cannot be understood apart from the five factors which are the common denominators of the process regardless of the type of organizational setting.[6] These factors are:

1. *The Act.* The communication act requires the use of symbols. Language symbols usually serve the purpose. But even a low level of understanding exists between people who do not speak the same language. Actions, facial expressions, intonations of the voice, and so on are sym-

---

[4] C. G. Browne, "Communication Means Understanding," in Keith Davis and William G. Scott (eds.), *Readings in Human Relations* (New York: McGraw-Hill Book Co., Inc., 1959), p. 331.

[5] Richard A. Johnson, Fremont E. Kast, and James E. Rosenzweig, "Systems Theory and Management," *Management Science*, January, 1964, p. 380.

[6] These factors are adapted from C. Merton Babcock, "A Dynamic Theory of Communication," *Journal of Communication*, May, 1952, pp. 65–68.

bolic conveyers which have meaning. But, effective action based on communication would be inhibited by the inability to understand the main vehicle for transmitting ideas which is, of course, language.

2. The Scene. The scene refers to the environment of communication. The scene determines what is said, what symbols are used, and often the *meaning* of what is said.

3. The Agent. Individuals who engage in a communication relationship are said to be the agents of communication. Typically, a sender and receiver are involved, frequently interchanging these roles as the communication situation develops.

4. The Agency. The media for communication constitute the agencies. Besides face-to-face oral communication such media as written orders and memos, bulletin boards, telephones, and public-address systems are found in business situations.

5. Purpose. The purpose of communication refers to the objectives sought by engaging in the communication process. Four goals have been noted:[7]

a) The functional goal. This goal is utilitarian. Information is transmitted so that some organizational objective can be achieved.

b) The manipulative goal. Communication is used in this case to maneuver people into accepting ideas which may or may not be in conformance to their own attitudes or values. Propaganda is an example of the manipulative use of communication on a mass basis.

c) The aesthetic goal. The purposes sought by this goal are creative. Communication is employed to enable a person to express his feelings and to interpret his sense of reality.

d) The confidence goal. This attempts to increase people's confidence in their environment. Scientific research falls in this category. Its purpose is to uncover and communicate findings regarding the nature of the world in which we live.

We must tarry briefly with the last factor in the communication process. The utilitarian or functional nature of organizational communication has already been noted several times. It should not be inferred, however, that all communication in an organization is utilitarian. Quite obviously, some organizational communication has manipulative overtones. But on a more noble level, communication is for some people both aesthetic and creative.

In any event, the demands made by the organization for functional communication, and the satisfactions an individual gets from engaging in communication, stem from different causes. For example, from the standpoint of the organization communication is utilitarian because it serves as a linking or coupling function. Without communication survival for the organization is impossible. But the utilitarian nature of communication

---

[7] Harry A. Grace, "Confidence, Redundancy, and the Purpose of Communication," *Journal of Communication,* Spring, 1956, pp. 16–23.

taken from the organization's frame of reference does not restrict individuals in the organization from using communication for personal satisfactions which are not utilitarian.

"Machiavellians" utilize communication for manipulating people to achieve their ends of status and power. But the communication process may also be used as an avenue of self-expression and creativity. It must be emphasized that the goals of communication as pursued by the organization and individuals in it are not necessarily inconsistent. An individual may derive creative satisfaction from a communication act, but, at the same time, he may also be serving the utilitarian communication purposes of the organization. This argument has another side, however. Communication ends of individuals may differ from the utilitarian objectives of the organization. Unscrupulous use of communication by a person to establish his power and prestige frequently is at odds with the utilitarian needs of the organization.

THE SETTING OF COMMUNICATION

The remainder of this chapter is devoted to the conceptual underpinnings of the communication process in human organizations. The major topics covered are the communication model, senders and receivers, the "distribution" system, communication dimensions, communication effectiveness and communication symbols.

The Communication Model

One author says ". . . a model is . . . a structure of symbols and operating rules which is supposed to match a set of relevant points in an existing structure or process."[8] From what has been stated before, in the previous section on definition, an administrative model of communication should contain:

1. Sources to generate information and receivers to assimilate it.
2. Vehicles to convey information—symbols.
3. A channel to distribute information.

In addition to these basic factors, a model also requires some approximation of the activities by which the communication act accomplishes organizational and personal goals. Communication is not homogeneous. Various types of communication activities are used to accomplish different ends in organizations. Using March and Simon's classification, communication activities are said to fall into the following categories.[9]

---

[8] Karl W. Deutsch, "On Communication Models in the Social Sciences," *Public Opinion Quarterly*, 16 (1952), p. 357.

[9] James G. March and Herbert A. Simon, *Organizations* (New York: John Wiley and Sons, Inc., 1958), p. 161.

1. "Communication for nonprogrammed activities." This category includes all individual "talking and listening" not associated with the utilitarian objectives of the organization or the job. The grapevine, gossip, and social conversation fall into this classification.

2. "Communication to initiate and establish programs, including day-to-day adjustment or 'co-ordination' of programs."

3. "Communication to provide data of application of strategies. . . ." Communication of this variety supplies information to decision makers enabling them to activate the programs developed in the second category.

4. "Communication to evoke programs. . . ." In this category, communication is used for motivating people. Commonly, this form of communication is found in superior-subordinate relationships and is the "on-the-job" method of getting work done. It is the communication activity which receives the most emphasis in management literature.

5. "Communication to provide information on the results of activities." This final category refers to communication which feeds back *control* information to decision makers from the point of performance.

Communication provides a utilitarian function for the organization by the activities covered in categories 2, 3, 4, and 5. These activities center in the generation (2) and implementation (3) of programs or plans of action. Category 4 notes the use of communication for motivating people

FIGURE 7–1

Elements and Activities Found in an Administrative Communication Model

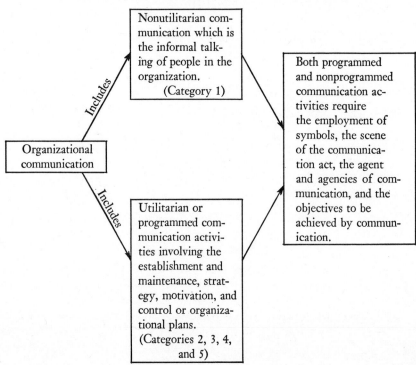

to accomplish the programs; and category 5 reveals the necessity for control to ensure programs are performed according to the standards established by the original plan. Within the complex of these formal (utilitarian) functions of organizational communication is category 1, pertaining to the informal "talk" or nonutilitarian communication which goes on in the organization.

Figure 7–1 illustrates the elements of a communication model. A statement and a diagram of a model, however, hardly do justice to the dynamic nature of the process itself. So the following sections consider in detail aspects of the processes and elements contained in the model.

Senders and Receivers: The Psychological Foundations and the "Social Matrix" of Communication

Encoding and Decoding   A simple approach to communication—which nonetheless has a good deal of merit—is that communication involves a sender who encodes his ideas into symbols and a receiver who decodes the symbols. The purpose of the process is to reconstruct the ideas of the sender in the mind of the receiver. This statement encompasses the entire notion of human communication. But the fact of its generality obscures much—for example, the psychological basis of communication.

The Psychological Foundations of Communication.   A person who sends information does so with the intention of having his ideas replicated

FIGURE 7–2
Restructuring an Ambiguous Communication Setting

(1)	(2)	(4)	(5)
Perceived unclarity in a communication situation giving rise to a tension between potential senders and receivers.	The creation of communication content by the sender	Specific reaction in the form of behavior by the receiver.	Reconstructing the communication setting as a result of effective action. Tension eliminated.

Transmission
(3)

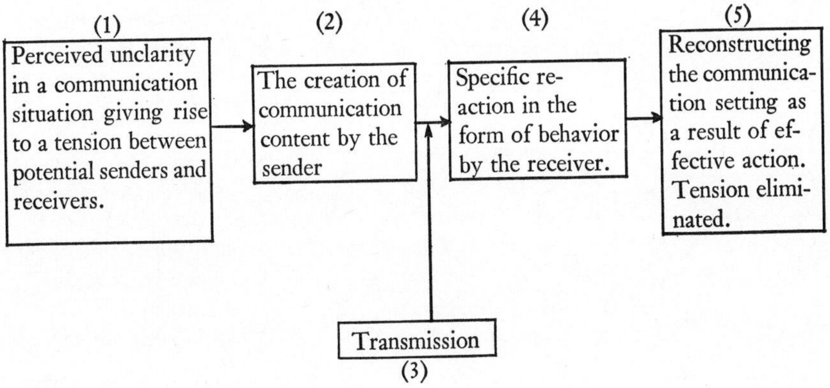

by those who he assumes have need of the type of information offered. The receiver accepts information with the expectation that it will satisfy his needs or demands in the communication situation.

Communicated content is a structured or patterned set of symbols designed to stimulate the sensory organs of the receiver. Content always exists in a communication setting which, according to Fearing, possesses physical, social, and psychological characteristics. These characteristics prompt and determine the behavior of both senders and receivers. The key aspect of the communication setting is that it is often hazy. This lack of clarity about the environment builds up "states of tension" between senders and receivers. Tension, in turn, creates a "need to communicate" and "a need to be communicated to."[10]

Figure 7–2 includes these ideas with some elaboration to demonstrate the dynamic psychological properties of the communication process. The process is traced as follows:

1. To begin, the parties in a communication situation perceive a lack of clarity and an ambiguity in the setting. Perceptions of this variety cause states of tension that can be resolved only through communication. Communication clarifies and gives definition to the situation.

2. The sender moves to alleviate the tension state by creating communication content. Content is a structured field of symbols which, it is assumed, has meaning for the receiver.

3. The content is transmitted to the receiver via some suitable channel. Administratively, the channels selected are those most readily adaptable to written or verbal language symbols.

4. In accord with the definition of administrative communication, effective action (it is hoped) is forthcoming.

5. If effective action is realized, the tension has been removed from the standpoint of management and the communication setting has been restructured and clarified. An equilibrating function has taken place.

An observation or two must be made about the equilibrating process mentioned in point 5. Effective action as seen by the manager does not necessarily constitute satisfaction of the communication needs of the receiver. Communication needs exist on different levels.[11] At one level, utilitarian communication is necessary for adequate job performance. Supplying this information can resolve states of tension caused by ambiguity in the content of job responsibilities.

At another level are tension states resulting from the individual's need to know the *reason* for his job activities and the overall role of these activities in the broader scheme of the total organization. The major difference between the levels of specific job knowledge and the purpose of the job is, perhaps, the difference that exists between "how" and "why." An individual's communication needs extend beyond the confines of job activities.

Although deeply rooted in psychological foundations, communication

---

[10] Franklin Fearing, "Toward a Psychological Theory of Human Communication," *Journal of Personality*, 22 (1953–54), pp. 73–76.

[11] For a recent research analysis see Herbert C. Kelman and Alice H. Eagly, "Attitude toward the Communicator, Perception of Communication Content, and Attitude Change," *Journal of Personality and Social Psychology*, January, 1965, pp. 63–78.

is also a social phenomenon. It is the basis of social interaction. The relationship between sender and receiver is not a simple one. The idea that the initial sender has control of the communication situation, with the receiver passively reproducing and responding to what is transmitted to him, is of course erroneous. What the sender sends is often conditioned by what he thinks the receiver will accept. And, further, the sender may constantly modify the content of his messages as the receiver feeds back reactions to him. Thus, communication has social implications. Senders and receivers are affected by and act upon the "social matrix" enmeshing the communication process.

Social Aspects of Communication. Man's social and cultural matrix may be considered in terms of space and time dimensions. But added to this are the symbolic language forms by which he perceives and describes his relationship in his matrix. Indeed, it is very hard to separate man's culture and his language forms. Human personality and behavior are in large part shaped by the symbolic systems impinging upon it. If a culture is without anxiety about its food supply, it would not have a language component to express this anxiety. But if a society knew nothing but privation, it is likely that its language would be filled with symbols relating to food and its acquisition. As we mentioned in concluding Chapter 3, *n* (achievement) is a pervasive cultural trait in American society. How many symbolic expressions, both abstract and concrete, can you think of which convey notions of success, accomplishment, and acquisition?

Ruesch and Bateson describe some of the dimensions of communication in the social matrix.[12]

Level I—Intrapersonal. Communication with one's self is intrapersonal. Intrapersonal communication is essential in cognitive activities. At first it might seem that this hardly fits the administrative definition of communication where senders and receivers are required. But if we look at Roger's approach of nondirective interviews as facilitating the process of internal communication to allow the individual to cope more effectively with his environment, we can see the value of this dimension in administration.

Level II—Interpersonal. This level is one of common familiarity in which one person communicates to another, such as a manager discussing a job assignment with a subordinate.

Level III—Group-Individual Communication.

a) The first situation in the category is the "one-to-many" case. In the administrative sense, the obligation of a president of a company to report his activities to the board of directors or stockholders is an example.

b) "Many-to-one" communication is the second situation in this category. Frequently decisions made by a committee are communicated to an individual for final action. The decision is jointly derived but its imple-

---

[12] This approach to the social aspects of communication is adapted from Jurgen Ruesch and Gregory Bateson, *Communication: The Social Matrix of Psychiatry* (New York: W. W. Norton and Co., 1951), chap. 2.

mentation is referred to an individual in higher authority. An executive committee referring decisions to a company president is an example of many-to-one communication.

Level IV—Group-to-Group Communication.

a) The first form of this communication is many-to-many, spacebinding messages. This type of communication is characterized by messages flowing between organizational segments. The information usually deals with on-going situations and frequently is coordinating in nature. Differences in functions performed in an organization may be regarded as separated by space. Communication used for transcending this space and coordinating activities is thought of as "space binding."

b) Time-binding messages constitute the second form of "many-

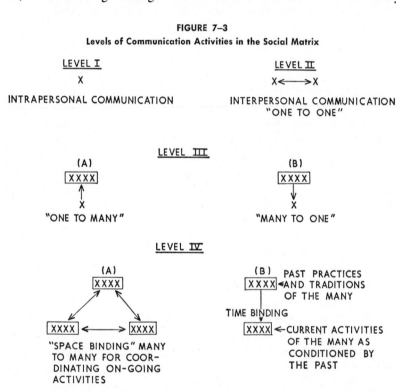

FIGURE 7–3
Levels of Communication Activities in the Social Matrix

to-many" communication. While space-binding messages are concerned with current management activities of coordination, time-binding messages link the present with the past. The traditions and policies—in short the image of a company—are a product of the "many" who have gone before the present group of executives.

Figure 7–3 schematically presents the aforementioned levels of communication. Note that each level except the first involves social interaction. Value judgments should not be inferred from the presentation of communication as levels. Level IV is no more important than Level III. If anything, the levels are ordered in terms of the complexity of the social interactions portrayed.

Each level, however, has social implications peculiar to it. Level II provides for close, personalized communication. This level offers the greatest opportunity for senders and receivers to modify their messages as the communication situation develops. Reactions to communication information on Level II are relatively more rapid than on the other levels.

Two social situations prevail at Level III. In the "one-to-many" case, the individual—say, a president of a company—may be communicating to a rather heterogeneous aggregate of people such as stockholders, or he may be communicating to a small, homogeneous group such as a board of directors. These two cases require distinctly different communication approaches.

The first case is often quite impersonal. Communication with stockholders is accomplished at annual meetings or through annual reports. The opportunity for feedback from the stockholders to the president is relatively low. Votes of confidence or no confidence in the form of proxies are the delayed reaction to company policy.

The second case—the president's communication with the board of directors—is considerably different. Here a more immediate reaction to communication is achieved in the intimate surroundings of meetings. Also, since this group is fairly homogeneous technical terminology is feasible for explanations of the operations of the business and the formulation of policy. The heterogeneous, detached nature of the stockholder group, then, requires general, impersonal, and nontechnical forms of communication from which feedback is infrequent. In contrast, the homogeneity and smaller size of the board allows the president to communicate in technical and specific terms with every expectation that the feedback from the group will be immediate and direct.

The second situation in Level III is "many-to-one" communication. A number of companies use formally constituted committees to generate policy and to thrash out problems. The results of these joint deliberations are relayed to individuals for action. The receiving individual can be either a member of the committee itself or a nonmember. He, further, can be situated above the committee in formal authority, at the same level, or below the committee.

Reactions by individuals to committee decisions are quite varied. A decision by a group is difficult for an individual to resist at best, even if his better judgment tells him to. In any event, a strong man in a status position above committee members is strategically placed to derive the greatest advantage from the committee's "combined mind." He can offset the weight of the committee by not yielding to schemes which he thinks are poorly conceived. Individuals at the same status level or below the committee in status may not be so fortunate.

Committees are the product of large complex organizations. They serve useful purposes from the standpoint of advice and coordination. But there are many dangers in their use, and not the least of these is the difficulty of pinpointing responsibility for decision. As Ernst Pawel observes:

> A committee is not just a group of men. A group of men, once they constitute a committee, form a mythical, mystic, mysterious, inaccessible entity whose decisions have the same force and effect as an Act of God and are equally beyond appeal.[13]

Of course, communication by the many to the one does not have to occur in the context of formally established committees. Informal pressures for conformity and acceptance of values exist throughout organizations. The result, however, is much the same as noted above. Mass opinion tends to lend authoritativeness to communication, regardless of whether in fact the judgment of the group is sound. Some people will form personal judgments that are inaccurate as long as they are told others are making the same judgments.[14]

At Level IV in situation *a*, the space-binding functions of communication serve coordinative purposes. This type of communication (called horizontal, at times) ties together diverse activities. Space-binding communication exists in the line organization among departments in all the organic functions. It also binds the staff organization to the line.

The concepts involved with situation *b* at this level are rather elusive but are nonetheless real. Through time-binding communication, the past "speaks" to the present in the form of history, established policies, and the organization "image." These heritages of past management provide either cherished traditions or burdensome problems for incumbent management. The past does indeed send messages to the present which have to be nurtured or lived down.

COMMUNICATION DISTRIBUTION SYSTEMS

Now that we have discussed some of the social and psychological foundations of communication and a definition of administrative communication has been established, thought must be given to the way information is distributed in organizations. Two models are offered as conceptu-

---

[13] Ernst Pawel, *From the Dark Tower* (New York: The Macmillan Co., 1957), p. 68.

[14] The problem of conflict between the individual's view of reality and social pressures is discussed by S. E. Asch, "Effects of Group Pressure upon the Modification and Distortion of Judgment," in H. Guetzkow (ed.), *Groups, Leadership, and Men* (Pittsburgh: Carnegie Press, 1951), pp. 177–90; and, T. D. Tuddenham, "The Influence of a Distorted Group Norm upon Individual Judgment," *Journal of Psychology*, 86 (1954), pp. 227–41.

alizations of organizational communication systems. They are the "circuit model" and the "network model."

The Circuit Communication Model

The simplest way to visualize an organizational communication system is the circuit illustrated in Figure 7–4.

FIGURE 7–4
The Communication Circuit

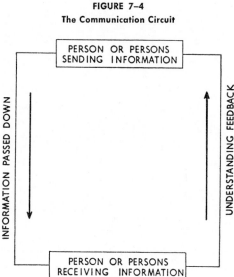

This model fits quite nicely into the definitions of administrative communication quoted earlier in this chapter. The model shows that for communication to exist both a sender and a receiver are necessary. Additionally, communication in this model relies on a *closed* circuit, requiring both the elements of downward passage of information and understanding feedback to be present. As a first approximation, this model represents the basic ingredients necessary for effective communication. It should be added that the model is indeed a first approximation.

The circuit model is quadratic, symmetrical, and continuous. It is quadratic in that four elements are basic to it; it is symmetrical because information emitted by the sender (ideally) is balanced by understanding evidenced by the receiver; and it is continuous because it portrays communication as an undisrupted interchange between the sender and receiver.

Newman advances the interesting idea that "although communication is . . . a circular process, circular should not be construed as continuous. . . . There need not be an unbroken, continuous relation among the sender, the signal, and the receiver . . . communication may be said to exist wherever there is a relationship effected between any two of the three factors involved, even though the third may be in abeyance."[15]

A diagram (Figure 7–5) is useful to explain Newman's point.

FIGURE 7–5
A Dyadic Communication Model

Brackets *A* and *B* identify communication dyads. These dyads may eventually link up to form a completed communication circuit. But their linking is neither direct nor continuous as the model in Figure 7–4 suggests.[16] Instead the two dyads may couple at different times and for different reasons in the organization.

The dyadic aspects of communication do not fundamentally change the circuit model. They modify it to accord more with the realities of communication in complex organizations. Certainly not all organizational communication is the personal, direct, and circular interchange which the simple circuit model implies. Administrative communication is frequently impersonal and is disconnected both in space and time from intended receivers.

It is important to appreciate how the communication process operates in the continuous, circular, face-to-face relationship. But it is equally essential to know the circumstances under which dyads link up to form systems in more complex communication situations. For this reason, the topic of the network model follows.

Communication Networks

The subject of communication networks brings this discussion to the topic of organization, and focuses on communication as a linking process—for as Rothstein says, "Organization presupposes the existence of parts, which, considered in their totality, constitute organization. The parts must interact. Were there no communication between them, there would be no organization for we should merely have a collection of individual elements isolated from each other."[17] Similarly, Dorsey points

---

[15] John B. Newman, "Communication: A Dyadic Postulation," *Journal of Communication*, June, 1959, p. 53. Grace also holds that communication occurs when a message is emitted regardless of whether it is immediately received and prompts action. Grace, *op. cit.*, p. 17.

[16] While the circuit model uses four elements, two of these elements—information and understanding feedback—are carried by the vehicle of a signal to link the sender to the receiver. So, in principle the same elements exist both in Newman's model and the circuit model.

[17] Jerome Rothstein, *Communication, Organization and Science* (Indian Hills, Colorado: Falcon's Wing Press, 1958), p. 34.

out that administration can be viewed as a configuration of communication patterns relating individuals and groups.[18]

A network is best visualized as a system of decision centers interconnected by communication channels. A network always has feedback features; that is, *control* of the system is accomplished by retroactive mechanisms. Feedback, through a communication network, allows for self-regulation of the system. By sampling the output, the system regulates the input in such a way as to maintain stability in the face of change. Feedback is a basic property of *cybernetic* systems. And the business organization is an example of one of the most complex of all such systems.[19]

Now, the circular model incorporates all the features of a network. In reality this model *is* a highly simplified network because it contains decision centers, information, and a feedback property. However, the network model is far more complex, containing numerous intermeshed loops which do not necessarily behave in a continuous, direct pattern. They act more as dyads than simple circuits. *Further, because of its complexity the network possesses greater capabilities for variety. It is able to assimilate a wider range of inputs, to operate on these inputs in diverse ways, and to produce a larger number of outputs.* For example, compare the intricate communication network shown in Figure 7–6 with the circuit model illustrated in Figure 7–4.

There is no need for a detailed explanation of Figure 7–6, but two points relative to this discussion should be mentioned.

1. Note that this production communication net is a highly complex system, containing all the communication elements discussed before. There are decision centers, indicated by the boxes or cells on the chart; information is present in the system in the form of various messages such as blueprints, records, and reports. Communication channels are shown by lines with arrows noting the flow. And finally, control or feedback information is present as customer complaints, tool receipts, system change recommendations, inventory balances, and so on.

2. Within the network some simple circuits are found. For example, order-dispatching requests for blueprints and the blueprint department's direct channel for returning completed prints constitute a simple circuit. But the communication relationship between order dispatching and the operating department is far less direct and continuous. The system corresponds more conveniently to the dyadic modifications introduced into the circuit model. Thus, order dispatching sends messages directly to the operating department, but the response from operating is far from continuous. Operating feedback to dispatching is routed through many different channels and departments which can be easily followed in Figure 7–6. Hence, the communication activities set

[18] John T. Dorsey, "A Communication Model for Administration," *Administrative Science Quarterly*, December, 1957, p. 310.

[19] For an excellent discussion of feedback see Stafford Beer, *Cybernetics and Management* (New York: John Wiley and Sons, Inc., 1959), chap. 4.

FIGURE 7–6

Communication in Intermittent Production

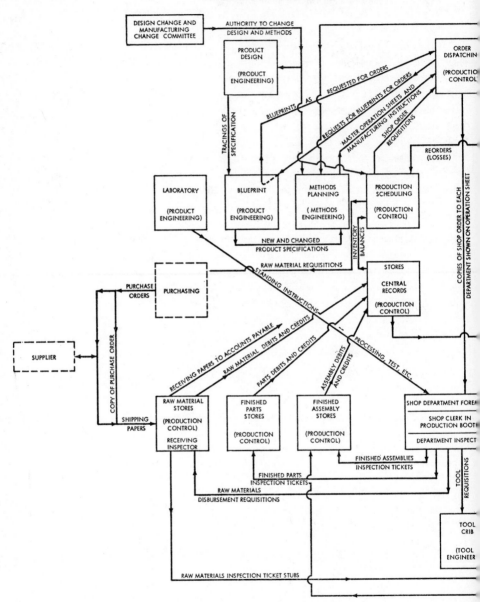

Source: Howard L. Timms, *Production Management* (Bloomington: Bureau of Business Research, Indiana University, 1958), p. 43. Reprinted with permission from Indiana Readings in Business, No. 22.

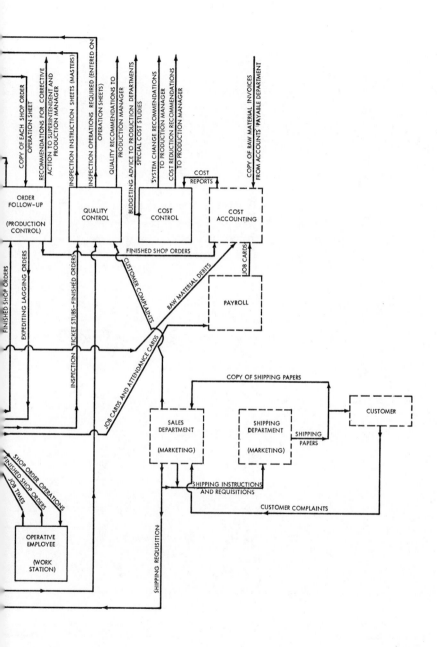

in motion by a message from dispatching to operating cause events to occur which are separated from dispatching by both space and time. Results of such initiating messages are neither immediately nor directly available to the sending department.

In summary, the network exists to accomplish *goals* set by decision makers. Movement toward these objectives implies the need for control information relative to the progress of the system in achieving its objectives. *Control functions operate through the feedback of information from strategic points of performance to the decision centers.* Therefore, as stated before, a network is the nervous system of an organization which, in turn, is an elaborate cybernetic mechanism. Cybernetics is not the exclusive property of engineers; rather, "cybernetics is about all manner of control, all kinds of structure, all sorts of systems."[20]

Finally, control via the feedback mechanism is the distinguishing feature of a true communication network. Decision centers utilize information feedback to appraise the results of the organization's performance and to make any adjustments to insure the accomplishment of the purposes of the organization. Additionally, feedback is crucially important for maintaining balance among the parts of the system. Feedback cues executives as to when changes are to be instituted.

COMMUNICATION EFFECTIVENESS AND EFFICIENCY

There are two things we need to know about the performance of communication networks.

1. We should know something about the *speed* and *accuracy* with which a network gets work done.
2. We should know the degree of satisfaction the participants in the network derive from it.

In other words, we are applying Barnard's criteria of the cooperative system to measure communication.

Several experiments have been conducted to test the effectiveness and efficiency of various arrangements of communication networks.[21] Following Dubin, these networks were tested in modifications of six patterns shown in Figure 7–7.

The serial patterns, vertical and horizontal, describe network communication linkages in the chain of command and on functional levels, respectively. The radial patterns show executive coordination of subordinate decision centers and the distribution of staff services. Note that

---

[20] Stafford Beer, "The Irrelevance of Automation," *Cybernetics*, 1 (1958), p. 295.

[21] See Harold J. Leavitt, "Some Effects of Certain Communication Patterns on Group Performance," *The Journal of Abnormal and Social Psychology*, 66 (1951), pp. 38–50; and M. E. Shaw, "Group Structures and the Behavior of Individuals in Small Groups," *Journal of Psychology*, 38 (1954), pp. 139–49.

communication links between decision centers do not exist other than with the focal unit; i.e., the coordinating center or the staff center. The circular network permits free communication and maximum participation in the decision process by units. It is the only one which does. The remaining three networks are hybrids more closely approximating formal organizational communication patterns.

The research which has been done on linkage patterns points to two conclusions.

FIGURE 7–7
Basic Linkage Patterns

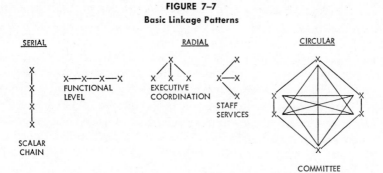

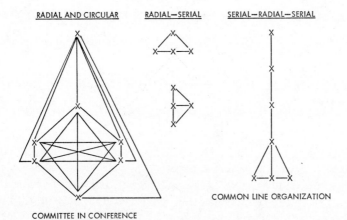

Source: Robert Dubin, "Stability in Human Organizations," in Mason Haire (ed.), *Modern Organization Theory* (New York: John Wiley and Sons, Inc., 1959), p. 223. Used with permission.

1. The fewer the links between centers the more effective organizational communication will be.

2. The minimization of the number of links in a network, while making for greater effectiveness, tends to reduce efficiency or the degree of satisfaction individuals find in the communication process. This is because the reduction of links increases centrality or authoritarianism. It has been found that the circular pattern contributes more to human satisfaction largely as the result of its participative character.

Thus, management is faced with a dilemma. Which is the most appropriate system to serve both the needs of the organization and the people in it?[22] The claims made for the circular pattern seem to tilt the balance in its direction. However, the amplification of participative activity has lethal consequences—both for people and for organizations. People may be happy "participating" because they are relieved from their primary obligations of production. Or even worse, production demands may remain while time is consumed by the compulsive sociality of the committee.

Yet, the research on the effectiveness of participation and group decision making is too formidable to be denied entirely. Some circumstances may require a committee-participative form of decision or joint consultation on problems. These conditions include highly involved technical problems or the coordination of complex organizations. Participation is also useful when it can be shown to improve both effectiveness and efficiency. However, group decision making or participation is not defensible as a pure "morale booster" if it interferes with the accomplishment of legitimate organizational goals.

A Note on Fayol's Bridge

Suppose we hypothesize a formal communication network which has the minimum possible number of links between units. It would look like this.

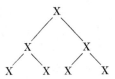

There are six links for the seven decision centers. This network is a combination of radial and vertical serial patterns. It is hardly effective, much less efficient. Although it minimizes links, it introduces artificial rigidities in communication because it lacks "legitimate" channels for cross communication between decision centers on the same functional level.

It was precisely to overcome this problem that Fayol proposed his classic bridge of horizontal communication.[23] His concept of cross communication was the result of studies as an industrial engineer of the hidebound traditions of communication in the French civil service. A diagram in Figure 7–8 illustrates the bridge.

If "H" wanted to communicate with "I" he would have to go up the

[22] For a further discussion of communication patterns and their relationship to morale and efficiency see Alex Bavelas and Dermont Barrett. "An Experimental Approach to Organizational Communication," *Personnel*, March 1951, pp. 366–71.

[23] Henri Fayol, *General and Industrial Management*, trans. Constance Storrs (New York: Pitman Publishing Corp., 1949), pp. 34–36. The original work appeared in 1916.

various levels through "A," and down again until he finally reached "I." Fayol observed that this method of communication was inefficient and time consuming. He therefore postulated the idea of lateral communication between persons performing functions on similar levels (in Figure 7–8, from "H" to "I").

This brings up a problem which can be resolved without too much

FIGURE 7–8
Fayol's Bridge

difficulty. We observe (Figure 7–8) that before the introduction of Fayol's bridge the communication network had eight links. After "legitimatizing" cross communication, the network had 12. According to the theory of linkage effectiveness, the network having more links after the bridge than before should be less effective. However, we have to recognize that the crucial determinant of communication effectiveness is the number of links a message must consume when passing from one decision center to another. H communicating with I before the bridge uses eight links; after the bridge just one.

Now, one might ask that if this is the case why not allow free communication throughout the network laterally, vertically, diagonally, and every which way? This reduces to one, the number of links any decision center would use communicating with another. The reason this is not done is simply that every organization in greater or lesser degrees must preserve the integrity of its formal structure of authority and responsibility.

In summary, Fayol's Bridge is in a sense a compromise between the minimum and maximum number of links in an organizational communication network. The minimum number of links unduly rigidifies the organization, the maximum number, 36 in the case of Figure 7–8, would destroy the authority structure.

THE INFORMAL DIMENSION OF COMMUNICATION

While formal communication exists to meet the utilitarian needs of the organization, informal communication is the method by which people carry on social, "nonprogrammed" activities within the formal boundaries of the system. Informal communication channels, commonly called the *grapevine*, are not always occupied with information oriented toward organizational goals.[24] Rather, the grapevine is a vehicle for achieving satisfaction of employees' personal objectives. Since personal and organizational goals are either consistent or inconsistent with each other, information on the grapevine reinforces or undermines an organization's objectives.

Simon points out that the grapevine generally performs a positive service to the organization.[25] For one thing, it provides an outlet for expression, thus satisfying a "need to communicate." Additionally, for the executive who can "tune in," the grapevine is a pulse of employee sentiment. Further, it offers a channel for disseminating information that cannot conveniently be sent through formal channels.

Irresponsibility is probably the most mischievous feature of the grapevine. Since the origin and direction of the flow of information on the grapevine is hard to pinpoint, it is difficult to assign responsibility for false information or morale-lowering rumors.[26] The speed at which the grapevine is capable of transmitting information makes control of invalid messages troublesome.

Grim as some executives picture the grapevine, it need not be considered a dangerous nuisance. The grapevine is a natural phenomenon; it cannot be destroyed. Fact can usually end rumors, and when principal communicators on the grapevine are identified they can provide a direct and personal channel of information to employees. Also, the information they feed back to the manager enables him to gauge the attitudes of employees.

Another aspect of informal communication is the *bypassing* of formal communication channels in the normal course of job performance. Some have said that if the usual channels of formal communication were not bypassed in the routine of the day-to-day work situation very little would get done, and *it* would take a long time.

Formal communication involves a good deal of regimentation. Superceding formal channels often expedites the accomplishment of plans.

[24] For a detailed account of the functioning of the grapevine, see Keith Davis, "Management Communication and the Grapevine," *Harvard Business Review*, September–October, 1953, pp. 43–49.

[25] Herbert A. Simon, *Administrative Behavior* (New York: The Macmillan Co., 1945), pp. 160–61.

[26] Festinger points out that rumors arise and persist because of ignorance or uncertainty about events which directly affect people. He develops three principles of rumors: (1) rumors begin in situations people find highly relevant to their own affairs; but these situations lie outside their control; (2) rumors always contain a central theme; and (3) when people accept the rumor's general content or theme, they will distort future happenings to conform with the theme. Leon Festinger (and others), "A Study of a Rumor: Its Origin and Spread," *Human Relations*, August, 1948, pp. 483–85.

Although formal channels are bypassed, the methods of going around them are usually quite well specified by custom and protocol. For example, two executives may communicate outside the formal channels, but the occasion for the communication is well defined.

Some of the elements which define when executives can bypass are:

1. The nature of the information as it pertains to a job situation. Some information is routed through a bypass; some is sent along the formal channels.

2. How well the bypass is established in tradition. Some bypasses are so well established they become quasi-formal channels of communication.

3. The recognition of the need for a bypass by higher level executives. Tacit approval for bypassing formal channels should be a matter of "unwritten" policy.

SUMMARY

We have occasions in many of the chapters to bring up the subject of communication. It was noted in the beginning of this chapter that it is a strategic concept. We go on now to the subject of status and role which introduces some of the ideas upon which an understanding of interpersonal relationships is based. Communication is the socializing process which accomplishes the link between man and his position in the social matrix.

Appendix: Information Theory

WEAVER[27] categorizes the subject of communication as a series of problems on three levels:

Level A—How accurately can the symbols of communication be transmitted? (The technical problem.)

Level B—How precisely do the transmitted symbols convey the desired meaning? (The semantic problem.)

Level C—How effectively does the received meaning affect conduct in the desired way? (The effectiveness problem.)

This chapter and Chapter 15 deal with communication problems on Levels B and C. The technical level (Level A) is discussed here.

Now it might well be asked, why complicate the subject of communication further by bringing up a theory outside the realm of human behavior? In the first place, there is no neat division between where the

---

[27] Claude E. Shannon and Warren Weaver, *The Mathematical Theory of Communication* (Urbana: University of Illinois Press, 1949), p. 96.

technical problems leave off and the other problems on Levels B and C begin. So although information theory has its most precise application in the domain of the communication engineer, some of its insights seem to be relevant to human communication problems. In the second place, some efforts are being made to extend information theory into theories of communication in human organizations, into semantics, and into psychology.[28] Therefore, since information theory is making inroads into both the behavioral and managerial sciences some aspects of it must be examined here.[29]

The labels attached to the basic concepts of information theory are among its most misleading features. For example, "noise," "redundancy," "channel," and "capacity" are fairly common words. Yet their most usual connotations do not apply to information theory. The communication engineer has a precise meaning for these terms.

Take the name of the field itself: "information theory." Normally, the word *information* conveys the idea that a given message contains *meaning* for the sender and the receiver. Whereas, in the field of information theory "information" has nothing to do with meaning.

These semantic difficulties should warn that "things are not as they seem" in information theory. But in both practical and theoretical circumstances the elements of information theory are:

1. Defined with precision.
2. Frequently observable and quantifiable phenomena.
3. Subject to experimentation with outcomes that can be predicted empirically and mathematically.
4. Available for concrete application in telephone communication systems, electronic computing apparatus, and control devices for automated equipment.

However, when it comes to applying information theory concepts to human behavior in human systems, precision breaks down, the phenomenon defies quantification, predictability becomes far more tenuous, and the regions for fruitful concrete applications rapidly diminish. To a great extent, bridging the gaps between *Level A* and *Levels B* and *C* is accom-

---

[28] For a sampling of some of this work see Anatol Rapoport, "A Logical Task as a Research Tool in Organization Theory," in Mason Haire (ed.), *Modern Organization Theory* (New York: John Wiley and Sons, Inc., 1959), pp. 99–117. For the use of the concepts in semantics see Dale D. Drum, "Change, Meaning, and Information," *Journal of Communication*, Winter, 1957, pp. 161–70. In the area of psychology see George A. Miller, "What Is Information Measurement?" *American Psychologist*, January, 1953, pp. 3–11. For an excellent managerial analysis of the relationships among information theory, system theory, and cybernetics see Stafford Beer, *Cybernetics and Management* (New York: John Wiley and Sons, Inc., 1959), and finally Adrian McDonough, *Information Economics and Management Systems* (New York: McGraw-Hill Book Company, Inc., 1963).

[29] For a nontechnical treatment of information theory see J. R. Pierce, *Symbols, Signals and Noise* (New York: Harper and Bros., 1961).

plished by analogy. And analogies may hide basic dissimilarities while revealing superficial similarities in seemingly parallel phenomena.

In spite of the dangers of carrying over concepts from the natural to the social sciences, some of the major contributors to the field of information theory feel this process can render useful insights into the problems of human organization and behavior. Both Norbert Wiener[30] and Warren Weaver,[31] for example, attest to the fact that information theory, cybernetics, and other associated areas possess sufficient generality to warrant their extension into most every facet of the animate universe.

What Is Information?

Perhaps it would be better to ask, what is the technical meaning of information? Information is a quantitative measure of the amount of order (or disorder) in a system. Since order and certainty are positively related, information theory yields a yardstick of the degree of certainty or uncertainty in a given system. The more uncertain a system the greater is its potential for varieties of behavior. Information introduces organization into the system—killing variety—thus making the system more predictable.

Information theory tells how much one needs to know in order to proceed from a state of uncertainty to a state of certainty about the organization of a system. As Miller puts it:

A well-organized system is predictable—you know almost what it is going to do before it happens. You don't acquire much information from a well-organized system. A perfectly organized system provides no information at all. The more disorganized a system the more you can learn by watching it. Information, organization, and predictability are all related.[32]

This leads to the conclusion that the price paid for greater degrees of organization is the cost of the information necessary to introduce more order or certainty into the system.

The next step in understanding the nature of information is to note its statistical character. It has been pointed out that the amount of information in a system is related to what you *can* say about the system, rather than what you *do* say.[33] Therefore, the more disorganized a system is the more you can say about it. Again, if a system is perfectly organized it is perfectly predictable. It has no variety. One does not have a *freedom of choice* in selecting messages from it because a perfectly organized system produces just one message.

Now, freedom of choice is related to the statistical nature of informa-

---

[30] Norbert Wiener, *The Human Use of Human Beings* (New York: Doubleday Anchor Books, 1954).

[31] Weaver, *op. cit.,* pp. 114–17.

[32] Miller, *op. cit.,* p. 3.

[33] Weaver, *op. cit.,* p. 100.

tion. In a situation where one selects alternative A from possible messages A and B, the amount of information derived is arbitrarily called one bit.[34] Realize, however, that message A itself does not yield one bit of information. Rather, it is the combination of alternative messages A and B that is capable of producing this amount of information. The measurement of information is, therefore, based on the *total* communication situation, not

FIGURE 7–9

Relationship between Number of Alternative Messages and
Number of Bits Needed to Move from Uncertainty to Certainty

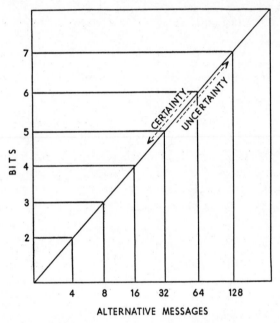

ALTERNATIVE MESSAGES

on specific messages or alternatives. Several examples are offered next to clarify this point.

Assume one wishes to move from uncertainty to certainty about a system which produces 128 equally probable messages. How much information, in bits, is required? The answer is shown in Figure 7–9. Seven bits are needed ($\log_2 128 = 7$). Also it is observed in this figure that one bit of information halves the number of alternative messages. Or, one bit of information is gained when the number of messages is halved.

The next example is more complex. Suppose a person is waiting on a

---

[34] A "bit" stands for *binary digit*, which is a unit of information measurement. While the ordinary method of counting is based on 10, the binary system uses the base of 2. The two digits, namely 0 and 1, can be used to correspond to yes-no, all-nothing alternatives. Technically, the measurement of information is the logarithm of the number of choices computed to the base 2. The amount of information in the systems with the following number of equally probable messages is: 32 messages—$\log_2 32$ or 5 bits; 16 messages—$\log_2 16$ or 4 bits; and so on.

floor for an elevator and there is no indicator showing the position of the cars. The bank in the building contains six elevators. The probability of any one arriving is one-sixth. The average amount of information gained by knowing which elevator will appear first is 2.58 bits.

Now imagine that the superintendent tells the waiting individual that two elevators are out of order. The number of alternatives is reduced to four and the system is able to produce just two bits of information. Thus, moving from six to four alternatives reduces the amount of information needed for certainty by .58 bits.

So far the elevator example assigned equal probabilities to the alternatives. Imagine that the situation changes so that the alternatives are not equally likely, exhibiting an array of probabilities as follows:

A	B	C	D	E	F
.1	.2	.2	.125	.125	.25

The average information in this example is computed by the formula:

$$H = -(p_1 \log p_1 + p_2 \log p_2 + \cdots p_n \log p_n).$$

Plugging the probability data in, $H = 2.497$ bits of information needed to produce certainty about the system. Note that this figure is slightly below the number of bits computed for six equally probable events. The reason is because alternative F weights the unequal system of probabilities a little more toward certainty. This phenomenon can be demonstrated more dramatically if these possibilities are used:

A	B	C	D	E	F
.001	.001	.001	.001	.001	.995

The average information needed for certainty in this case is only .057 bits. The F alternative makes the system almost perfectly predictable. Very little information, therefore, is necessary to order it further.

Thus, the more disorganized a system is the more information it is capable of producing. Rapoport summarizes these points by saying:

. . . .[The] 'amount of information' can be equated to the 'amount of disorder.' That is not to say the information is a carrier of disorder. On the contrary, information is the carrier of order. What is meant by the equivalent is that the more disordered a portion of the world is, the more information is required to describe it completely, that is, make it known. Thus, the process of obtaining knowledge is quantitatively equated to the process of ordering portions of the world.[35]

The Concept of Entropy

That information is a measure of disorder, and that disorder in a system is measured in terms of probabilities, lead to the second law of thermo-

---

[35] Anatol Rapoport, "What Is Information?" *ETC: A Review of General Semantics,* Summer, 1953, p. 260.

dynamics and entropy. One of the most interesting features of information theory is its parallel to the concept of entropy in physics. The formula used to calculate the amount of information in a system, $H = \Sigma P_i \log P_i$, is structurally similar to the equation used to solve entropy problems in thermodynamics.

Entropy expresses the tendency for the organization of any closed system to deteriorate, to become more shuffled, more chaotic. Entropy describes, in relative before-after terms, the inevitable movement of a physical system toward greater degrees of randomness (often called the point of highest probability). This can be demonstrated by a simple example.

Visualize a tank of water divided by a removable partition. On one side of the divider the water is colored with blue ink, the other side with red ink. If the partition separating the different colors of water is raised, the colors merge into an overall purple hue. The entropy of the system has increased. Before the removal of the partition, a form of order existed with the red-ink molecules separated from the blue. But after the change, the molecules distributed themselves evenly throughout the tank, resulting in a single color.

It is quite natural to expect this experiment should end this way. Finding that the colored waters remained in their respective positions, retaining their identity after the removal of the divider, would be exceedingly unusual. Generalizing, systems tend to approach their highest probability, which is greater randomness as opposed to greater organization.

The implications of this law are enormous. Life itself is an improbable form of existence, death being statistically a more "natural" condition. Entropy has only one direction and it is the inevitable movement toward chaos. Wiener views the universe as caught in the inexorable current of entropic disaster, while life, in the broadest sense, is locally swimming upstream.[36]

The vast generality of the "second law" encompasses information theory. Where a system is highly organized the entropy—and hence the information—is low. A small entropy figure represents a system capable of little variety. As randomness increases, so also does the amount of information needed to restructure the system.

In the process of communication, messages are transmitted with a certain entropy value at their origin. When the messages are received it is found that the entropy value is higher, indicating that somewhere in the transmission process random interference of noise has been introduced. In a sense, it can be said that information has been lost, and further that the organization of the original message has deteriorated.

Entropy, from the standpoint of the receiver of a message, is related to the amount of information gained. Information is equal to initial igno-

---

[36] Wiener, *op. cit.*, chaps. 1, 2.

rance less final ignorance.[37] So if the entropy value of the received message reflects a large increase relative to the entropy value at its source, the difference between initial ignorance and final ignorance is not great and little information has been gained. All this means is that one major problem of the communication engineer is to combat the "natural decay" of information, so that the difference between initial and final ignorance is maximized.

Wiener has a valuable observation as a summarization of this section on entropy:

> The commands through which we exercise our control over our environ-
> ment are a kind of information which we impart to it. Like any form of
> information, these commands are subject to disorganization in transit. They
> generally come through in less coherent fashion and certainly not more
> coherently than they were sent. In control and communication we are always
> fighting nature's tendency to degrade the organized and to destroy the mean-
> ingful. . . .[38]

Noise and Communication Channels

The "natural decay" or increasing entropy of information is due largely to noise. Noise is the introduction of undesirable uncertainties some-where in the transmission process—static on a radio is an example. Noise or equivocation refers to "lost" information. Coding messages in various forms can reduce the ill effects of noise, but noise can never be eliminated entirely. There will always be some uncertainty about the message at the receiving end.

Noise can be combated by repeating. However, repeating means add-ing to the bulk of signals the communication channel must handle. Com-pensating for noise by repeating reduces the efficiency of a channel because greater capacity must be added to carry a larger bulk of signals. Repeating, therefore, cuts down the rate of information flow. This poses a problem of compromise to the communication engineer. He must balance the system in terms of bulk and excessive sensitivity to noise.[39]

Redundancy

The fact that noise cannot be eliminated or entirely compensated for by a code brings up the function of redundancy or repeating. As Miller states, "Redundancy is an insurance against mistakes."[40]

---

[37] Y. S. Touloukian, *The Concept of Entropy in Communication, Living Organisms, and Thermodynamics* (Purdue Engineering Experiment Station, Research Bulletin 130), p. 16.

[38] Wiener, *op. cit.*, p. 17.

[39] Brockway McMillan, "Mathematical Aspects of Information Theory," in *Current Trends in Information Theory* (Pittsburgh: University of Pittsburgh Press, 1953), p. 6.

[40] Miller, *op. cit.*, p. 9.

All codes have a certain amount of redundancy, because they have structure. Since structure implies a departure from chance, it follows that all codes must repeat. Redundancy is the opposite of randomness. It is anything that makes a code system predictable. Language is a code itself, so the remarks that follow pertain to language.

The English language is roughly 50 percent redundant, which means that books and lectures are about twice as long as they would be if the language was 100 percent efficient. However, the brain is constructed such that it could not handle the information flow from a language much less redundant than 50 percent.

Drum mentions two sources of redundancy in English:[41]

1. The General Level of Redundancy. At this level redundancy is attributed to the statistical nature of language—"A"s occur more frequently than "Z"s, "I"s more often than "R"s, and so on. It is certain that each "q" will be followed by a "u." If hundreds of letters of the alphabet were put in a bowl according to their frequency of appearance in the language, and then randomly withdrawn, a gibberish looking something like English would appear. The reason is, of course, the statistical structure of the language.

2. The Syntactical Level.

a) Formal syntax or grammar limits freedom of choice, introduces structure, and hence makes language more predictable. For example, "the men are going;" not, "the men is going." The plural form of the main verb can be predicted from the grammatical structure of the language.

b) Many words can be used with grammatical correctness, but in terms of context only a few make sense. This is known as the contextual level of redundancy. For example, "the snow is falling;" not, "the snow is running."

Thus a certain degree of redundancy is imposed by the structural limitations of language, or of any code for that matter. This accounts for the fact that even though a radio program is intermittently interrupted by static the listener is able to construct the sense of the message being transmitted. The same principle holds for all codes in a variety of communication systems.

Information Theory and Administrative Communication

The behavioral sciences have a propensity for borrowing concepts from the natural sciences, regardless of whether the connections are real or imaginary. The temptation is great, indeed, to apply the concept of entropy to information as it flows through organizational communication channels.[42] It seems rather useful to think of naturally increasing random-

---

[41] Drum, *op. cit.*, pp. 167–69. He also mentions two other sources—the semantic and the pragmatic—which are not discussed here.

[42] In fact, management could be considered as source of "negentropy." That is, management is constantly combating the natural tendency of systems to become more disorganized. Management tries to reverse the direction of entropy.

ness of administrative communication during transmission as an explanation of communication failure. But how is the physical concept of increasing entropy in administrative communication to be distinguished from failures caused by filtering, distortion, semantic differences, misrepresentation, short circuiting, and dozens of other afflictions of the communication system? In the generalized notion of entropy such distinctions are not necessary because increasing entropy of information is a result of human and nonhuman interferences. In the practical, operational sense, however, it is still quite fruitful to think of communication breakdowns in a more specific way. For example, if misrepresentation of information is a problem it should be recognized as such and treated by the executive in a straightforward way.

Consider, next, the problem of channel capacity and communication overload. An executive may experience communication overload because of his limited abilities and not because the channels are jammed with messages. How, then, is the technical capacity of a system to be distinguished from individual differences? For that matter, how is the capacity of an administrative communication channel to be expressed quantitatively in the first place?

What can be said about noise? The technical meaning of noise has no real counterpart in administrative communication. Unwanted additions to administrative communication are probably analogous to noise. But how useful is this analogy? Cannot the same phenomenon be understood as conveniently with the more conventional theory of filtering?

These objections and more are summarized nicely by McMillan who says ". . . one must be careful to distinguish between proved relationships among precisely defined concepts on the one hand, and speculative relationships suggested by the names of these concepts on the other."[43] Confusing the technical meanings of information theory with administrative processes is a pitfall that should be recognized and avoided.

Yet, after all this has been said, language and communication are at the core of administrative practice. Information theory is intimately bound up with the concept of organization itself. Information plays a crucial role in the notion of cybernetics which is basic to human organizations. Thus, information theory supplies a powerful conceptual tool for management plus being useful in attacking specific problems of human communication—provided the range of these problems is carefully delineated.[44] Finally, there is a feeling that information theory is the theoretical linkage between various systems which exhibit feedback characteristics. If such is the case, and progress is made in determining the precise application of these ideas to administrative communication, then revolutionary insights into the management process itself will evolve.

---

[43] McMillan, *op. cit.,* p. 14.
[44] See, for example, Rapoport, *op. cit.,* pp. 91–114.

CHAPTER 8

Status and Role Concepts

WE HAVE CONSIDERED the individual and the function communication performs in linking him with positions in his social matrix. It is appropriate now to look at two concepts which are directly related to the matrix itself. These concepts are status and role. They are inseparable as they are sides of positions the individual occupies on a social matrix. Analytically, however, we treat these concepts under different headings in this chapter.

Hans Speier observed, "A man's honor neither springs from his personality nor clings to his deeds. It depends upon other men who have the power to bestow honor on him and a will to pay it."[1] How dramatically this is demonstrated in the Soviet Union where a person, though dead, may oscillate between adulation and oblivion depending on the policy of the incumbent administration!

Status is of foremost concern in human consciousness. Achieving honorific positions is a goal toward which people devote countless hours and considerable energy. But unlike attitudes, motives, and interpersonal communication, status is not generated by the individual. It is something, similar to honor, which is given by others. Status is socially defined and granted.

STATUS

Status has two connotations. First, it may be thought of as a ranked order of rights and duties of the kind found in the formal structure of an organization. This view of status is *objective*. Second, status has a private, *subjective* connotation. For example, one in his own mind can judge another individual. This personal status judgment is not necessarily related to the formal status position that the person being judged holds in the organization.

Thus status may apply to a position in a social structure distinct from the individual who occupies it; or it may apply to a private evaluation of an individual by another. These status connotations are not unrelated, of

---

[1] Hans Speier, "Honor and Social Structure," *Social Research*, February, 1935, p. 74.

course, because a private evaluation of another may very well determine his career in the formal, or objective, structure of an organization. This is particularly true when a superior forms opinions of his subordinates.

The Objective Connotation of Status

In the objective sense, status is considered as a position involving rights and duties arranged in a structure of human interrelationships. A particular status is something apart from the individual who occupies it.[2]

Status systems refer to the total structure of an organization, including a hierarchial pattern of rights and duties. The rights and duties, and their relative position in status hierarchies, are determined by the value systems of institutions.[3] For example, an organization has various positions carrying rewards, authorities, and obligations. Also, these positions are ordered in relation to each other according to the importance assigned to them by the organization.

Thus, a president and vice president have specific functions to perform, but the value placed on the president's job is greater than that given the vice president's position. This example could be carried to all the positions in a business organization. The point to keep in mind is that both the *specific* obligations and rewards for status positions, as well as the relative values assigned to them, are determined by administrative decision. *Management imposes the status hierarchy.*

The Subjective Connotation of Status

The subjective aspect of status concerns how people make status judgments of others. Man constantly evaluates those with whom he comes in contact. This behavior is a process of making *status judgments*. From these private judgments an individual receives a status in a plant, office, or executive group.[4] Status from this point of view is an individual's position in a social system resulting from the judgment of others regarding him.[5]

---

[2] Linton points out that role is the dynamic counterpart of a status position. An individual is given a status through a social process; but when he begins to discharge the obligations of this position he is said to be playing a role. Status and role, thus, are inseparable. Ralph Linton, *The Study of Man* (New York: D. Appleton-Century Co., 1936), pp. 113–14.

[3] The hierarchial aspect of status is discussed at length by Emile Benoit-Smullyan, "Status, Status Types, and Status Interrelations," *American Sociological Review*, April, 1944, pp. 151–61.

[4] The status one receives may be translated into a position in the formal organization, or a position in an informal organization, or it may simply remain one person's opinion of another.

[5] Status is approached this way by Herbert Goldhammer and Edward A. Shils, "Types of Power and Status," *American Journal of Sociology*, September, 1939, p. 179; and George C. Homans, *The Human Group* (New York: Harcourt, Brace and Co., 1950), p. 179. This method of viewing status presumes application to both formal and informal evaluations. That is, people are placed by the judgment of others into status positions involving the rights and duties connected with their jobs. Also, people are ranked in terms of private evaluations of others regardless of their duties.

The Criteria Underlying Status Judgments. People's status judgments are based on criteria. A judgment is a form of measurement through which status decisions are made by comparing an individual against certain standards. According to Talcott Parsons, five standards are used to measure status.[6] Briefly described they are:

1. *Birth.* A person may hold a certain status simply by being born into a particular family, social class, race, or sex. A president of a company may hold his position because a tradition passes the presidency through the family.

2. *Personal qualities.* One person may be differentiated from another, status-wise, because of age, strength, intelligence, or just being a "good guy."

3. *Achievements.* A person may be accorded status because of his accomplishments. A president of a corporation may hold a high status among his fellow businessmen because his leadership results in success for his company.

4. *Possessions.* "Possessions" refer to an individual's belongings. The kinds and amounts of such belongings may be used as a basis for judging status.

5. *Authority.* Authority is considered as the right to command action from others. The extent of authority is an important measure of status in business.

Not all individuals or groups at all places and at all times are going to weigh each of these standards the same. Different weights are assigned to these standards by the groups and individuals with whom one comes in contact. This accounts for the fact that a person can have a "high" status position in one group and a "low" status position in another.

The purpose of making status evaluations is to associate a person with a position on a "status scale" which ranges between two extremes—high and low. A person's position on the scale results from the "score" he makes when evaluated. The method of evaluation may be described as a comparison process. Each person brings to a social situation a "status profile," which is some weighted combination of the status-measuring characteristics mentioned above.

Now, the people with whom an individual associates have norms or standards also comprised of the same characteristics. The degree to which the "profile" of the individual matches the norms of the evaluating group determines the status of the person being measured. This process can be clarified by a diagram, shown as Figure 8–1.

The profile the individual brings to the evaluating situation is, in this case, heavily weighted on "personal qualities." This individual is a likeable sort, long on personality and roughly average on the other four qualities. The superior evaluating this person is likely to rank him about average because the achievement factor emphasized by him is not predominant in the individual's profile. However, his fellow employees will probably give this individual a high status because of the close match of his profile with their measuring norms.

---

[6] Talcott Parsons, *Essays in Sociological Theory Pure and Applied* (Glencoe: The Free Press, 1949), pp. 171–72. Parsons also mentions a sixth category of power which is status achieved by illegitimate means.

The diagram suggests another important fact about status. Many different statuses are possible for an individual. Indeed, a person can have as many different statuses as he has contacts with people.

Once a person has a status assigned to him he is not doomed forever to that particular status. He may change his profile in such a way so as to make it conform more closely with the norms of those doing the evaluating. For example, the mythical character in Figure 8–1 could improve his "achievements" and, with all the other factors remaining equal, raise his status in the eyes of his superior.

FIGURE 8–1

The Process of Status Evaluation

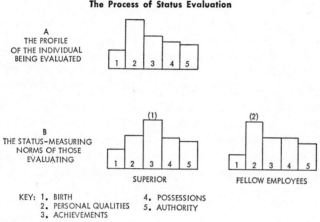

KEY: 1. BIRTH   4. POSSESSIONS
          2. PERSONAL QUALITIES   5. AUTHORITY
          3. ACHIEVEMENTS

As might be guessed, the process of making status evaluations is rather arbitrary. When evaluating others, people do not apply the status-measuring criteria in a uniform way. In other words, people's judgments of the profile of others vary even though the situation in which the evaluation takes place does not vary. Two individuals, for example, performing the same function, might be evaluated by their superior as having high status for different reasons. The boss may defer to one because he happens to be the son of the president of a company; the boss might respect the other because of his achievements on the job.

Status determination is not a unilateral process. An individual entering a status-evaluating situation can cause those measuring to readjust the weights placed on their evaluating norms, just as pressure from a group or individual can cause the individual being evaluated to modify his profile. This last point is associated with the reciprocal relationship which exists between the individual and the evaluating group. It is analyzed in greater detail under the topic of role.

Status Systems

Status systems incorporate all status positions in an organization into an overall pattern of relationships. Every status position can be plotted as a point on a matrix having both vertical and horizontal relationships to points representing other status positions.[7] The horizontal status system is called *functional;* the vertical status system is called *scalar.*

Functional Status Systems.   Functional status is based upon the *job or task.* Functional status systems disclose which positions are on the same level in an organization. This type of system is in no way predicated on the right to command. A functional position has no authority over other positions on the same level. Again, functional status is derived from the job and its horizontal relation to other jobs of equivalent value. Figure 8–2 depicts a horizontal status system.

FIGURE 8–2

An Example of a Functional Status System

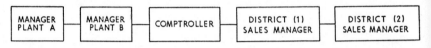

Scalar Status.   The essential feature of scalar status is that it carries the *right to command* others. Scalar status bestows command privileges on individuals occupying positions in a vertical system of relationships. The president of a company has a higher scalar status than the vice presidents. Hence the president has authority to command action from the vice presidents, and so on through all the superior-subordinate positions down the line. This type of system is shown in Figure 8–3.

FIGURE 8–3

An Example of a Scalar Status System

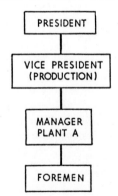

The Status "Pyramid."   A typical formal organization is a combination of scalar and functional systems assuming a form roughly like a pyramid. The sample organization chart in Figure 8–4 demonstrates the pyramid character of the combined status systems.

---

[7] This treatment of status systems follows Chester I. Barnard, *Organization and Management* (Cambridge: Harvard University Press, 1949), pp. 207–44.

This figure shows the functional levels of the organization and the scalar chain of command. Note that each executive position on the vertical hierarchy has both functional and scalar status. But observe the positions at the bottom of the chart shown in dotted lines. Obviously the positions occupied by operative employees, clerks, and salesmen have functional status. As for their scalar status, of course these positions do not

FIGURE 8–4

Sample Organization Chart Combining Functional and Scalar Status Systems

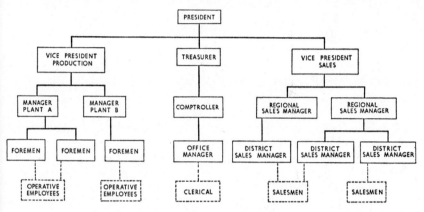

carry the right to command. However, the concept of scalar status must not be narrowly restricted to include only the command privilege. Scalar status also should be interpreted to imply the obligation to report to a superior. This being the case, it is evident that the positions at the bottom level of the status pyramid simultaneously carry functional and scalar status.

Other Status Relationships.   In addition to the basic status systems just discussed, other forms of ranked positions exist in a business organization. One example is the ranking of jobs according to pay grade determined by job-evaluation methods. An employee could move from job classification "A" to classification "B" with an increase in pay and most likely a change in function. This status arrangement, however, in no way implies that a change in classification for pay purposes includes scalar authority over employees in a lower classification.

The case of the "working supervisor" presents an interesting status problem. This position goes by many names such as lead man, straw boss, set-up man, and others. The working supervisor is between the foreman and the operative employees. He is actually classified as operative employee, but his position is slightly senior to them. The position has scalar authority including obligations for training new employees; setting-up for production runs; and acting—by virtue of skill—as a "consultant" for production problems which might occur on the line.

This position does not include other important scalar prerogatives such as the right to discipline, fire, give pay increases, and so on. The working foreman, thus, is in sort of a status never-never land.[8]

The formal structure of an organization presents myriad cases of hybrid status relationships, such as line-staff, the "assistant to," liaison work, and master-apprentice systems.

Status Systems and the Formal Dimensions of Communication. The flow of information in formal organizations follows routes roughly prescribed by scalar and functional status relationships. Along the scalar chain, or vertical communication dimension, move action evoking messages downward and control information upward. Sending and receiving information on the horizontal dimension corresponds to communication among various positions on a functional status level. The chief purpose of horizontal communication is coordination of plans and programs. This is achieved by interdepartmental exchange of data.

Status Symbols

People are status conscious, although it is probably more accurate to say that people are conscious of the status symbols they possess or lack. Status symbols are externalizations of the basic social processes of ranking regardless of whether the processes are subjective, objective, or a combination of the two.

Once a status position is acquired, "badges of office" are granted. These badges are status symbols and act as tangible evidence of the rank and function of people in an organization.

The symbols of formal organizations are easiest to describe. In business, titles serve as status indicators. The title "vice president of sales" has a twofold message. First, "vice president" says the individual occupies a high rank in the *chain of command*. Second, "sales" tells interested parties the function or job the individual performs in the company.

But titles relate only part of the story of an individual's status. At best they are rough indicators, particularly when the middle management "jungle" is viewed. Here other symbols tend to become more important. External trappings of office such as the size of the desk; name in the company telephone directory; a secretary; the floor on which the office is located; gold, silver, or brass spitoons—all are evidence of a rank in the formal structure. While subtle, these symbols are quite tangible. They show the shadings of status gradients in an organization.

A neat description of status symbols in a bank is given by John P. Marquand in his novel *Point of No Return.*

Though you seldom talked of salaries at Stuyvesant, your social status was obvious from the *position* of your desk. Charles occupied one of the *two flat mahogany desks* that stood in a sort of *no man's land* between the *roll-top*

---

[8] For a larger treatment of this subject see George Strauss, "The Changing Role of the Working Supervisor," *Journal of Business,* July, 1957, pp. 202–11.

desks of the officers and the *smaller flat-tops* of lesser executives and secretaries crowding the floor of the bank *outside* the cages. A *green rug* extended from the officers' desks, *forming a neat and restricted zone* that *just included* Charles's desk. . . ."[9]

Without knowing any more about Charles and the Stuyvesant bank than this passage reveals, it is still easy to pinpoint his position in the status structure of the company.

Although fun can be made of the elaborate forms and rituals connected with the use of status symbols, their importance as a social phenomenon must not be disregarded.[10] Few grasp the abstract meaning and the logic behind the concepts of status in organizations. But status symbols, as the concrete product of judgmental and ranking processes, have real significance for organizational participants. Rewards are often made in other than money terms. People weigh external evidence of success heavily. Accomplishments do not taste so sweet unless others know about them. Status symbols represent achievement; if symbols are not awarded, many would suffer from severe cases of "status anxiety."

In summary, the importance of status symbols may be expressed as the organizational purposes which they serve.

1. *Motivation.*   Status symbols act as honors or rewards for achievements. As such, they provide incentives to motivate people toward greater accomplishments.

2. *Identification.*   Status symbols make it easier to determine who holds authority and performs differentiated functions. The greater the degree to which specialization of functions is carried the more important status symbols become in order to identify who does what in an organization.

3. *Dignification.*   Status symbols add dignity to a position and support authority in it.

4. *Stabilization.*   Status symbols solidify rank, authority, and areas of functional specialization, and this facilitates regularization of work patterns.

While the context of the discussion implies formal organizations, it should not be inferred that status symbols are their exclusive property. Indeed, status symbols are used by small groups in less obvious ways. But they are present nonetheless and perform the same four services just mentioned.

Status Passage

Status passage is a basic social process by which the change of status of an individual is regularized.[11] The route of status change for a child as he

---

[9] John P. Marquand, *Point of No Return* (Boston: Little, Brown & Co., 1949), p. 29. Reprinted with permission. Italics are mine; they indicate the symbols mentioned in this short paragraph.

[10] For a further discussion of status symbols see Erving Goffman, "Symbols of Class Status," *British Journal of Sociology,* December, 1951, pp. 294–304.

[11] This discussion is drawn from Anselm L. Strauss, "Transformations of Identity," in Warren G. Bennis, Kenneth D. Benne, and Robert Chin (eds.), *The Planning of Change* (New York: Holt, Rinehart and Winston, 1961), pp. 548–58.

matures from schoolboy, to college student, to a career in business, to marriage, to fatherhood, and eventually to death is lined with cultural road marks showing the way he should travel to ease his passage as he makes status transitions. Now, of course, not all pitfalls are clearly indicated. Some may be obscure or ambiguous. Others may not exist at all. Often, to help with these rough segments, the older person who has traveled the route comes to the aid of the younger. It is common in many walks of life for the young man to have a patron, a high-status friend, coach him as his career evolves. Kildare does have his Gillespie.

Because there are specified functions to be performed in formal structures, and because the people who are presently filling these functions will eventually either be promoted, or quit, or retire, or die, most organizations institutionalize the process of status mobility. This means that organizations prepare the way for individuals who must undergo status changes. The person's passage is facilitated by indicators showing where he is going and where he should be at certain points of time corresponding to his age. Now the route of status passage is not necessarily the same as the hierarchy of status positions shown on the organizational chart. The literature on career progress makes this clear.

Martin and Strauss present an interesting study of organizational status passage patterns.[12] In their view, as an organization matures it evolves career lines which are open to individuals seeking advancement. They describe these lines as branches on a tree, with some terminating at lower management levels, fewer moving through middle management, and still fewer going all the way to top management.

The status passage of an individual in an organization requires a series of vertical and horizontal steps. Horizontal movement from one function to another is designed to give the manager a broader background in the organization. Vertical mobility, of course, constitutes the payoff by status changes to positions of greater authority and responsibility. But each move is, in a sense, ritualized since it is considered a training and testing point where the manager is evaluated. If he performs well he is in line for another move. If he does not live up to expectations, his mobility probably is terminated.

The interesting feature of established career progressions is the timetable by which an individual can gauge his progress. Martin and Strauss observe, "Acceptable age ranges are identifiable for the various strata. . . . A person who does not progress in accordance with these age timetables may know . . . that his potential for higher levels of management has been judged unfavorably."[13]

---

[12] Norman H. Martin and Anselm L. Strauss, "Patterns of Mobility within Industrial Organizations," *Journal of Business*, April, 1956, pp. 101–10. A study of mobility patterns which stresses the element of independence from ritualistic passage routes is by William R. Dill, Thomas L. Hilton, and Walter R. Reitman, *The New Managers* (Englewood Cliffs, N.J.: Prentice-Hall, Inc., 1962).

[13] *Ibid.*, p. 109.

Even within this model of a well-structured promotional system the individual retains some discretion and control over his career. In any organization a person has available to him a number of alternative channels or career lines from which he may select. It is largely up to the individual to appraise these alternatives and select the channel which he feels will be the most beneficial to him in the realization of his ambitions. In the stable organization, however, *he selects from established career lines; he does not make his own.*

Thus far, individual progress is predicated on possession of technical competence, favorable judgment of superiors, and appropriate selection of a career alternative. Another factor emphasized by Martin and Strauss is the role of sponsorship. Sponsorship is the support lent by one person to another in order to facilitate a career. The sponsor, usually an executive higher-up in the chain of command, pulls his protégés up the ladder.

Here again, the judgment of the subordinate executive (the protégé) enters into his promotional pattern. A career often is greatly enhanced by the happy wedding of a protégé and a powerful sponsor. But there are also dangers in these arrangements. A sponsor may lose ground in organizational transitions and power shifts, in which case the protégé is placed in an extremely tenuous position. It is not only high-level executives who are affected by organizational personnel changes; also affected are constellations of people, high and low, who have formed alliances.

One consequence of organizational reshuffling is, of course, being fired. However, it often happens that an executive who at one time appeared to be a "hot prospect" in the organization has had his lustre tarnished. Instead of being fired, his failure to perform up to expectation or his loss of power might result in being "cooled out." "Cooling out" is a face-saving device by which the executive is "kicked upstairs" or "banished" to an innocuous position where he can do no damage. The cooling-out process may be only temporary, in the event an executive has moved too fast too soon, or it may represent a terminal point in an executive's upward mobility.

Status Congruency and Perceived Status Differentials

The reader should not leave the last section with the idea that status passage somehow *effortlessly* allows an individual to make positional changes in his social matrix. Anyone who has experienced life realizes this is not true. Change, even under the most desirable circumstances, causes social and psychological dislocations which must be restored in new status positions.

As one changes status, one often changes reference groups. This is routine in formal organizations. The extent to which one making passage into a new group perceives the status of the group as compatible with his own, and the group concurs in this perception, we have status congruency. The individual has a high degree of social certitude because his position is secure, established, and unambiguous in terms of the subjective status judgment of his associates. This condition is important in formal organizations. As Homans says,

Congruence facilitates social ease in the interaction among men, and so when they are working together as a team, a congruent relationship between them, by removing one possible source of friction, should encourage their joint efficiency. Up at least to middle levels of congruence . . .[14]

While small group behavior is treated at length before, we must not pass the opportunity to note the function played by status congruency in formation of these groups. People tend naturally to group where they perceive status congruency. The basis of the perception may be occupational—secretaries will associate with secretaries, not with file clerks. Or it could be 101 other socially differentiating factors which condition choice of affiliation in small groups such as age, sex, marital state, affluence, and education.

The perception of status differentials will tend to limit mobility between primary groups either because the individual recognizes his status is not congruent with others or the group will not accept him as a member. This phenomenon is at once a built in stabilizer of interpersonal relationships and a source of conflict between the individual and the organization. We turn now to the subject of role.

ROLE

At the beginning of this chapter, the inseparable nature of status and role was noted. Every status has a role, and every role has a status. While this point is straightforward enough, the concept of role is complex.

Role, on the face of it, is a collection of activities peculiar to a position or function in society at large, a community, a formal organization, a social club. Thus an individual occupies many roles, respectively, citizen, husband and father, chief systems analyst, treasurer of local alumni society. Each of these roles, and others which a person plays, has a counterpart status. Each role, as well, has, as defined by the society, community, and organization, certain *rights, duties, and obligations* which comprise both the costs and rewards of participation.

Dimensions of the Concept of Role

Role has three dimensions.[15] The one stressed depends often on the behavioral science persuasion of the person discussing the subject. If he is

---

[14] George C. Homans, *Social Behavior: Its Elementary Forms* (New York: Harcourt, Brace & World, Inc., 1961), p. 264. Beyond the middle point of congruency task performance will fall off. See Stuart Adams, "Status Congruency as a Variable in Small Group Performance," *Social Forces*, 32 (1953), pp. 16–22.

[15] The three "usages" of role are adapted from Daniel J. Levinson, "Role, Personality, and Social Structure in the Organizational Setting," *Journal of Abnormal and Social Psychology*, March, 1959, p. 172.

a sociologist, or perhaps an anthropologist, he will approach role as something outside the individual. Role would be considered as a set of social pressures which direct and support an individual in the action he takes in an organization. Coutu defines role in this sense. Role is a ". . . socially prescribed way of behaving in particular situations for any person occupying a given social position or status."[16]

If the behavioral scientist has a psychological orientation, he probably will look upon role as an individual's conception of the part he plays in an organization. Using this point of view in an experimental situation, Gerard observes that in any social situation an individual will tend to evaluate the degree to which his behavior has fulfilled the expectations of the role he has played.[17]

The third view of role, which is popular currently, is that of the social psychologist. The ". . . concept of role concerns the thoughts and actions of individuals, and, at the same time, it points up the influence upon the individual of socially patterned demands and standardizing forces."[18]

The reciprocal and normative nature of role is stressed in the social psychologist's point of view.[19] For example, a small work group has expectations of the type of behavior it anticipates from members of the group. These expectations are values or norms commonly held by members of the group.[20]

An individual who seeks association with a group must sense what its values are and modify his behavior accordingly. But, as Bakke observes, the individual is also capable of modifying the expectations of the group.[21] What results is a "fusion process" which changes both the group and the individual so that their separate values may be reconciled.

From these definitional dimensions, we can develop a topology for role concepts as shown in Figure 8–5. We assume that each dimension defines role similarly, but the effect of role on the individual is seen differently.

Deterministic. Role is seen here as a dominant influence on behavior. The assumption is that if the content of the role is known, the behavior of individuals playing the role is predictable. *Behavior is role determined.* Thus, if we know the role content of, let us say, "father" in a primitive

---

[16] Walter Coutu, "Role-Playing versus Role-Taking: An Appeal for Clarification," *American Sociological Review*, April, 1951, p. 180.

[17] Harold B. Gerard, "Some Effects of Status, Role Clarity, and Group Goal Clarity upon the Individual's Relations to Group Process," *Journal of Personality*, (25) 1956–1957, p. 475.

[18] Levinson, *op. cit.*, p. 170.

[19] See Aidan Southall, "An Operational Theory of Role," *Human Relations*, 12 (1959), pp. 17–34.

[20] Frederick L. Bates, "Position, Role, and Status: A Reformulation of Concepts," *Social Forces*, 34 (1955–56), p. 319.

[21] E. Wight Bakke, "Concept of the Social Organization," in Mason Haire (ed.), *Modern Organization Theory* (New York: John Wiley and Sons, Inc., 1959), pp. 60–61.

society, then we would be able to predict the behavior of all fathers play-ing this role in that society. Similarly the content of jobs which is highly specified in modern business or government organizations permits us to predict what any individual performing these jobs will be doing when he is occupied with the formal aspects of his functions.

Particularistic. This view of role focuses not so much on the formal content of the role as specified culturally and organizationally, but upon

FIGURE 8–5

Dimensions of the Role Concept

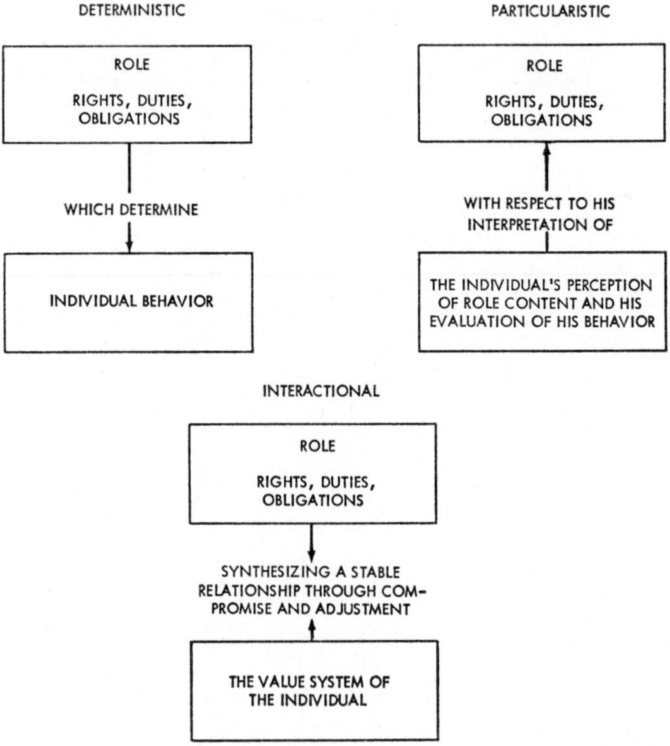

DETERMINISTIC

ROLE
RIGHTS, DUTIES, OBLIGATIONS

WHICH DETERMINE

INDIVIDUAL BEHAVIOR

PARTICULARISTIC

ROLE
RIGHTS, DUTIES, OBLIGATIONS

WITH RESPECT TO HIS
INTERPRETATION OF

THE INDIVIDUAL'S PERCEPTION OF ROLE CONTENT AND HIS EVALUATION OF HIS BEHAVIOR

INTERACTIONAL

ROLE
RIGHTS, DUTIES, OBLIGATIONS

SYNTHESIZING A STABLE
RELATIONSHIP THROUGH COM-
PROMISE AND ADJUSTMENT

THE VALUE SYSTEM OF THE INDIVIDUAL

how the individual *perceives* the role or roles he is required to play and how the individual *evaluates* his performance in light of this perception.

Interactional. This approach concerns outcomes resulting from the merger of individual-group behavioral vectors. The mutual modification of value norms of both the individual and the group is the chief matter of attention. Bakke's concept of the fusion process nicely summarizes this dimension.

This topology is, of course, an oversimplification. Two points must be amplified before a misunderstanding is created. First, not all behavioral scientists work in such a vacuum that they are prevented from adopting useful approaches in other areas. So it should not be thought that sociologists or anthropologists are exclusive devotees of the deterministic approach, or that psychologists are wedded to the particularistic dimension if, say, the interactional provides a better explanation for a given event. Second, the three dimensions as presented in Figure 8–5 tend to admit only a one-sided interpretation of the behavioral consequences of the relationships depicted. For example, a "stable relationship" is not always the outcome of the interactional dimension. Compromise and adjustment may never occur in some individual-group transactions. Conflict is the behavioral product of this case.

Or, role may be ambiguous. It may present an individual with contradictory obligations. Hence, behavior cannot be predicted in the sense implied in our initial discussion. Rather, anxiety, or in extreme cases, action paralysis may occur in the individual. We mention these points merely to warn the reader that much human woe comes from role pathologies.

Some Administrative Applications of Role Theory

For administrative purposes human behavior cannot be treated only by a sociological fashion which views an individual's actions as determined by social pressures. Further, the psychological approach of individual perception of role expectations is not a complete explanation of human behavior. Probably the most satisfactory point of view is the one offered by the social psychologists, which stresses the reciprocal relationship that exists between the individual and the role expectations.

Expectation Forces. Following this approach, the individual is influenced in his actions by two major sources of role expectations—the formal demands made by the organization, and the informal ones made by the groups contacted by the individual in the work situation. Thus both formal and informal expectation forces make behavioral demands on the individual.

As a result of these demands, the individual attempts to structure the social situation and to define his place in it. This process is called *role definition*. Role definition, as Levinson notes, is an aspect of personality and is expressed in terms of basic values, opinion of one's self, objectives in life, and attachment to an occupation. The purpose of role definition is to guide the individual in his pursuit of goals and to help him obtain work satisfaction.[22]

This approach, however, is somewhat oversimplified. For as Sarbin observes, "role expectations are bidimensional. . . ." For every expectation a formal or informal group might have a reciprocal expectation or demand is made by the individual on these groups.[23] Additionally, as

---

[22] Levinson, *op. cit.*, p. 178.

[23] Theodore R. Sarbin, "Role Theory," in Gardner Lindzey (ed.), *Handbook of Social Psychology* (Cambridge: Addison-Wesley Publishing Co., 1954), Vol. I, p. 255.

could be anticipated, the groups themselves can be expected to interact, each affecting the other's expectations. Figure 8–6 shows the interacting of relationships these preliminary remarks suggest.

The outcome of the pattern indicated in Figure 8–6 is the fusion process, which, in turn, is a fragment of Bakke's total theory of social organization. He says that the reconciliation of expectancies brought by the fusion process acts ". . . to maintain the integrity of the organization in the face of divergent interests of individuals, groups, other organizations, and the organization itself. . . ."[24]

FIGURE 8–6
Role Expectations and Their Interactions

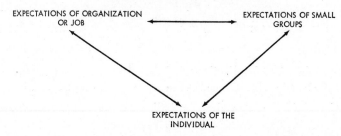

Management should note several things regarding expectation forces:

1. The job is not the only force which makes demands on individuals. The informal organization acts as an expectation force as well. At times informal demands may seem more imperative to the individual than formal job requirements.

2. Each individual will attempt to define the roles expected of him. His "accuracy" in the definitional process can determine his satisfaction and performance on the job. Management can facilitate this process by defining task requirements.

3. Management can anticipate that the three sources of expectations— formal, informal, and individual—will interact and modify each other.

The Significance of Empathy.   Empathy refers to an individual's *role-taking* ability.[25] It is a process whereby an individual "puts himself in another's shoes." There are three general ways, listed by Turner, which an individual can empathize:[26]

1. An individual can *unwittingly* adopt the other's standpoint as his own. The role-taking individual identifies himself with the other.

2. The other person can remain as a purely *objective* consideration to the

---

[24] Bakke, *op. cit.,* p. 60.

[25] Role taking and role playing are distinct processes. Role playing refers to overt behavior in which an individual performs what he conceives to be the content of a role.

[26] Ralph H. Turner, "Role-Taking, Role Standpoint, and Reference Group Behavior," *American Journal of Sociology,* January, 1956, pp. 318–21, 326.

role-taking individual. He understands and interprets the other's role, but he does not allow the role to become his own. In this case the role-taking individual *does not* identify.

3. The role-taking person allows the attitudes of the other to become his own and *consciously* adjusts his behavior as he sees how the other is reacting to it. This is a reflexive or adaptive act in which one modifies his own behavior as he observes the counteraction of the other.

Role Conflict. Role conflict results when an individual is faced with two roles which are incompatible.[27] He cannot meet the expectations of these roles simultaneously, and thus a conflict ensues between them. The seriousness of the conflict depends on two factors:

1. The nature of the situation, including the degree to which the roles are incompatible, and the rigidity with which the expectations are enforced.

2. The personality of the individual, including his adjustment to the situation and his ability to ignore some of the demands of one role or the other.[28]

An individual in an organization is required to play a number of roles. Traditionally, good management practice tries to ensure that role conflict does not occur in formal job requirements, because of the consequent inefficiencies and employee dissatisfactions.

As far as possible, well-managed organizations spell out the functions required of employees and arrange that these functions are not incompatible. Also, the principle of unity of command is framed to counteract the problems which would arise from a number of superiors having different role expectations from the same subordinates.

However, modern organizations are so complex that it is practically impossible to eliminate all sources of role conflict. One example is the production foreman who is faced with certain productivity demands by his immediate line superior. At the same time, a staff organization—quality control, for instance—is making demands on him in terms of quality expectations. Frequently these two demands are inconsistent and the foreman is faced with a quality-or-quantity dilemma. Whichever route he chooses, someone is likely to label him as incompetent.

In addition to role conflict between functions within the formal organization, there is also the problem of role conflict between the expectations of the formal versus the expectations of the informal organizations. Output restriction is a convenient example of this situation. Output restriction is a deliberate effort, informally enforced by the group, either to produce below standards set by management or not to produce as much as possible under the standard for fear it may be unfavorably revised.

An individual coming into such a situation is faced with two sets of

---

[27] See John T. Gullahorn, "Measuring Role Conflict," *American Journal of Sociology*, January, 1956, pp. 299–303.

[28] J. W. Getzels and E. G. Guba, "Role, Role Conflict, and Effectiveness: An Empirical Study," *American Sociological Review*, April, 1954, pp. 164–66.

demands. Management wants as much output as possible. The informal organization pressures the individual to restrict his output to some limit that they, not management, consider appropriate. Hence role conflict results!

What does the individual do? On the one hand he may go to either extreme. He can join forces with the output restricters, or he can commit himself to be a rate-buster. On the other hand, the individual may vacillate or try to find a niche somewhere between these two extremes. In speaking of restricters and rate-busters Whyte notes that by far the majority of employees in a particular situation studied by him were "men in the middle." They were pulled in one direction by the goal of higher productivity and in the other by the goal of the restricting work group.[29]

Role conflict, no matter what its origin, is a source of individual frustration and a threat to the integrity of the organization. Management has a greater opportunity to iron out problems of role conflict when they are caused from unclear job definitions or chain-of-command relationships: direct action to adjust the organizational structure is possible. But adjustments are less clear and direct when role conflict is caused by line-staff jurisdictional questions or from formal versus informal demands on the individual.

Role Effectiveness.   Role effectiveness is something of a counterpart of role conflict. Role effectiveness is a concept which deals with the clarity of the role and the individual's ability to perceive it and play it accurately.[30] Regarding an individual's role perception, Steiner states two propositions:[31]

1. . . . the more knowledge an individual has concerning the intention, preferences, and beliefs of other persons, the more effectively he can participate in group activity with these persons.

2. . . . groups composed of individuals with accurate social perceptions will be more efficient than groups composed of members with less accurate social perceptions.

These propositions, according to Steiner, are true only if group members are motivated to cooperate, the social perception of individuals is relevant to the activities of the group, members are free to alter their behavior as a result of their perceptions of others, and behavioral changes result in a more closely knit social organization.[32]

Steiner feels that achieving the goals implied by these propositions is

---

[29] William F. Whyte, *Money and Motivation* (New York: Harper and Bros., 1955), pp. 46-49.

[30] For an interesting discussion showing the reaction of individuals in different status levels under varying conditions of role clarity, see Gerard, *op. cit.*, pp. 475-88.

[31] J. D. Steiner, "Interpersonal Behavior as Influenced by Accuracy of Social Perception," *Psychological Review*, 62 (1955) p. 268.

[32] *Ibid.*, p. 273.

remote. But they do constitute legitimate criteria for administrative actions to achieve a cooperative system. Certainly programs aimed at improving communication, leadership efficiency, and the climate of organizational decision making are involved, in part at least, with improving the role effectiveness of participants.

CHAPTER 9

Concepts of Social Influence:
Authority, Power, and Leadership

SOCIAL INFLUENCE is a behavioral transaction in which a person or group is induced by another person or group to act in conformance to the influencing agent's objectives, values, norms, or standards. In this chapter we are concerned with some forms of influence (or control) over behavior. The terms, influence and control, are close conceptually.

Sources of influence can be found in status, possession of information, access to communication channels, and personality. Influence may also be derived from small groups, formal bureaucratic functions, and decision activities in organizations. We treat the first group of influence sources in this chapter and the second group systematically in subsequent chapters.

Social influence concepts can be viewed in four frameworks.

1. Person to person.
2. Person to group.
3. Group to person.
4. Group to group.

There is a close connection between the concepts treated in this chapter and the next on decision making. Indeed, the placement of certain subjects, like the "zone of acceptance" is somewhat arbitrary, but for convenience and balance we elect to treat it in Chapter 10. The reader is advised to consider this chapter and the next as a conceptual unity because the goal of influence is to shape and change the decisions which people make.

Authority, power, and leadership form an influence syndrome in organizations. It is impossible to separate them in a concrete situation. They are mutually interacting and reinforcing. For analytical reasons, we must make an effort to see each in terms of its components, and, then, toward the end of the chapter form a few generalizations about these processes. We begin with a discussion of authority, turning to power and influence, and finally to leadership itself.

AUTHORITY

Max Weber made the classic analysis of authority. He saw it as the willing, unconditioned compliance of people resting upon their belief that it is legitimate for the superior to impose his will on them and it is illegitimate for them to refuse obedience.

The key word in this statement is legitimate. The extent to which people *believe* in the legitimacy of authority determines the amount of positive incentives or coercive measures a superior must employ to secure compliance to his aims. Blau points out that the very use of incentives or sanctions is evidence that authority is not accepted either altogether or in part.[1] An interesting problem is what conditions are necessary to produce the perception of legitimate authority. According to Weber there are three grounds for legitimating authority: tradition, charisma, and legal (or rational).

Tradition

Traditional authority rests in the perception that a certain person, class, or caste is destined to rule by some preordained right. This perception may be found in the acceptance of a political system or it may be based on religious belief. Regardless, those who are in the ruling position obtain compliance by virtue of the fact that those who follow subscribe to the cultural values which support the ruling structure. Authority based on tradition is static—it supports the status quo.

Charisma

Charisma is tied in with the notion of change usually brought about by an individual who has the personal ability to produce support of followers who believe in his goals. Change may be directed against the established traditional system of authority. Charismatic authority is legitimate in the sense that the individual makes it so. The property of charisma is thought to be a configuration of personality traits which enables the possessor to obtain compliance of his followers because they believe that the goals he seeks ought to be the goals they should strive for as well.

Legal (Rational)

Rational authority also involves change. But the change evoked by this process is not in response to a particular person. Rather it is change based on the emerging needs of a bureaucratic organization. People possessing rational legitimate authority secure compliance to their goals because they are technically (functionally) equipped to spell out what sort of ends are

[1] Peter M. Blau, "Critical Remarks on Weber's Theory of Authority," *The American Political Science Review,* June, 1963, p. 312.

necessary to be pursued for the good of the system. Followers accept these prescriptions because of the acknowledged expertise of the decision maker who is selected for his ability, in the sense of being technically qualified, to perform those functions required to further the rational progress of the organization.

These concepts of legitimate authority stand in juxtaposition. On the one hand is tradition which is static, preserving the established order. On the other are charisma and rational authority dedicated to change. In a concrete organizational setting all three types of authority are displayed. They stand not so much in equilibrium relationships, that is, forces of tradition balancing forces of change. Rather, instead we find organizational tension and flux resulting from the interplay of these authority types.

Origins of Authority

Now it is useful to see how the concepts of legitimate authority apply to organizational situations. In this context authority is thought either to orginate at the top of the organization and pass down through the process of delegation or to originate at the bottom of the organization and move, through the consent of those led, to the top of the organization. Let us examine these theories in some detail.

The Top-Down Theory. We begin this discussion by asking where administrator "X" in some executive function of an organization gets his authority. The answer most likely would be "from his superior next in line in the chain of command." If we trace the roots of delegated authority they lead us to the chief executive. Assuming a business organization, we can push beyond the executive hierarchy to the board of directors, from there to the stockholders, and if we persist we find the ultimate legitimacy for authority in the laws of the land supporting the rights of private property.

This theory of authority is closely allied with the concept of traditional legitimacy. Every organization which has a formally structured system of authority rests upon tradition to some extent. This is so regardless of whether one traces authority to private property or to God, as in the case of the divine right of kings.

Society recognizes the ultimate source of authority as legitimate and accepts the outcomes of the distribution of this authority throughout social institutions. So as people at one time widely accepted and complied with the "ruling and teaching" powers of the church exercised through the stewardship of the clergy, now they comply with the formal prescriptions of professional administrators who are agents of the owners of property.

The Consent Theory of Authority. Authority is proposed in this theory as emanating from those led rather than from the delegation process in hierarchial systems. This theory, as the name indicates, is based upon the acceptance by followers of the authority exercised by those in super-ordinate positions. The idea essentially is that authority is meaningless unless consent is secured from subordinates. Action is impossible without the willing cooperation of those who are led to act.

In the strict sense of the definition employed by Weber, the only possible origin for authority is the consent of those who follow. Bottom-up as it were! This holds true regardless of whether the grounds for legitimacy are traditional, charismatic, or rational. This brings up a semantic problem which needs some analysis at this point.

At times authority and authoritarianism are confused. Authoritarianism is a management style, a personal way of implementing power, which has acquired a negative connotation largely because it is thought less able to achieve organizational goals and to produce human satisfaction than other leadership forms. In our analysis authoritarianism is more closely associated with power than with authority.

We must remember that power is connected with such practices as the use of incentives or coercion to secure action toward goals. The more a superior is required to use incentives or coercion the less his subordinates have accepted the legitimacy of his authority. Naturally, the most efficient and economical way of gaining compliance is by voluntary, willing submission to superordination. Coercion and incentive programs are always more costly than if people are spontaneously motivated to achieve goals which they perceive as created by legitimate authority.

Chester I. Barnard was one of the first in administrative circles to give a systematic statement of the consent theory of authority.[2] However, it is not entirely clear whether his position was a reaction to the dysfunctional consequence of *authoritarianism* or a reaffirmation of Weber's concept. There are elements of both in his analysis. His approach was eclectic if anything. But there is strong evidence indicating his preference for a democratic explanation of the authority phenomenon. His argument runs that since all formal organizations are founded on the consent of those governed the administrators of these organizations should act consistently with this foundation. In other words, managers would be better able to achieve the goals of the cooperative system if they tapped the democratic roots of authority in the decision process rather than unilaterally imposing their will on the people subordinated to them. Based upon a democratic assumption about the origins of authority, Barnard prescribes the kind of management style required, which of course includes a greater degree of permissiveness than allowed by autocratic practices.

Beyond this Barnard caught the effectiveness-efficiency implications of legitimate authority versus the use of power to motivate subordinates. He believed the main vehicle for legitimating authority in organizations is

---

[2] Chester I. Barnard, *The Functions of the Executive* (Cambridge: Harvard University Press, 1939), chap. 12. But for an earlier work see Mary P. Follett, *The New State* (London: Longmans, Green and Co., 1920).

communication. If people think that messages they receive are legitimate, they will accept the source which issues them as a legitimate authority and act accordingly to pursue goals which will satisfy their needs and the organizational needs. This holds whether the authority is rational, traditional, or charismatic. However, there are hints throughout Barnard's work that the ground upon which he seeks legitimacy is bureaucratic rationality.

To summarize the discussion of authority to this point we noted first that authority in its three legitimate forms evokes willing compliance from followers. Second, various kinds of legitimate authority are found in the same organization at the same time. Change within this framework may often be attributed to the interaction of individuals exercising different kinds of authority. Third, power becomes an essential ingredient in achieving action when those led perceive deficiencies in the legitimate authority of superiors or in the legitimacy of the institutions which bestow authority on individuals.

Is Authority Impersonal?

The answer to this question is yes if one consults the classic works in the field of administration. It seems, however, that these writers were focusing on either traditional authority or rational authority. Consider Fayol's view as an example.[3] He treats authority as a right to exact obedience by virtue of a position on the chain of command. Obviously if subordinates accept the traditional basis of hierarchial authority, they will accept the legitimacy of the various command functions with the hierarchy.

Mary Parker Follett inclines more to the functional or rational view of authority.[4] She emphasizes the impersonality of authority in the sense that the expertise required in a function stays with it regardless of personnel changes. The rational demands of the formal organization are not predicated on the particular abilities of individuals but in the activities themselves.

In any concrete bureaucratic system both traditional and rational authorities are present. They are indeed impersonal. They are also reinforcing in the sense that authority of position casts an aura of legitimacy about the function being performed. That the reverse is true as well is nicely developed by Feld in a research study dealing with information and authority in military organizations.[5] The access to intelligence and operational data by functional staff specialists at times endows these people with

---

[3] Henri Fayol, *General and Industrial Management,* trans. Constance Storrs (New York: Pitman Publishing Corp., 1949), p. 21.

[4] Mary P. Follett, "The Illusion of Final Authority," *Bulletin of the Taylor Society,* December, 1926, p. 244.

[5] M. D. Feld, "Information and Authority: the Structure of Military Organization," *American Sociological Review,* 24 (1959), pp. 15–22.

the authority to command, if not officially at least instrumentally, because their superior information often "takes precedence over formal rank as a determinant of organization status."[6]

The case of charisma is not quite as clear. Charismatic authority, as a first approximation, stems from the character of the individual. It is a personal thing. However, Shills makes an important point noting that people will often attribute the property of charisma to a person in a position of vast authority such as president, pope, dictator, or king.[7] This may happen even though the individual does not in fact have the magnetism which Weber implied as necessary in the charismatic personality. Thus the source of charisma is in some instances the awesome impersonal authority possessed by a few individuals in political and economic life. But in most other circumstances the personal interpretation of charisma is likely to be the most correct.

POWER AND INFLUENCE

As Weber saw authority as willing compliance, he viewed power as a form of domination. That is, power is an individual's ability to impose his will on others despite resistance. We have seen that in the absence of total compliance, power fills the vacuum to secure action. In most administrative situations, it is realistic to suppose that executive behavior rests upon some combination of accepted authority and power. Yet the relationship between power and authority is a most difficult one to form conceptually.

French-Raven Analysis

French and Raven[8] have a well-known approach which is useful to initiate discussion. They define power in terms of influence, and influence in terms of psychological change. Influence is the *control* which a social agent exercises on others. They say that the strength of power a person possesses in a given system is his maximum *potential* ability to control. Obviously it is a matter of discretion how much of this potential a social agent chooses to exercise. An important concept is based on this idea. *Power is latent influence; while influence is power in action.*

The basis upon which power rests is a crucial part of the French-Raven analysis. They see power stemming from five sources.

1. Reward Power. Reward power is the number of positive incentives which the social agent is able to offer others. Now reward power depends

---

[6] *Ibid.*, p. 20.

[7] Edward Shills, "Charisma, Order, and Status," *American Sociological Review,* April, 1965, pp. 199–213.

[8] Much of the following material is based on John R. P. French and Bertram Raven, "The Bases of Social Power," in Dorwin Cartwright and A. F. Zander (eds.), *Group Dynamics* (2d ed.; Evanston: Row, Peterson and Company, 1960), pp. 607–23.

not only on some absolute quantity (of money for instance,) but also on the *perception* by those influenced of the number of positive rewards they think a potential social agent can muster. Thus, an administrator may have a certain amount of absolute power to offer salary incentives within the established range on a given job. But he may or may not be perceived as possessing the ability within the organization to get the ranges changed or to have a positive influence in advancing the careers of his subordinates.

2. Coercive Power. The analysis of coercive power is similar to reward power, only it is the opposite side of the coin. It stems from both the absolute and perceived expectations that punishment will follow if one does not comply with the aims of the power agent.

Reward and coercive power have positive and negative administrative valences. But it is frequently difficult to distinguish between the two. Often administrative strategy requires the use of both to secure compliance. Depending on the situation, too much coercion may cause those subject to power to leave the social agent's field of influence entirely.

3. Legitimate Power. Legitimate power stems from, "internalized values . . . which dictate that [a social agent] has a legitimate right to influence . . . and that [one] has an obligation to accept this influence."[9] This kind of power rests upon cultural values, acceptance of a social structure, and the delegation of power by one possessing it to another to act as his agent.

4. Referent Power. Referent power is based on the identification of those influenced with one who is influencing. This feeling of value oneness may be, but is not necessarily, reciprocated.

5. Expert Power. Possession of functional expertise is the foundation of this form of power. The strength of power in this instance is in large part based on the perception of the influence of the knowledge had by the influencer cast against his own knowledge of a given field and some absolute standard.

We should be struck in this discussion by the obvious parallel between legitimate, referent, and expert forms of power and the Weberian categories of authority: traditional, charismatic, and rational. Reward incentives and coercive sanctions are truly power instruments, whereas the other French and Raven classifications are so similar to Weber's as to blur any distinction.

By the very nature of the formal organization a person may have legitimate authority in one or a combination of its Weberian forms. At the same time, the formal system endows those within its administrative hierarchy with access to and the right to use power in order to secure compliance in the likely event that voids exist in subordinates' perception of the legitimacy of authority.

The use of power is subtler than the carrot-stick analogy leads one to

---

[9] *Ibid.*, p. 616.

suppose. Certainly raw coercion and elementary financial appeals are part of every administrator's kit of motivational tools. They may lie, however, well below the surface of interpersonal relations in modern organizations. On this theme Blau points out an important variation in the use of power which is profitable to note.[10] He observes that subordinates may be *obligated* by superiors. In this process superiors may extend their sphere of influence over those under them. Because of his administrative position, a superior often has access to higher managerial echelons, staff specialists, information, channels of promotion, and control of appraisals, all of which constitute power prerogatives which stem from his status in the organization.

If strategically employed, these power privileges can gain the goodwill of subordinates. The advantages subordinates derive simultaneously obligates them to comply with the wishes of the superior. A symbiotic relationship ensues from this interaction and becomes institutionalized in the sense that an equilibrium system of mutually shared expectations arise between superior and subordinates. On occasion the obligated group will impose the norms of this compliance relationship on recalcitrant types who might turn up in its influence field.

Out of this complex set of transactions a kind of "willing compliance" to authority emerges, but it is a long way from the sort which Weber and Barnard visualized. While the "acceptance of authority" is rooted in the group, it is based upon the group's perception of the reality of power prerogatives resting in superordinated positions, whose ultimate support may be traced to larger institutional forces like the economic, political, social, and legal establishments.

Whatever are the power-authority accommodations reached between superiors and subordinates, they are modifiable by interaction with change-producing conditions in the environment. So while equilibrium of expectations is often achieved it may be altered, by bringing in a new superior for example, in which case a new accommodation must be evolved that probably will include a new set of expectations. No small part of the kind of coalition reached between a manager and those he supervises depends on the leadership variable.[11] For this reason we take up the subject of leadership next as part of the influence process.

LEADERSHIP

Few areas in the behavioral sciences have attracted as much attention as leadership. In the past, theories of leadership gained ascendancy only to give way eventually to newer postulates. Even now there is hardly a coherent body of doctrine which may be labeled the theory of leadership.

[10] Blau, *op. cit.*, p. 312.

[11] See Robert H. Guest, "Managerial Succession in Complex Organizations," *The American Journal of Sociology*, July, 1962, pp. 47–56.

In spite of this difficulty most students of the subject agree that they address themselves to seven major questions, with varying degrees of emphasis, in their research and writing.

These questions are:[12]

1. Why do people subordinate themselves to a leader?
2. What are the sources of the leader's power?
3. How and why do leaders arise?
4. What motivates leaders to lead?
5. What are the functions of the leader?
6. What determines leadership effectiveness?
7. Are there any common denominators of leadership behavior and leadership characteristics?

As we review the research and theory of leadership in this section, answers to some of these questions emerge. Our objective is not to propose a theory of leadership here, but, rather, to give some of the conceptual developments in the area.

Definitions of Leadership

Because those who research the leadership phenomenon use different methods of investigation, there is little agreement on operational definitions in the literature. Nevertheless it is useful to look at some of the definitions which have been proposed since they give a feel for the major conceptual problems confronted by those concerned with this study.

Stogdill defines leadership as ". . . the process of influencing the activities of an organized group in its efforts toward goal setting and goal achievement."[13]

He points out that in a leadership situation three elements are presumed to constitute minimum social conditions. The first is the presence of a group; second, a common task or group objective; and third, a differentiation of responsibility. Leadership, to Stogdill, is a segment of group organization. Organization as such is based on the division of functions which must be performed. The distinctions among organizational roles, founded on functional differentiation, are essential to the existence of leadership. Without the separation of activities there is no opportunity for the leader to coordinate the efforts of group members toward accomplishing an objective.

The emphasis Stogdill places on structured roles and on functional differentiation leads one to conclude that at least a place to start investigating leadership is with people in formal positions in organizations. This is certainly his argument in the Ohio State Studies in Naval Leadership. In one respect it is correct to say that Walter Reuther is the leader of the

---

[12] Warren G. Bennis, "Leadership Theory and Administrative Behavior: The Problem of Authority," *Administrative Science Quarterly*, Vol. 4 (1959–60), p. 261.

[13] Ralph M. Stogdill, "Leadership, Membership and Organization," *Psychological Bulletin*, January, 1950, p. 4.

United Automobile Workers. But this approach tends to obscure the interpersonal dynamics in leadership. While people may indeed be leaders of their organizations, we cannot generalize and say that all those who occupy headships are leaders in a true sense.

Bennis sees leadership as ". . . the process by which an agent induces a subordinate to behave in a desired manner."[14] He describes five elements contained in this definition.

1. The agent—an actor in a leadership role.
2. The process—sanctions, incentives and moral suasions by which the leader induces action.
3. The subordinate—the agent must perceive what needs the subordinates wish satisfied, and he must control the means for granting satisfactions.
4. Induced behavior—the process of influence implemented by sanctions and incentives.
5. The manner—the avenues of obtaining a goal.

Bavelas shifts the focus of analysis away from the *setting* of leadership toward the *act* of leadership itself. According to him leadership acts are those which enable the group to achieve its objectives by giving assistance in making choices. ". . . leadership consists of uncertainty reduction."[15] Gibb also affirms this position.[16] He concludes that any group will have a leadership function to fill. Leaders in turn may be identified by the frequency with which they perform these acts.

The irreducible minimum of a leadership act is found by returning to the concept of uncertainty reduction. Another way of putting this idea is that a leader will behave so as to structure a previously ambiguous situation for members of the group. Uncertainty may be thought of as a lack of structure. By supplying structure, by crystallizing goals and objectives, an individual performs a basic leadership activity.[17] More is said about this in a subsequent section on leader behavior.

---

[14] Bennis, *op. cit.*, p. 295.

[15] Alex Bavelas, "Leadership: Man and Function," *Administrative Science Quarterly*, March, 1960, p. 495.

[16] See Cecil A. Gibb, "Definition of the Leader," in C. Gratton Kemp (ed.), *Perspectives on the Group Process* (Boston: Houghton Mifflin Company, 1964), pp. 190–97.

[17] Some interesting lessons may be learned in this respect from experiences with the so-called structureless group. Use of the structureless group as a selection device for army officers is traceable to German military psychology in the 1920's. The process works rather as follows. A small group of officer candidates is assembled after the initial phases of selection are completed. They are brought together with no other apparent purpose than to discuss areas of common interest. At first the group flounders because of its hazy goal and lack of organization. But during the meeting an individual appears who directs the group into channels of fruitful analysis. The leader who arises actually "structures" a previously unstructured situation and reduces the group's uncertainty about the direction it is to proceed in the session.
During these activities the formal conference director, who usually remains passive throughout the proceedings, observes the group's and the leader's behavior. The expression of attitudes by individuals which are most desired in military

There are many modifications of this approach in modern executive selection and training methods. However, the idea behind the use of these techniques remains much the same as developed by the German psychologists. This idea is to allow normal group processes to identify potential leaders.

Leadership Determinants

Given the premise that all groups, formal and informal, require leadership functions to be performed, the question arises which asks what it is that determines who will lead and who will follow? Historically, several leadership theories addressing themselves to this question have been popular. Some of these theories have been discredited, others have been retained in modified form, and still others are emerging as research continues. The leadership theories discussed in this section with exception of the first may be found in current literature. They are not all acceptable, however, to the numerous schools of leadership thought. For example, the traitist approach finds limited approval among those who are committed to the situational theory.

The "Great Man" Approach. This theory attaches extraordinary powers to the character of the great man. Because of the form it assumes this approach frequently is called the biographical approach. Perhaps the first famous exponent of this method was Plutarch in his *Lives.* Now while the capacity for greatness is not equally distributed, by studying the lives of outstanding people it is thought that one might find clues for success on a more modest scale. While little credence is placed in this theory as offering a generalized explanation of leadership, it stands as a precursor to a far more popular approach.

The Trait Approach.. Dealing with the personal characteristics of leaders, the trait approach represents one of the earliest attempts to organize a coherent theory of leadership. Many studies have been conducted which posed the question to "acknowledged leaders," what personal qualities are important in influencing the action of others? From answers to questions like this, endless lists of traits have been compiled. Needless to say they offer little comfort to those seeking universal attributes of leaders. In a study of just these kinds of lists some 17,000 one-word descriptions of leader qualities were assembled. While the trait approach finds little favor among the more sophisticated scholars of leadership[18] it is

---

leadership are carefully noted and credited to those persons' behalf when the final choice of candidates for officer training is made. It might be added that the traits looked for by observers are carefully identified and validated against the traits evidenced by successful military leaders. See H. L. Ansbacher, "German Military Psychology," *Psychological Bulletin,* June, 1941, pp. 370–92; and "The History of the Leaderless Group Discussion Technique," *Psychological Bulletin,* Vol. 48 (1951), pp. 383–91.

[18] For a thorough critique of the trait approach see Alvin W. Gouldner, *Studies in Leadership* (New York: Harper and Bros., 1950), pp. 21–25.

surprising how often it appears in management and marketing literature in reference to desirable qualities of salesmen, sales managers, and administrators in general.

The Modified Trait Approach. Although the trait approach has limited value, continued research appears to have uncovered three personal qualities which show up often in leadership studies. These qualities are intelligence, communication ability, and sensitivity to group goals. Intelligence is defined in the conventional way, as the global ability to think in abstract terms. Communication is the ability to verbalize to members of the group and to those outside it, group values and goals. And sensitivity reflects an individual's awareness of a group's needs and his ability to facilitate group effort in achieving them.

These characteristics are not absolute; they are relative to the group. Thus leaders are often found to be more intelligent, better communicators, and more sensitive relative to other members of the group. Further, these three qualities are combined in a personality configuration. It is not sufficient, for example, for an individual to have high intelligence relative to the group if he is not also aware of group thinking. Or he may be sensitive to group values but he may not be able to articulate them. Thus, as one study points out, the leader is one who knows the thinking of the group best and is able to verbalize it. Leadership refers to the ability to abstract relevant determinants of group behavior in order to move the group to action.[19]

A fourth quality, observed by Hollander and Webb, is interesting as it refers to the relationship between leadership and followership.[20] They note that leadership and followership nominations, sociometrically derived, are closely related in a positive direction. The more desired followers tend to be at the upper extremes of leadership distribution. That good leaders also are good followers makes sense in an organization because of its hierarchial structure. Managers must look to others above and below themselves for decisions and performance, respectively.

As a methodological note it should be observed that research on leadership qualities usually requires that the study group be separated into those perceived as leaders and nonleaders, or good and not-so-good leaders. The actual slotting of people into one or the other categories rests on decisions by a person in formal authority over the group, as a supervisor, or by peer nominations of the group, or by a combination of these methods. Of course, the initial criteria for the division is established by the researchers

---

[19] C. G. Browne and Richard P. Shore, "Leadership and Predictive Abstracting," *Journal of Applied Psychology*, April, 1956, pp. 112–16. See also Kamla Chowdhry and Theodore M. Newcomb, "The Relative Abilities of Leaders and Non-leaders to Estimate Opinions of Their Own Groups," *Journal of Abnormal and Social Psychology*, January, 1952, pp. 51–57.

[20] E. P. Hollander and Wilse B. Webb, "Leadership, Followership and Friendship: An Analysis of Peer Nominations," *Journal of Abnormal and Social Psychology*, March, 1955, pp. 163–67.

themselves who enter the study with preconceived values about what constitutes leadership.[21]

The Situational Approach.   The situational view of leadership has many exponents. This approach is based on the notion that traits are not the main determinant of who will rise in a leadership setting; rather, the situation or the environment is the relevant variable. Thus, a leader in one situation may not be a leader in a different situation regardless of the traits he possesses.

The situational approach is valuable because each organization has a certain uniqueness in spite of the fact that organizations have structural similarities as well. The uniqueness of an organization corresponds to its personality. Research following the situational approach focuses on the personality of the organization as a whole as well as on its parts.

The functional character of leadership is closely allied to the situational approach. It is possible for almost anyone to become a leader if circumstances allow him to perform activities designated by the situation. Hence, if the situation is one of emergency a leader might arise to fulfill the functions demanded in this case. And the individual who appears in this role might not ordinarily be the same one who carries out leadership functions over the group in stable situations.

The functional aspect of leadership requires researchers to investigate how leadership activities are distributed in an organization. It requires, further, a probe of the organization's power structure to determine, why one individual, out of a number of presumably qualified individuals, is propelled into a leadership role.

Elaborating on the functional aspect of leadership in an attempt to reconcile the situational and traitist approaches, Allport indicates that the ". . . role of personal traits is greater in situations that are 'unstructured'—where, for example, the task assigned to the group is discussion rather than skilled action. Personal traits are less important when the task . . . concerns a mechanical or technical problem."[22]

Generalizing on the status of the situational and traitist approaches to leadership, Bavelas says: "The status of trait and situational leadership research can be summed up in this way: (1) The broad similarities which hold for a great number of organizations make it possible to say useful things about the kind of person who is likely to become a leader in any of these organizations, and (2) the unique characteristics of a particular organization make it necessary to analyze the situational factors that determine who is likely to become a leader in one particular organization."[23]

---

[21] Bavelas, *op. cit.,* p. 492.

[22] Gordon W. Allport, *Pattern and Growth in Personality* (New York: Holt, Rinehart and Winston, 1961), p. 179.

[23] Bavelas, *op. cit.,* p. 494.

Becoming a Leader

From the previous discussion we deduce that there are two polar conceptions of how an individual assumes a leadership role. (1) Following the traitist orientation, the individual takes over the role because of personal characteristics and abilities. (2) Along the situationist line, the group thrusts one of its members into the role. By a little sophistry, it is possible to convert a situationist argument to a traitist or vice versa. For example, the situationist might say that the only reason an individual could take over the role was because the group allowed it to happen. But the traitist would counter that the group allowed it because a clever person wanting the role manipulated them into accepting him as leader.

This is the kind of ideological argument which can never be resolved. But on the conceptual level, we can say from the traitist standpoint the individual is viewed as an active ingredient pursuing the leader role, the group being on the passive side in either accepting or rejecting the bid. We find the emphasis reversed in the situationist camp. That is, the group is the active component selecting one of its peers through the dynamics of consensus to lead. And, of course, given a change in the situation a new consensus may be necessary to pick a new leader.

Clearly neither the traitists nor the situationists can dominate the play of explaining how leaders become leaders. Another tack is required. Some time ago Gibb indicated that in selecting a person for a leadership role, the choice of the specific individual depends more on the nature of the group than on the personality of the individual. However, the main determinant of who shall lead is the relationship between the group and the individual at a particular time.[24] While this sounds like the situationist theory over again, it is in fact not. It has been called the "interactional" approach.

This theory takes as a point of departure the individual and his *social space*. Social space is defined as the *field* in which an individual is attempting to interact with others. Playing upon this field are numerous forces such as the task orientation of the formal organization, the systems of power and authority, the goals and values of informal groups, and the specific personal traits, values, and aspirations of other persons occupying social space in the field. Out of the interaction among these forces the field generates its own peculiar equilibrium in which an important variable is the leadership structure. This structure comprises various roles which a person or persons must fulfill to preserve the equilibrium of the field. The extent to which individuals are able to attract to themselves a following because of a "fit" between their personal traits and the demands of field

---

[24] Cecil A. Gibb, "The Principles and Traits of Leadership," *Journal of Abnormal and Social Psychology*, July, 1947, p. 268.

forces determines who ends up with the leadership roles and who follows. This returns us to the idea expressed earlier in the section on definition that we know leaders by the acts they perform and nothing more or less.

Leadership Roles

Defining leadership in terms of acts performed directs us to a discussion of leadership roles. We saw before that the minimum act of leadership is ambiguity reduction, or stated positively, structure initiation. Beyond this Stogdill cites nine other acts which are associated with leader functions.

1. Integration—acts which tend to increase coordination.
2. Communication—acts which tend to increase understanding and transmission of information.
3. Production emphasis—acts oriented toward volume of work done.
4. Representation—acts which promote group representation with outside organizations.
5. Fraternization—acts which make leaders part of the group.
6. Organization—acts which lead to the differentiation and prescription of duties.
7. Evaluation—acts which pertain to distribution of rewards and punishment.
8. Initation—acts which result in changes of group activities.
9. Domination—acts which disregard the ideas of persons or group members.[25]

These activities are difficult to accomplish to the satisfaction of all, especially if the leader role is filled by a single person. Not only is the leader faced with conflicting expectations originating from within the group, he also may find, that the expectations of his group as a whole conflict with the demands of outside groups. This is basically a conflict situation. Commenting on it in the context of the formal organization, Stogdill says: "Leadership is concerned with problems of human performance and interaction. . . . The leader in any actively operating organization is constantly confronted by discrepancies between the demands of organization and performance of organization. This means that the leader is concerned with the co-ordination (restructuring) of interactions and performances as necessary in order to accomplish the tasks at hand."[26]

Stogdill's distinction between leadership problems of "human performance" and "human interaction" is suggestive of a multiple leadership concept in task-oriented situations. Frequently one encounters the popular notions of the natural leader and the designated leader. The natural leader achieves this role primarily as the result of group consensus. In this

---

[25] Ralph M. Stogdill and Alvin E. Coons, *Leader Behavior: Its Description and Measurement* (Columbus: Bureau of Business Research, Research Monograph #88, Ohio State University, 1957), pp. 8–9.

[26] Ralph M. Stogdill, *Leadership and Structures of Personal Interactions* (Columbus: Bureau of Business Research, Monograph #84, Ohio State University, 1957), p. 3.

process the group selects one of its own members to serve in an *informal* leadership capacity.

The designated leader is one who is appointed to serve in a formal capacity as an agent of the organization. Such appointments to executive positions in a conventional line organization result from the delegation process. Frequently they are labeled supervisory or executive headships. Now those who serve as natural leaders have gained group acceptance and have the legitimacy of their authority established. However, there is

FIGURE 9–1

Elements of Informal versus Designated Leadership

POSITIONAL AUTHORITY
(TRADITIONAL + RATIONAL)

	+	−
+ PERSONAL ACCEPTANCE	1 FORMAL LEADER (NATURAL + DESIGNATED)	2 INFORMAL LEADER (NATURAL)
−	3 DESIGNATED HEADSHIP	4 FOLLOWER

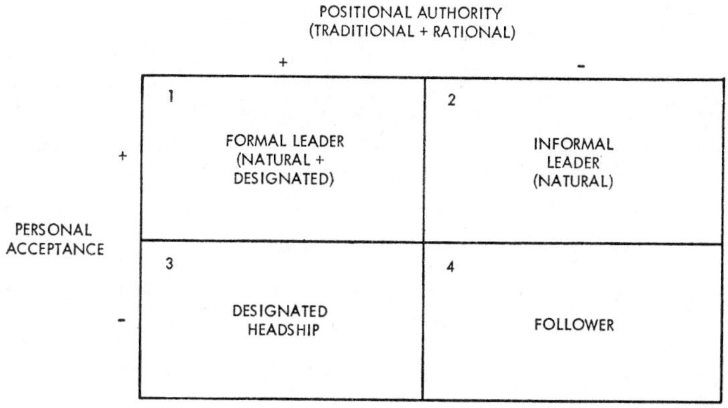

Source: Amitai Etzioni, "Dual Leadership in Complex Organizations," *American Sociological Review,* October, 1965, p. 691. Used with permission.

nothing in this approach to preclude an individual who is designated to a headship from gaining group acceptance either.

This is certainly possible if the group recognized that distinct clusters of leadership activities need to be performed; i.e., those associated with maintaining group integration and solidarity on the one hand and getting the job done on the other. Thus the role of facilitating human interaction might fall to one person and the role of facilitating human performance to another. The so-called natural leader often fills the first role cluster and the designated leader the second.

Etzioni comments on this point in an article dealing with dual leadership.[27] His position is that in complex organizations shared leadership is the most likely behavioral pattern encountered. This is contrary to the view expressed in much leadership literature which suggests that all leadership functions are (or should be?) centered in one person. In developing his analysis, Etzioni compares the elements of informal versus designated leadership. Figure 9–1 presents his diagram showing the basis of his

---

[27] Amitai Etzioni, "Dual Leadership in Complex Organizations," *American Sociological Review*, October, 1965, pp. 688–98.

argument. The designations of his variables are modified to conform to the language of this chapter.

A person with personal acceptance without positional authority of the formal structure is the natural (informal) leader. Conversely an individual with positional authority but without personal acceptance falls into a designated headship. Etzioni calls one with both positional authority and personal acceptance a formal leader. Those lacking the two are followers.

In complex organizations, the most improbable leadership patterns in an influence field are (1) and a combination of (2) + (3). The most probable is (2) and (3). That is, the natural leader and the designated head share leadership roles. However, as we have said, a person designated a head, can evolve into an accepted leader for purposes of task facilitation.

The organizational implication of this line of analysis is that groups are more likely to be both effective and efficient if both types of leadership are provided, the roles performed by different individuals. However, there are strong suggestions that this outcome is modified by group expectations conditioned by the prevailing leadership climate. For instance, the more highly conditioned the group is to an authoritarian climate, the more it anticipates that the designated head initiate acts aimed at achieving interaction and performance.

Berkowitz, in a study of shared leadership, observed that the groups analyzed indicated a general expectation that the designated leader should be the sole behavioral leader. When the leader did not perform as expected other members of the group took over and filled the vacuum. However, leadership sharing, in these instances studied, was accompanied by a decrease in group solidarity and satisfaction.[28]

While there may be some question about the effectiveness and efficiency outcomes of shared leadership, there can be little doubt about dual leadership as a fact of organizational life. There is always the problem of potential conflict between leaders sharing as they do essential roles in an influence field. Their relations are conditioned by the relative availability of resources and distribution of organizational power. The one who commands the most resources and power is the most likely to give the group its primary orientation either toward solidarity or toward tasks. But that there is a primary orientation does not exclude the other role; it simply is subordinated.

The relationship between the group and the leaders (natural and designated) is reciprocal. The leader has to perceive group needs and to direct the group toward their gratification. In turn, the group must feel that the leader is adequate in this role. In a study of naval recruits, Henning and Economos observed three forms of behavior associated with an informal leadership role.[29] The first type was one in which the leader was thrust up

---

[28] Leonard Berkowitz, "Sharing Leadership in Small Decision-Making Groups," *Journal of Abnormal and Social Psychology,* April, 1953, pp. 231–38.

[29] Kenneth K. Henning and Gus L. Economos, "Patterns of Natural Leadership: A Research Study of Informal Organizations" (an unpublished manuscript, 1962).

by the group to serve in what was perceived to be an emergency situation. The second type was the leader who took over the role on his own initiative; his tenure persisted as long as the group recognized him. The third type of leader planned his strategy "behind the scenes" and made his play for leadership when he felt the group was ready. It is interesting that of the second and third types of leaders, the most durable in resisting challenges were those who accepted the formal goals of the Navy.

It might be hypothesized from this study that informal leaders who arise in stable formal organizational settings and who accept the goals of the formal organization tend to remain in leadership capacities longer. They are best equipped to help the group reconcile its own needs with those of the formal organization. This is a key function because groups in military or business surroundings often have few alternatives but to conform to the strictures of the environment. The individual is most likely to persist in a leadership role if he is able to direct the group through formal organizational and technological mazes, showing it how to gain some satisfactions at the same time. In this respect, there is no inherent conflict between formal and informal leadership.

Commenting on this point, relative to an assembly-line situation, Whyte says: "The technological environment is so overwhelming that nothing the foreman can do would really make the workers like the work they do. Nevertheless, it is possible for him to modify to a degree the impact of this environment upon the workers. To the extent that he does so, he can build favorable sentiments toward himself."[30]

SUMMARY AND CONCLUSIONS

Some of the main points developed in this chapter must now be brought together. A useful device is to make some generalizations with respect to the questions asked at the beginning of the leadership section.

1. *What are the sources of a leader's power and authority?* This question was amended slightly by adding the notion of authority. The answer is clearly that the source of a leader's authority is in group consent and acceptance of legitimacy. The power to reward and punish is an inherent prerogative of authority. Nothing is found in the leadership concept to suggest that it is an enduring role. However, organizations are structured so that individuals are supported in headships although they are unable to secure the willing compliance of followers. In this case we speak of domination based upon power.

2. *How and why do leaders arise?* Largely, as we have seen, a unique combination of personal qualifications plus group perception and acceptance of these qualifications allow a person or persons to produce and maintain equilibrium in an influence force field where leadership is a

---

[30] William F. Whyte, *Money and Motivation* (New York: Harper and Bros., 1955), pp. 46–49.

crucial variable. The relative importance of the group propelling a person into, versus the individual actively pursuing, a leadership role is situationally determined.

3. *What are the functions of the leader? Why do people subordinate themselves to a leader?* We considered two general leadership functions: interaction facilitation and performance facilitation. We saw as well that in task-oriented groups these roles may be shared by different people. People subordinate themselves, that is they will comply to the leader, because they accept the legitimacy of the functions performed. When dual leadership exists, there may be different grounds for acceptance, *but this in no way undermines the concept of voluntary compliance.* One person is accepted as a behavioral facilitator, the other as a task facilitator.

4. *Are there any common denominators of leadership characteristics?* Yes, to the degree that research has pointed out such quantitative factors as intelligence, communicative ability, and sensitivity. But it must be recognized that there also are qualitative aspects to these traits in terms of their pattern or configuration in personality. Of equal importance are the equilibrium demands, of a given influence field, that determine which pattern is most suitable to meet the needs of the situation.

CHAPTER 10

Decision Concepts

DECISION MAKING is one of the principal determinants of individual, small group, and formal organizational behavior. As we have indicated the concepts treated in this chapter are allied with those of social influence and the concepts of balance discussed in the next chapter. This latter instance is so because it is through decisions that people and organizations adapt to their environment.

The structure of this chapter is straightforward. In it we consider basic decision concepts, individual decision making as it relates the person to organizations, and organizational decision programs. The focus of the chapter is on the behavioral dynamics of decision theory. We do not deal with the more technical statistical and operation research applications in the decision-making field.

INTRODUCTORY CONCEPTS

Regardless of the level of decision making, the process involves certain common ingredients.[1] They are (1) a search process to discover goals; (2) the formulation of objectives after search; (3) the selection of alternatives (strategies) to accomplish objectives; (4) the evaluation of outcomes.

The Search Process

In the search process, an individual or organization undertakes to find a new goal or goals because of dissatisfaction with outcomes within an existing goal structure. The present payoff structure growing out of the present set of goals is, in other words, less than an individual's (or organization's) level of aspiration. March's and Simon's model of adaptive behavior is useful to demonstrate the role of search in the decision process.

The search process is evoked by a low level of satisfaction as the

---

[1] See for example, Stephen H. Archer, "The Structure of Management Decision Theory," *Academy of Management Journal,* December, 1964, pp. 269–73, and Howard E. Thompson, "Management Decisions in Perspective," in William E. Schlender, William G. Scott, and Alan C. Filley (eds.), *Management in Perspective* (Boston: Houghton Mifflin Company, 1965), pp. 135–38.

diagram shows. The lower the level of satisfaction the more intensive is the search for new goals. The degree of satisfaction depends on the outcomes (expected value of reward) as does the level of aspiration. Satisfaction is achieved when payoffs correspond to the level of aspiration. However, as we have seen in Chapter 3, since favorable experience with outcomes from goals often raises the level of aspiration, a new discrepancy

FIGURE 10–1

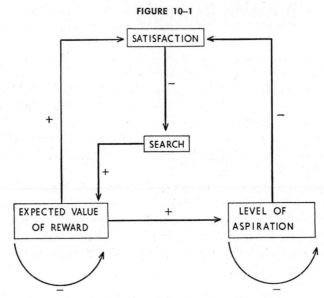

Source: James G. March and Herbert A. Simon, *Organizations* (New York: John Wiley and Sons, Inc., 1958), p. 49. Used with permission.

might again appear between rewards and aspiration level setting the search process in motion again.

Formulation of Objectives

Objectives, whether personal or organizational, are values which are desired by the decision maker. Usually, it is useful as a first approximation to view the decision maker as attempting to maximize or minimize values such as profits, losses, costs, salary, rate of advancement, or output. This approach, based largely on traditional economic theory of rationality, has been criticized. Simon, for instance, introduces the concept of "satisficing" which he offers as a substitute for the maximization concept. He observes:

Psychological studies of the formation and change of aspiration levels support propositions of the following kinds. (*a*) When performance falls short of the level of aspiration, search behavior . . . is induced. (*b*) At the same time, the level of aspiration begins to adjust itself downward until goals reach levels that are practically attainable. (*c*) If the two mechanisms just listed operate too slowly to adapt aspiration to performance, emotional behavior . . . will replace rational adaptive behavior.[2]

We can conceive of goals, out of this framework as "states of tension" providing the motivation impetus to behavior.[3] There is little in psychological theory to suggest that outcomes have to be maximized in order to reduce or even eliminate the intensity of the drive. Indeed the theory of aspiration, as we have seen, indicates adaptive flexibility whereby goals may be raised, lowered, or changed in the light of experience.[4]

The theory of value maximization proposes an objective predictive model of behavior within a very narrow framework of adaptive modes. Most of the constraints of this model result from the rigid assumption regarding the relationships among economic variables. Satisficing, according to Simon, allows a richer model of adaptation which is closer to a more natural (realistic) explanation of decision behavior. For example, simply recognizing the lack of information necessary for rational decisions makes satisficing a more acceptable explanatory device.

Strategies

Once a goal, or hierarchy of goals has been established, the decision maker prepares a repertory of alternatives for achieving his aims. For any given alternative, and there may be an infinite range of possibilities, is associated a decision system comprised of an outcome, a probability, and a value. With four alternatives, for example, there is:

$$
\begin{array}{cccc}
A_1 & O_1 & P_1 & V_1 \\
A_2 & O_2 & P_2 & V_2 \\
A_3 & O_3 & P_3 & V_3 \\
A_4 & O_4 & P_4 & V_4
\end{array}
$$

In each case a payoff (outcome) is computed, a probability of payoff occuring arrived at, and the subjective value of the strategy decided.

As an illustration let us suppose a person, Mr. X, is bitten by a dog and must make a decision to have rabies shots or not.[5] The shots, as X knows, are painful, inconvenient, expensive, and even dangerous because of the remote chance that death might occur from them. The experience of having shots cast against the possibility of dying from rabies represent extremes on X's value scale.

---

[2] Herbert A. Simon, "Theories of Decision Making in Economics and Behavioral Science," *The American Economic Review*, June, 1959, p. 263.

[3] See William J. Gore, *Administrative Decision-Making* (New York: John Wiley and Sons, Inc., 1964), pp. 38–41.

[4] The adaptation of organizational goals in the face of changing environment is developed by James K. Dent, "Organizational Correlates of the Goals of Business Management," *Personnel Psychology*, Autumn, 1959, pp. 365–94.

[5] I am indebted for this example to my colleague Professor Robert Weigand, who three weeks before this was written did not know the difference between an Airedale and a ring-necked pheasant, but does now. One bites.

Given these alternatives, X must have *information* on probabilities and outcomes in order to decide. Assume a dog is caught that X is fairly sure, but not positive, is the culprit. The presence of doubt about the dog is crucial. If there is certainty in this respect, and the dog is in custody, then the observation period will definitely establish the health of the animal. Based upon what we take as objective probability data, here is X's decision tree.[6]

If X is optimistic he will not undergo shots because the ultimate outcome, the probability of death, is remote in either situation of right or

FIGURE 10–2

Mr. X's Decision Tree

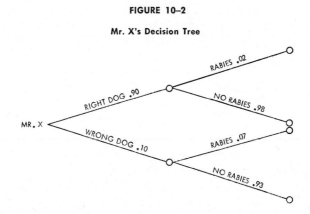

wrong dog. X reasons that in nine chances out of ten the dog is the correct one, and since the dog under observation is a neighborhood pet the probability of it being rabid is very low. And even in the unlikely event the dog that actually did the biting got away the chance that it is rabid is still quite low based on experience factors in the area. Thus according to X's value system incurring the small risk of rabies is more desirable than pain associated with the shots. Thus he chooses the no-shot alternative.

Instead of X, let us assume a Mr. Y is in the identical situation, bitten one-half hour later by the same dog. But Y is a pessimist. While the same probability information is available to Y, in his eyes a chance of one in ten error about the dog and the higher risk of rabies among strays leads him, according to his value scale to take shots and endure the pain to secure positive protection. Several important concepts are derived from this simple example.

Risk. The nature of risk is such that the probability of an event occurring or not occurring can be assigned. Both X and Y we

_____

[6] Although these figures are purely imaginary, let us suppose they represent reliable public health data on rabies for the region in which the incident occurred. The probability information on the right-wrong dog is based on a dog census for the area. We assume that X identified the breed, thus limiting the field of candidates considerably.

assume are confronted by the same objective probability data. But X thinks that since the chance of rabies is trifling he avoids the shots. Y perceives the same probability but he still does not want to run even this small chance and so he acts accordingly. This differential behavior does not stem from the probability data per se. Rather, it is a function of the value systems of X and Y respectively.

This case is analogous to another which has to do with the probability of being killed in an air crash on a commercial carrier. The objective probability data, which has been computed and available to all, is very much against such a calamity happening. Yet there are people who refuse to fly for the very reason that they fear a crash. They choose other modes of transportation, like driving, even though the danger of accident with injury or death is higher. You might say this is not rational. But there is no claim, of course, that values are rational in any objective sense.

Some might argue that optimism or pessimism is reflected in probability data itself. That is, an optimistic person would say, "I think it is a 90 percent chance we got the right dog, *in the absence of any concrete probability data to the contrary.*" Whereas the pessimistic person would be more doubtful feeling the chances were only 50–50. Now while the resulting decisions of X and Y likely will be identical to those postulated in the face of objective data, the line of reasoning is quite different. Under the conditions which we have just stated, X and Y are mixing value data and probability data. This is wholly erroneous in risk analysis, but is quite appropriate in the discussion of uncertainty.

Uncertainty. The nature of uncertainty is such that it is not possible to assign a probability to the occurrance of an event. This is because of either lack of information about the event, or the nonrepeatable character of the event, or both. Archer sums it up this way:

> Uncertainty in decision theory describes all shades of knowledge of the probability distribution of the states of nature ranging from near accurate estimates based upon objective experience to an extreme case in which no knowledge exists. It is this type of model which most frequently applies to management decision. Uncertainty varies from the extreme of no information up to but excluding the condition of risk in which the probability of the states of nature is known. Short of risk conditions, exists uncertainty.[7]

Selection of strategies under uncertainty conditions requires the application of judgment, opinion, belief, subjective estimates of the situation, plus whatever objective data is available. The estimates of probability and payoff (P and O) become hopelessly dependent upon the values of the decision maker. The concept of "subjective probability" is introduced into uncertainty situations as a shorthand notation that a strategy has been selected using decision criteria which are not entirely rational. Hence, subjective probabilities regarding strategies may vary among decision

---

[7] Archer, *op. cit.,* p. 276.

makers confronting the same situation. In short, under risk we can separate O and P from V. We cannot do this under uncertainty.

Uncertainty ranges between total ignorance at one end of an extreme
to either, but not including, risk or certainty at the other. We dispel
uncertainty with information.

Information.   In the appendix to Chapter 7 the inverse relationship between information and uncertainty is discussed. Information, in the language of that section, serves to structure (reverse the entropy) of a
previously unstructured situation. We emphasized in this appendix that
information is construed in the narrowest quantitative sense. However,
here we must relax somewhat from the engineering position and allow

FIGURE 10–3
Information and Uncertainty Reduction

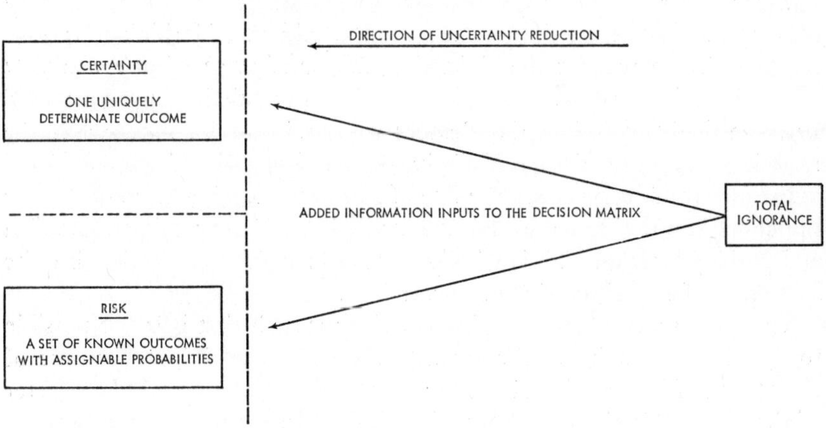

that information, although imperfectly measured and qualitatively defined
in an administrative setting, similarly structures an uncertain environment
for the decision maker. It permits him to make better decisions assuming
effectiveness criteria is measured by the relationship between payoffs and
goals. Therefore the decision maker wishes to reduce uncertainty or, if
possible, to convert it to a state of either certainty or risk. That this is
accomplished through the medium of information is highlighted in Figure
10–3. This figure requires several observations:

1. The nature of "added information inputs" is data concerning outcomes and probabilities of given strategies. Suppose a decision maker
begins acquiring information at the point of "total ignorance" or at some
other point to the left of it. He may be unsure at this time whether added
information will lead him to the risk state, the certainty state, or for that
matter, leave him at some advanced condition within the uncertainty state.

2. Of course it is clear, or should be, that a decision maker may never
"cross the dotted line" to either certainty or risk states regardless of how

much information he acquires. More information may improve decisions within the uncertainty state. Beyond this the decision maker may never learn what the nature of a particular decision is. But he may avoid the error of using risk assumptions for a decision which more correctly lies in uncertainty.

3. The amount of information the decision maker actually acquires depends on some marginal (or satisficing) calculus, in which he compares information cost to the value of uncertainty reduction. Naturally, we must think incrementally in terms of so many units of information for so many units of uncertainty reduction. It is unlikely that we can go from say total ignorance to some arbitrarily desirable point of uncertainty in a single leap.

It is tempting to introduce some marginal analysis at this point "to explain" why a decision maker acquires just so much information. This approach explains the phenomenon as the marginal cost of the information acquired equaling the marginal value of the uncertainty reduced. However, this subject is best put off to Chapter 15, where it is discussed at some length in an appendix on "Communication and Centralization of Organization." But we should note here that the *need* for information may be as much *psychological,* in view of the qualitative character of most administrative decisions, as it is technical in some quantitative sense. This then would suggest that the need for information is *satisficed* at points other than where "the cost of information equals the value of uncertainty reduction." Most of the literature leads us to believe that these points are somewhere before the point of maximization.[8]

The Evaluation of Outcomes

The final element of the decision process, after the search has been made, goals set, and strategies determined, is the evaluation of outcomes. This process has been variously called the measurement of effectiveness or the rationality criteria. One of the problems with which we are confronted is that there is apparently no rationality criteria apart from decision rules.

Since there are many families of decision rules (or decision frameworks) there are also many criteria for effectiveness, which do not necessarily carry over from one set of rules to the next. If we accept this position, then one way to measure rationality is to compare the outcomes of decisions to the goals of the decision maker. This yardstick of rationality is based on the *consequences* of decisions. Thus, if the set of rules is "good," that is, if it produces outcomes which meet the objectives of the decision maker, then rationality is established by definition. This is what Bross calls the *pragmatic principle.*[9]

---

[8] This is the implication in Simon, *op. cit.,* p. 271.

[9] Irwin D. J. Bross, *Design for Decision* (New York: The Macmillan Company, 1953), pp. 29–32.

Note that this principle subjects neither the decision process nor the goals of the decision maker to rational scrutiny. It does not insist that a set of decision rules have internal consistency or that goals conform with some "objective" standard of behavior. The presuppositions of conventional logic and conventional culture are *not* standards of rationality so far as the pragmatic principle is concerned.

The pragmatic principle is deceptively simple, since it does away with difficult problems by abolishing absolute standards. Goals become merely datum of rationality measurement, not themselves subject to rationality analysis.[10] So we must say that *given these goals*, such and such is a rational strategy to produce the sought for outcomes. If it does not work out so well, then there is a more *rational strategy*. But how about a more rational goal? Since goals are relative, how can one talk about one goal being more rational than another? The pragmatic principle, like positivism, is oriented in spirit toward conservatism. It is more compatible with what is, than with what ought to be.

With these basic concepts behind us, we turn next to the subject of individual decision.

INDIVIDUAL DECISIONS

With emphasis we say that the material covered in this section represents just a humble fraction of available information on individual decision processes. Such information ranges in scope from computer simulation experiments in decision analysis, through neurophysiology and biochemistry, to work in psychology. Our focus here is on certain classes of decisions which underlie an individual's choice to (1) participate in an organization and (2) produce for an organization.[11]

Decisions to Participate

An individual undertakes an inducement-contribution calculation when making an organizational participation decision. If he has arrayed before him the alternatives to join or not to join an organization, or several organizations, he weighs what he *perceives* to be:

1. The reward structure of the organization, that is, all the inducements, economic, psychological, and social, present and future, against
2. The expectations of the organization which constitute the role structure or the contributions he must make present and future.

---

[10] Rationality analysis can point to the desirability of certain goals over other goals. But again the concept of desirability introduces value systems and so this does not really help much except in scientific fields, and a few administrative situations where the decision field is ethically neutral.

[11] For this section we rely heavily on James G. March and Herbert A. Simon, *Organizations* (New York: John Wiley and Sons, Inc., 1958), chaps. 3 and 4.

Considering for now simply the initial decision to join or not to join an organization, we can say:

(1) $C > I \rightarrow$ the individual will not participate and will continue his search for *alternatives*.

(2) $C = I \rightarrow$ the individual is neutral to alternatives before him and will continue acquiring *information* on which to base a decision.

(3) $C < I \rightarrow$ the individual will participate in the organization which produces this perception.

Within the dynamics of the organization the individual may change his initial evaluation. If he finds, after experience, that contributions exceed inducements he will resume his search for alternatives and eventually change organizational affiliation. Satisfaction is closely connected to the inducement-contribution relationship. Factors which the individual perceives as lessening the satisfaction he derives from a particular organization will cause him to become mobile. If we are talking about an employment situation, then the ease of movement among organizations is affected by a number of variables, including economic conditions, and the age, sex, and training of the person.

So, the predictions we can make on the basis of $C > I$ and $C < I$ are fairly clear regardless of whether we are considering a person's initial decision to participate or a decision to remain in an organization as a participant. When we look at the $C = I$ relationship, some interesting problems are posed. For instance, can we expect that an initial $C < I$ perception may change to a $C = I$ perception? If so, what can we say about behavior under these circumstances?

The answer to the first question is, of course! Many after a time are confronted in job situations with the perception that their contributions are about balanced by the inducements offered. Such being the case, what are the consequences? One possibility is that a search for new alternatives either in or out of the organization may be motivated. Another possibility is that the individual may accept the situation at face value, do enough to retain organizational membership, and channel remaining energies elsewhere.

Burns made a very interesting study of the behavior of executives who experienced a termination of their career progress below the level of their expectations. At times, people will take refuge in a clique, where with the reinforcement of others in similar circumstances, an effective retreat from occupational status is accomplished. Speaking of such an executive clique Burns says, "their clique had a specifically protective reassurance purpose . . . [the executive] . . . furnishes himself and others with assurances that he in fact succeeded but the system was rigged against him, or that failure is not final but an episode in progress towards success, or that the status is one that he has not really claimed, or one in which it would be vulgar to succeed. . . ."[12]

Burns shows in his study how the clique acts as a countersystem to moderate the impact of failure. But more importantly the devaluation of their role in the executive's eyes does not mean they are paralyzed in its performance. The carryover of years of routine in addition to accumulated responsibilities of home and family are sufficient to motivate them to continuing satisfactory performance. They have important stakes in their positions which they are not likely to sacrifice just because their present $C = I$ perceptions do not accord favorably with the optimistic $C < I$ perceptions they had when they first joined the organization.

Thus, while a person's role perception changes, his aspirational levels also change often enough to bring about the equivalence between contributions and inducements. As Burns's analysis nicely points out such a change will not necessarily motivate an individual to change formal organizational connections. Rather efforts which might have been directed toward occupational success may be diverted to interests outside the occupation, including the maintenance of satisfaction producing informal work associations.

There is still another dimension to the inducement-contribution analysis with respect to the individual's acceptance of and compliance with legitimate authority. We may postulate that a person more likely than not will accept the legitimacy of the authority of his superior in a formal organizational setting if he also sees his participation producing greater rewards than contributions. The reverse holds true as well. The kind of leadership provided has much to do with satisfactions derived.

But we may ask how an individual is apt to respond to authority if he perceives his contributions equaling inducements. Following Barnard's conceptual scheme, he suggests that an individual is confronted by three possibilities when evaluating the orders of a superior.[13] There are those orders which are clearly unacceptable, those on the neutral line of acceptability: i.e., barely acceptable or unacceptable, and those clearly acceptable. Obviously the degree of acceptability or unacceptability of orders depends upon the individual's perception of the legitimacy of the superior person's authority. In the language of the last chapter, a high degree of positive compliance is likely to be forthcoming in response to orders from an individual enjoying considerable legitimacy in his position.

Now according to Barnard, the last group of orders, those which are clearly acceptable, lies within the *zone of indifference*. He says that:

The zone of indifference will be wider or narrower depending upon the degree to which the inducements exceed the burdens and sacrifices which

[12] Tom Burns, "The Reference of Conduct in Small Groups: Cliques and Cabals in Occupational Milieux," *Human Relations,* November, 1955, pp. 472 and 474.

[13] Chester I. Barnard, *Functions of the Executive* (Cambridge: Harvard University Press, 1938), pp. 168–69.

determine the individual's adhesion to the organization. It follows that the range of orders that will be accepted will be very limited among those who are barely induced to contribute to the system.[14]

Barnard's use of the term zone of indifference is unfortunate. It suggests a neutrality or passiveness toward authority and the orders stemming from it. However, this is far from Barnard's intended meaning. To him clearly acceptable orders receive positive compliance because they, ". . . lie within the range that in a general way was anticipated (by the individual) at time of undertaking the connection with the organization."[15]

Based on this line of analysis, we diagram in Figure 10–4 the relations which exist among the contribution-inducement variables and the authority compliance variables. Figure 10–4(a) shows authority is not perceived as legitimate and the individual probably will leave the organization as soon as an opportunity appears. Figure 10–4(c) depicts a wide range for the zone of indifference indicating acceptance of authority plus willing compliance to it. The neutral range in Figure 10–4(b) indicates that under circumstances where $C = I$ compliance to orders is secured less because of acceptance of legitimate authority and more as the result of the *power* exercised by persons vested with organizational position.

Decisions to Produce

Motivation to produce is a function of the character of the evoked set of alternatives . . . the perceived consequences of evoked alternatives . . . , and the individual goals . . . in terms of which alternatives are evaluated.[16]

The evoked set of alternatives means that each individual has frames of reference founded on his personality structure. Stimuli impinge upon the individual, evoking certain reactions. The reactions to production motivations depend on the "set" of psychologically based alternatives called forth by a stimulus.

Along with these alternatives are the systems of expectations and values interpreted by March and Simon as the perceived consequences of alternatives which might be selected by the individual as a course of action. Not every alternative will be weighted similarly by the individual. Some alternatives may appear more acceptable than others because of an individual's preconceptions. These preconceptions have strategic importance. Human behavior can be influenced (manipulated!) by changing an individual's value system.

Finally, decisions to produce are partially a function of individual

---

[14] *Ibid.*, p. 169.

[15] *Ibid.*, p. 169.

[16] March and Simon, *op. cit.*, p. 53.

FIGURE 10–4
The Zone of Indifference and Decision Variables

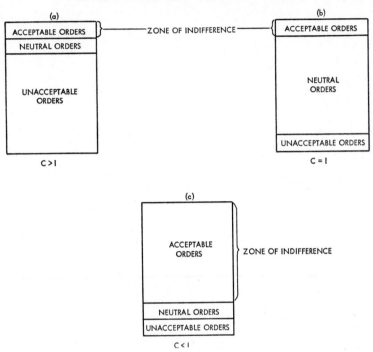

goals. An individual enters an organization with objectives in ordered arrangement. But these objectives are not immutable. He can be, and is more frequently than not, influenced by the groups, formal and informal, with which he comes in contact. The influence process conducted by the group is, of course, a method by which it preserves its integrity. More is said about the decision to produce in Chapter 14 which deals with productivity dynamics.

This section treated decisions as internal variables oriented around the individual but affected by the social and economic conditions of the organizational environment. Looked at this way decisions which an individual makes can be influenced by administrators through modifying organizational structure and climate. The decision process is an independent variable upon which the survival of the organization is based. From this point of view the organization is thought of as having inherent to its structure the ability to maximize survival needs through its decision processes.

ORGANIZATIONAL DECISIONS

Organizational decisions may be considered as the ways by which organizations adapt to change. March and Simon view such adaptation decisions as either routine or innovative.[17] The question is, under what circumstances will an organizational adjustment to change be quasi-automatic or routine, and under what circumstances will the adjustment be innovative? The answer lies in two interrelated considerations: the nature of the change itself, and the range of programs available to the organization for adjusting to changes. (A "program" means an established plan of action.)

The first circumstance deals with the routine adjustment to change. As shown in Figure 10–5, a change impinges on an organization. It perceives the change and identifies its nature. In this case, the change is identified as

FIGURE 10–5
Routine Adjustment of an Organization to Change

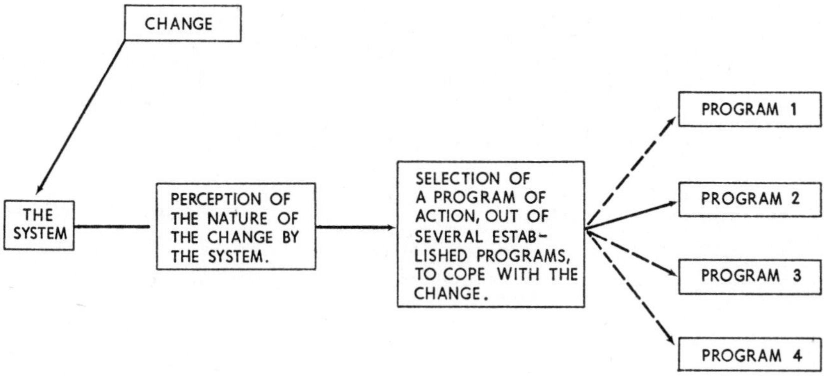

one which can be handled by using a program—program 2—in the organization's repertory of programs, 1, 2, 3, and 4. Thus, the system's adjustment to change becomes a routine, or quasi-automatic, matter of selecting one out of an established range of programs to cope with change. To summarize, if the change is perceived by the system as coming within the purview of established programs of action the adaptation made by the system to the change generally will be routine, or quasi-automatic.[18]

The second circumstance involves innovative or creative adaptation efforts. The need for innovation arises when adaptation to a change is outside the scope of the existing programs that keep the system in balance. The organization has to evolve new programs in order to maintain its internal harmony.

New programs are created by trial-and-error search for feasible alternatives of action to cope with a given change. But innovation is subject to two limitations, at least. First, the organization cannot simultaneously adapt all aspects of its structure to change. That is, certain aspects of an organization's structure have to be held stable, while other, more critically

---

[17] *Ibid.*, chaps. 6 and 7.
[18] *Ibid.*, pp. 139–40.

affected areas of the system are adjusted. As March and Simon state, ". . . in order for an organization to behave adaptively, it needs some stable regulations and procedures that it can employ for carrying out its adaptive practices."[19] Therefore, the process of innovation presupposes stability in certain segments of the system. By its very nature innovation cannot immediately extend to the total organization.

Second, innovation is limited by the quantity and variety of information present in a system at a particular time. For innovative purposes, new combinations of alternatives depend on four factors. The first of these is the possible range of output of the system, or the capacity of the system to supply information. Obviously, decision makers are limited in innovative activity by the capacity of the system to supply data. Alternatives, from which new programs of action are created, arise from the information available in the system. As this information is limited so also are the possibilities for finding appropriate action alternatives.

The second factor limiting innovation is the range of information available in the system's memory. Most human organizations have facilities for storing information, usually in the form of performance records, accounting data, historical information on competition, and the like. Also included in the memory of the system are past solutions to problems of change which appear to be similar but are not identical to the problem at hand. The capacity of the storage centers is not unlimited; therefore, the ability of the system to call on its memory of suitable action alternatives is restricted.

The third factor deals with the operating rules (programs) governing the analysis and flow of information within the system. This limitation on the use of information is similar to the first mentioned above. The use to which information is put for innovative purposes is regulated by the policies of the system. Some action alternatives may be distinct possibilities for change adjustment, but if they fall outside the policies of the firm they will be discarded as unusable.

The fourth factor is the system's ability to "forget" previously learned solutions to problems of change. This interesting limitation means that a system with too good a memory might narrow its behavioral choices to such an extent that innovation is stifled. Previously learned, old programs might be brought into play for an adjustment to change when newly innovated programs are necessary. Often this is what is meant when an organization is termed "inflexible"—it is incapable of learning for purposes of long-range adjustments.[20]

It is wise to leave the decision process at this point. The subject of organizational adaptation takes us directly to the concepts of balance.

---

[19] *Ibid.*, p. 170.

[20] For further discussion see Mervyn L. Cadwallader, "The Cybernetic Analysis of Change in Complex Social Organizations," *The American Journal of Sociology,* September, 1959, p. 156.

11

Balance Concepts

A SERIES of related concepts concerning organizational stability and adaptation to change are treated in this chapter. Some of the concepts elaborated here have been touched on previously. However, we intend to go into greater detail, developing several new notions.

BALANCE

Balance is an administrative concept. It has specific reference to human organizations and the elements comprising them. Before we deal directly with balance, it is best to consider certain preliminary ideas which bear on it.

The Black Box

The *black box* is an interesting idea found in the literature of physics and, more recently, in cybernetics.[1] It is particularly relevant to the analysis of complex organizations. The black box is a device for converting inputs into outputs. But the operations it employs to transform inputs are quite obscure. Indeed, the black box is never fully knowable! Its inscrutable nature is produced by two important properties:

1. The internal structure of the black box is highly complex. Elementary cause-effect relationships are impossible to find. The mind simply cannot comprehend the multitude of interconnections and interdependencies which exist among its parts through its linkage system.

2. The black box defies investigation of its innards because if it is tampered with it will change its internal properties. The significance of this statement should not be underestimated. It implies that experimentation with the black box could be futile, since the experimenter is not entirely certain his results are properly relevant to what he wished to study in the first place.

---

[1] For an excellent discussion of the black-box concept see W. Ross Ashby, "General Systems Theory as a New Discipline," in William E. Schlender, William G. Scott, and Alan C. Filley (eds.), *Management in Perspective* (Boston: Houghton Mifflin, 1965), pp. 396–400; see also Stafford Beer, *Cybernetics and Management* (New York: John Wiley and Sons, Inc., 1959), esp. chap. 6.

Thus, about all that can be known about the way the box functions is to observe what is put in and see how it comes out. From the changes occurring in the input, inferences can be drawn about the processes within the box which actually wrought the changes. As a consequence, incomplete knowledge of the box is obtained indirectly.

In spite of all this, the black box is not as stubborn as it seems. The black box is a system. And all systems have structures which lend them a certain degree of predictability. Therefore, the black box is not altogether capricious in its behavior. It can be ascertained that in response to certain inputs the black box will produce specified outputs. How this is accom-

FIGURE 11–1

The Balancing Process as It Appears to the Outside Observer

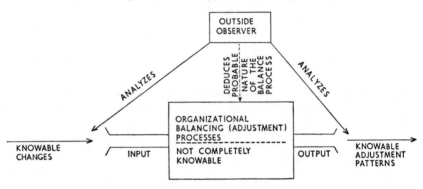

plished is not completely describable; in fact, for practical purposes it is not really necessary to know much about the internal operations of the box. Desired outputs can be had by modifying *strategic* inputs.

Human organizations are similar to the black box because: (1) they convert inputs of productive factors into outputs of goods and services; (2) they are often highly complex; and (3) they tend to rearrange their structure as a response to the introduction of foreign influences.

To elaborate point three: assume an organization is being observed by a detached, objective viewer who is making inferences about its operations. Now, suppose an experiment is undertaken to check the accuracy and validity of the conclusions arrived at through the observations. No matter how careful the experimenters are they inject a new element into the organization by their presence. In so doing, they rearrange the interactional patterns in such a way that they cannot be positive they are experimenting with the "same" organization previously observed.

Thinking in terms of the subject of this chapter, imagine that a change occurs in an organization. The change is arbitrarily called an input, although some may prefer the word "stimulus." The organization reacts, and an adjustment to the change follows. The adjustment is the output. Figure 11–1 shows that the outside observer can make some deductions regarding the balancing process by knowing the nature of the change (input) and by dissecting the adjustment (output). Complete understanding of the process, however, is hidden from the observer.

Next the observer decides to include himself as part of the organization to test the validity of his deductions by experiment and to gain a greater insight into the process of balance itself. He cannot, however, be assured that the adjustment process is the same after he has joined the organization. The best which can be said is that if the inputs and outputs are the same under both the conditions of observation and those of experiment, the investigator may be fairly confident that his presence has not affected the balancing process. He feels he has the right to say he understands it. The investigator's confidence is reinforced because his experiments support his observed deductions, *and* he has, in fact, been observing and experimenting with identical situations.[2]

What does all this mean for administrators? Is it true that their efforts to facilitate adjustment to change are futile, because organizational reactions to change are complex and unknowable? The answer to this question fortunately is no. Desired reactions to change (output) are obtained by controlling the changes (inputs) themselves. Management regulates the nature of changes so that the adjustments accord with the objectives of the organization and satisfy the needs of the people in it.

From an analytical standpoint, balance is an elusive concept. But as a result of observation, deduction, experimentation, intuition, and analogy some things can be said about the black-box process of balance. Generally, balance is considered as a process which reconciles and maintains structural interrelationships among the many forces and elements that make up the organization. Balance is a condition where there is accord among the objectives of individuals, the informal organization, jobs, and the formal organization. It is a process which acts to insure system stability in face of changing conditions which are either internal or external to the organization. The first definition treats balance in a management context specifically. The second definition has greater generality and is found frequently in the literature of the behavioral sciences. In essence the two definitions refer to the same process.

---

[2] The problem of observer interference in experimental situations has been mentioned in the Prologue. It is an issue not likely to be resolved in the behavioral sciences, but it at least should be recognized. The phenomenon of interference, in the form of experimental bias has been explored in an imaginative study by Robert Rosenthal *et al.* It was demonstrated in these studies that biases in research results, based upon certain preconceptions of those who formulated an experiment would still appear even though the formal work with subjects was three times removed from the originators of the study. See Robert Rosenthal, Gordon W. Persinger, Linda Vikan Kline, and Ray C. Mulry, "The Role of the Research Assistant in the Mediation of Experimental Bias," *Journal of Personality*, 31 (1963), pp. 313–35; and Robert Rosenthal, "On the Social Psychology of the Psychological Experiment: The Experimenter's Hypothesis as an Unintended Determinant of Experimental Results," *American Scientist*, 51 (1963), pp. 268–83.

Concepts Related to Balance

Equilibrium and, more recently, homeostasis are terms often encountered in the behavioral sciences. They pertain to concepts which are similar to balance. Balance, equilibrium, and homeostasis have some important differences. A little closer attention to the latter two ideas casts some light on balance and its administrative applications.

Equilibrium. Equilibrium refers to a state of adjustment between opposing forces. It also describes a tendency of a system to move toward a condition where the forces or influences in it are resolved. Two kinds of equilibrium are applied to social phenomena—static and dynamic.[3]

Static or stationary equilibrium is a situation where the environment of the system is held constant over a period of time. Dynamic equilibrium implies change and the ability of the system to preserve its internal structure of relationships despite a changing environment. Neither of these two forms of equilibrium carries the meaning that activities internal to the organization cease.

The equilibrium concept was borrowed from physics and has had a long tradition of application to economics. Somewhat more recently equilibrium has been used to describe processes in psychological and sociological research and theory. Pareto noted the usefulness of the idea in application to social systems, observing that systems have the tendency to return to a state of equilibrium if their original adjustment is disturbed.

Homeostasis. This word is derived from the Greek and means "steady state." It has been borrowed from biology and refers to a process by which a system regulates itself around a stable state. But as Penrose observes, "Strictly speaking, the basic principle [self-regulation] is not a biological one at all in spite of the name given it. It is a general principle of organization, examples of which may be found in biology, in mechanics and in social organization. . . ."[4]

Self-regulation requires feedback and control, both operating in such a way as to minimize the adverse effects of change on a system. On the surface, it appears that equilibrium and homeostasis are quite similar. However, all equilibrium states do not involve homeostasis. *Constancy does not imply feedback.* Davis[5] cites an example of a system moving through several states as follows: 10, 9, 8, 7, 6, 5, 4, 3, 2, 1 . . . . . ! If these states are not dependent on each other, and are equally probable, it is

---

[3] For a discussion of various types of equilibrium see David Easton, "Limits of the Equilibrium Model in Social Research," *Profits and Problems of Homeostatic Models in the Behavioral Sciences* (Chicago Behavioral Sciences Publications #1) (1953), pp. 26–40.

[4] Edith Tilton Penrose, "Biological Analogies in the Theory of the Firm," *American Economic Review*, December, 1952, pp. 804–19.

[5] R. C. Davis, "The Domain of Homeostasis," *Psychological Review*, Vol. 6 (1958), p. 10.

predictable that the next state is 0. The stability or equilibrium of this system is not dependent on a feedback mechanism.

Following Davis, homeostasis has feedback as its basic feature. That is, some energy must be taken from a latter part of the system and introduced in an earlier part so as to oppose the change produced there by the original input. In human systems information is analogous to energy and is a major part of feedback. Data pertaining to the status of a given result in terms of objective accomplishment are fed back so that modification of action can be made if necessary.

FIGURE 11–2
The General Principle of Feedback

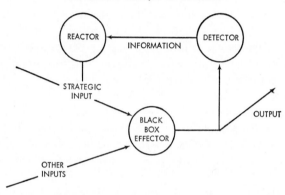

Source: Adapted from Pierre de Latil, *Thinking by Machine* (Boston: Houghton Mifflin Co., 1957), p. 50.

Thus, feedback is a process of retroaction whereby activities are modified in terms of what has been accomplished and what still needs to be done in order to reach a goal. Figure 11–2 illustrates the general principle of feedback.

The operational sequence of a feedback system is as follows.

1. The *detector* is sensitive to variations in the output produced by the black box (the effector); if variations exceed tolerance limits programmed during the planning function, information is sent by the detector to the reactor.

2. The *reactor* is sensitive to the reception of this information and is capable of adjusting the strategic input. It is important to note that in order to achieve outputs which conform to standards it is usually not necessary to change *all* the inputs. There may be one input, or input mix, which, if altered, will result in a change to an acceptable output condition.

To summarize what has been said so far, equilibrium has inherent to it the notion of the resolution of opposing forces. Homeostasis also incorporates this idea, but adds to it the matter of self-regulation. Both these concepts offer a useful way of viewing the interdependency of parts of a system. They are, however, not complete in themselves. They describe ends—constancy or stability under changing conditions. They do not specify particularized means whereby these ends are achieved.

Stability in the Simple System

Mills offers the adjustment process of an uncomplicated system as a first approximation explaining the means used by organization to preserve stability. He points out that at least three conditions are necessary for stability.[6]

First, all possibilities of behavior can be controlled. That is, all relevant behavioral alternatives which may emerge in reaction to change fall within the spectrum of the established control machinery. Control can assume numerous forms, including formal regulation through policies, standards, and rules. The informal organization exercises control over behavior by the group through norms, values, and sanctions of conduct.

Second, the system is able to allow for constructive change even though such a change may deviate from established norms. A discriminating ability between constructive and destructive changes is necessary because stability in a system does not imply stagnation. Indeed, stability may be dependent in some cases on the facility with which an organization is able to adapt to change. Adaptation requires the modification of organizational relationships.

Third, the system has a feedback mechanism. Once a change from standards is sensed evaluative action is initiated, and if necessary offsetting strategies are introduced.

Under these circumstances, the simple system would operate something like this:

$$A \qquad\qquad\qquad B$$
$$1 \quad 2 \quad 1 \quad 2 \quad 1 \quad 2\text{—change—control—}1 \quad 2 \quad 1 \quad 2 \quad 1 \quad 2$$

Starting with the pattern A a change is introduced. The control system is activated offsetting the change and preserving the structure of the system as indicated by pattern B.

Obviously, this is an oversimplification. But the example does at least point up some essential features of the stability process. All organizations have internal controls designed to maintain a harmonious relationship among the parts. Any change or deviant form of behavior will be interpreted in terms of the threat it poses to the stability and continuity of the system. If the organization interprets the change as a menace to its integrity actions will be set in motion to counterbalance the change.

The performance of the simple system is limited by at least four conditions.[7]

First, the effectiveness of the stability process is restricted by lack of

---

[6] Adapted from Theodore M. Mills, "Equilibrium and the Processes of Deviance and Control," *American Sociological Review*, October, 1959, pp. 673-74.

[7] *Ibid.*, p. 677.

information regarding the change. Because of this limitation, change-combating strategies may be totally ineffective for the preservation of stability.

Second, each system, like formal organization, is composed of subsystems which may be pressed into an unwanted readjustment because of the power exerted by one subsystem relative to the other. For example, an informal organization could be forced into a realignment of its values, status positions, and standards of conduct because technological change is forced on it by the formal organization. The informal group may resist and strive to maintain its established structure. But the power exerted by the formal organization is too strong to withstand. The informal organization capitulates grudgingly. A tenuous truce emerges.

Third, the individual seeking personal ends can undermine stability. Individual goals are not necessarily integrated with organizational goals. The amount and the way in which personal objectives deviate from those of the system determine the extent to which stability is reduced.

Fourth, the system buys stability at a price. Feedback and control cost, if not in dollars then in some other value. The value of stability is weighed against the cost of control. If the cost is too high for the value derived, then some stability is sacrificed.

Some suggest that we look at the human organization as a cybernetic system.[8] Such a point of view is useful particularly in the context of the subjects being considered here and in the previous chapter on decision making.

Cybernetics raises several questions regarding the system.

a) How are decision centers connected, and how are they maintained? Corollary to this question: what is the structure of the feedback system; that is, how is control information transmitted from the point of performance to the decision centers?

b) What information is stored in the system and at what points? Corollary: how accessible is this information to the decision-making centers?

c) How conscious is the organization of the operation of its own parts? To what extent do the policy centers receive control information with sufficient frequency and relevancy to create a real awareness of the operation of the segments of the system?

d) What are the learning (innovating) capabilities of the system?[9]

Answers to the questions posed by cybernetics are crucial to understanding the decision, balancing, and communication processes in systems. Although cybernetics has been applied largely to technical-engineering problems of automation, the model of feedback, control, and regulation in all systems has a good deal of generality.

---

[8] See Beer, *op. cit.*, esp. chap. 16; and Gordon Pask, *An Approach to Cybernetics* (New York: Harper and Bros., 1961), chap. 8.

[9] These questions are adapted from Karl W. Deutsch, "On Communication Models in the Social Sciences," *Public Opinion Quarterly*, 16 (1952), pp. 368–70.

The Nature of Balance

Balance is a valuable concept. Unlike equilibrium and homeostasis, which are largely automatic mechanical, electrical, or biological processes, balance pertains to cognitive and administrative properties of open systems like the individual and the human organization.

Balance at the Level of the Individual. Some psychological literature is devoted to balance theory as it applies to the motivation of behavior. While motivation is discussed in Chapters 3 and 14, it is viewed here in a somewhat different light.

Pilisuk observes that attitudes are cognitions with signs. That is, attitudes have positive and negative valences. An odd number of negative signs in an associative cluster of attitudes (a set) produces a state of "cognitive dissonance" which leads to a behavioral action aimed at restoring balance, i.e., an even number of negative signs in the attitudinal set.[10]

There is nothing especially mysterious about this. Imagine that you are an office worker with a strong dislike toward a union which is attempting to organize your company (negative valence). You have a friend of long standing with whom you share a good many activities (positive valence). At the time of the union organizing effort you find that your friend also dislikes unions (negative valence). The resulting set is:

1. You dislike unions (−).
2. You have a friend (+).
3. Who dislikes unions (−).

For you there is no cognitive dissonance and no behavioral motivation to restore balance to the set.

Suppose, however, you favor unions and you have a friend who dislikes unions. The new set is:

1. You favor unions (+).
2. You have a friend (+).
3. Who dislikes unions (−).

The individual now may adopt one of three strategies, or a succession of strategies, to restore balance in this attitudinal set. He might (1) try to

---

[10] See Marc Pilisuk, "Cognitive Balance, Primary Groups, and the Patient-therapist Relationship," in Warren G. Bennis *et. al.* (eds.), *Interpersonal Dynamics* (Homewood, Ill.: The Dorsey Press, 1964), pp. 486–89. See also Leon Festinger, *A Theory of Cognitive Dissonance* (Evanston: Row, Peterson and Company, 1957), esp. chap. 1.

We must inject a critical note here. The theory of valences is deceptively attractive at the *logical* level because it is predicated on the assumption that man acts to acquire symmetry in his attitudinal clusters. What is underplayed is that on the *existential* level people may ignore unsymmetrical (odd number of negative valences) attitudinal sets as relevant behavioral motivators. That is, an ideological issue, like unions, might be avoided among friends differing in values. It may not be allowed to enter the realm of interpersonal relations. What we are saying is since so many variables are involved at the existential level of behavior a concept which is based upon a restricted number of value cognitions may suffer greatly as a predictive device.

convert his friend to like unions, (2) change his own mind about unions, or (3) drop his friend. In any case, the important point is that imbalance in an attitudinal set, or cognitive dissonance as Festinger calls it, will motivate behavior directed at resolving the disequilibrating forces.

Balance at the Level of Organizations. Balance is a goal of conscious managerial effort. Therefore, it is an administrative concept as well as a psychological one. It has reference to the major components which comprise complex formal organizations. There are four distinct components.

1. The *individuals* in organizations as independent "open systems" in themselves.

2. Organizational *roles* which include for work-oriented organizations, jobs, functional processes, and even the physical equipment necessary to do the jobs.

3. *Small groups,* or the informal organizations which supply need satisfactions to their members apart from formal job requirements. These organizations have status and role systems often independent of formal status differentiations.

4. The *formal* organization which is the overall status hierarchy plus structure, policy-making, and coordination activities.

These elements are interdependent and can be viewed by an administrator from a number of frames of reference: he can think of these factors

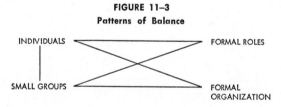

FIGURE 11–3
Patterns of Balance

in terms of their interaction in the organization as a whole, in a division, or within his own department. A convenient way of looking at balance is through the patterns-of-balance diagram.

The purpose of this diagram is to show that there are ten areas of conflict or harmony of *objectives* among the factors on the chart. Each element on the chart has objectives which may or may not be in accord with the objectives of the other elements.[11] The objectives of any one element—say, individuals—can conflict or be in balance with the objective

---

[11] Except in the case of "job" and "formal organization" where it is assumed for the sake of simplicity that jobs which are no longer useful will be eliminated. Job elimination and consolidation are largely technical problems. However, even this relationship has behavioral overtones. Jobs may not be dropped, or redundant functions may be added, because of the personal power of individuals in the organization. Empire building is an example of this situation. An individual may expand his activities to enhance prestige. The jobs which are created do not serve to meet the objectives of the organization. Rather, they may indeed be in conflict with its objectives.

of the other elements. As a result, the objectives of one element in the diagram may be in conflict with one other element, two others, or all of them. But, for that matter, an element can also be in balance with all the other elements.

The balance concept is not an automatic, problem-solving device. It is a way of demonstrating the interdependencies which administrators face in complex organizations. Achieving and maintaining balance among organizational components, is, of course, an administrative responsibility. The primary obligation rests with those who have supervisory responsibility. They are the ones who "manage" systems of interpersonal relations.

Management is the human instrumentality which consciously acts to produce balanced organizational relationships. While equilibrium and homeostasis are useful for conceptual purposes, they are impersonal and automatic. The processes which maintain body temperature at a fairly constant level are homeostatic. But the functioning of sweat glands is hardly similar to the administration of an organization.

An open system like an organization either changes or it fails to survive.[12] The only way to exist in a changing environment is for the organization itself to change. Balance pertains to management's ability to modify formal systems and the operational climate of the organization in face of shifting technological, economic, and social conditions.

Obviously, the caliber of management is a key variable associated with adjustment to change. But even the best management is limited to the extent it can accomplish such adjustment. Limitations are inherent in the system itself. These limitations are very similar to those noted in this chapter with respect to simple systems. Additionally, it can be said that the rate management is able to adjust to change is, in part, dependent on the way in which the organization has structured its method of solving problems. Ideally, the structure should be such that it encompasses the widest range of possible changes which might arise. However, something less than the optimum must be accepted because of limitations on organization resources and human ability to foresee the future.

In addition to all this, balance is a time-oriented concept. A balanced organization is one which:

1. Exhibits continuity with the past. The past contributes to stability by giving the organization an identity.

2. Affords management control over the present direction and amount of change in policy, structure, personnel, and physical facilities.

3. Offers a workable degree of predictability for the future. As we have said before, organizational change is predicated on stability of some parts while undergoing modification of other parts. Predictability of certain balanced relationships is essential to planned change.

---

[12] In fact Bennis has pointed out that flexibility is the key criterion for judging organizational health. Warren G. Bennis, *Changing Organizations* (New York: McGraw-Hill Book Co., Inc., 1966), pp. 50 ff.

PART IV

Problems and Issues in the Analysis

IT WOULD BE CONVENIENT if each of the chapters in this part could be paired with another in Parts II and III. We then could analyze certain administrative issues and problems by associating them with a particular cluster of concepts. But this is not possible. We might claim, for example, that the chapter on motivation, productivity, and incentives is the counterpart of Chapter 3, "Personality Dynamics and Motivation." It could be argued that the individual is motivated, makes decisions to produce, and is influenced by incentives. No doubt this is true. But the overall logic is not impressive because we know that there are many forces in the social territory which shape an individual's behavior. Productivity and motivation may be discussed in conceptual terms drawn from a number of sources in previous chapters, for instance, leadership, decision making, and small group influence. The same can be said for the other subjects which pose problems and issues for administrators. We can discuss them fruitfully in several conceptual dimensions.

We select in this part of the book subjects for discussion which represent either or both normative and action problems for administrators. These problems and issues are not arbitrarily chosen. They are enduring matters which have been scrutinized at length in the literature of administration and the behavioral sciences. We can hardly ignore, for example, such issues as bureaucracy and the recommendations for modifying the organization. Nor could we overlook the insistence by numerous writers that the organization of work be made more compatible with the needs of the individual.

Part IV has subparts which contain three main classes of problems and normative issues. The first deals with problems of organizational change. The second discusses problems of influence and the third concerns relevant issues at various levels of management.

The reader should study the issues not only in terms of what is on the remaining pages, but also in terms of what he feels can be derived from preceding chapters in application to these problems. This suggests, therefore, that matters dwelt on in Parts I, II, and III are key conceptual foundations to this part.

The connections between chapters in this part are loosely drawn. But there is one common theme. It is implicit throughout these chapters that the type of organization providing the framework for the problems and issues is large in size and fairly bureaucratized in structure. A predisposition of this sort could be challenged. But the trends toward large organizations are evident in business, government, labor, and voluntary nonprofit organizations. So this commends the orientation of this part to issues as they appear in the perspective of the large organization.

PART IV-A

Problems and Issues in the Territory

CHAPTER 12

Bureaucracy

THE TARGET of organizational change is bureaucracy. It has been the subject of criticism for a number of years; and recently it has come under intense attack by the advocates of planned change. Since this subsection is concerned with "changing the organization," it is a good idea to have a notion of what it is changing from. Specifically, the reaction, led by the industrial humanists, is against formalization and the "ideal" of rationality in administration. Thus industrial humanism stands as a counterfoil to classical organization theory of which bureaucracy is a prime manifestation.

THE SCOPE OF THE STUDY OF BUREAUCRACY

The study of bureaucracy has proceeded along two lines.[1] First, the traditional approach is the study of bureaucracy as an administrative tool. This view is attributed to Max Weber.[2] The bureaucratic organization is seen in this respect as a mechanism for the achievement of goals. To Weber, the bureaucracy is the epitome of rationality. No other form of organization, to him, could grind out goal accomplishment better. The second and a somewhat more recent view is concerned with bureaucracy as an instrument of power and influence. Within the context of this view are a number of subtopics including the effect of human behavior on the so-called rational organization instrument, the modification and stagnation of bureaucratic goals, the internal power plays of bureaucratic functionaries, and the relationship of bureaucracies to society as a whole. In short, the study of bureaucracy in this sense looks at the *process* and *implications* of bureaucratization rather than the static characteristics of the machine itself.

Why Do Bureaucracies Develop?

A civilization must reach a certain degree of maturity before bureaucracies emerge to exert a significant influence on the life patterns of people

---

[1] See S. N. Eisenstadt, "Bureaucracy, Bureaucratization, and Debureaucratization," *Administrative Science Quarterly*, 4 (1959–60), p. 303.

[2] See Max Weber, "The Essentials of Bureaucratic Organization: An Ideal-Type Construction," in Robert K. Merton *et al.* (ed.), *A Reader in Bureaucracy* (Glencoe: The Free Press, 1952), pp. 18–27.

in a society. The institutions in society must be differentiated in terms of the role they play. Differentiation takes place along functional lines; for example, the separation of the economic functions from the family. In this case, the family is no longer the locus of the production of goods and services. Instead, such activities are centralized in specialized institutions.[3]

Once differentiation occurs the selection of individuals to perform tasks in bureaucracies is based on possession of the necessary qualifications for adequate dispatch of the duties. In other words, bureaucracies require that individuals, to "qualify" for their roles in differentiated organizations, possess specialized forms of training and education.

The society as a whole must be in a position to supply the resources for support of bureaucratic organizations. As such, society is expected to underwrite bureaucratic activities. Theoretically, therefore, the bureaucracy has to pursue socially acceptable goals.

Implicitly, a society which is ripe for bureaucratization is highly complex, exhibiting considerable interdependence among its parts. Under these circumstances social needs can best be met by marshaling and administering resources in centralized bureaucratic organizations. Some social demands requiring centralization are imposed from the outside, like war. Other demands are internal, such as when agricultural, employment, or tax problems are thought to be more efficiently solved through centralization of authorities.

Many bureaucracies exist in a modern society: governmental bureaucracies, military bureaucracies, labor bureaucracies, and business bureaucracies, to name a few. Within these institutional segments are discrete bureaucratic organizations which represent aggregations of power in competition with other bureaucracies for resources which supposedly will be channeled to meet some social need. However, with proliferation bureaucracies are propelled into a power situation. The bureaucracy in a mature society must engage in activities which enhance its power and its ability to compete with other bureaucracies for a favorable allocation of resources. Thus, the accumulation of power and the wielding of influence are adjuncts of bureaucracies in mature societies regardless of whether these societies are totalitarian or democratic.

BUREAUCRATIC ORGANIZATION

The term "bureaucracy" can be taken to apply to all sizes and types of formal organizations. Thus, bureaucracy is part of the general extension of organized activities into most facets of life in our society. The study of bureaucracy consists of the analysis of formal organizational structures, of human behavior within these structures, and of power and influence.

---

[3] See Eisenstadt, *op. cit.*, pp. 305–8; and Peter Blau, *Bureaucracy in Modern Society* (New York: Random House, 1956), pp. 27–44.

The words "bureaucracy" and "bureaucrat" are emotionally charged. They conjure up a gigantic governmental organization of monumental inefficiency peopled with lazy, narrow-minded functionaries. This stereo-type centers on shortcomings. Actually, bureaucracy is a characteristic possessed to a greater or lesser extent by most formal organizations. In this discussion, therefore, it seems to be far more fruitful to speak of a degree of bureaucratization rather than of bureaucracy or nonbureaucracy in an absolute sense.

Bureaucracies neither have to be large nor do the people in them have to display a uniform type of behavior which is supposedly repugnant to "nonbureaucratic" behavior. Bureaucracies have only two elementary characteristics—rules which prescribe and govern functional relationships; and rules which prescribe and govern behavioral patterns and desirable habits of members of the organization. It can be seen readily, therefore, that the concepts of bureaucracy extend to just about every formal organization in an ordinary person's experience.

The Characteristics of the "Ideal" Bureaucratic Instrument

As stated earlier, one method of studying bureaucracy is as a tool of administration. In this respect, the framework of analysis differs little from that applied to conventional formal-organization theory. However, there are several points stemming from bureaucratic analysis worth men-tioning here.

Weber, in his treatment of bureaucracy, emphasizes its superiority over other organizational types. The source of this superiority is based in rationalization and the utilization of technical knowledge. As a result, the bureaucracy is able to achieve the highest degree of efficiency for accom-plishing objectives. The ideal bureaucracy has, in the Weberian sense, the following characteristics.[4]

1. A clear division of labor is found in which regular tasks are distributed in a fixed way and legitimatized by recognition as official duties.
2. Functions are arranged hierarchically, resulting in a chain of com-mand—the scalar principle.
3. All activities in the bureaucracy are governed by abstract rules which are applied uniformly in particular cases.
4. Officials of the bureaucracy act impersonally in the application of rules to the internal affairs of the organization and to contacts outside the organiza-tion.
5. The selection criteria for employment applicants are based on the quali-fications of the applicant relative to objective standards for the job set by the officials of the bureaucracy.

Weber implies that any deviation from the ideal bureaucratic frame-work reduces the efficiency with which the organization operates. Yet it is

[4] As cited in Blau, *op. cit.*, pp. 28–32.

difficult to consider these standards meaningfully if they are taken in an absolute sense. It is more plausible to talk of the degree of bureaucratization in formal organizations. In this regard, Carl Friedrich presents six criteria which are useful as tests of the extent of bureaucratic development.[5] They are:

1. *The degree of functional differentiation:* How far has the division of labor gone in an organization?

2. *The degree of centralization of control and supervision:*

   a) How complex are the organizational problems of coordination and communication? The greater these problems are the more bureaucratic the organization has become.

   b) How many levels are there in the scalar chain? The larger the number of levels of subordination the more bureaucratic the organization.

3. *The degree of qualification for office:* To what extent have the requirements for employment in specific tasks been spelled out according to objective standards?

4. *The degree of objectivity:* How much pride do employees of the bureaucracy derive from recognition of their technical competence by fellow bureaucrats? (Technical competence in this sense means mastery and application of bureaucratic rules and procedures.)

5. *The degree of precision and continuity:* How much do employees adhere to precedents and routines essential to the preservation of complex administrative machinery?

6. *The degree of discretion:* To what extent do employees exercise judgment in making known or withholding information of a special character to the public at large? Presumably a bureaucratic organization of a high degree restricts information to a greater extent than a bureaucratic organization of a lesser degree.[6]

On the basis of these six standards some degree of bureaucratization is evident in formal organizations of many different sizes. However—although this cannot be taken as a general rule—the larger the organization becomes the more bureaucratic it becomes. Sometimes this statement is assumed to be a self-evident truth, but it is interesting to investigate possible reasons underlying it. Clues might be found in the notion that larger organizations are more stable than smaller organizations. Caplow offers several points in support of this idea.[7]

---

[5] Carl Joachim Friedrich, *Constitutional Government and Politics* (New York: Harper and Bros., 1937), pp. 32–40.

[6] Merton says, "Bureaucracy is administration which almost completely avoids public discussion of its techniques, although there may occur public discussion of its policies." Robert K. Merton, "Bureaucratic Structure and Personality," in Robert K. Merton *et al.* (ed.), *Reader in Bureaucracy* (New York: The Free Press of Glencoe, 1952), p. 363.

[7] Theodore Caplow, "Organization Size," *Administrative Science Quarterly,* 1 (1950–51), pp. 501–2.

1. Large organizations afford more chance for greater vesting of interests than small organizations.

2. Large organizations tend to support each other. Society generally will not tolerate the collapse of a large organization.

3. Large organizations frequently have a wide range of activities so that disaster to one activity does not jeopardize the entire organization.

4. Large organizations apparently devote a greater proportion of their resources to the maintenance of their internal operations such as communication, control, and coordination. Through making these allocations the large organization has greater control over its continuity and ultimate survival than the small organization.

Caplow's stabilizing influences add up to these conclusions about bureaucratic tendencies in large organizations.

1. Vested interests make the crystallization and perpetuation of rules governing functional relationships, procedures, and behavioral patterns more convenient.

2. Society preserves the large organization because it cannot stand the consequences if the organization should be lost. Thus, society at the same time supports implicitly the intensification of bureaucratic practices which grow as the organization grows in protected surroundings.

3. Through multiplication of activities and objectives the bureaucracy enhances its survival prospects. Diversification enhances stability. For example, the March of Dimes organization continued even after the discovery of the Salk vaccine because it changed the objectives of its program.

4. By having command over considerable resources the large organization can take steps to insure its integrity over time. It can structure and run its internal operations more effectively and it can exercise more power and influence in society than can the small organization.

Some Facets of Bureaucratic Behavior

The six criteria of bureaucratization fall into two categories. The first three are impersonal *expectations of bureaucratic organizations.* That is bureaucracies are expected to have specialization of labor, centralized authority as the method of coordination, and a rational program of personnel administration which is expressed in the criteria as "qualifications for office." Next are the three personal criteria concerned with the *behavior expected of those who hold bureaucratic positions:* objectivity, precision and continuity, and discretion. Of these six criteria, the rational program of personnel administration is pivotal in the analysis so we focus on it.

The Rational Program of Personnel Administration. The recruitment, selection, placement, transfer, promotion, and release of personnel are involved in this aspect of bureaucracy. It provides the link between the functional and coordinative needs of the organization and the way people are expected to act who are employed by such an organization. In other words, people are sought who will perform functions with objectivity, discretion, and precision. This criterion presumably assures the organization of a flow of individuals who are both technically and emotionally equipped to discharge effectively the responsibilities of their position. Two issues are raised. One concerns selective versus saturative policies of choosing people for bureaucratic posts. The other relates to the classic reconciliation of authority-capacity variables in bureaucratic positions.

1. *Bureaucratic Recruitment.* Early forms of bureaucracy were selective in the sense of recruiting members from special segments of society. Thus, the military, the church, the government tended to draw recruits from certain social strata to the exclusion of others. This situation is dangerous in a democratic sense. The selective bureaucracy appeals to a segment of society which Smith says to be "atypical"[8] since the values of the segment may not represent the values of the whole society. Thus society's values are subjugated to rule by a group whose standards and goals are not representative. All in all, the more selective bureaucratic recruitment is the greater the chance that socially beneficial ends are jeopardized.

The alternative of selective recruitment is saturative. Through saturative recruitment the bureaucracy draws employees from a wider social cross section. This does not mean, however, that the bureaucracy has become less concerned about the "qualification for office" standard. It simply has offered the opportunity to compete for positions to more people from many layers of the social structure.

In order to compete, aspirants for jobs must have access to the education or training necessary for meeting the qualification requirements. There is some evidence that bureaucracies are drawing employees from a broader base. Formal education has been a force in making this transition possible.[9] Access to education, then, is the first step toward saturative bureaucracy. Ideally, the more saturative the bureaucracies in our society are the more likely they will be to administer their affairs in the public interest rather than for a restricted clique.

2. *Authority-Capacity.* The classic position with respect to these variables is discussed in Chapter 5. Recall the assumption that the optimum relationship between the two is equality. It is based on an operational definition of authority as the totality of the content of a position—both command and functional. Capacity refers to the personal abilities of individuals to perform up to the expectations of roles. One objective of the rational program of personnel administration is to bring about this equivalence. Of course, responsibility for administration of the program rests with "line" executives with the help of "staff." Naturally, in an

---

[8] Edmund Arthur Smith, "Bureaucratic Organization: Selective or Saturative," *Administrative Science Quarterly*, 2 (1957–58), pp. 361–75.

[9] Joseph R. Gusfield, "Equalitarianism and Bureaucratic Recruitment," *Administrative Science Quarterly*, 2 (1957–58), pp. 521–41.

organization having a high degree of bureaucratization, "personnel guidelines" in the form of rules, procedures, and policies circumscribe executive action.

Dysfunctional Consequences of Bureaucratic Behavior

The centralization of authority for control purposes, the emphasis on reliability in the behavior of bureaucrats, the dependence on rules for uniformity, and objective application of policies create results which are unanticipated and unwanted. These results are discussed at length by various authors. Most influential has been the work of Gouldner, Selznick, and Merton whose models are treated at length by March and Simon in their book *Organizations*.[10] In general these scholars say that bureaucratic processes produce inherent contradictions. Let us look briefly at three aspects of the argument.

The Dysfunction of Structure. Merton focuses on bureaucratic problems of control. The response of the bureaucratic official in terms of uniformity, objectivity, and precision and continuity needs of the organization creates the problem of rigidity of behavior with respect to the clients of the organization.

The emphasis bureaucracy places on structural maintenance leads to sanctification of procedure and to domineering attitudes of officials. Although apparently quite unlike, these two structural pathologies have one thing in common: the frequent failure of the bureaucratic functionary to separate means from ends. Procedures which are means become ends for the functionary who is imbued with the sanctity of impersonal application of abstract rules.

Restricted to the domain of his function, resulting from the division of labor, the bureaucratic official often becomes domineering when dealing with the public. While acting within his own province he gives the impression that he actually speaks for and represents the character of the entire organization. Such behavior is self-defeating for a bureaucracy which ultimately relies on public support for its existence. It is interesting in this respect to note the care which large protected utilities exercise when instructing employees in "proper" behavior in customer relations.

Dysfunctions of Subordinated Groups. Just as the total bureaucratic organization is a center of power so also are suborganizations within the structure power centers. Subordinate power centers can arise as typical informal organizations or they can appear as power groups by virtue of their position in the formal organization. In either event, the power adhering to these subgroups may be sufficient to detract the bureaucracy from its major purposes, by displacing resources into the accomplishment of the subgoals of special interest cliques.

---

[10] See James G. March and Herbert A. Simon, *Organizations* (New York: John Wiley and Sons, Inc., 1958), pp. 36–52.

Selznick describes the process underlying goal displacement.[11] He observes that the division of labor requires the delegation of authority to minor officials. Such delegations set the stage for a division of interest between those who initiate action (the top authorities) and those who carry out action (the intermediate authorities).[12]

The initiator most often is prompted in policy formulation to pursue ultimate organization goals. Whereas the intermediary, having another social position and role, is sometimes prompted to seek goals which are different from those set on top. As a consequence a struggle ensues between these groups for control over the organizational mechanisms which will enable each group to solve the problems of their own special interest.

Because the intermediaries possess skills, technical qualifications, and proximity to the machinery of implementation in the organization, they are in a strategic position to dominate in the power struggle. If this occurs, the intermediate group is able to establish the goals for the entire organization, leaving higher officials to rubber-stamp lower-level decisions.

Thus the organization moves away from its original purpose toward aims which are internally generated by lower-level executives. There is no doubt that this situation is pathological from the standpoint of organizational effectiveness and social relevance. It is representative of a case where the *actual* center of power does not correspond to the formal center of power; that is, the individuals occupying the top positions in the structure are not the people who make decisions regarding the purposes and directions to be assumed by the organization.

This situation usually does not arise where top administrators are able to retain the right of review and control, plus sufficient proximity to intermediate organizational levels for effective appraisal of performance in the light of policy. A situation of this sort is more probable when top management *abdicates* control or becomes so *distant* from the point of policy implementation that adequate appraisal is nearly impossible. Both these conditions go hand-in-hand. The implication is that the larger the organization grows the more likely it is for the center of power to devolve on the intermediate levels, in which case the organization tends to depart from its original purposes. Hence, the bureaucratic machine becomes the instrument for the satisfaction of special interests rather than an efficient device for achieving social goals.

---

[11] Philip Selznick, "An Approach to a Theory of Bureaucracy," *American Sociological Review*, February, 1943, pp. 51–52.

[12] A distinction is made between a division of interest and a division of interpretation. The former involves a conflict in objectives between two groups; the latter pertains to a breakdown in communication between two groups. See David M. Levitan, "The Responsibility of Administrative Officials in a Democratic Society," *Political Science Quarterly*, 61 (1946), p. 568.

An associated dysfunction in this category is suboptimization. In this situation, the performance of a subordinated unit of an organization is maximized to the net disadvantage of the total system. This is often the result of giantism and system complexity which is caused by purely technical difficulties in determining objectives and the allocation of resources. Management science is aimed at correcting these problems if they fall in this class. But the problem may also be the result of "empire building." Frequently, organizational "audits" are used to find these cases and adjust them. However, audits and suboptimization tendencies are subject to the conditions of internal power plays, and trading and bargaining among executives. So the use of audit groups to ensure compliance to objectives, policies, and regulations is not necessarily the answer to behavior which moves counter to the overall efficiency aims of the organization.

Dysfunctional Character of Rules. The bureaucratic use of rules to secure uniformity in administrative practices generates, according to Gouldner, a tendency for functionaries to perform at the lowest minimum acceptable level (because unacceptable behavior has been defined). This in turn creates superior-subordinate tension which causes closer supervisory practices attended by more rules and authoritarian leader behavior.

Thus, we see that bureaucratic imperatives for control of behavior give rise to events which actually impair the functioning of the organization. Rules give rise to more rules and autocratic behavior. Uniformity produces rigidity in client relations. The emphasis on precision and continuity sets the stage for goal displacement and suboptimization. All in all, the bureaucratic form of organization appears less than ideal in Weber's sense, as a means for accomplishing goals. However, there are two more issues of greater concern which we treat next.

Goal Displacement or Goal Succession?

It must be clear by now that bureaucracy is a tool by which people solve problems. As such its life is predicated on the accomplishment of socially acceptable ends. But as an organization endures and grows it, at times, remains merely figuratively associated with the purpose it was originally constituted to achieve. New goals emerge. This transition of objectives is what is meant by the displacement or succession of goals. On the one hand, succession of goals refers to the healthy adaptation of the organization to meet changing needs. The accomplishment of past goals becomes the foundation supporting new and socially relevant objectives. On the other hand, goal displacement pertains to a switch from the pursuit of social ideals to a conservative policy which values the preservation of the organization for the sake of preservation.[13]

Many years ago Robert Michels wrote a significant book called *Political Parties* in which he proposed the "iron law of oligarchy." His thesis is

---

[13] For a discussion of goal succession and displacement see Blau, *op. cit.*, p. 95.

that bureaucracy is fundamentally opposed to democratic ideals. Further, he says there is an inevitable tendency as organizations get larger to become more tyrannical and stagnant with the final cost borne by society. The organization comes to exist for itself; bureaucratic preservation emerges as an end of the first priority. With such a displacement of goals, Michels concludes that, "THAT WHICH IS oppresses THAT WHICH OUGHT TO BE."[14]

At the heart of the issue of goal displacement or succession is the matter of responsibility. A bureaucracy is not responsible if it exists for itself only nominally serving the public which supports it. The responsible bureaucracy is one which is able to adapt its ends to meet changing social needs. The basic question is: where are the sources of pressures in society for responsibility?

Some look to the impersonal free market as the source of pressure for organizations operating in the economic segment of society. Others find the electorate as the source of pressure forcing responsible behavior on government bureaucracies. And still others look to the membership of unions as the source of pressure on labor leaders.

Where the public fails to exert pressure for responsible performance a vacuum is created allowing for the exercise of irresponsible power by administrators. Rapoport has observed that, "There is hope only if the players of the power game are to some extent receptive to public pressure."[15] It must be added, however, that the motives to exert pressure for responsibility in administrative leadership have to be stirred first. As Blau notes, in our complex civilization innovation and progress may be obtainable in the future largely through the bureaucratic mechanism. The challenge to the public is to maintain sufficient vigilance to ensure that bureaucracies move in the direction of socially valuable goal succession rather than socially futile goal displacement.

Democracy or Autocracy?

Of concern in a democratic society is the way institutions comprising it are run. The issue seems to be whether democracy in subsidiary units of American society is necessary for the preservation of democracy in the state as a whole. Without much reflection, the inclination is to say, "it is." But on second thought, this is found in only a few so-called democratic states. Many organizations making them up are autocratic. Business, government, military, and numerous unions are far from meeting democratic ideals.

Thus, there is not a unity of opinion among writers on the relationship between the practice of democracy in component social institutions and

---

[14] Robert Michels, *Political Parties* (New York: The Free Press of Glencoe, 1958; first published 1915), p. 418.

[15] Anatol Rapoport, *Fights, Games, and Debates* (Ann Arbor: University of Michigan Press, 1960), p. 308.

society as a whole. Some feel it is the key for achieving the ideals of political equality and economic opportunity. Others say that democracy is possible in a state without widespread democratic practices in its major institutions.

This issue is one which cannot be resolved here, if it can be settled at all. However, the major arguments follow so the reader may determine some of the dimensions of the issue.

Pro:

1. If democracy is a superior form of political organization, it should levels of human satisfaction are possible.

2. When people have an effective voice in organizational affairs, higher levels of human satisfaction are possible.

3. If policy initiators break contact with organizational participants they will lose the source of creativity and innovation which contribute to healthy goal succession.

4. Whenever power is present, in the hands of organizational administrators, it should be offset by democratic processes.

Con:

1. Most organizations have not had sufficient experience with systems of checks and balances which provide truly effective democratic controls for protecting member rights.

2. Most major organizations in our society are hierarchial, hence disposed to autocracy. In part, this has resulted from the fact that the problems which an organization faces can be more efficiently handled by a centralization of authority.

3. Certain organizations, like the military, function better if removed from the diffuse pressures of democratic life.

4. The need for unity in the face of external conflict does not admit democratic practice.

No doubt the trend today, inspired by liberal humanism, is away from autocratic bureaucratization. Apart from pure idealism, however, Bennis says, "that democracy in organizations is inevitable," because the nature of work and the people who do it have changed.

CHAPTER 13

Modifying the Organization

IN THE LAST CHAPTER and in Chapter 5 we discussed the nature of bureaucracy and the character of formalization at length. The assumptions and processes comprising the so-called classic model of organization have dominated administrative thought for many years. In spite of the fact that bureaucracy has dysfunctional aspects, suppressive authoritarianism, and often results in goal displacement, it has not been supplanted by a viable system of work organization. However, much of the traditional is passing, on the level of theory, and there appears emerging another view of more appropriate forms of organizing to achieve objectives. This change is captured nicely by Bennis when he speaks of the theme of his recent book.

The burden of this book rests upon the premise that this form of organization [the classic form] is becoming less and less effective, that it is hopelessly out of joint with contemporary realities, and that new shapes, patterns, and models—currently recessive—are emerging which promise drastic changes in the conduct of the corporation and in management practices in general. So within the next twenty-five to fifty years, we should all be witness to, and participate in, the end of bureaucracy and the rise of new social systems better able to cope with twentieth-century demands.[1]

Two dynamics lie at the root of the change which Bennis forecasts. One is the expanding influence of democratic liberalism which provides the philosophic foundations for industrial humanism. The other is technological which is transforming the nature of work.

THE QUESTION OF ORGANIZATIONAL CLIMATE

The goal of industrial humanism is the restoration of the individual's opportunity for self-realization at work. Needless to say, industrial humanists see the bureaucratic organization, based as it is on dominance, depriving the individual of this chance. The classic organization is characterized by strong functional and superior-subordinate systems of interdependency. These systems are bonded through the scalar principle by formal authority and power.

[1] Warren G. Bennis, *Changing Organizations* (New York: McGraw-Hill Book Company, Inc., 1966), p. 4.

In such settings, the freedom of subordinates is considerably constrained with respect to their superiors. Instead of freedom, a state of dependency exists which is crucial and often objectionable. It is crucial because the integrity and effectiveness of the organization rests upon coordination, which according to classic principles, is best achieved through unity of command in a determinate hierarchy. It is objectionable because it is thought to produce dysfunctional consequences for the organization itself, for the community which the organization serves, and especially for the people who participate in the system.

In this last respect the individual, according to Evan, who is deprived of any rights of recourse beyond his superior, is "highly motivated to fulfill his superior's expectations even at the expense of his own ideas and wishes in order to insure positive appraisal and associated rewards."[2]

Thus, because of superordinate control of the reward system, a stifling kind of conformity is induced, creating:

1. Dependency of the subordinate on the superior, resulting in,
2. The frustration of the subordinate's freedom of self-expression, leading to,
3. The blocking of the individual in his search for self-actualization through work.

All in all the individual's quest for psychological maturity is forced by organizational demands to give way to authority, discipline, and dependence.

We examined in Chapter 2 some aspects of industrial humanism. We may summarize what we observed there by saying that the industrial humanists are concerned with providing offsetting measures to the oppressive authoritarian tendencies in organizations. Their arguments have persuasiveness given the assumption that any large organization which impedes by one way or another the mobility of its members more naturally than not evolves tyrannical, or at best paternalistic, relationships between superiors and subordinates.

The industrial humanists share with others a social philosophy which provides the basis for this premise. A correspondence exists between legal philosophers, like Roscoe Pound, and industrial humanists. It rests in a view that society is no longer able to offer boundless opportunities for the individual *merely through guaranteeing him his liberty*. The day of Horatio Alger's hero, seeking his fortune on the limitless frontier, is over. Instead, they see human wants and expectations increasing, but, seemingly, without a correlated increase in each man's confidence that he will be allowed an equal chance to participate in the means for satisfying his expanded desires within the framework of traditionally structured and administered organizations.

Pound puts it this way, talking about the evolution of legal thought.

---

[2] William M. Evan, "The Organization Man and Due Process of Law," *American Sociological Review*, August 1961, p. 543.

Security no longer means simply that men are to be secure in freely taking advantage of opportunities abounding to them. Men begin to assert claims to equality of satisfaction of expectations which liberty itself does not afford them. . . . Jurists began to think in terms of human wants or desires or expectation rather than of human will. . . . They began to think of the end of law not as a maximum of self-assertion, but as a maximum of satisfaction of wants.[3]

The spirit of this argument is caught by the industrial humanists. There is no question that they see their philosophy and their ways of implementing it as a liberating, democratic force in such important segments of our society as business and government administration. This is the motivation behind McGregor's Theory Y which proposes an integration of individual and organization goals;[4] it underlies laboratory training; it is the foundation of participative management.

Industrial humanism is a philosophy "beyond liberty" in the 19th-century use of the term. It is an approach presumably in step with the 20th-century imperative which addresses itself to the most serious problem in administrative theory—the reconciliation of demands for democracy and self-determination with the need for control in intensely interdependent organizations.

More generally industrial humanism is an example of the desire in the mid-20th century to bring freedom from oppression and the chance for self-determination to all men regardless of whether they live under a dictatorship or work in a large organization. Professor Waldo says that if these tendencies are seized a New Democracy in public and private administration may emerge.[5] We see in Chapter 16 how this philosophy has become instrumental in guiding the content of many executive development programs in business and government. Out of it stems as well other structural modifications planned to alter organizational climate to correspond more to the democratic ideal.

SHIFTS IN THE OCCUPATIONAL CHARACTER
OF THE WORK FORCE

The repressive tendencies of autocracy cannot simply be wished out of existence by democratic idealism. Something must be happening to the work done in organizations so that bureaucracy makes less sense as a way of organizing it. Apparently there is. Bennis, at least, sees the rise of the "professional" as so basic a change that new forms of organizations must be created to accommodate his special needs.

[3] Roscoe Pound, *An Introduction to the Philosophy of Law* (New Haven: Yale University Press, 1922), pp. 32 and 42.

[4] See Douglas McGregor, *The Human Side of Enterprise* (New York: The McGraw-Hill Book Co., Inc., 1960), esp. chap. 4.

[5] Dwight Waldo, "Development of Theory of Democratic Administration," *The American Political Science Review*, March-June, 1952, pp. 83–84.

That there has been a change in the character of the work force is undeniable. Whether or not we call it professionalization is a choice of words. A union friend reports that 12 years ago, when he worked for a large aircraft manufacturer, two thirds of the employees were classified as production, and one third office and technical. Today, the same company, enjoying greater prosperity than before, employs 15,000 fewer people, with one third of the remainder considered production personnel and two thirds office and technical.

This situation reflects what has been going on to a greater or lesser degree in all of American industry. There has been a transition to the employment of larger numbers of technicians, engineers, scientists, office, and administrative personnal. The causes are not difficult to find. On the one hand technological advancement in products and production methods resulted in premiums placed on those scientifically and technically trained. On the other hand, the so-called "information explosion" created by the demand for data for all kinds of uses brought about the technological revolution of the office. With these changes came the systems planners, analysts, programmers, and all the support people needed to run the machinery of data processing.

These trends in manufacturing, service, and government activities are not abating. They are steadily intensifying. We have reached the point now in employment ratios where production workers are exceeded by administrative and scientific personnel. This transition accompanied by the generally higher levels of education of the work force make the repressive aspects of organization life less acceptable to the new generation of employees.

We might call what is happening a challenge to formal authority. Administrators have not ignored the potential affects of this challenge. The acceptance of modifications in organizational and managerial behavior is evidence that the traditional structure of formal authority creates dangerous inequalities in the distribution of satisfaction to the people in organizations. Dangerous to the extent that if changes in the motivational climate and in the nature of incentives are not introduced the effectiveness of the organization as a cooperative system will be impaired. Thus, the demands for restraint on arbitrary authority and reducing the stifling organizational atmosphere will not go unnoticed. They will become imperative as the nature of the work force continues to change. The enlarging numbers of scientists, administrators, and technicians will give their support to the swelling desire for freedom and satisfaction within organizations.

PLANNED CHANGE

We have seen in the Prologue the differential impact which pure and applied research has had on administration. Growing largely out of the applied branches of the behavioral sciences is the newer notion of action research. The concept of planned change and action research are similar; both are extensions of clinically oriented applied research which should be recalled as the distinctive feature of the human relations movement.

Action and applied research similarly are employed to solve client problems. They differ in that applied research ordinarily assumes static roles for the behavioral scientist (called a change agent) on the one hand and the client on the other. That is, the scientist is given a specific job to do. When he finishes it, he turns in a report. After a ritual round of conferences about the report the consultant departs leaving the client to implement the recommendations or not as he sees fit.

In action research the roles of the parties are reversed. The client becomes the researcher looking for causes of problems uncovered by initial investigations. While the scientist, as a change agent, plays an executive role where implementation of recommendations becomes the key activity.

Of course, at the start the client assumes a dominant position by stating the "problem" to be looked into. But as a going interaction between change agent and client evolves, mutual confidence develops which is likely to produce deeper insights into the original problem. Indeed, it is not unusual for a redefinition of the problem area to occur.

One of the early examples of this approach is the work done by Coch and French reported in their paper "Overcoming Resistance to Change."[6] Briefly, a garment manufacturing firm was having difficulties with turnover and performance recovery rates of employees who had their jobs switched perfunctorily. After an initial survey of the situation and identification of the sources of trouble, the researchers recommended a program of participation in the decision processes and communication to help gain employees' acceptance of change.

The consultants worked closely with management installing the program and following up to determine the effectiveness of the recommendations. The research and the program which followed brought about a material improvement in the work situation reducing turnover and hastening employees' progress toward standard productivity on reassigned jobs. A bonus which neither the change agents nor the client could have forecast was that this work would become classic.

Advances have been made in the behavioral sciences since the Coch and French study. The modern scientist has at his disposal more data and research generalizations about behavior upon which to base change recommendations. Beyond this those who subscribe to the planned change approach are more articulate in their philosophy. For one thing they do not deny that they have a value orientation which they bring to the client system. This is certainly a break from the positivistic heritage.

---

[6] Lester Coch and John R. P. French, Jr., "Overcoming Resistance to Change," *Human Relations*, 1948, pp. 512–32.

Ideologically fundamental to the value hierarchies of most change agents (and change agents have different value scales) is (1) a bias against bureaucratic norms and the rational model of human motivation, (2) a bias toward democracy and participation leading to opportunities for individuals in organizations to experience a wider scope of satisfactions.

Out of these biases stem the goals which are most often sought by change agents.[7] By their interventions they hope to modify the client system:

1. To improve interpersonal competence of managers.

2. To change values so that nonlogical human attitudes and sentiments are considered legitimate as opposed to only the rational bureaucratic.

3. To develop understandings between and within groups to reduce tension.

4. To develop more effective team management.

5. To improve methods of conflict resolution.

6. To promote the notion that human organizations are open, organic, systems rather than closed machines.

To accomplish these objectives for clients, behavioral scientists in the role of change agents, usually employ a combination of three methods which are ideally welded into a change program. The first method is *consulting*. The behavioral scientist integrates himself in the environment, pointing out problems to clients and articulating them so they are understood. The change agent uses himself as a role model of change in the hope that his behavior will be emulated by the client. The second method is *research*. The data collected in on the spot problem areas are used as a starting point, a catalyst, for discussion among the change agent and the participants in the area of the organization where the information is obtained. The third method is *training* by which the interpersonal competencies of clients are developed.

Of these methods, *training* as a way of inducing behavioral change has the longest history and is, therefore, the most familiar and widely used. Roethlisberger traces the evolution of training as a method of inducing behavioral change from the human relations approach to the modern T-group sensitivity training approach.[8]

Two major problems are likely to grow out of an approach which involves as deep an involvement of the parties as does the planned change methods. One of the observations often made by behavioral scientists is

---

[7] Warren G. Bennis, "Theory and Method in Applying Behavioral Science to Planned Organizational Change" (presented as keynote address to the International Operational Research Association) (Cambridge, England: September 14, 1964) (mimeographed), pp. 26–31.

[8] Fritz J. Roethlisberger, "Contributions of the Behavioral Sciences to a General Theory of Management," in Harold Koontz (ed.), *Toward a Unified Theory of Management* (New York: McGraw-Hill Book Co., Inc., 1964), p. 41.

that those who use them as change agents do not really want change. For whatever reasons they may have in bringing in behavioral scientists in the first place, the closer the researcher gets to the core of the client's problems, the more resistance he is apt to encounter. All this may have nothing to do with the qualifications of the researcher or the adequacy of his methodology. In fact, if the client's commitment to change is not there, the more competent the researcher, the more resistance he will meet. This situation is most evident when the anticipated relationship between scientist and client is an action one, rather than merely one in which the scientist is expected to perform an intelligence or data collection role. Given an initial agreement between scientist and client to induce change, then the scientist has the obligation to exercise whatever tactics which are professionally at his disposal to overcome client resistance. This includes interpretation of resistance to the client as possibly symptomatic of deeper organizational difficulties.

This is how the situation looks at times from the side of the change agent. How about from the side of the client? A change agent joins an organization as an expert in the diagnosis and treatment of human problems. In the relationship which ensues between administrator and scientist, we often find the executive more at the mercy of the expert than he is the objective facts of the behavioral situation which he wants explained and, presumably, changed.

This is so because the expert brings to the relationship sets of concepts with the inevitable jargon with which the administrator has mostly a superficial acquaintance. More than this, however, are the normative preconceptions which the change agent introduces in an action research setting. Potential for conflict between client and scientist is always present over value judgments which are not explicit initially but become so after the research undertaking is well along.

Few would disagree that changes which improve the interpersonal competence of executives, reduce organization tensions, raise the effectiveness of team management, and so on are good. But it seems that the feeling of some change agents is that the formal organization, be it in business or government, is a pathological institution whose executive "inmates" need treatment.[9] Needless to say, this negative set would cause a good deal of resistance on the part of the client unless it was carefully concealed by the change agent.

Sofer's[10] position on the process of inducing change is rather extreme. He emphasizes that a change agent would find psychotherapy and clinical

---

[9] One author speaks of an executive development program for *n* achievement as an "educational or treatment" process, using the words interchangeably. David C. McClelland, "Toward a Theory of Motive Acquisition," *American Psychologist*, May, 1965, pp. 321–34.

[10] C. Sofer, *The Organization from Within* (London: Tavistock Publications, Ltd., 1961), pp. 141–44.

experience in a mental hospital useful. Now in fairness we must say that Sofer stresses the *method* of analysis for consultants working to change formal organizations. There is no direct implication that the people in the organization are insane or anything of the kind. But this qualification does not help much in another respect.

There is a question of whether analysis has caused any greater than chance incidence of recovery in cases of individual neurosis or psychosis. That is, some research has indicated as many instances of spontaneous recovery in control groups as in experimental groups undergoing analysis.[11] Now we come to this problem which we pose but do not discuss. Given the somewhat dubious value of analysis in treatment of individuals, what reliance can we place on psychoanalytic methods to bring desired organizational changes?

The need for change has not gone unheeded. Numerous proposals for modifying the organization are on record. One such instrument, management development, is discussed in Chapter 16. At this point we examine other schemes: decentralization, performance appraisal, job enlargement, and appeal systems.

PARTICIPATIVE MANAGEMENT AND THE PRINCIPLE OF SUBSIDIARITY

It has been pointed out in many places that organizations would perform more effectively if higher groups left to lower groups within the same system decision powers and functions which they could handle best. Not only would organizations work better achieving their goals, but the dignity and freedom of people in these organizations would rise to higher levels, and human satisfaction concomitantly would advance. This is the principle of subsidiarity and it is identical in spirit to the philosophy of participative management and decentralization. It promotes, as Golembiewski keenly observes, "a sense of partnership in and responsibility for" the affairs of the organization.[12] In short, it allows self-determination instead of lockstep conformity to the whims of a central authority. Thus the principle of subsidiarity must be a pivotal doctrine of industrial humanism and the cornerstone of the modified organization. It is the high road to democracy in administration. Its chief form of expression in the literature is as participation and decentralization.

What Is Decentralization?

We review in the appendix to Chapter 15 some of the reasons for decentralization. Cost, product line, market area, and communication are

---

[11] The basic reference is H. J. Eysenck, "The Effects of Psychotherapy: An Evaluation," *Journal of Consulting Psychology*, 16 (1952), pp. 319–24.

[12] For an excellent discussion of the normative and action problems of decentralization see Robert T. Golembiewski, *Men, Management, and Morality* (New York: McGraw-Hill Book Co., Inc., 1965), chaps. 7 and 8.

technico-economic determinants which underlie decisions to disperse production facilities, distribution activities, and administrative centers in order to achieve efficiencies in the performance of an organization. Now, of course, *true* decentralization requires more than merely spreading out the operations of an organization. However, there is some confusion in the literature, as well as in public relations press releases, about what happens in the decentralization process.

An organization with geographically or functionally distinct divisions may still be centralized. *The responsibility for the judgmental aspects of work is retained by central authorities.* The result is a tall organization, close supervision (imposed either by immediate superiors in the chain of command or elaborate staff control groups responsible to higher central authorities), and narrow spans of control.

The only valid estimate of decentralization is the degree to which *decision making* is delegated to subordinate command units, and, in turn, to individuals in these units. The qualitative results of decentralization are flatter organizations, more general supervision, and wider spans of control.

The *process* by which decentralization is achieved is unequivocal. It is accomplished by the *delegation of authority*. Delegation, which is the dynamic behind the scalar process, is the method by which the authority of subordinate command units (and managers) is conferred and defined. Now the degree of decentralization is a function of the amount of authority delegated. In Golembiewski's words:

> How much authority is conferred and what conditions hedge that grant: these determine the degree of "centralization-decentralization." When much is conferred and the grant is not restricted by detailed controls, then the delegation is decentralized. While delegation cannot be avoided, the specific pattern of delegation can run the full spectrum from rigid centralization to extreme decentralization.[13]

While the theoretical-definitional aspects of decentralization can be stated pretty neatly, its meaning in a concrete sense is more difficult to determine. For instance, suppose at an arbitrary time a firm allows its department managers to make capital expenditures of $1,000 without having the approval of higher authorities. Then at a later date, this amount is increased to $2,000. Has decentralization occurred? If not, how about an increase to $5,000? Or $10,000?

The moral of this little story is that the problem of making judgments about the degree of decentralization in an organization is the problem of deciding what are the *criteria* of decentralization. It is obvious that these criteria are not universal; they differ from organization to organization.

---

[13] *Ibid.* p. 256.

Further, decentralization standards will tend to shift in value and, indeed, change within an organization. At one time, capital expenditure decisions may be a crucial criteria; at another time, in the same organization, the freedom of executives to choose between internal versus external sources of supply may become the pivotal issue.

The criteria problem casts the decentralization issue into a highly relative analytical framework. Decentralization must be relative to before and after organizational states. But it seems necessary as well, that executives themselves perceive that the degree of judgmental discretion which

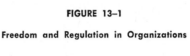

FIGURE 13–1

Freedom and Regulation in Organizations

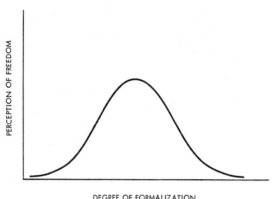

PERCEPTION OF FREEDOM

DEGREE OF FORMALIZATION

they exercise has increased. So decentralization has its subjective side in addition to the measurement of objective criteria. Subjectively decentralization reduces the problem to individual differences.

This does not take us too far afield because it is true that the goal of decentralization in the modified organization is to increase peoples' perception of freedom. The issue is how far constraints can be relaxed in order to achieve a workable balance between freedom and control, acknowledging that both are necessary.

Figure 13–1 suggests an answer. This figure relates perception of freedom to the degree of formalization. The "degree of formalization" scale represents the extent to which an organization specifies—usually in the form of written documents—rules, regulations, procedures, and policies governing job behavior. The "perception of freedom" scale shows the attitudinal effect upon people in that organization. One might expect the relationship between these variables to follow a pattern similar to the one in Figure 13–2.

While this may hold in some organizations, research seems to indicate that the relationship in Figure 13–1 is closer to the truth in work-oriented organizations. In a careful study, covering a span of four years, Comrey, Pfiffner, and High[14] found that people prefer some formal direction in their work environment. This direction should not be so meager that the environment is nearly structureless. If this is so, people would perceive little freedom because they are afraid to act, fearful of doing something wrong and bringing adverse responses from their superior. They need enough information so that they are secure in understanding the general dimensions of work requirements in order to anticipate the reactions of their bosses and to know the criteria used to evaluate their performance.

FIGURE 13–2
Freedom and Regulation in Organizations

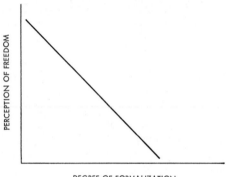

Decentralization, in a behavioral sense, is not a compromise between centralization and chaos. It is a bona fide third alternative in the management of people which is most relevant to the modified organization. It combines flexibility with the formal requirements of discipline in such a way that people see their freedom to act as maximized since they know the limits of their responsibilities within the jurisdiction of their authority.

Further, as research tends to suggest, decentralization is a way of reconciling the demands for human self-determination and administrative control because it is consistent with individual needs and expectations in a work-oriented environment. Finally, decentralization is the principle of subsidiarity in action. Because as Kline and Martin put it, "The real test as to whether freedom prevails is this: *will the superior support the subordinate in carrying out the task in a manner different from that which he himself would have used?*"[15] If the subordinate is free to act,[16] with the

---

[14] Andrew L. Comrey, John M. Pfiffner, and Wallace High, "A Survey of District Rangers," *Personnel Psychology*, Winter, 1954, pp. 533–47.

[15] Bennett E. Kline and Norman H. Martin, "Freedom, Authority, and Decentralization," *Harvard Business Review*, May–June 1958, p. 71.

[16] The above authors make a distinction between the "authority to act" and the "freedom to act." They observe that even though authority may be delegated to make decisions within a prescribed jurisdictional area, a centralized organizational

knowledge that he has his boss's confidence, then authority has been delegated to the degree that a true decentralized management pattern is operational in an organization.

The Participative Management Syndrome

It has been said that Romania is not a country; it is a state of mind. Much the same can be attributed to participative management even though many programs have been suggested to encourage it. It is a state of mind, a posture assumed by executives toward subordinates, supported by organizational philosophy, that people do better, are happier, and goals met more effectively, if participants have something to say about matters which affect them directly.

Participation, like delegation and decentralization, is an inspiration of the principle of subsidiarity. It draws upon individual resources in the decision process. It consciously and systematically involves the individual resources in the decision process. It consciously and systematically involves the individual in organization decision activities to the extent of his abilities. The advantages that this kind of managerial leadership has to offer people and organizations is amply documented by research.

In this respect, participation is not peculiarly a product of administrative systems. Rather, the roots of participation are traceable to the work of John Dewey and Kurt Lewin in the field of education. They discovered that educational goals and the process of learning are facilitated by a permissive climate in which a person has flexibility in seeking his own objectives and is able to proceed in the process of learning at a rate that is consistent with his abilities.

In its broadest sense participation implements the aims of democratic administration by enhancing the degree of self-determination had by people in organizations. It is a reaction to repressive, autocratic leadership forms which direct the actions of people toward goals by means which are unilaterally determined by centralized authority-power centers. This reaction is expressed in all kinds of organizations regardless of whether their purposes are educational, religious, governmental, or economic.

DEPENDENCE AND CONFORMITY: PERFORMANCE REVIEW

In the unmodified structure, the control held by the superior over the reward system and the method of appraising the performance of those under him is an instrument of power which is almost absolute. It has led writers like Douglas McGregor[17] to take "uneasy glances" at the ways

---

climate may exist because an executive feels it necessary to seek, defer to, or try to second-guess the boss's wishes and opinions on how he would handle a situation. So, while formally the organization looks decentralized, in terms of decision power, it actually is quite centralized in the way decisions are made.

[17] See Douglas McGregor, "An Uneasy Look at Performance Appraisal," *Harvard Business Review*, May-June, 1957, pp. 89–94.

used to determine the effectiveness of people on the job. Power of this magnitude, unrestrained in any realistic sense, places the superior in the position to "god-play" with the careers of his subordinates.[18]

These conditions make those who are appraised considerably dependent upon superiors. They must try to second-guess "what the boss wants," conform to the impressions gathered throughout the course of the relationship, then wait and see. We have already observed how Evan feels conformity of this kind often forces the individual to hide his own ideas and wishes, and that the consequences of this could be undesirable for all involved.

Beyond being a conformity inducing practice, typical methods of performance appraisal, following a "merit-rating" format, may be used as an instrument for repressing the aspirations of subordinates. The classic example is in the book *The Caine Mutiny* when Captain Queeg destroyed the hopes of his officers for transfer to better posts by giving them mediocre ratings. Where there is no effective avenue of appeal, then performance appraisal looms as an oppressive and restrictive device. It coupled with the right of the superior to withhold rewards and to take disciplinary action increases the potential for inequity in the unmodified organization.

The question then is what alternative exists to conventional methods of appraisal. After all executives have to make some judgments about the performance of their subordinates. This is extremely difficult in most situations, apart from those where effectiveness is based on tangible productivity standards like a sales quota or the number of pieces made per hour.

Appraisal by Results

Performance appraisal cannot be eliminated. It is a valuable management tool. As McGregor has shown, performance appraisal has three purposes.[19]

1. It serves an *administrative* function by giving executives an idea of how their subordinates have done.

2. It is *informational* in the sense that subordinates get an idea of how they are doing. It should tell them where their strengths and weaknesses lie.

3. It is *motivational* because the standards which are implicit in appraisal are goals for which the individual is supposed to strive to achieve.

The inadequacies of traditional methods of appraisal reduce its value in these areas. Power produces the dysfunctional consequences of conformity offsetting the motivational purpose. The unilateral setting of goals by

---

[18] Thomas L. Whisler, "Performance Appraisal and the Organization Man," *Journal of Business*, January, 1958, pp. 19–27. For a comprehensive treatment of performance appraisal see Thomas L. Whisler and Shirley F. Harper, *Performance Appraisal Research and Practice* (New York: Holt, Rinehart and Winston, 1962).

[19] McGregor, *Human Side of Enterprise, op. cit.*, pp. 82–87.

superiors frequently result in unrealistic and unaccepted standards of performance. The cut-and-dry format of merit-rating appraisal does not adequately measure the subjective elements of performance which they allegedly are designed to evaluate. What is more such rating variables as personal appearance, judgment, ability to deal with others, cost consciousness, and so on are only incidently related to the actual results achieved by a ratee. Finally, the secrecy in which the superior fills out the merit-rating form serves no useful purpose as an informational guide for subordinates.[20]

These objections and others have prompted an approach to appraisal called management by objectives or results. The key elements in this approach are:

1. A commitment to the idea that appraisal will be objective, based on measurable standards. The use of vague subjective attitudinal reference points are dropped.

2. An understanding that the objectives set will not be unilaterally imposed. Each executive along with the advice and approval of his superior will participate fully in setting objectives for his unit for a time period.

3. The actual rating of the executive after the time period will be done in consultation with the ratee. During the rating session, all aspects of the executive's performance are gone over.

In a study of performance appraisal comparing the traditional unilateral ratings approach with the participative goals approach, Blake and Mouton[21] observed differences along three dimensions of superior-subordinate interpersonal relationships. The variables studied were teamness, satisfaction, and responsibility for change. The participative approach produced positive results. That is, it pulled superiors and subordinates together in seeking solutions to common problems (teamness). It created a climate of greater collaboration resulting in higher levels of job satisfaction for both parties, and finally it caused subordinates to feel a greater degree of responsibility for inducing changes in the organization. This is in place of leaving the decisions for change making solely on the shoulders of the boss.

Managing by results submerges power beneath the surface of interpersonal relationships. It emphasizes self-determination in goal setting, and reduces the influence of coercion and domination implicit in the more traditional forms of judging performance. As such, it plays an important role in the modified organization.

THE JOB AND THE MAN: JOB ENLARGEMENT

Antispecialization of work is a major theme upon which industrial humanism has dwelt for years. According to the classical view, the divi-

---

[20] Dale D. McConkey, "Measuring Manager by Results," *Personnel Journal,* December, 1962, pp. 540–41.

[21] Robert R. Blake and Jane Srygley Mouton, "Power, People, and Performance Reviews," *Advanced Management,* July-August, 1961, pp. 13–17.

sion of labor is supposed to result in productive efficiency. This has been the argument anyway since the time of Adam Smith and his famous description of pin-making. The specialization opponents are quick to point out the dysfunctional consequences of over rationalizing work. The critical view has been well-documented by research. Authorities have shown that one of the major causes of job dissatisfaction is the routine, repetitive character of jobs.[22] It leads to lower productivity, higher turnover, and absenteeism. Additionally others have said that typical factory work retards the psychological development of man toward self-

FIGURE 13–3
The Job Enlargement Process

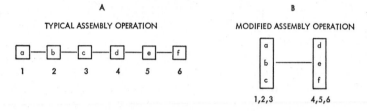

actualization,[23] and, what is more, it violates human dignity and is destructive of human values.[24]

The specific program for organizational modification which has come from these concerns is called *job enlargement*. In its elementary form, it involves the reorganization of work so that the number of operations an employee does are increased. Additionally, of course, the time cycle required for the completion of a unit of work is lengthened. It may be viewed as follows in Figure 13–3 representing an assembly operation.

Situation A represents the conventional case of a horizontally organized production line. Each worker (1, 2, 3, etc.) does a single operation (*a*, *b*, *c*, etc). In the modified case, Situation B, work is reorganized vertically in units. Here each worker does three operations as a more or less independent block over a longer span of time.

Needless to say, such a change would require considerable modification in the engineering of production systems, to say nothing of the philosophy of the organization itself regarding its administrators' perception of the obligation they owe employees for providing a climate of job satisfaction. However, the supporters of job enlargement feel that it pays dividends in higher productivity and morale with all its attending benefits. The payoff, they say, stems directly from increasing workers' spans of

---

[22] For example see C. R. Walker and R. H. Guest, *The Man on the Assembly Line* (Cambridge: Harvard University Press, 1952).

[23] The major source here is Chris Argyris, *Personality and Organization* (New York: Harper and Bros., 1957), esp. chap. 7.

[24] O. A. Ohmann, "Skyhooks (with Special Implication for Monday through Friday)," *Harvard Business Review*, May-June, 1955, pp. 31–41.

discretion and providing the opportunity for greater interaction with other workers.

Some Voices of Dissent

Those opposed to specialization say it causes the isolation and anonymity of the worker. This, in turn, is a basic source of dissatisfaction. Émile Durkheim, as we have said in Chapter 5, did not see the division of labor producing this result. As a matter of fact, rather than a cause of *anomie* Durkheim thought that the division of labor would be a force for collaboration.

More recently, Kennedy and O'Neill[25] found in an opinion study of employees in an automobile plant, that workers on assembly operations did not have significantly different levels of job satisfaction than utility personnel or supervisors which could be attributed to job differences. This study is particularly revealing because the automobile industry has often been used as an example of the epitome of job routinization. Nevertheless, employees who had greater freedom of movement and job variety did not show much more favorable (unfavorable) attitudes toward their job than those who did not.

In an excellent article, MacKinney, Wernimont, and Galitz[26] summarize their case against the antispecialization group by pointing out that:

1. The antispecialization school has not proved their contentions about worker dissatisfaction with a high degree of scientific rigor.

2. In any event, it is not proven, even admitting workers are dissatisfied with their lot, that job rotation and job enlargement would change dissatisfactions much.

3. Job enlargement does not account for the facts of individual differences. The question is job enlargement for whom? Everyone: This is hardly realistic. Yet, if a general revision of work organization was undertaken by a firm this would result.

The authors' alternative for a cure of job dissatisfaction is vocational counseling, scientific selection and placement, and personnel development. Adding to this we may comment, that job enlargement made more sense when work dominated a person's life as it did in years past. Life for the adult worker tended to be the factory for ten or more hours a day, six days a week. But with the reduction of hours, and the increase in the standard of living, American workers have *alternatives for satisfaction and fulfillment outside their jobs.* Thus, it seems that the problem shifts to utilization of leisure time, accompanied by better attempts to educate and

---

[25] J. E. Kennedy and H. E. O'Neill, "Job Content and Workers' Opinion," *Journal of Applied Psychology,* 42 (1958), pp. 372–75.

[26] A. C. MacKinney, P. F. Wernimont, and W. O. Galitz, "Has Specialization Reduced Job Satisfaction," *Personnel,* January-February, 1962, pp. 16–17.

place people in the right jobs with the chance for development according to their interests and abilities.

The real significance of job enlargement grows out of changing technology, rather than attempts to reorganize work within the framework of existing technologies. In some respects, traditional systems of production, suboptimized around the machine and the manufacturing process, take man as a given. Some of the more naïve approaches to job enlargement are suboptimized around the man. It seems what the modified organization requires is a form of work organization which stresses the productive system, that is, the man-machine relationship. In this respect, job enlargement plays a major role by ensuring the compatibility of the system to the needs of the men in it. By so doing the efficiency of the system is focused on. And this is where the emphasis should be in any work-oriented undertaking.

CONFLICT RESOLUTION AND APPEAL SYSTEMS.[27]

Appeal systems have an important role in the modified organization. They provide participants with an alternative channel of communication upward, around the chain of command, so that redress of complaints and grievances may be had. They relieve individuals to some degree from dependence upon and conformity to the whims and wishes of superiors. They reduce, at once, the control of the superior over the subordinate while allowing the subordinate avenues to seek justice by means other than the conventional hierarchy. In this respect, appeal systems are ways of implementing *due process of law* in organizations.

Relatively little systematic attention has been given to the judicial functions of management and judicial procedures in organizations. This knowledge gap of administrative behavior is apparent when we survey the large amount of literature pertaining to policymaking and the implementation of plans and programs. These activities are, of course, the legal equivalents respectively of legislative and executive functions.

The major premise in this discussion is that the administrative organization, regardless of its institutional setting, is as much a legal system as it is an economic, social, or decisional system. Accepting this premise orients this discussion to the view that administrators in business, government, military, labor, and other formal organizations do not just make and execute organization law, but they maintain a system of justice as well. This may be self-evident. Nevertheless, the nature of these systems and their place in the modified organization has not received much attention.

---

[27] This section is based on the author's recent book. See: William G. Scott, *The Management of Conflict* (Homewood, Ill.: Richard D. Irwin, Inc., 1965). See also Wendell French, "The Nature and Problems of Organizational Justice," *Proceedings of the Academy of Management*, December, 1964, p. 102.

Judicial systems have two main components. One concerns the actions and the sanctions which are brought against members of a society or an organization who have allegedly transgressed its law. Disciplinary policies and practices in personnel administration are examples of this in business and government organizations. While common, this judicial activity is not dwelt upon here. The second component of judicial systems involves the ways individuals may seek redress if they feel their rights have been abrogated by another. Thus we are interested in exploring formal systems unilaterally created and maintained by management to afford organizational members an avenue of appeal when they think they have been treated unjustly by an agent of the organization.

These systems need to be described. Their frequency should be noted in relation to other variables such as the size and activity of organizations in which they appear. And most importantly, they ought to be explained, hopefully with the scope of a model which is generally familiar.

We may legitimately ask such questions as the following about appeal systems.

1. What are the similarities and differences between business and nonbusiness programs in terms of origin, policy, and form of implementation?

2. What are the procedural patterns followed by business and nonbusiness appeal systems?

3. What relationship is there between organization size, the opportunities for individual mobility, and the existence of formal appeal procedures?

4. What explanation can be offered for the existence of these programs?

This section proposes to answer questions like those above. It is directed to the formal and procedural features of organizational appeal systems and the logic which exists to explain them. No attempt is made here to evaluate the effectiveness of appeal programs or their psychological and social impact upon organizational participants. While these matters are in themselves very important, they are more effectively treated after the nature, logic, and determinants of formal appeal systems are uncovered.

The following hypotheses are made with respect to the relationship between formal appeal systems and the organizations in which they are found.

1. Formal appeal systems are associated with large organizations in the sense that the larger the organization the more likely it is to have an appeal system.

2. Formal appeal systems arise out of the structural and environmental determinants of reduced mobility and increased dependency of organizational participants.

3. Formal appeal systems are indifferent to organizational objectives. They are found in private business, union, religious, military, and government organizations.

Evidence drawn from business and nonbusiness organizations is presented to test these hypotheses. Additionally the data collected is used to develop an explanation of why these programs exist within the structure of bureaucratic-type organizations.

The Appeal Issue: A Problem of Explanation

Many organizations recognize the *right* of individuals to seek redress of complaints and grievances and provide for this right to be exercised through appeal mechanisms aimed at conflict resolution. The policies underlying appeal systems are analogous to civil guarantees of *due process of law*. While due process is adequately explained in traditional jurisprudence, it does not have the same explanatory status in theories of administrative organizations.

Three reasons for the presence of appeal systems in organizations have been suggested.

1. They are used as an antiunion measure by management.
2. They are an attempt to humanize the organization by giving subordinates an alternate channel of communication around superiors. This channel is available if the subordinate feels he was victimized and his rights transgressed.
3. They are a logical outcome of organizational growth and formalization. As such they represent an unexplored aspect of formal organizational theory.

The Appeal Systems in Nonbusiness Organizations

Four organizations are selected for study of the appeal rights granted to members. While the United Automobile Workers, the Roman Catholic Church, the United States Army, and federal government agencies represent a most diverse sample of organizations in terms of their objectives, they do have factors in common which enable us to make generalizations about their appeal programs.

We can say with respect to similarities among these organizations that:

1. They are large and complex.
2. They restrict the mobility of their members.
3. They are highly formalized in the "classic" bureaucratic sense.
4. They centralize authority to a considerable degree.

As anticipated by our hypotheses, appeal systems were found in these organizations which gave union members, clerics, military personnel, and government employees the *right* to bypass supervision if they desired redress of real or imagined transgressions. Though procedurally the appeal mechanisms were different in each organization, they had several principles in common.

1. In each case, the rights of the organization membership were spelled out in formal documents analogous to statutory law. The union has its constitution,

the church canon law and the constitutions of orders, government agencies have manuals and the regulations of the Civil Service Commission, and finally the military has Army Regulations and the Uniform Code of Military Justice.

2. All the organizations support the principle of nonsuspension of administrative decisions during the time an appeal is being heard. If this principle is not operational the formal authority of the organization would be undermined.

3. Typically these organizations stressed the local handling of disputes, reserving appeal to higher administrative segments just in serious cases or when settlement is not reached on the local level.

The existence of appeal systems in these organizations is evidence of a modification of the classic organizing prescriptions for the sake of making justice in organizations instrumental. In this respect, some separation of legal power exists. That is, the judicial function is separated from the legislative and executive to some degree on lower organizational levels.

We find that this separation, while not as complete as it is in civil life, is present in rudimentary form so that some rough equity is possible, freeing subordinates from the burden of absolute authority of their superiors.

Appeal Rights in Business Organizations

This part of the discussion is based upon a survey of 1,800 business firms sampled according to industry and firm size. The research universe included small, medium, and large companies in the manufacturing, finance, retail, public utility, extractive, and transportation industries. The survey instrument was designed to produce information on the following subjects.

1. We wished to know first if the company had a *formal* policy covering employee appeal rights and what the mechanisms were that the employee had access to for processing his complaints.

2. Next we were interested in the specific form of the appeal right and the procedures by which this right could be exercised by the employee. We wanted to discover if the grant was made simply as a policy statement, or if the grant included both a policy and a step-by-step procedure. Respondents were asked to include with the completed questionnaire relevant sections of policy manuals and employee handbooks.

3. Finally we asked if the firm had any other provisions than a formal program for handling employee complaints. This allowed those firms which did not have written formalized programs to state their informal, traditional practices.

This survey brought nearly 800 replies from the 1,800 sampled firms. The relevant findings of this study are:

1. Significant proportion of companies (275 of 793) recognize the principle of an employee's right to appeal through the use of an upward channel of communication *alternative to the chain of command*.

2. To insure that the rights recognized by the company are understood by employees a policy is promulgated. This policy, whether formal or informal, puts management on record that it considers legitimate the bypassing of the chain of command for expressing a grievance.

3. In cases where appeal procedures are associated with appeal policies, line executives abdicate some of their authority to veto the decisions of subordinates. This consequence is inherent in the logic of a step-by-step appeal apparatus. Higher levels of management could not reverse a settlement reached at a lower level of the appeal system without risking the destruction of the entire program. Ninety-one firms indicated that they formalized, in terms of written policy and procedural statements, employee appeal rights.

4. Very little was said by responding companies about what they recognize as appealable and non-appealable matters. Apparently in most cases the many things which constitute work related complaints are appealable. This indicates the absence in business organizations of a "statutory base" of employee rights of the kind we found in the constitutions and the like of non-business organizations.

5. Though other levels are not ordinarily specifically excluded, most of the appeal programs examined seem designed for the nonexempt employee.

6. Most of the appeal programs examined fix the responsibility for the settlement of complaints and disputes on a step-by-step system, using varying combinations of line and staff executives in ascending degrees of authority, who hear cases and render judgments. Only two instances were found in which an outsider was brought in at some stage of the procedure for his judgment.

7. An association was discovered between the size of the firm and the existence of a formalized appeal system. The larger the firm the more likely it is to have one.

8. An association also seems to exist between high mobility industries and the tendency to show a low frequency of appeal activities. The reverse seems to hold as well. However, we must hasten to add that these conclusions are tentative because of the problem of obtaining mobility data on gross job changes on inter- and intra-industrial cross sections.

Synthesis and Explanation

Based on the data, we feel that:

1. Formal appeal systems are peculiarly associated with large organizations.

2. They arise from conditions which reduce the mobility and increase the dependency of organizational participants.

3. These systems appear ubiquitous. They are found in many kinds of organizations.

Testing hypotheses about appeal systems is, however, just one aim of this study. The other is to explain appeal phenomenon. Three explanations appear possible: antiunion, humanistic, and the formal. We feel that the most satisfactory model is the formal approach to organizational analysis which is the theoretical bulwark of classic administrative thought.

This model cannot be accepted without modification because the existence of appeal systems undermine two cornerstones of the classical approach. They are the principle of unity of command and the principle of a determinate hierarchy. Any system which officially legitimates bypassing the chain of command is a direct attack on these basic principles.

In order to explain appeal systems in the framework of the classic model, we have to refer to a higher principle—the principle of coordination. As organizations grow, they tend to formalize. And formalization introduces rigidities into the administration of policies. Certainly in the management of human resources in large organizations, *uniformity* is desirable. But, at the same time, flexibility is necessary as well. So far as our findings are concerned appeal systems satisfy both the requirements for uniformity and flexibility. They permit all organizational members equal access without prejudice to uniform procedures for settling disputes. But within the procedural mechanisms, there is room for tailoring solutions meeting the need for flexibility in individual cases. This approach for resolving conflicting forces in organizations accords with Chester I. Barnards prescriptions of effectiveness and efficiency for creating and maintaining a cooperative organizational system. If subprinciples have to be sacrificed to achieve the higher imperative of coordination, then it is entirely within the spirit of the classic model to do so.

Conclusions and Some Unresolved Problems

Appeal systems are in a real sense a way by which aggrieved people may, in Adolph Berle's words, have access to the "conscience of the organization." Actual and potential conflict is always present in human systems. Because of this, methods for resolving conflict, and often directing it into constructive channels, evolve. The regularization and institutionalization of conflict by both formal and informal means is essential to organizational maintenance.

In most cases, informal methods of appeal provide an adequate and simple approach to conflict settlement. But as organizations grow, and if the mobility of their members tends to decrease, informal conflict resolution is often paralleled by formalized policies and procedures which serve similar ends. These programs are generated by processes which are explainable in classic organizational terms. We strongly emphasize, however, that formal procedures do not replace informal methods.

The difficulty with most formalized programs is that frequently the people for whom they are designed do not believe it in their interest to use them. This is because:

1. They fear reprisal if they bypass their superior even though they are guaranteed immunity.

2. They believe that the standards of justice by which the system is governed are so close to the normative values of the organization that the chance for "equity" is weighted against them.

The causes of these negative perceptions are twofold. First, most formal organizations are biased toward centralization creating an authoritarian climate. Second, a real separation of legal functions does not exist. That is, the people who participate in judicial proceedings are the same as those who make and execute policy and who control the reward and punishment system.

There is a vast difference between the forces which give rise to formal systems of appeal and the spirit with which they are administered once they come into being. Formal systems of appeal undivorced from a centralized autocratic administrative atmosphere will not be productive of much in the cause of organizational justice. We suggest that appeal systems will function more effectively if they go hand-in-hand with a lessening of centralized authority and a greater separation of legal functions. Of course, the optimum climate for the viable operation of appeal systems is democratic. Thus appeal systems appear to be the judicial arm of democracy in the modified organization.

PART IV-B

Problems and Issues in Influence

14

Productivity Dynamics

MOTIVATED PRIMARILY by the survival drive, but also by social and psychological needs, man "rents" his muscles and his brain. He enters into an agreement, usually with the highest bidder, to exchange his physical and intellectual assets for money. The process whereby he fulfills his part of this agreement is work. Formally defined, ". . . work is the totality of prescribed and discretionary activities that a person does in discharging the responsibilities he has contracted to undertake in order to earn his living."[1]

In our society, man has won the struggle for pure existence. The "affluent society" has obscured work as the elemental activity of simple survival. Instead, social and psychological needs and derived work motives have interposed themselves between survival and man. In short, work now means more to man, and it offers him a richer variety of satisfactions. The essence and purpose of work have not changed, but the social and psychological content of work has assumed different meanings for man. A man is judged by the work he does, and invariably his status is linked to the functions he performs in an "employee society."[2] Work determines the individual's position in the social hierarchy.

A "normally" motivated person wishes to climb as high as possible on the social ladder, and money is the most convenient way of doing it. Money has not lost its significance as the medium for moving up in the world. As such it is a basic incentive. But money is sought not just for pure survival; it is a resource to buy the symbols of social status which are appropriate to an individual's role and function in society.

For years it has been an accepted axiom in economics that money is paid for the creation and distribution of goods and services. And, in some vague way, the amount of money which an individual receives for his efforts is related to the value of his contributions to the affairs of an organization.

While it is impossible to deny this hypothesis some writers feel that this

---

[1] Elliott Jaques, *Measurement of Responsibility* (Cambridge: Harvard University Press, 1956), p. 85.

[2] See Peter Drucker, "The Employee Society," *American Journal of Sociology*, January, 1953, pp. 358–63.

concept of wages is incomplete. Some look on money as a "bribe" to overcome the unpleasant factors in the work environment. Another writer's view is that, "The amount of money an individual . . . may earn is dictated by the amount of loss he is expected to avoid by the use of his discretion, rather than by the amount of value he creates."[3]

These and other approaches to a wage rationale range over a span of concepts starting with the conservative motto, "A fair day's pay for a fair day's work," to the revolutionary position, "Abolition of the wage system and emancipation of the working class."

The many theories and solutions offered for the wage issue are a sign that work and wages are interrelated, complex matters with explosive content. While it is admitted that "man does not live by bread alone," the disputes which arise over the means by which man earns money to buy bread (and much else) are substantially in the forefront of contemporary labor-management relations.

From the standpoint of modern scholarship it is felt that the issue of wages as it relates to motivation has been treated by the more traditional-minded in a misleading, indeed, erroneous manner. Personal decisions to produce for an organization need to be explained in a more general way which requires recognition of incentives other than simply economic.

March and Simon point out that to understand motivations behind decisions to produce we must consider three behavioral variables.[4]

1. A decision to produce or not depends upon the sets of alternatives evoked by incentives. In other words an individual considers what alternatives he has to the production incentives offered by a given organization.

2. Simultaneously the individual weighs the values of the alternatives in terms of the outcomes which he perceives associated with them.

3. Finally, the individual casts the alternatives and their consequences against his personal expectations and aspirations in order to derive decision criteria.

Thus motivation to produce is a function of the alternatives evoked, their values, and their congruency with the goal structure of the individual. Within the framework of this model, we look at the problem of motivation in work-oriented organizations. This leads us in this chapter to consider the issues of incentives, group influence, organizational climate, and morale as they are related to productivity.

THE NATURE OF INCENTIVES

An *incentive* is a stimulus which incites action. In its broad usage "incentive" is applicable to any inducement, material or nonmaterial,

---

[3] Jaques, *op. cit.*, p. 112.

[4] James G. March and Herbert A. Simon, *Organizations* (New York: John Wiley and Sons, Inc., 1958), pp. 52 ff.

which impels, encourages, or forces a person to perform a task to accomplish a goal. *A psychological reaction is the primary effect of an incentive. Its secondary effect is behavior.*

Each individual responds uniquely to stimuli. His sentiments regarding an event are determined by elements of heredity and experiences old and new. Thus, each individual looks on an incentive in light of associative clusters called attitudes.

But between sentiments and behavior are motives. Motives are unsatisfied needs which prompt an individual toward the accomplishment of specifiable goals. Motives determine a line of action; incentives (rewards) are the forces which induce the individual to pursue an objective to fruition.

It is useful—although perhaps an oversimplication—to think of a motive as an inner force and an incentive as an outer force operating on an individual. Motives and those forces which are perceived by the individual as incentives are interwoven in a personality configuration. The matching of appropriate incentives to motives will result in behavior by an individual.

It is evident, then, that anything which induces an individual to produce in an organization can be generically called an incentive, (sanctions are merely the negative side of a motivational system).

Man in a work situation is motivated in part by economic needs. For the performance of tasks he is offered monetary incentives which are scaled both to the type of work done and to the quantity and quality of the work. The economic incentives provided "outside" the individual are supposed to satisfy the "inner" motives based upon economic needs.

The relationship between economic motives and financial incentives is hardly one-to-one. If it were, then the axiom, "A fair day's pay for a fair day's work" would constitute more than an emotional appeal. But as it is, the measurement of work and pay defies precise calculation. However, even if such precision were possible, the appropriate adjustment of wages and human effort still would not be forthcoming. Interwined with the work-wage relationship are economic-political forces of power and market domination on the parts of labor and management which make "fair" adjustments in wages and effort utopian.

Reduced to its basic ingredients, however, money incentives are inducements which constitute means for evoking action. For centuries money has been the common denominator expressing the relationship between the effort expended by the individual and the value derived therefrom by the employer.

Therefore, the money-motivation issue is an important one and requires attention. But we cannot leave the subject here. In the latter part of this chapter, we take up the broader issue of the relationship between morale and productivity and treat the effect of other motivational variables on the decision to produce.

THE EVOLUTION OF WAGE INCENTIVES

The Industrial Revolution along with the closing of the frontier shattered the ideal of individualism in America in the late 19th century. Modern technology, mass production, mass employment, and huge investments placed considerable pressure on the owners and managers of industrial enterprises to improve profitability. Methods were sought to boost output per unit of capital and per unit of labor.

Technological improvements, standardization, and revolutions in transportation and communication increased the efficiency of industrial processes. These developments alone were not adequate, however, because human inefficiency partly neutralized the gains resulting from engineering advancements.

It was entirely reasonable, therefore, that the embryonic school of scientific management turned upon the "human factor" of production as the next logical step in improving the efficiency of the industrial undertaking. Operating under the notion that human behavior responded predictably to inexorable economic laws,[5] the scientific management pioneers developed several incentive systems to tie productivity of the individual worker to his paycheck. Taylor, the Gilbreths, Gantt, and Emerson are associated with wage incentive plans and with the development of scientific measurements upon which such plans are based.

Frederick W. Taylor, of course, stands off from the other pioneers as the founder of the scientific management movement. It is not surprising that one of his most important contributions to the "mechanisms" of this movement was the differential system for piecework payment. But regardless of the type of time or piecework incentive plan, all systems are based on the fundamental notions that man is motivated by money and there is a direct relationship between how much a person is paid (or allowed to earn) and how hard he will work.

The "human factor of production" could scarcely remain relegated to a theoretical economic limbo no matter how advanced incentive plans became. More than any one other piece of research, the Hawthorne studies drove home to management that man is a basic modifier of plans, directives, and policies. In the same vein, the human element could not be considered as without influence on wage and incentive systems.

The impetus provided by the Hawthorne studies prompted behavioral scientists to study human response to wage incentives in terms of broad organizational contexts. Profiting by this work, personnel administrators and wage specialists have modified, to some extent, their orthodox approaches to wage incentives by introducing new concepts or rediscovering old ones, like profit participation plans.

The inadequacies of monetary incentives have led management to seek

---

[5] Rationality is the pursuit of economic gain and mutual interest of employer and employee in productivity.

new ways to motivate employees. These efforts have combined to produce "families" of financial and nonfinancial incentive programs in many
organizations.

No matter how well conceived a program of incentives is, the troublesome fact persists that all such programs create unanticipated adverse
reactions by individuals and groups in the work environment. But in spite
of their shortcomings, a multitude of incentive plans are in operation.

HUMAN PROBLEMS OF INCENTIVE SYSTEMS

An enterprise is made up of interrelated but independent variables
which function best in a state of balance with each other. Disturbances to
a balanced system are often generated within the system itself. A factory
is an example of this sort of system; an incentive program, and the
industrial engineers who administer it, may well be the sources of disturbing influences which upset the equilibrium of the shop system.

A financial incentive system, particularly one that is time based, is a
logical economic program which management uses to achieve higher
productivity at lower unit cost. It is also a system which if fairly administered results in higher earnings for the "average" to "better-than-average"
employees.

Workers, however, do not necessarily react logically to incentive plans.
Their attitudes toward these programs are colored by nonlogical sentiments, particularly in time-based systems where the pace of work and
the pay are geared to standard times established by rate setters. The
operative employee is concerned with the effects of these programs on
him, not only financially but also in terms of his status in the organization.[6]
Some problems generated by the individual time-based systems, are considered in this section.

The Time Determination Problem

In such incentive systems as the Taylor, Emerson, and Gantt plans, and
in other plans which are modifications of these three, discontinuities are
present in wage payment curves at certain standard output levels. This
means that above the standard output level the worker has the opportunity to increase his earnings substantially by added increments of productivity. The use of discontinuities as an incentive to higher levels of
achievement is contrasted with straight piecework plans where additional
increments of pay are simply a linear function of output.

This point is brought out to emphasize the need for accurate time and
rate determination by the industrial engineer. If the rate is "loose" the
"average" worker can reach the high pay segment of the curve with
comparative ease. The result is increased production costs and lower

---

[6] For an excellent discussion of incentives and their effect on the social system see
William F. Whyte, *Money and Motivation* (New York: Harper and Bros., 1955),
part 4.

efficiency. When the rate is too "tight" workers have difficulty in reaching high incentive earning, causing morale problems due to frustration with the "system."

The "rate setter" is a crucial figure not only because of the technical need for adequate standard determinations but also because of his effect on the human "equilibrium" in the shop. In the eyes of operative employees, the rate setter (or time-study man) is an individual to be feared, hated, avoided, or fooled, depending on the situation. The foreman also reacts to the visits by representatives of the industrial engineering department with a certain trepidation. He knows that *he* must sell his workers on rate changes instituted by the engineering department.

The industrial engineer and his corps of rate experts and time-study men create difficulties not only for those who are working on the shop floor. The job content of the industrial engineer is itself problematical and is often viewed critically by the industrial management writers.[7] The main criticism stems from the fact that the methods used currently for the measurement of human application have not eliminated subjective elements in the determination of rates.

Time-study men employ techniques to develop standard times for jobs. But none of the procedures, regardless of their complexity, are free from subjective judgments of the rate setter. Human judgments, and therefore human error, are often involved in rate calculations.

As equally significant as the technical faults in time determination is the interaction of the rate setter with workers and foremen on the production floor. The foremen in particular consider "visitors" from the industrial engineering department as intruders—an attitude which fuels the fire of line-staff conflict.

For his part, the worker may be unnerved by the rate setter or time-study man at his side. Although the employee studied is supposed to represent an "average" worker operating at "normal" speed, it is likely that the worker will not maintain a normal production pace but will slow down instead.

The behavior results from conscious intent or subconscious apprehensions caused by a mixture of attitudes including:

1. Fear of the unknown.
2. A desire to maintain an established financial and status position.
3. Resentment of being studied.[8]

---

[7] See for example, R. Blackwell, "The Impact of Work Study on the Operative," *Time and Motion Study*, July, 1956, pp. 12–14; and William F. Whyte, *op. cit.*, chap. 3.

[8] It is difficult for a worker to appreciate the impersonality of the time-study-rate-setting process. The industrial engineer is interested in the job, not the person who happens to be performing it at the time. This fact, however, has not been adequately communicated because a worker inevitably feels it is *he* who is being observed and resents it.

When a staff man from industrial engineering appears the worker is immediately on his guard. He does not fully understand what is going on during the rate-setting process, but he is aware of shop lore which convinces him that this person "is up to no good." Regardless of how much reassurance is given to the workers by management that time determinations are for their own welfare, the general reaction is "who's kidding whom?" This worker cynicism toward the rate-setting process is reinforced by the industrial engineer and his staff. They are highly specialized, technical people who sincerely believe in the infallibility of their slide rules, stop watches, equalization factors, fatigue coefficients, and so on. They pay little heed to the human "guinea pig" under their scrutiny.

It is amazing that the methods used for time determination—which are inherently inaccurate and create many human problems when applied— have been so widely accepted in industry. They may be better than nothing, but their shortcomings are embarrassingly highlighted by the ingenuity of the worker in beating the system.[9]

The strong negative feeling of workers toward time-based incentive plans has a long history. It cannot be doubted that Taylor, Gantt, the Gilbreths, and others who developed systems of this nature were motivated by the desire to improve efficiency and to pay workers adequately for their efforts. But the other side of the picture involves the cases of abuse where the techniques of time determination and rate setting were used to speed up operations and cut pay unjustly. It was in the 1920's when the term "efficiency expert" received the onerous connotation of one who rigged jobs by mysterious time determination techniques to squeeze the last ounce of energy out of the workers.

Problems of Time-Based Systems

Although not a time-based system, daywork is a logical starting point for the considerations of this section. Daywork is the oldest and still most commonly used method of compensation. However, it does not provide much incentive for higher efficiency or greater output. A worker receives the same pay, per day or per hour, no matter how fast and accurately he works.

This situation may frustrate ambitious individuals because paywise they are classed with slow, disinterested employees. This problem points to management's failure to appraise jobs correctly and to establish standards which relate individual competence to wages.[10]

Daywork is used most often because it is impossible to apply piecework or time-based methods of incentive rewards to certain types of jobs.

---

[9] See Whyte, *op. cit.*, chaps. 5, 6.

[10] Elmore Peterson and E. Grosvenor Plowman, *Business Organization and Management* (3d ed.; Homewood, Ill.: Richard D. Irwin, Inc., 1953), p. 483.

These are jobs requiring "brainwork" and "judgment," or other elements which are not conveniently reduceable to "objective" measurement.

Inequities of daywork and hourly methods of pay are well known, and the flagrant abuses of these systems have prompted wage and hour legislation. But the law has not completely eliminated the chances for unfair practices on the part of management; and it certainly has not overcome worker unfairness to management through "soldiering" on the job.

Piecework. Straight piecework is widely used because it is simple to administer and so uncomplicated that it is easily grasped by the least intelligent worker. The worker can compute his paycheck in advance since he knows his output and the value of each piece he has produced. Further, the relationship between production and earnings is unequivocal. Each piece produced reflects a constant pay increment.

Though this plan is simple enough it is not without human problems. In some circumstances workers are paid for actual output even if production stoppages are outside his control. The combination of union efforts and minimum wage legislation has reduced this problem by guaranteeing workers a specified hourly amount regardless of the work flow. Such provisions require management to reduce "downtime" to a minimum.

When piecework rates are based on standards coming from time studies, the shortcomings inherent in time-measurement practices appear. The problems of loose and tight rates have been discussed already. Tight rates, or rates *perceived* as tight, generally produce dissatisfaction in the workers affected. Serious conflicts also arise when management tries to change established rates from loose to normal levels. Such attempts are interpreted by employees as attacks on their paycheck and status.

Further, the tightening of loose rates affects the morale structure severely. Even employees who are not immediately involved in the change are fearful that their own jobs will eventually be studied and re-rated. All this conjures up old slogans of speedup and sweatshop. Thus, adjustments of loose rates pose a real problem for management in communicating to employees the reasons for changes which may lie in improvements in the production processes or technological advancements.

Generally it is comparatively easy for a worker to reach the "average" level of output under a piecework system. However, to go beyond this point is difficult and not particularly desirable from the employee's standpoint because he is compensated at the same rate per piece. Thus simple piecework does not provide a strong incentive to reach a plateau of output above standard. This feature of straight piecework is not encouraging to workers capable of producing more than average.

The worker shies off from high output levels for another reason which is put well by a German saying, "*Akkord ist mord,*" or "Piecework is murder." This warning, taken to heart by many workers, admonishes not to overdo efforts to make money because of the strain that the system places on the physical and mental health of the individual.

INCENTIVES AND THE SOCIAL SYSTEM

The routine of introducing a new employee to his co-workers triggers an interesting set of group reactions. It is assumed that before entering the work situation the new employee is oriented by his foreman to the workings of the incentive system, especially if it is a time-based plan. Once the individual is on the job he is taken in hand by members of his work group and instructed in how the plan "really" works.

At the start, the new employee is treated by his foreman as an economically motivated, passive man who "obviously" wants to earn as much as he can on the job. Later, under the tutelage of his fellow workers, he sees the incentive plan's social and psychological aspects.

To the older employees, the newcomer represents a change, a potential source of disturbance to their social system. They are willing to accept him in their ranks if he is inclined to subscribe to their rules of behavior.

Research has shown that the phenomenon of output restriction is a form of group behavior.[11] It is not a random practice of disgruntled individuals in its significant manifestations. Therefore, if group norms demand restriction of output in order "to belong," the individual faced with these demands is also confronted by several dilemmas:

1. Loyalty to management or acceptance by the group.
2. Desire to earn more money or the desire to derive nonmonetary satisfactions from group membership.
3. Protection and companionship of the group or the loneliness of "going it on his own."

Reporting on a study of individual reactions to incentive systems. Whyte observes that the *majority* of individuals in a work group do not make a commitment to either extreme—the small number of "rate busters" on the one hand and the output restricters on the other.[12] The majority are "men in the middle," as he calls them, oscillating between conformance with the rules of the incentive system and conformance with the norms of the restricters.

No general solutions seem possible in these cases, given the "ground rules" of incentive systems based on measured output. An individual's

---

[11] Groups practice output restriction for several reasons:

1. They restrict output so as not to kill a "gravy job"; that is, a job in which workers can make and exceed standard output with comparative ease. The logic is that if workers consistently earn high-level bonuses, the job will be restudied and the loose rates tightened.

2. Workers goldbrick on "stinker" jobs, jobs with tight rates, where standard output is difficult to achieve. They know they will earn a guaranteed minimum regardless of how much they produce. Their restriction of output is a form of protest against the tight rates. For an elaboration of these points see Whyte, *op. cit.*, pp. 20–27.

[12] See *ibid.*, pp. 46–48.

response to money as an incentive is learned and naturally he will react strongly toward it. But this response cannot be easily separated from other learned responses to other incentives such as group support and protection, and group pressure. Conflicting incentives such as these are often the cause of conflict in the industrial environment.

Deeply rooted in the philosophy of all incentive systems is the aim of integrating the interests of management and the workers. The lowest common denominator of these interests is productivity. From it, wages are derived for employees and profit for management. The point has already been made that there is more to motivation than money. If "economic man" is not dead he is at least resting in a dormant state. Money is still an important motivator but it is far from being the only force for promoting the cause of mutuality of interests.

The concept of mutuality of interests is something of a myth which management has endorsed at least from the time Charles Babbage put it into print. By digging deeply enough, one is able to find a bit of truth in most myths. It is man's economic needs which have provided the fragment of truth that has dominated management's attitude toward and understanding of human motivation for years.

To the extent that man is motivated by money there is a possibility that a mutuality of interests does exist on an economic level and that an integration of interests can be accomplished through financial incentives. But a harmony of interests is illusory if rewards from the work situation are framed in terms of money alone. The social and psychological planes of human motivation, which are entwined with economic motivations, need to be considered in any far-reaching program of incentives. The absence of such considerations has been the curse of conventional piecework and time-based incentive programs. Though widely used, they seem to have the propensity to disrupt, rather than to weld, the interests of various human segments of an organization.

For this reason we turn next to other aspects of the work environment which contribute to human satisfaction and productivity. These sources of motivation have often been lumped in the literature under the concept of morale.

MOTIVATION AND MORALE

For sometime a direct relationship between morale and the motivation to produce was accepted as a self-evident truth. That is, it was assumed that high morale results in high motivation and low morale in low motivation. Recent research on the matter has questioned the generality of this assumption, placing the relationship between morale and productivity more in the realm of an issue than a precisely verifiable law.[13] To under-

[13] See Arthur H. Brayfield and Walter H. Crockett, "Employee Attitudes and Employee Performance," *Psychological Bulletin*, September, 1955, pp. 396–424.

stand the nature of the issue it is necessary to know how the variables in the problem are treated by those doing research on the subject.

Productivity

Productivity presents fewer problems of definition and measurement than morale. Productivity is usually quantifiable in terms of an input-output ratio for research purposes. As Kahn and Morse define it, "productivity is the number of units of work accomplished in a given period of time."[14]

This method of defining productivity is simple and direct. Furthermore, it is quite adequate for gathering data and making appraisals of work groups which are producing a tangible, measurable output in a given time period. However it must be noted that this approach to productivity is wholly inadequate when it comes to measuring the output of executive personnel. Typically, the executive, functioning in either a line or staff capacity, does not work under the rigorous demands of a production line.

The executive's output is often intangible and is frequently creative, which are two conditions that defy quantification. So, unfortunately, research in the morale-productivity relationship has been largely concentrated at the operative level. Any generalizations which are made on morale should be accepted as applying to production employees and not to employees at higher levels in companies.

Morale

While the matter of productivity can be treated rather summarily, such is not the case with morale. Definitional and methodological problems inherent in morale research and measurement result, it seems, from the lack of an explicit, universally acceptable definition of morale. In addition, widely varying sampling techniques and criteria measures of morale are probably a major reason for the conflicting findings of many research reports treating the morale-productivity relationship.

Three Approaches to the Problem of Definition. 1. The *"classical"* approach stems from the "needs psychology" school. Personal determinants of morale are emphasized in this approach. Needs are visualized as emanating from the ultimate problem of human survival. Thus, satisfaction of basic needs is seen as a primary morale factor.

2. The *psychological approach* stresses the hierarchial and dynamic nature of needs. When basic needs are satisfied, then higher motives, such as accomplishment, recognition, and participation, emerge to dominate an individual's behavior. High morale from this point of view results from a continual satisfaction of the so-called "higher" motives.

3. The *social approach* to morale is a product of the work of Elton

---

[14] R. L. Kahn and N. C. Morse, "The Relationship of Morale to Productivity," *Journal of Social Issues*, 1951, p. 10.

Mayo and the Hawthorne researchers. Morale is considered as a social phenomenon caused by the strong desire of man to be associated with his fellowman. Thus, morale is determined by the social situation at work.[15]

A number of operational definitions of morale have resulted from these three basic approaches. For example morale has been defined as:

a) . . . the extent to which an individual's needs are satisfied and the extent to which the individual perceives that satisfaction as stemming from his total job situation.[16]

b) . . . the sum of satisfactions which the individual experiences because of his membership and involvement in an organization.[17]

c) . . . the attitudes of individuals and groups toward their work environment and toward voluntary cooperation to the full extent of their ability in the best interests of the business.[18]

d) . . . a predisposition on the part of persons engaged in an enterprise to put forth extra effort in the achievement of group goals or objectives.[19]

And on and on it could go! The probability of arriving at a generally accepted definition of morale is unlikely. However, for reasons of research and analysis of employee attitudes and morale it is necessary to have an operational definition, but with the realization that this definition would not be acceptable for other situations.

The current feeling is that morale is multidimensional, no matter what definition is finally assigned to it. Zaleznik, Christensen, and Roethlisberger, for example, list five determinants which form morale dimensions. They are the technical (formal) organization of the group, the social structure of the group, individual task motivation (willingness to work), rewards for performance, and satisfactions from group acceptance.[20]

It is commonly held among authors that *morale is a result of a composite of factors including the personality structure of the individual, the social organization of the work situation, the type of leadership used, the formal nature of the job, policy, incentive systems, and the physical environment of work.*

[15] The three approaches to defining morale are found in Melany E. Baehr and Richard Renck, "The Definition and Measurement of Employee Morale," *Administrative Science Quarterly*, 1958, pp. 159–60.

[16] Robert M. Guion, "The Problem of Terminology," *Personnel Psychology*, Spring, 1958, p. 62.

[17] Kahn and Morse, *op. cit.*, p. 8.

[18] Keith Davis, *Human Relations in Business* (New York: McGraw-Hill Book Co., Inc. 1957), p. 444.

[19] Egon E. Guba, "Morale and Satisfaction: A Study in Past and Future Time Perspective," *Administrative Science Quarterly*, 1958–59, p. 198.

[20] A. Zaleznik, C. R. Christensen, and F. J. Roethlisberger, *The Motivation, Productivity, and Satisfaction of Workers: A Prediction Study* (Boston: Graduate School of Business Administration, Harvard University, 1958), p. 35. For other listings of morale dimensions see Gerald M. Mahoney, "Unidimensional Scales for the Measurement of Morale in an Industrial Situation," *Human Relations*, 1956, pp. 7–9; and Baehr and Renck, *op. cit.*, pp. 175, 176.

The Four Factors Included in the Multidimensional Morale Approach.

1. *Personality Structure.* The first morale factor, personality structure, brings attitudes and motives to the surface of the discussion again. Motives and attitudes underlie the will to work and, of course, productivity. The degree to which the existing work situation satisfies an individual's work motives will determine, at least in part, the state of his morale. The satisfaction of employee motives in the work situation crosscuts the entire range of human desires for work, including the social, psychological, and economic motives.

2. *The Social Organization on the Job.* As stated earlier, one of man's strongest motives is to be associated with his fellowman. Identification of an individual with a group has considerable influence on his behavior and morale. The study by Zaleznik and associates has pointed out that workers who were being rewarded by the group with regular membership tended to be highly satisfied, regardless of their rewards by management. Those who were not rewarded by the group gave evidence of low satisfaction.[21] William C. Schutz, in another study, found high morale and group efficiency to be based on compatibility in interpersonal relations.[22]

3. *Leadership and Supervision.* Any number of studies can be cited to support the direct relationship existing between morale and supervision. Notable work in this field has been conducted by Likert. The widely held view, which Likert champions, is that supportive, participative leadership elicits the highest morale-productivity situations.[23]

Much of the research Argyris summarizes backs up Likert's conclusions.[24] But it must be emphasized that the supportive-participative approach to supervision should not be taken as a "soft" approach. Indifferent leadership or leadership which casts aside all formal control patterns can produce low morale conditions.[25]

4. *Formal Aspects of Organization: Job Functions, Company Policies, and Incentives.* In addition to the above factors, the formal aspects and demands of the work situation must not be overlooked as influential elements determining morale. Argyris has a thesis that the nature of the work done is a basic determinant of morale. Individuals derive greater satisfaction from challenging jobs rather than routine, monotonous ones.[26]

---

[21] Zaleznik, Christensen, and Roethlisberger, *op. cit.*, p. 285.

[22] William C. Schutz, "What Makes Groups Productive?" *Human Relations*, 1955, pp. 429–65.

[23] For example see Rensis Likert, "Measuring Organizational Performance," *Harvard Business Review*, March–April, 1958, pp. 41–50.

[24] Chris Argyris, *Personality and Organization* (New York: Harper and Bros., 1957), pp. 188 ff.

[25] Robert L. Kahn and Daniel Katz, "Leadership Practices in Relation to Productivity and Morale," in D. Cartwright and A. Zander, *Group Dynamics Research and Theory* (Evanston: Row, Peterson and Co., 1953), pp. 612–27.

[26] Chris Argyris, "The Individual and Organization: An Empirical Test," *Administrative Science Quarterly*, September, 1959, pp. 145 67.

Among others, Super supports this view in a research study from which he concludes that varied and interesting jobs prompt workers to express attitudes of greater satisfaction in what they are doing.[27]

Besides the job itself, morale is further affected by the overall work environment set by management through the medium of policy. Such policies cover the total employment situation. They include not only tangible "fringe" benefits but also statements of *operating* policy recognizing human dignity and individual worth.

Coupled with policy is the reward system of incentives endorsed by the organization. Viteles defines incentives as "situations which function in arousing dynamic forces in the individual, or arrangements of conditions introduced with the expectation of influencing or altering the behavior of people."[28]

Incentives, so viewed, are considerably broader than "incentive pay plans" or "piecework plans." Incentives arouse motives by appeal to *all* the sources of human motivation.

Three points have to be underscored in conclusion. First, morale is closely connected with the satisfactions an individual hopes to derive from work. Need satisfactions do not have to be forthcoming immediately, but they have to be anticipated by the individual as quite probable of occurring.[29]

Second, morale is often dependent on the relationship of the individual to the group. Group acceptance or nonacceptance frequently determines whether an individual has high or low morale. But membership in a group depends on the willingness of the individual to pursue group goals. The third conclusion arises as a corollary to this observation.

A problem which often appears in the work situation is a conflict between group and individual goals. Goal conflict frequently results in low morale for individuals. To illustrate this point, Stagner has four examples shown in Figure 14–1 which indicate various morale conditions.

Maximum morale results in condition "A" where group and individual goals are perceived as being the same, and where these goals can be achieved by the same process. The other cases result in lower morale. This leads Stagner to conclude, "The task of the person who wishes to raise morale within an organization is to create situations in which group and individual goals coincide to the maximum extent possible."[30]

---

[27] D. Super, "Occupational Level and Job Satisfaction," *Journal of Applied Psychology*, 1959, pp. 547–64.

[28] Morris S. Viteles, *Motivation and Morale in Industry* (New York: W. W. Norton and Co., 1953), p. 76.

[29] One writer feels that high satisfaction must precede high morale; that is, a person first has to have experience with satisfaction before he will have high morale. See Egon Guba, *op. cit.*, pp. 195–209.

[30] Ross Stagner, "Motivational Aspects of Industrial Morale," *Personnel Psychology*, Spring, 1958, p. 70. It is evident that "group goals" refer to the goals of both the formal and the informal groups.

FIGURE 14–1

Various Morale Situations Resulting from Individual-Group Interactions

A
MAXIMUM MORALE

B

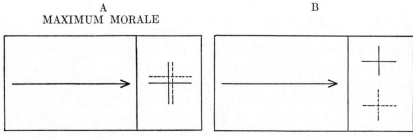

Group goal and individual goal achieved as part of the same process

Group and individual goals closely associated but not achieved simultaneously as part of the same process

C

D
MINIMUM MORALE

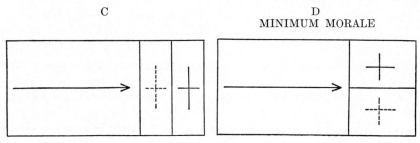

Obtaining group goal necessary before the individual's goal is achieved

Individual and group goals perceived as separate and are obtained separately

KEY: $+$ = INDIVIDUAL GOALS; $\cdots+\cdots$ = GROUP GOALS

Source: Ross Stagner, "Motivational Aspects of Industrial Morale," *Personnel Psychology,* Spring, 1958, pp. 67–68. Reprinted with permission.

Morale and Productivity

The question of the relationship of morale to productivity can be re-opened now that some of the intricacies of the morale problem have been investigated. The morale and productivity variables may exhibit four logically possible relationships. These relationships are shown in Figure 14–2.

Situations "A" and "D"—high morale and high productivity, low morale and low productivity—are kinds of relationships predicted by the Law of Effect. Just because the Law of Effect has been shown not actually to be a law does not mean that it is unusual to find direct relationships between morale and productivity. Giese and Ruter, for example, using objective measures of morale, found a direct and slightly positive relation between morale and productivity for retail employees.[31]

Further, the findings in the Hawthorne study revealed a direct relationship between morale and productivity. An improved change in worker attitudes were reflected in productivity increase. The relationships found by Mayo and associates is not purely a matter of changing attitudes, however. Higher productivity is an outcome of the whole work environment where needs are met, where employees have satisfactory associations with fellow employees, and where the supervisor maintains informal social relationships.[32]

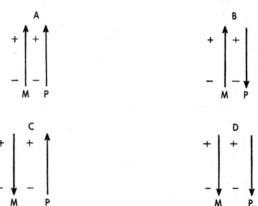

FIGURE 14–2
Relationships between Morale and Productivity

Situation "B" represents a case of high morale and low productivity. As Davis observes, this condition results from a supervisor feeling that employees must be kept happy at all costs.[33] The consequence might well be falling production with soaring morale.

Situation "C" perhaps appears unusual because of the low morale-high productivity relationship. The cause of a condition like this results from an overwhelming emphasis on output and a disregard for the feelings of employees. Sustained production pressure through forced sign out of work and close supervision would produce this situation easily.

Goode and Fowler[34] report an interesting example of such practices. The company they studied failed to maintain its equipment adequately, and safety practices were neglected. New employees were given little training. They were fired if they did not achieve standard output in a

[31] William James Giese and H. W. Ruter, "An Objective Analysis of Morale," *Journal of Applied Psychology*, October, 1949, pp. 421–27.

[32] For example, F. J. Roethlisberger and William J. Dickson, *Management and the Worker* (Cambridge: Harvard University Press, 1939), pp. 84–86.

[33] Keith Davis, *op. cit.*, p. 182.

[34] William J. Goode and Irving Fowler, "Incentive Factors in a Low Morale Plant," *American Sociological Review*, 1949, pp. 618–24.

given period of time. Wages were low. Workers also did not receive the usual fringe benefits common to the area. Finally, stability of the work force was absent—turnover was high.

These conditions would produce low morale if anything could. Nevertheless, output was high as measured by objective standards against similar companies. The authors concluded that in spite of poor working conditions, informal group pressure (brought about by the key personnal placed by management among the operative employees),[35] and overt management action (produce or be fired), productivity was pushed to high levels.

Besides the four morale relationships just discussed, two other morale situations have been found to exist. The first of these two shows no relationship, neither direct nor inverse, between morale and productivity. Katz and associates report that a study of office workers reveals, "Neither intrinsic job satisfaction, satisfaction with the company, nor financial and status satisfaction was found to be directly related to productivity."[36]

The second additional morale situation can be called the circular relationship. In a study of small military units, Medalia and Miller concluded that, "Unit operating efficiency is a factor associated with morale . . . standing in a mutually reinforcing relationship to morale."[37] Leadership may act to increase morale or efficiency, but the increase in efficiency then reacts to improve morale, which then acts to further improve efficiency, and so on.

Thus, under certain conditions morale and productivity are reciprocal. This point has also been noted by Haire and Gottsdanker when they say, "To be sure, as soon as we get into the problem we find that it is somewhat circular, for just as morale may lead to high production, high production may lead to good morale."[38]

It is fairly clear from the foregoing that high morale is no longer considered as a prerequisite of high productivity. But more than this, the *nature* of the relationship between morale and productivity is open to serious questioning. Is it direct? Is it inverse? Is it circular? Or, is there any relationship at all between the two; are they independent variables?

Generalizations are impossible to make. At best, the morale-

---

[35] This situation is "human relations" in reverse. Management used the key personnel as informal leaders within operative ranks to motivate workers to high production levels. The informal leaders were agents of management rather than individuals selected by their peers through natural group processes.

[36] Daniel Katz, Nathan Maccoby, and Nancy C. Morse, *Productivity, Supervision and Morale in an Office Situation*, (Ann Arbor: Institute for Social Research, University of Michigan, 1950), p. 63.

[37] N. Z. Medalia and D. C. Miller, "Human Relations Leadership and the Association of Morale and Efficiency in Work Groups: A Controlled Study with Small Military Units," *Social Forces*, May, 1955, p. 349.

[38] M. Haire and J. S. Gottsdanker, "Factors Influencing Industrial Morale," *Personnel*, May, 1951, p. 445.

productivity relationship is situational. Thus, morale and productivity must be studied in the specific work environment with research tools adapted to each situation.

WORK SATISFACTION AND MANAGEMENT RESPONSIBILITY

Sound management practice is firmly committed to promoting both morale and productivity. Employee satisfaction and productivity are goals which management must seek. They are values of a high order.

The best route to achieving these dual objectives—which may be recognized as conflicting at times—is through an enlightened type of motivation. Enlightened motivation by management accepts the diversity of human motives and attitudes. It also attempts to work through the personalized forms of individual motivations (states of tension, unmet needs).

In addition, enlightened motivation takes the social structure of employee groups as a given factor. That is, management should recognize that such groups exist, and that efforts to destroy them could result in a morale crisis. Groups are in themselves molders of attitudes and conditioners of behavior. They carry values and forms of satisfactions for which management cannot offer substitutes.

Finally, morale and motivation at lower levels of an organization reflect the morale, attitudes, and motives of executives at higher levels. Morale filters down from the top; the morale of a subordinate tends to be responsive to the morale of his immediate superior. Thus, the entire management corps must be conscious of its own morale. And what is more important, policies and operating behavior must be a true expression of high morale throughout the executive ranks.

High morale is a goal in itself no matter what its relation to productivity. But the approach for achieving high morale must be consistent with the basic economic objectives of the firm. Reference to Barnard's concept of "effectiveness" and "efficiency" in an organization is appropriate for concluding this chapter.

An organization is effective if it accomplishes its ends. But the organization is efficient if it satisfies the derived work motives of the individuals in it. An organization can be either effective or efficient; however, an organization must be *both* effective and efficient to build a cooperative system.[39]

---

[39] Chester I. Barnard, *The Functions of the Executive* (Cambridge: Harvard University Press, 1938), pp. 19–21, 82–83.

CHAPTER **15**

Communication Breakdown

AFTER COVERING the conceptual foundations of communication in Chapter 7, we now turn in this part of the book to some problems and issues of information handling which arise in administration. The first part of this chapter dwells on problems of communication failure and suggests approaches for overcoming them. Toward the end of the chapter we consider the issue of communication acceptance, which asks the question of how far can a person's "view of reality" be manipulated in order to influence him toward organizationally determined goals. The chapter's appendix treats the problem of organizational centralization or decentralization from a communication orientation. Special emphasis is given in the appendix to the economics of informational systems.

COMMUNICATION FAILURE AND REMEDIES

Communication has many pathological states which beset administrators. In general, communication difficulties arise from one or a combination of the following five causes:

1. The nature and functions of language.
2. Deliberate misrepresentation.
3. Organization size and complexity.
4. Lack of acceptance.
5. Failure to understand.

Almost all communication breakdowns can be traced to these five causes. The first set of communication problems analyzed is *distortion and filtering*. Probably the severest and most frequent communication breakdowns result from these diseases of the communication system. Technically, distortion is caused by the nature of language while filtering is produced by deliberate misrepresentation. Filtering and distortion occur both in the vertical and horizontal communication dimensions.

Distortion

Distortion is largely a semantic problem. The amount of distortion contained in any communication act is a function of three variables—the relative efficiency of language, the type of language employed, and the degree of incongruency in the frames of reference of the sender and receiver.

Distortion occurs because of the inadequacy of language to carry precisely the ideas of the sender, and because of the inadequacy of the sender to frame his ideas in correct language. Not much can be done to improve the efficiency of language commonly used in ordinary written or oral communication; but a great deal can be done by improving the sender's facility to work with what he has. In short, the human use of language can be bettered although the basic structure of language itself is not susceptible to rapid change.

Messages sent up and down in an organization have to be *translated* to suit the levels at which they are received. Top policymakers tend "to speak a different language" than those on levels below them. But general policies have to be implemented down the line, so a translation process occurs in order to relay policies from top to bottom.

However, something is usually lost in the translation, to say the least. The very nature of language does not allow precise translation of ideas from one level to the next. This inability to bridge organizational levels by precise translations cannot be entirely overcome. However, the distortion resulting from the inefficiency of language can be minimized. One way is for the executive to get a feedback from receivers to check whether they have truly understood the content of a message. (The role of "listening" as it relates to understanding is discussed later.) Redundancy is another technique the sender can use to reduce the distortion in message content. A technical treatment of redundancy is found in the appendix on information theory.

Distortion also occurs because of differing frames of reference. People in various organizational functions perceive problems differently. Sales people tend to view business problems from the marketing standpoint, the plant manager from the manufacturing standpoint, and so on. The technical staff presents a magnification of this situation.

Apart from the differences in jargon of various specialists there also is a difference in the "thinking apparatus" of one organizational group compared with another. The confusion which results from the clash of different frames of reference is apparent in the day-to-day communication of the line with the staff.[1] The staff has been trained to think in terms of the logic of its speciality. For example, establishing or adjusting job standards is a matter of logical procedure. The staff expert feels he can set, by scientific measurement, fair standards on the job. It is, however, not his responsibility to sell the standards to the men; this is the foreman's job. So the foreman and the staff man may often clash on standards. Both try to

---

[1] For an example see Melville Dalton, "Managing the Managers," *Human Organization,* 3 (1956), pp. 4–10.

communicate their feelings to the other. Neither succeeds, because they are talking on two different planes—two different frames of reference. The staff man speaks the logico-experimental language of work measurement; the foreman uses the emotive language of operative supervision.

Analogous to the communication barriers erected by differences in technical frames are the social barriers which result in distortion up and down the scalar chain. Social barriers come from what sociologists call *social distance*. For reasons of specialization, the staff man does not think the same as the line executive. For social reasons, the superior does not think the same as his subordinate. The boss has a different frame of reference than the people working for him. One research study[2] shows that between the boss and subordinate most communication breakdowns occur because:

1. The two do not rank job responsibilities similarly in order of importance.
2. There is little agreement on relative priorities of job requirements.
3. There is little agreement on future changes in the job content of subordinates. Subordinates see fewer possibilities for change than the boss.
4. There is a great lack of agreement on obstacles and problems the subordinate faces. The boss seldom knows the problems which are of the most concern to his subordinate.

Another study[3] found that people on different levels in the organization have dissimilar criteria for making status evaluations of others. For example, upper management based its evaluation on class distinctions and background. Lower management felt power was important as a status criterion. And operative employees looked for reliability and authority as bases for making status judgments.

In any event, social distinctions created by authority levels in the organization separate communication groups. This forces each group, and the individuals in it, to adopt a particular frame of reference in forming and interpreting communication. Obviously, the greater the similarity of frames of reference the less likely will be distortion stemming from social distance. Empathy is one method by which social distance is overcome. The ability to project one's self into the other's frame allows the sender to formulate his message so it will be understood by the receiver.[4]

For the reasons just mentioned, distortion is found in the horizontal and vertical communication dimensions. Filtering, because of its peculiar nature, is more apt to appear in the upward flow of communication.

---

[2] Norman R. F. Maier, "Breakdowns in Boss-Subordinate Communication," *Communication in Organization: Some New Research Findings* (Ann Arbor: Foundation for Research on Human Behavior, 1959), p. 22.

[3] Harry C. Triandis, "Similarity in Thought Processes and Boss-Employee Communication," *Communication in Organization: Some New Research Findings* (Ann Arbor: Foundation for Research on Human Behavior, 1959), p. 29.

[4] Lester T. Arnopol, "Attitudes Block Communication," *Personnel Journal*, February, 1959, pp. 325–28.

Filtering

Filtering is the conscious manipulation of "facts" to color events in a way favorable to the sender. It is interesting to note that "coloring" takes place primarily in upward communication, because this direction of flow carries managerial control information. Management evaluates performance as a result of what it hears via the upward channel. The motivation, then, to misrepresent the true situation is strong—stronger, of course, than in downward or horizontal communication where the motives for altering messages seem less imperative from a personal standpoint.

No one likes to appear incompetent in the eyes of his boss. Subordinates study their superiors with great care to find out what they approve or disapprove, what they want to hear, and what their interests are. Then they tend to filter their upward reporting and send their superiors the material most likely to be acceptable. Filtering involves sins of omission as well as commission.

Upward communication carries more than filtered and unfiltered control information. Planty and Machaver[5] note that the upward information flow also contains:

1. Problems on which subordinates need help.
2. Suggestions for operating improvements.
3. Subordinates' opinions about jobs, associates, and the company.

This list may be summarized by saying that much of the content of upward communication is nonlogical. Upward communication is peculiarly susceptible to opinions, gripes, and complaints. It is a channel of emotional expression for people down the line.

This channel has been formalized to some extent by grievance machinery in unionized firms. Systems of this sort operate for the benefit of operative employees. Management, however, "contaminates" upward communication channels just as frequently as do operative employees. No amount of formalization can eliminate emotive language and misrepresented information from upward communication.

Of course, there are many ways management can attempt to separate fact from fiction and logico-experimental language from emotive. Tighter formal controls over the sender of control information can reduce deliberate misstatements of facts. However, the degree to which checking on subordinates can be carried is obviously limited. The simple notion of "span of control" is an example of an important limitation.

Numerous suggestions have been made for unclogging formal upward communication channels by reducing the amount of emotive language found in them. Likert feels filtering can be cut down by building con-

---

[5] E. Planty and W. Machaver, "Why Doesn't Somebody Tell Me These Things?" *Supervisory Management*, October, 1958, pp. 5–6.

fidence and sources of expression through teamwork.[6] In much the same vein, Planty and Machaver observe that "unless superiors are particularly receptive, subordinates may prefer to withhold or temper bad news, unfavorable opinions, and reports of mistakes or failures."[7]

The recommendations for reducing filtering include:

1. Tighter controls to ensure that upward communication contains a realistic estimate of the actual situation.

2. Building confidence by teamwork so subordinates see how their reports fit into the overall picture of company operations.

3. Developing receptivity on the part of superiors to alleviate subordinates' fear of failure.

4. Improving the sensitivity of management to the problems, opinions, and feelings of subordinates so another method of expression is available to them besides the formal channel.

Organizational Audit Groups.[8] Numerous large organizations have introduced control staff activities which are allowed to bypass the chain of command and go directly to various points of performance to gather

FIGURE 15–1
Audit Staff Relationships

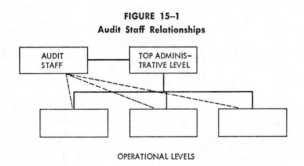

OPERATIONAL LEVELS

data on operations and relay it to evaluative functions on higher command levels, see Figure 15–1. Even though these staff groups are called audit functions they often have little to do with pure accounting. They gather information of all kinds designated as important by top administration. These staff groups may be either established on a permanent or on an *ad hoc* basis.

Audit staffs provide "instant" and presumably unbiased information on a relatively narrow, often highly technical, range of activities at lower organizational echelons. They are also a positive control factor which helps ensure compliance with organizational regulations. These groups

---

[6] Rensis Likert, "A Motivation Approach to a Modified Theory of Organization and Management," in Mason Haire (ed.), *Modern Organization Theory* (New York: John Wiley and Sons, Inc., 1959), pp. 195–200.

[7] Planty and Machaver, *op. cit.*, p. 5.

[8] For a comprehensive treatment of this activity see Leonard R. Sayles, *Managerial Behavior* (New York: McGraw-Hill Book Co., Inc., 1964), pp. 93–103.

typically are independent of the chain of command, in the sense that they are responsible only to the highest organization authorities.

Examples of this activity are many. The Inspection Service in the Internal Revenue Service is almost a classic case. The Inspection Service has two functions:

1. Internal audit—designed to ensure procedural compliance in operations to the specifications of the manuals in order that uniformity in the administration of the tax law is achieved.

2. Internal security—designed to ensure high standards of personnel behavior. It investigates allegations made against employees of the IRS.

The channel of upward communication which the audit staff opens is calculated to reduce the tendency and the effects of filtering. In summary, we have observed that this problem becomes particularly acute when (1) the distance between top and lower echelons of the organization widens, (2) as the organization grows in size and complexity, (3) as the operations of the organizations disperse geographically.

However, as a formal organizational device to overcome problems of communication, it also produces dysfunctional consequences of its own. We cannot ignore the fact that the audit staff can be, and in some cases is, a tension-inducing activity. Its extraordinary powers of investigation may create uneasiness among those who are on the receiving end of the audit.

Communication failures caused by filtering and distortion are connected to the nature and function of language and the problem of conscious misrepresentation of facts. The next three classes of problems—overload, timing, and short-circuiting—are largely related to organization size and complexity.

Communication Overload

It is common that an executive is literally buried in administrative communication. Communication at times becomes so heavy that an executive is saturated. He cannot absorb or adequately respond to all the messages impinging on him. This problem brings up the *principle of sufficiency*.

Sufficiency pertains to the regulation of communication to ensure an optimum flow of information to executives. Communication thus should be regulated in terms of both quality and quantity. Sufficiency is implemented by what Dubin calls the "monitoring effect."[9] The monitoring unit acts as a valve which both clears information in order of priority and condenses all messages so that only the relevant information is channeled to executives up the line. In a sense, middle management is a monitor of information between the point of operation and top management.

Weil illustrates the sufficiency principle by drawing his example from reporting by engineers and scientists to higher levels of line management.

---

[9] Robert Dubin, "Stability of Human Organizations," in Mason Haire (ed.), *Modern Organization Theory* (New York: John Wiley and Sons, Inc., 1959), pp. 247–48.

Figure 15–2 reproduces his model. Note that a monitoring of information occurs at each level of transmission in this process. The reports marked with asterisks are prepared by a service group which performs both specialized work in the development of the report and a monitoring function.

FIGURE 15–2

The Principle of Sufficiency and Progress Reporting of the Scientific Staff Organization

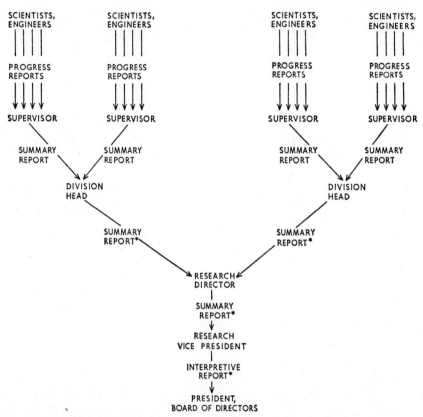

Source: B. H. Weil, "The Role of the Information-Service Group in Internal Communication," in T. E. R. Singer, *Information and Communication Practice* (London: Chapman and Hall, Ltd., 1958), p. 57. Used with permission.

The principle of sufficiency is supported by the hoary management "exception principle" applied to the field of communication. The exception principle states that only significant deviations from standards, procedures, and policies should be brought to the attention of the superior. Put another way, subsidiary units or subordinate individuals should handle all matters coming in the scope of their jurisdiction. Thus, the superior should be communicated with only on matters of exception and not of standard practice. This principle is implicit in business organizations founded on the military line structure.

Timing

When asked what his greatest communication problem is one executive answered, ensuring that all people who are affected receive a message at the same time. Timing involves two major considerations: the strategic release of information, and the simultaneous, or—as the case may be—correct sequential, receipt of information by individuals or organizational units.

The Strategic Release of Information. Communication sets in motion the machinery for accomplishing objectives. The timing of information release is part of the strategy of decision making. Messages are received and reacted to in various ways at different times by the same people. Politicians are very aware of the timing factor when they try to pick the most opportune moment to release their message. The time selected should have the greatest possible psychological impact. The executive must be conscious not only of the psychological consequences of communication timing but also of the adverse effect poorly timed information has on the organization.

Coordination of the Release of Information. Business communication is such that receivers must get information either simultaneously or in a sequential order. The interdependency of the parts of an organization requires established patterns to maintain the receipt of information.

In addition to the technical operating matters associated with communication coordination are the status problems. If five individuals of equal rank are supposed to receive information simultaneously, status difficulties may occur when one receives information before the others. Although it may not be intended, the four could interpret this act as lowering their status positions.

Short Circuiting

An organization may apply all the known theories of communication with little effectiveness if consideration is not given to the routing of messages. *Who* is to be communicated with is as important as what, when, and how the message is stated. Frequently, "who" will determine the content and route of a message.

Short circuiting is a common failure of the routing mechanism. Short circuiting means someone has been left out of the communication chain who normally should be included. Figure 15–3 is an example of this problem. Assume the department manager informs a staff representative of an impending layoff without telling the foreman. The staff man "leaks" the information to the operative employees. The foreman, being short-circuited, is in no position to answer his employees' questions about the situation. Although the foreman was informally rather than formally short-circuited the results are equally unfortunate for him. The foreman's

FIGURE 15–3
Short-Circuited Communication

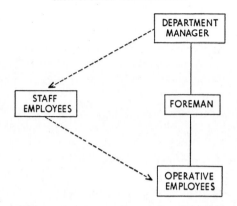

status is lowered because he does not have information on matters of importance to his subordinates.[10]

Growth causes the problems associated with communication overload, timing, and routing increase at more rapid rate. Organizational growth generates both information and the amount of paper with which an executive must deal. It also results in complexity of the timing and channeling of information in the system. Recently, a number of organizations have used electronic data processing equipment to alleviate some of the difficulties of communication flow. The appendix to this chapter discusses the issue of decentralization from the standpoint of electronic data processing (EDP).

Acceptance

Administrative communication fails not only because of language problems, misrepresentation, or difficulties of size. Two additional causes—lack of acceptance and lack of understanding—also contribute to failure. This section and the next are devoted to these topics.

Receipt of information does not guarantee acceptance. Acceptance is a psychological phenomenon based on, among other things, the needs, motives, experience, and education of the receiver, plus the environment in which he finds himself. Escher comments that, "Since unconscious selection [of information] is closely allied to our psychological needs and desires, it may be said quite aptly that we hear what we want to hear and reject what we don't want to hear."[11]

---

[10] The quasi-formal system of communication bypasses, discussed in Chapter 7, is a form of short circuiting. But the bypass, as it was established, facilitates the operation of the organization. Short circuiting in the present context assumes that the individual left out of the communication flow needs the information for operating and morale purposes.

[11] Albert J. Escher, "But I Thought . . . ," *Supervision*, July, 1959, p. 24.

Assuming that the content of a message is understood, acceptance of the message's statement is a desirable—but not a necessary—prerequisite of effective action. From the standpoint of "democratic leadership," acceptance carries the force of a value; that is, people will be happier doing things they accept. Nonacceptance, however, does not preclude effective action. People do many things quite efficiently even though they neither agree nor accept the rightness of their act. A manager may not "accept" a sales policy, but he operates under it because of loyalty, or fear of the loss of his job, or the transient nature of the undesirable policy.

Several factors condition human acceptance of communication. They are:[12]

1. *Reality.* This very important factor refers to the individual's appraisal of the situation in which he finds himself. Reality is a person's definition of his environment. Reality for one may not be reality for another. But the relevant reality in this case is the one which the *receiver* defines for purposes of his acceptance or nonacceptance of the contents of a message.

2. *Ambiguity.* All communication is susceptible to varying interpretations. The receiver may not have a clear idea of his "reality," or the content of the communication may be unclear in itself. In any event, lack of clarity results in ambiguity. And the more ambiguous a communication situation the less likely the receiver will be to accept a message.

3. *Credibility.* A good deal of communication is accepted as a "matter of faith" in the sender. The trustworthiness of the source of information is an important variable promoting or hindering acceptance.

4. *Congruency.* The congruency factor applies to the relevancy of the communication to the needs, motives, and values of the receiver. Acceptance in this case depends on whether the information in a message conflicts with or reinforces the receiver's values and his social, psychological, and economic needs. Obviously, conflict between the contents of the message and the receiver's value-need system lowers the probability of acceptance.

These factors are clearly interrelated. A person's view of reality defines what information is ambiguous, who is credible, and what communication is congruent with his needs and values. So it seems that the manager who wants acceptance of his communication should work first on his subordinates' definitions of reality. If these definitions can be changed to conform with the manager's (or organization's) view of reality, then higher levels of communication acceptance are reasonably assured.

This statement, however, only points out the strategic factor for the executive to work on. It says nothing about accomplishing changes in reality definitions. A variety of techniques is available, ranging from

---

[12] These factors are adapted from Franklin Fearing, "Toward a Psychological Theory of Human Communication," *Journal of Personality*, 22 (1953–1954), pp. 81–84; and Robert Zajonc, "Distortion at the Receiving End," *Communication in Organizations: Some New Research Findings* (Ann Arbor: Foundation for Research on Human Behavior, 1959), p. 6.

private informal discussions to brainwashing, with participation, training, and "group dynamics" in between.

Changing people's perceptions of reality is an extremely delicate practice; its implications extend far beyond the topic of communication. On the surface, nothing is particularly wrong in tampering with another's view of reality. Indeed, changing the perspective of an individual's outlook on the world is the main function of education. In business, a manager has the obligation to his company, to himself, and to his employees to educate them in the affairs of the company. And the employee has the reciprocal obligation to change his views. This is all part of maturing in business.

Yet, there are boundaries beyond which the manager and the organization must not trespass. Loosely, these limits are the views held by a person regarding his private life. The fundamental integrity of the individual rests upon keeping his organization life and his personal life separated as much as possible. Political ideals, religious principles, cultural pursuits, and family life are private matters which must not be forced into some preconceived mold to suit the whims of the boss or the policies of an organization.

As noted before, numerous tools are available for changing individual perceptions of reality and gaining acceptance of a newly defined situation. These tools are simply means to an end. The ends sought are defined by an executive, or policy, or by both interacting. The ends may be good or bad, noble or ignoble. If the ends are questionable, the application of the tools is questionable. If the ends are good, but the tools are used to manipulate people into accepting ideas which do not normally accord with their principles, the use of the tools is still ethically questionable. Ends do not justify means.

Teamwork has often been cited as an effective device for changing an individual's perception of reality, and achieving acceptance as the result. A rather lengthy quote from Likert serves as a starting point for showing a problem or two connected with the use of this device.

The fact that an effectively functioning group presses for solutions which are in the best interest of *all* of the members and will not accept solutions which unduly favor a particular member or segment of the group, is an important force in the group pattern of organization. . . . It provides the president, or the superior at any level in an organization, with a powerful managerial tool. This tool is very effective in dealing with the problem of how to handle special requests or favors from subordinates, including requests which the subordinate may feel are legitimate but are not in the best interest of the organization. In the man-to-man operation, the typical line organization, . . . the chief sometimes finds it difficult to turn down such a special request from a subordinate. Sometimes he may be virtually blackmailed into approving it. With the group pattern of operation, however, the superior can readily handle such requests, by merely telling the subordinate to submit his proposal to the group at the next staff meeting. This usually will kill requests for unreasonable favors or treatment.[13]

All this is nothing new. Using group pressure to force individual nonconformists back into line is well-known. The process Likert describes goes something like this in practice. The manager gains the confidence and acceptance of the group. He sets goals and spells out proper forms of behavior to reach the goals. Then the "well-developed team" takes over, pressuring the individual into conformity with its standards, which in Likert's case are also the standards of the manager.

Of course, Likert recognizes the imperative of preserving individual integrity. But the fact is that executives who set goals are not infallible. The executive working through a "well-developed team" can secure acceptance of his errors in judgment by individuals who under other circumstances might dispute them. Thus, the "well-developed team" cuts both ways. On the one hand, it can relieve the executive of a lot of petty annoyances. On the other hand, it can stifle initiative and preserve an untenable status quo.

The Problem of Understanding

Communication takes place through symbols which activate the senses. However, administrative communication most commonly refers to symbols that stimulate the higher senses of sight and hearing. Communication symbols, therefore, are classified as words, pictures, and actions. One of the main reasons for communication failure is a receiver's lack of understanding the symbols.

Understanding is a subjective mental function. A good example of understanding breakdown is a story from World War II. An aerial gunnery student was taking a ride in a plane for the first time. Although the pilot was enjoying the trip, the student was terrified. While in the air, the pilot pointed over the side of the plane to an object below. The student interpreted the action as the realization of his worst fears— something was wrong with the plane and he should jump for his life. This he did.[14]

Lack of understanding is caused—as in the example of the gunnery student—by differences in meaning assigned to communication symbols by a sender and a receiver. Naturally, achieving uniformity in the interpretation of symbols is a major problem for managers who are trying to transmit ideas to others. As noted already, language communication symbols are relatively imperfect media for conveying ideas. No receiver is able to translate symbols into the precise meaning a sender intends. However, the margin of difference between the sender and receiver can be minimized, see Figure 15–4.

---

[13] Likert, *op. cit.*, p. 197. Quoted with permission. Italics mine.

[14] Mason Haire, *Psychology in Management* (New York: McGraw-Hill Book Co., Inc., 1956), pp. 76–78.

FIGURE 15–4
Guides for Improving Understanding through Listening

Responsibilities of the Sender	*Listening Obligations of the Receiver*
1. He considers his status position in relation to the receiver.	1. He thinks ahead of the sender, trying to anticipate where the discussion is leading and what conclusions will be drawn.
2. He considers the receiver's opinion of him.	2. He weighs and evaluates the evidence the speaker is presenting.
3. He considers the background of the receiver.	3. He reviews and summarizes the points as they are covered in the discussion.
4. He considers both his and the receiver's attitudes toward the message by empathizing.	4. He listens between the lines, concentrating on meaning and not just the words.
5. He considers the language the receiver will understand.	5. He appraises the message in terms of his and the sender's attitudes toward it.
6. He is constantly aware of the impact of his words on the receiver.	

Source: Points adapted from Harold P. Zelko, "An Outline of the Role of Listening in Communication," *Journal of Communication*, Fall, 1954, pp. 72–75; and Ralph C. Nichols and Leonard A. Stevens, "Listening to People," *Harvard Business Review*, September, 1957, pp. 87–88.

Interviewing is closely allied with listening, although they have different objectives and methods. Listening is a generic term associated with every communication act.[15] Interviewing is more formal. It is both a technique to achieve understanding and a therapeutic method to solve personal problems.

Interviewing is defined as a planned discussion between persons.[16] However, the actual process of interviewing is more complicated. Interviewing programs are either directive or nondirective. The directive interview, sometimes called a structured interview, has a list of questions to ask. This sort of interview is used to gather specific information rapidly.

The nondirective interview has a different intent and method. The nondirective interview gathers information regarding the feelings and attitudes of the interviewee. It can be used to produce information of value to the organization, such as morale data derived from depth interviews, or it can be used as a therapeutic device, enabling the interviewee to identify and solve his own problems. In either case, the interviewer acts merely as a sounding board, asking no leading questions and giving no hints regarding the directions the interview could take. In fact, the interviewer should have no specific direction in mind.

---

[15] In the usual sense, listening is applied to face-to-face oral communication. But the rules for listening, given in Figure 15–4, are easily adapted to written communication.

[16] Harold P. Zelko and Harold J. O'Brien, *Management-Employee: Communication in Action* (Cleveland, Ohio: Howard Allen, 1957), p. 93.

The nondirective interview usually generates considerable information regarding the attitudes, interests, suggestions, needs, complaints, and personal goals of people. Also, interviewing of the nondirective variety has value in helping employees with their personal problems. However, one major danger of this form of interview, is that of turning inward an employee's legitimate complaint, so that he views his inability to "accept or adjust" as a personal shortcoming. Organizations and the executives running them are not perfect, and the burden for failure should not be forced upon unsuspecting employees.

This part of the chapter has pointed out some basic communication difficulties which occur in practice. Some of the causes for them have been identified and remedies suggested. Also, certain normative problems associated with, but extending beyond, the communication process have been noted. The appendix to this chapter departs from the tone of the immediately foregoing material to discuss the issue of centralization vs. decentralization in the light of changing communication theory.

Appendix: Communication and Centralization of Organization[17]

Communication assumes many forms in an organization. It is not a homogeneous phenomenon. A common classification of communication activities is the formal and informal. Informal types of communication include the grapevine, talking, rumor and gossip. These forms of communication are specifically excluded from consideration here. Attention is focused on formal communication activities which serve as connectors, linking the various formal functions within organizations. Thus, *communication is delineated in this discussion as a formal organizational process that includes the generation, transmission, assimilation, storage and retrieval of information.*

DECENTRALIZATION

It is convenient to discuss decentralization decisions first in this analysis. Decentralization is the complementary antithesis of centralization. Decentralization involves the division of an organization into autonomous

---

[17] This appendix with a few changes is taken from William G. Scott, "Communication and Centralization of Organization," *The Journal of Communication*, March, 1963, pp. 3–11. Used with permission.

or semiautonomous decision units where performance responsibilities and control are vested in subordinate organizational units.

Determinants of Decentralization

Traditionally business organizations have decentralized for one or more of the following reasons.

Cost. The cost factor is operative when the size of an operation becomes uneconomical. Economists refer to this as diseconomies of scale.

Product Line. This factor is operative when management considers that it is more efficient to manufacture and market a product through autonomous or semiautonomous product divisions.

Market Area. At times management considers it advisable to manufacture and market through regional divisions geographically decentralized.

Communication as a Determinant of Decentralization

Communication as a decentralization determinant is the consequence of organizational size and complexity. The larger an organization becomes the greater is the strain that is placed on its communication network. The traditional determinants mentioned above still significantly affect managerial decisions to decentralize; the communication determinant, however, is a growing factor in decentralization decisions. The object is to explain why this is so. The first step in the explanation is communication growth.

COMMUNICATION GROWTH PATTERNS

All organizations need information in their communication channels. As an organization grows, it is to be expected that its information needs will increase. *But the parallel growth of an organization and its need for information do not exist in a one-to-one ratio.*

Information behaves in such a way that when it is present it generates intensification of its own use. Hence, administrative information acts as an "autocatalyzer" by accelerating its own increase. An analogy may be drawn with railroad networks. Early railroad networks created a transportation form. The existence of this type of transportation generated accelerated use demands beyond the capacity of the existing network. This, in turn, required expansion of the railroad system. Figure 15–5 shows a hypothetical pattern of communication growth. The phase of extensive development refers to the accelerated quantitative growth of information. The intensive phase of development refers to qualitative improvements in administrative communication. More is said later of these phases of information growth.

If the central thesis of this argument is correct, that information is indeed an autocatalyzer, then the obvious conclusion is that the information requirements of an organization grow at a more rapid rate than the effective capacity of its communication channels. This phenomenon in

FIGURE 15–5
Pattern of Communication Growth

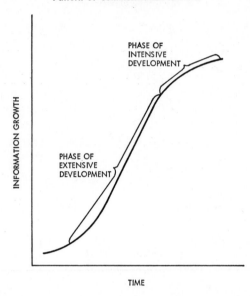

turn causes deterioration in administrative decision capability in the following concrete ways:

1. Communication overload of executives.
2. Inadequacies of information storage and retrieval.
3. Impairment of feedback processes.
4. Dislocations in timing strategic release of information.
5. Uneconomic utilization of existing capacity in communication networks.

It is largely for these reasons and other communication dysfunctions, when they are observed to be growing, that management starts considering a move from a centralized decision system to one which is decentralized. This, of course does not formally explain the logic behind decisions to decentralize. In order to do so, it is necessary to backtrack a bit and discuss the expansion of communication channels under a scheme of centralization.

EXPANSION OF COMMUNICATION CHANNELS

The typical managerial response to increased informational demands is to expand the size of administrative communication channels. The usual way this is done is to add more clerks, office machines, and technical staff positions. But channel expansion of this sort cannot go on indefinitely. Theoretically management will incrementally expand its communication capacity until the cost of the last increment of capacity equals the value of

FIGURE 15–6

Channel Size as a Function of Cost and Information Value

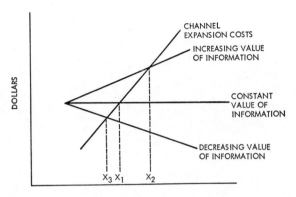

CHANNEL SIZE IN TERMS OF INFORMATION HANDLED

the information derived from it, see Figure 15–6. All this adds up to the point that if administrators acted rationally they would not buy any more information than what they could justify in terms of cost.[18]

These comments require us to make a closer examination of the value and cost variables.

The Value of Information

Incremental units of information may be perceived by administrators as worth more, the same as, or less than preceding units. As Figure 15–6 shows, if informational value is upward sloping, then executives will spend a greater amount in terms of total cost to expand channel capacity. The reverse is true if information decreased incrementally in value.

The "State of Communication Art"

The cost curve of channel expansion in Figure 15–6 represents a constant, or given, state of communication technology. Changes in the technological process would shift the cost curve. Obviously administrators would like to shift the curve to the right since it would allow for greater information flow without uneconomically increasing the cost of information.

Figure 15–7 shows just such a change in technology (C to C′) moving capacity from X_1 to X_2.

While the inference cannot be drawn directly from the above analysis, it has often been observed that new communication technologies have a qualitative impact on the value of information as well as a quantitative effect on channel size. That is, with increasing channel capacity, a new

---

[18] As we noted in the appendix to Chapter 6, this line of analysis is followed by Herbert A. Simon, "Theories of Decision Making in Economics and Behavioral Science," *American Economic Review*, June, 1959, pp. 269–70.

FIGURE 15–7

Changed Technology and Channel Expansion Cost

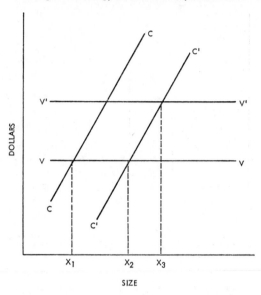

SIZE

technology shift increases the value of information to V' as shown in Figure 15–7 creating an equilibrium point at X_3. Thus, changes in the art and science of information handling tend to shift channel expansion cost curves to the right as well as to cause a movement upwards along the new curve.

STAGES OF COMMUNICATION TECHNOLOGY

Figure 15–5 indicates the general pattern of information growth in organizations. Figure 15–8 is an elaboration of the general pattern associating segments of the curve with particular forms of communication technology.

These stages are described as follows:

Handicraft Stage

The most primitive form of communication technology is identified as the hand-processing of organizational information. Included are such communication matters as sales reports, production data, inventory data, accounts receivable, billings, credit and elementary filing systems for information storage and retrieval.

Mechanization I

As information demands increase, technological change is required. This generally involves introduction of basic accounting and office ma-

FIGURE 15–8
Information Growth and Stages in Communication Technology

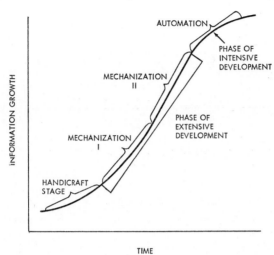

chines plus changes in the procedures of paper processing. Also more advanced filing systems are introduced to facilitate the storage and retrieval of information. At this stage personnel dealing with communication activities are increased.

Mechanization II

Information breeding on itself grows at an explosive rate requiring a higher level of technology. At this point, still more advanced mechanized equipment is incorporated in the network such as IBM tabulating machines. This equipment again allows for the expansion of capacity. The use of cards improves the system's information storage and retrieval capability. Interestingly enough still more personnel are added.

Automation

The mechanization stages do not constitute a real revolution in communication technology. The introduction of electronic data processing does. In mechanization, machinery is bought to fit a system, the modification of the system to the machinery is relatively minor. Whereas, the use of EDP requires a revolutionary change in the structure of the systems and procedures of an organizational communication network.

The promise of EDP is the ability to perform more meaningful operations on greater quantities of information in shorter time periods. Also EDP allows the "memory" of an organization to expand and eases the burden of recall or retrieval of information from storage. A further expectation is that EDP will provide a beneficial capital-labor substitution which will be reflected in favorable cost-information-value ratios.

Each of the three stages in the development of communication technology beyond the handicraft stage represents an attempt by management to shift the channel expansion cost curve to the right. The mechanization phases, however, may be considered evolutionary efforts that create organizational crises if carried too far within the context of a centralized structure. The nature of these crises, and how they are overcome, is discussed next.

THE SIGNIFICANCE OF COMMUNICATION TECHNOLOGY IN DECENTRALIZATION DECISIONS

The analysis that is appropriate to the subject of information processing differs little from the analysis which is applied to manufactured goods. In reality, we are dealing with two aspects of the production function. The one which interests us is concerned with paper; the other is concerned with nuts and bolts, automobiles and television sets. This is perhaps the reason why the development of communication technology parallels the evolution of manufacturing technology.

Throughout the evolution of communication mechanization, we observe improvements in machinery, growing clerical forces, and expansion of technical staff groups. During the phase of extensive communication development, the emphasis is on the quantity of information processed within given time boundaries. The extensive development phase does not necessarily result in improved information quality. Whether or not decision makers get better information quality during this phase is a function of how much money management spends on interpretive staff organizations.

It is not meant that mechanization increases or decreases error rates. Rather more information is processed by mechanization; but consolidated, interpretive analysis resulting from the manipulation of the raw data does not come from machines used in the mechanization stages. This kind of quality information is supplied to the key decision centers by technical staff groups that take the data produced by the machines, refine it, interpret it and pass it in finished form to top line management.

However mechanization can go just so far in effectively meeting the information needs of a growing organization. This is especially true in industries like insurance where their production function is exclusively paper processing. Given an accelerated growth in informational demands, there comes a time when conventional communication networks using many clerks and mechanized equipment face one or all of four crises.

Space Crisis. With the addition of machines, clerks, and interpretive staff to a limited space, a point is reached where it is impossible to expand the capacity of a centralized communication network by conventional methods.

Quality Crisis. Mechanization is limited in its ability to supply the *kind* of information needed by line management to make decisions involving many variables. As noted above, expensive staff groups have to be interposed between the place where information is generated and the places where decisions are made.

Time Crisis. Under the most advanced forms of mechanization, the time required may be too long for the generation, interpretation, and dissemination of information for strategic policy decisions and executive implementation. Staff work is often terribly slow and tedious.

Growth Crisis. The above three crises add up to one grand crisis from the standpoint of an organization. This crisis is that centralized, mechanized communication systems may limit organizational growth.

For these reasons, some managements have found themselves in the position of having just two alternatives for overcoming these crises. The first is the decentralization of the organization into independent or semi-independent communication units. This alternative simply breaks the large centralized communication network into smaller more manageable ones. The second alternative is to revolutionize the centralized communication network by EDP. By adopting this alternative the advantages of centralized control are retained but the crises of mechanization are reduced.

CONCLUSION

Of course managements' actions about communication centralization decisions does not follow unvaried patterns. Under some circumstances, administrators may decide that decentralization is a wiser and more economic course of action, as opposed to continued centralization with EDP. In any event, many types of centralization-decentralization decisions are possible. For example:

1. A previously decentralized organization moves back to centralization.

2. An organization contemplating decentralization goes into EDP and remains centralized.

3. A centralized organization contemplating EDP decides against it and decentralizes.

4. An organization decides to retain decentralized functions but reduces the scope of these functions or eliminates some functions by recentralizing certain activities in the field, i.e., credit, billing, payroll, inventory control, manufacturng allocated to multiplant operations.

As we move into the area of partial centralization, recentralization, or decentralization suggested by item 4, we find endless possibilities for combination. This is particularly true of giant organizations where total centralization of activities is out of the question.

In conclusion it must be noted that the conventional reasons for decentralization still exist and are compelling factors in management decisions quite apart from communication. The issue is that decentralization for cost economies, and efficient market or product exploitation has been faced by management for years. The limits and the nature of these problems therefore are fairly clear. However, in communication, management encounters a rather new dimension affecting decentralization policy. Consequently, the alternative solutions to the problem of communication are not as obvious as those associated with the other three decentralization determinants. It appears, however, that EDP biases the trend of organizational structure toward centralization. This is a reversal of the decentralization trend of organizations after World War II.

CHAPTER 16

Management Development

MANAGEMENT DEVELOPMENT has two distinct eras: BST (Before Sensitivity Training) and AST (After Sensitivity Training). Although sensitivity training chronologically overlapped other approaches since the end of World War II, it has become a dominant influence in training philosophy in the 1960's. We can say confidently that the 1950's was the period when conventional training activities in human relations were preeminent.[1] While this decade has felt increasingly the impact of methods and philosophy conceived initially in the National Training Laboratories. We will be more specific about this as we move along.

Since the Hawthorne studies, management has been interested in human relations as a legitimate field in which training should be done. Management gets things done through people, so the saying goes. If this is the case, then it is expedient that managers sharpen their "human skills." The hope has been in the past that by the use of appropriate training techniques managers would find out something about why people act the way they do. But what is more, training has also carried the promise of improving management's ability to deal with people.

Much has happened in the training area since the end of World War II. The 1950's can be considered as the "golden age" of human relations training programs. They were held with equal frequency on the premises of business firms and on the campuses of universities offering executive-development programs. Managers participating in these development activities had the chance to learn a little bit about the sociology of the informal organization, something about psychology, and often a considerable amount about leadership. These programs combined several techniques of presentation. The lecture-conference method was employed to cover the content of the subject matter. The case approach and role playing were used to give participants an opportunity to experience the ideas they had learned.

---

[1] For a capsule history of human relations training see: Fritz J. Roethlisberger, "Contributions of the Behavioral Sciences to a General Theory of Management," in Harold Koontz, *Toward a Unified Theory of Management* (New York: McGraw-Hill Book Co., Inc., 1964), pp. 54–58.

Late in the 1950's, management's interest in human relations training waned—and *not* because management felt that "good human relations practice" was no longer important. Rather, the causes were many and complex. Some of them are noted below.

First, human relations training had assumed the proportions of a fad. The management of organizations went into programs of this general nature without a very clear idea of the training needs of the participants. Motivations were strong to get on the bandwagon, and as a result human relations programs were hastily conceived. Then the recession of 1957 prompted the management of many companies to cut back on these programs. While sitting out the recession management had the chance to reflect on the nature of its executive-development activities. The upshot was the elimination of weak programs and the planning of future ones on a sounder base.

Second, the objectives of early human relations training programs were none too clear. Advised by researchers doing studies in democratic-participative leadership, management felt that somehow conferees in programs should be made more permissive toward their subordinates. Also, management felt that participants in these programs would profit from a general understanding of human motivation and group behavior. This type of knowledge helped, it was felt, to round out the education of the executive. Finally, management thought that simulation of human relations problem situations through case analysis and role playing would give program participants an opportunity to develop their human skills in a setting where mistakes in relating would not carry serious on-the-job repercussions. From this experience it was hoped that the participants would learn something they could carry back to their jobs to make them better human relations practitioners. In short, most human relations programs had the objective of improving the executives' human skills.

Third, human relations programs were endorsed enthusiastically by management and they were vigorously implemented. But little if any follow-up was attempted to discover whether or not the program met its objectives. Lack of control over results was a serious deficiency. This absence of adequate control was attributable to a number of factors: (1) the nature of human relations itself is pretty nebulous; (2) since the objectives of human relations programs were rather fuzzy it was difficult to set tangible standards to provide the basis for control; and (3) the effects of training on participants often would be delayed. Tangible improvements in the individual's ability to manage might not appear for a considerable period of time. And even if improvements were noted they would be difficult to attribute to the program alone. Thus, because of the inadequacy of effective control measures over human relations programs, management had to be content generally with the "warm glow of satisfaction" when the program was over, knowing that it had done all it could to improve the ability of the participants "to relate" successfully with others.

Management has had the opportunity to reappraise its policies on human relations training in the light of its rather spotty success with past programs and in the light of the newer developments in the behavioral sciences and training techniques. These changes have subordinated the skills approach to training in human relations to reach a more sophisticated level of abstraction regarding human behavior and a more sensitive one regarding an individual's role in a social system.

Before trends in management development in the behavioral sciences are dwelt on at length, some ideas pertaining to the philosophy and scope of training are considered.

PHILOSOPHY AND SCOPE OF TRAINING

Training Defined

The word "training" has many meanings. To some writers in the field of personnel management training means developing manpower for particular jobs.[2] Other writers interpret it more broadly, including training for adequate job performance *and* extending an employee's intellectual range through general education.[3] Still other writers speak of an overall area called development which they divide into education and training. Training in this instance means fitting the man to the job, whereas the purpose of education fits the man to his environment off and on the job.[4]

Searching management literature for an operative definition of management training in the behavioral sciences is quite futile. By its nature, such programs crosscut the definitions of training and education given above. In one sense, an understanding of the behavioral sciences at the skill level and at the level of concept fulfills the requirement of the training definition because the presumption is that knowledge and ability in this area will help a manager do a better job. In another sense, a knowledge of the behavioral sciences is essential for the executive from the standpoint of its educative overtones. An awareness of the scientific findings relating to organization theory and the theory of personality is essential for executives who are moving in complex social and business environments.

These remarks provide a background for an operative definition of management training programs oriented toward the behavioral sciences. *Training in the behavioral sciences is an activity which has as its goal individual achievement of greater job effectiveness, improved interpersonal relationships in the organization, and better adjustment of an executive to his total environment.*

[2] Dale Yoder, *Personnel Management and Industrial Relations* (4th ed.; Englewood Cliffs, N.J.: Prentice-Hall, Inc., 1956), chap. 9.

[3] William W. Waite, *Personnel Administration* (New York: The Ronald Press Co., 1952), pp. 219–40.

[4] Arthur M. Whitehill, Jr., *Personnel Relations* (New York: McGraw-Hill Book Co., Inc., 1955), pp. 121–51.

Thus, the immediate goals of training aim at improving individual job effectiveness and the climate of interpersonal relations in organizations. By necessity training must be oriented toward organizational objectives. It is the purpose of training in the behavioral sciences to equip executives with the knowledge and attitudes toward human behavior to improve their ability to run their own command unit and relate it successfully to others in the organization. *In short, training seeks a change in the behavior of the trainee.*

The more distant aim of training ties into the broad function of education and its role in executive development. The modern administrator is concerned with a wide range of social relationships which extend beyond his job. He cannot be content with fairly simple human relations formulations. His needs include the ability to generalize from basic research information and to perceive interconnections among a variety of behavioral forms.

Four Aspects of Training in the Behavioral Sciences

Like most forms of training, programs in the behavioral sciences aim to transmit information, develop attitudes, and improve skills.[5] Another facet of training, representing a fairly recent shift in emphasis, is the marked interest in the development of managerial conceptual abilities in the behavioral sciences. Each of these training facets is next discussed in turn, but it should be recognized that there is a considerable amount of overlapping among them.

Transmitting Information. The essential element in most training programs is content. The purpose of training is to impart to the trainees information drawn from a body of knowledge. Training in the behavioral sciences, therefore, transmits to participants information relating human personality and motivation, the process of communication, organization theory including small group processes, leadership, and so on. Fields like sociology, psychology, social-psychology, and anthropology are relied upon by the program developers and conference leaders to supply the material.

Development of Attitudes. Closely linked to the imparting of knowledge is the development of attitudes. Actually, it is more accurate to say *changing* the attitudes of participants. People go into training programs with certain preconceived ideas about leadership, the grapevine, the function of status, and the informal organization. The attitudes management trainees have regarding these factors and others in the organization environment determine executive effectiveness as a leader.

Experts in behavioral science training feel it is not sufficient just to impart knowledge in these fields. It is also necessary to work on changing the participants' attitudes on human behavior. Thus, the training aspect of

---

[5] See Herbert J. Chruden and Arthur W. Sherman, Jr., *Personnel Management* (Cincinnati: South-Western Publishing Co., 1959), pp. 153–54.

attitude development is an important part of programs. It is, however, the most difficult to execute effectively.

Development of Skills. Assume that in a given training program a considerable amount of information has been transmitted to participants, and that in the progress of training their attitudes have been changed. In other words, the first two aspects of training were accomplished well. Is the program then a success? The answer probably is "no," because the trainees have not yet had an opportunity to develop "human skills" in the application of the material imparted to them. Consequently, the next logical phase of training is skill development.

Some argue that the development of skills in the use of human tools derived from training must come from on-the-job experience. Classroom simulation of human problems through case studies and role playing, it is claimed, is inadequate even when conducted under the supervision of a training expert. Nevertheless, those in the training field are constantly working on new devices and techniques which endeavor to fill the need for realistic forms of classroom experiences where skills can be developed. More is said about this facet of training later in the chapter.

Conceptual Level. The notion that training or education in the application of the behavioral sciences to management practice should be conducted on a higher level of abstraction is a fairly recent development. The objective is to move training a step or two beyond direct application to a level of greater generalization. The idea is to develop managers who can *think* in behavioral science terms.

TRAINING AND THE INFLUENCE PROCESS

No one will quarrel with the proposition that the purpose of training is to change peoples' behavior. Furthermore, few will deny that the way it is done is through selected inputs of information, attitudes, and skills. Where problems arise is when we ask, what is the best way of making these inputs? And why are we changing people anyway? The first question is instrumental. The second is normative. We deal with them in this order in the remainder of this chapter.

The Model of Influence

Changing behavior requires a planned program of influence. The minimum requirements of such a program is set out by Schein.[6] The elements of his influence model serve nicely as criteria for judging various conventional training instruments and recommending others.

Much of the content of this model is based upon learning theory which has achieved a fair degree of substantiation over the years. This model is predicated on the assumption that an individual is ready for change. That

---

[6] Edgar H. Schein, "Executive Development as a Process of Influence," *Industrial Management Review* 11.11 (1961), pp. 61–64.

is, the person who is to participate in a program has training needs which he more or less recognizes and wants satisfied. This certainly does not mean that an individual is fully conscious of his training needs or has defined them for himself in any great detail. Rather, it indicates that training approaches and program content differs depending on a persons' organizational function, his level of career progress, and his stage of psychological and social maturity. Thus training has to be tailored according to the readiness of the person to absorb it.

The model also presupposes that a behavioral change is preceded by a change in attitudes, which is entirely consistent with the concepts of personality and motivation discussed in a previous chapter. Therefore, the target of the influence model is the attitudinal cluster selected for modification. Hence if a change in leader behavior is sought, then the program attempts to change the trainees' preconceptions of what constitutes effective leadership. Granting all of this, the model of attitudinal influence has three steps.

Unfreezing. The initial step breaks existing attitudes by altering the influences which play upon a personality. Essential to this step is the *isolation* of the individual from associations which reinforce the attitudes selected for change. Isolation is coupled with training pressure to change and a reduction of an individual's fear of change.

Changing. The second step introduces the individual to new attitudes and values which the influence process seeks to instill. This step is also most effectively accomplished in an isolated setting. The outcome desired at this stage is individual *identification* with the new values. At this point, hopefully the trainee achieves a tentative commitment to these values. However, another outcome is possible. It is the *internalization* of the new values which is not a true form of commitment. When one internalizes he simply accepts an attitude and a mode of behavior *ad hoc*. That is, he learns an appropriate framework of action and problem solving which is useful to him in the organizational setting he finds himself. He does not identify with these values in the form of commitment.

Refreezing. The last step crystallizes the new attitudes and values in the personality of the individual. This requires continual reinforcement by the organization seeking the change in the first place. It can be accomplished by genuine interpersonal relationships among members of the organization who hold the same values. However, if the environment to which the person returns is antagonistic to these values, then the individual may lapse into his old attitudes and ways.

Training Programs

Given the influence model, how does management training in the behavioral sciences measure up? To what extent does the "typical" program satisfy the requirements of the model and where does it fall short? We are, of course, talking about those programs which are primarily intended to improve executive ability in the sphere of interpersonal competence.

Shortly after World War II "human relations training programs" were grasped by management as the answer to their people problems. All too often these expectations were not fulfilled. The results management assumed would be forthcoming did not, and indeed realistically could not, materialize. Probably the greatest block to sound management development is that programs frequently were instituted for reasons apart from the avowed aims of management. There must be a total organizational commitment to the goals of a program if any lasting change in behavior is sought. This, of course, means that the organizational climate must be supportive of the new attitudes instilled in the attitudinal change process. This requirement of the refreezing phase is generally not met.[7]

The ultimate guide to program effectiveness is the degree of behavioral change it is able to secure in the participants' on-the-job performance. However, effectiveness is predicated on concrete program objectives, meaningful content, qualified instruction, motivated participants, and control of training results.

The motivation and control factors are the most forsaken of all the conditions underlying program effectiveness. Programs are structured *not to meet the training* needs of participants but to reflect the prejudices of training officers. Nothing undermines a program more than the feeling on the part of the participants that their training serves little purpose from the standpoint of their needs. In other words, participants are not *ready* for the kind of training which confronts them.

The follow-up failure is a flagrant deficiency in most programs. Typically, little effort is made to determine how far a program has gone in achieving the objectives set for it. The absence of adequate appraisal of a program's impact on behavior is a shortcoming of most conventional human relations training.[8] Asking whether or not trainees liked the program or are satisfied with the content, instructors, and the physical facilities is almost worthless as a control measure. Most responses are positively biased. The real measure of effectiveness is the extent of behavioral change.

Organizational training directors usually can justify the objectives of their programs. "We want to make our executives more effective leaders by instilling a democratic style. Or we want them to improve their communication abilities. Or we want them to be better at resolving conflicts." These are aims in the interpersonal competence area which will

---

[7] See James N. Mosel, "Why Training Programs Fail to Carry Over," *Personnel,* November–December, 1957, pp. 56–64. Mosel offers an interesting appraisal of the shortcomings of foremen training.

[8] The results have not been reassuring in cases where serious scientific attempts have been made to discover the affect of training on attitudinal change. See Edwin A. Fleishman, Edwin F. Harris, and Harold E. Burtt, *Leadership and Supervision in Industry* (Columbus: The Ohio State University, 1955).

provoke few objections. Additionally, training officers are most conscientious about the content, instructors, and methods used in their programs. But they squirm when questioned closely about control.

The lack of meaningful follow-up is not entirely the training director's fault. It is actually symptomatic of the incongruency which exists between the kinds of executive behavior which pay off, conditioned by the organizational climate, and the desire to improve the surroundings in which work goes on. Many training people feel that programs emphasizing democracy in leadership, participation in decision making, and freedom of communication will create an atmosphere for realizing greater organizational effectiveness and higher individual satisfaction.

Most top administrators agree with this in principle. After all they approve the financial support. Yet there is little proof that what is done in training carries over to job performance. People may be unfrozen and changed in training, but it is not difficult to predict what will happen when they return to an environment which is unprepared to accept their new attitudes.

To summarize, programs which have been aimed at improving the interpersonal competence of executives have been far from successful in the past because:

1. They have not clearly defined the training needs of participants. There has been a tendency to lump different executive types into a "canned" development program. Many executives simply are not prepared to accept what they hear in these programs.

2. Program appraisal has been so weak, that deficiencies in on-going training activities are not identified. This may be in part a defensive reaction by some training directors to the impossible incongruity between program philosophy and organizational reality.

3. The authoritarian, task-oriented environment has not changed so that the trainee finds little support for new democratic, participative attitudes even if he does accept them.

Clearly then, in terms of programs in general, there are serious shortcomings in the identification of executives who are "ready" for training and in the refreezing of new attitudes on the job.

Training Environment and Methods

Most of the better financed training programs have heeded the influence model's insistence that isolation is essential to the attitudinal unfreezing and change phases. Whenever possible trainees are taken out of the job and home environment for periods of a few days to several weeks. There is no question that isolation from distractions makes the job of changing old attitudes and implanting new ones easier. So the isolated training setting in a hotel, or training center, or university campus has become an established practice. However, the methods to accomplish the unfreezing and changing of attitudes vary widely.

A large number of training techniques have been used. They range from the simple lecture through the incident, conference, case and role playing methods. No purpose is served by elaborating on these techniques. Most personnel management textbooks explain them adequately. But there are two points of criticism which can be made about these more conventional devices.

First, where there is heavy reliance on lecture-conference discussion methods emphasis is placed on transmitting information. A kind of "rational" appeal is made to the trainee to change his attitudes about such matters as individual motivation, group behavior, and leadership style for example. Hopefully, the persuasion is sufficiently forceful and the evidence overwhelming enough to cause the individual to modify his behavior.

Second, those techniques which stress "reality practice" like roleplaying, cases, and incidents, while engrossing for participants, often do not follow through with a "message" of how observed behavior bears relevance to on-the-job situations. Further, much gimmickery is found in offshoots of these devices. Too frequently the end is to entertain rather than to change.

In tracing the evolution of training methods in human relations programs, we find increasing emphasis on the participation of the trainee. Instead of passively listening to lectures, he is discussing ideas in a conferencelike setting, or he is working on a case, or he is role playing. This reflects the notion that the more trainees actively *participate* in the development of subject matter, the more *involved* they tend to be in the values which the program seeks to impress. Since it is the purpose of training to replace old values with new, involvement is *the* desirable goal of training methods. At this stage though, trainee needs, program content, and methods are inseparable. In other words, it takes a high degree of congruency between needs, content, and method at the point of involvement to achieve trainee identification (or internalization) of the new value system.

The fact that participation and involvement are related, but separate, phenomena has eluded many responsible for training activities in the past. Participation tended to be viewed as an end in itself. The appeal often heard in training planning sessions was, "let's get everybody interacting." This is not difficult to do with a captive audience where the alternatives may be to interact and participate or to be bored to death. In any event, in proper hands most training methods can create considerable amounts of participation and interaction. But the extent of actual trainee involvement in the values and objectives of the program was largely left to chance. Therefore, it is misleading to interpret active participation in training sessions as involvement, much less commitment to a program's behavioral change goals.

To summarize, the conventional methods of unfreezing and changing attitudes, even in an isolated setting, are highly problematical. This is a source of concern for researchers and practitioners alike. Current thinking is aimed at methods to achieve greater involvement in the goals of change which training hopes to induce in executive behavior. The commoner techniques have not been ignored, in this respect, nor has participation been de-emphasized. Rather new approaches to training philosophy and methods have evolved.

Sensitivity Training

Sensitivity or laboratory training is a fairly recent innovation in executive development. It has grown out of the work of applied group dynamics[9] and is often associated with the program of the National Training Laboratory in Group Development.[10] The training approaches developed by researchers in these activities have been applied to industrial programs in a number of forms.[11] The objectives of sensitivity training, however, are basically the same.

It has been repeatedly observed in this chapter that the purpose of training is to change behavior. In the realm of human interrelationships as in no other sphere of human interest are attitudes fixed and loaded with explosive content. The aim of most human relations training is both to make executives more effective in their ability to relate to others and to accomplish organizational goals through the efforts of people. It is something of a self-evident truth that executive behavior in human undertakings is a matter of attitudes which are effective or ineffective from the standpoint of motivating people. Therefore, human relations training attempts to change attitudes so that ultimately behavior itself will change. However, programs in the past enjoyed a rather low level of success in effecting anything like a lasting or even initial change in attitudes.

Sensitivity training attempts to accomplish the end of behavioral change through a philosophy and technique of training which is best described as a concern with "how"—how a trainee appraises himself, how a group behaves, how another would react in a given situation. In short, sensitivity training has as its purpose the development of an executive's *awareness* of himself, of others, of group processes, and of group culture.

The core of a laboratory program is the T-group. From the standpoint of those who design and sponsor the program, the T-group's purpose is to help people:

---

[9] See D. Cartwright and A. Zander (eds.), *Group Dynamics: Research and Theory* (Evanston, Ill.: Row, Peterson and Co., 1960).

[10] See National Training Laboratory in Group Development, *Explorations in Human Relations Training: An Assessment of Experience, 1947–1953* (Washington, D.C.: National Education Association, 1953).

[11] For example see Irving R. Weschler, Marvin A. Klemes, and Clovis Shepard, "A New Focus in Executive Training," *Advanced Management*, May, 1955, pp. 19–22; and Michael G. Blansfield and W. F. Robinson, "Variations in Training Laboratory Design: A Case Study in Sensitivity Training," *Personnel Administration*, March–April, 1961, pp. 17–22, 49.

(1) to explore their values and their impact on others; (2) to determine if they wish to modify the old values and develop new ones; and (3) to develop awareness of how groups can inhibit as well as facilitate human growth and decision making.[12]

To the trainees the T-group, or the small group into which they are put, appears objectiveless and structureless at the start. But as they interact, structure and objectives emerge. In viewing this, the trainee can get an understanding of small group processes and his impact on them. At the same time, through communication and feedback with and from other members of the group, he learns about himself as seen through the eyes of others. By being told frankly how his behavior and attitudes are "read" he has opened alternatives for change.

From this experience, hopefully an individual will see behavioral shortcomings in himself and others which impair interpersonal relationships. If a person experiences failure in relating with other members of the group, and is told why by the group, he then may change his attitudes, and ultimately, his behavior in order to interact more successfully. Obviously these kinds of laboratory experiences can generate a high degree of individual involvement because a person's basic assumptions about his own behavior and other's is directly challenged.

The end of lab training is to enhance *authenticity* in human relationships. This can only be accomplished in a setting where there is a high degree of individual awareness and acceptance of other people. In Argyris' words, ". . . an individual's growth and learning (on the interpersonal level) is inexorably tied up with his fellow man."[13] Thus authenticity comes from the *relationship* between aware and sensitive individuals who have reached maturity in interpersonal transactions.

Laboratory programs differ widely in design. They may incorporate varying amounts of lecture, conference, case studies, and role playing. They may vary also in the degree of structuredness. But to repeat the central feature of these programs is the T-group which exists to accomplish the purposes mentioned above.

Now, we have been treating the lab method as though its main target of change is the individual. Most certainly the individual is one target. The other is the organization, or more precisely, the social system.[14] There are many changes which lab training could induce in organizations. Organizational climate could be improved so that individual change gets reinforcement instead of antagonism. The point we dwell on here, how-

---

[12] Chris Argyris, *Interpersonal Competence and Organizational Effectiveness* (Homewood, Ill. Dorsey Press, 1962), p. 156. This is a basic reference in laboratory training.

[13] *Ibid.*, pp. 20–21.

[14] For an excellent treatment of this point and other aspects of lab training see Warren G. Bennis, *Changing Organizations* (New York: McGraw-Hill Book Co., Inc., 1966), esp. chap. 8.

ever, is the use of the lab method to improve the setting for conflict resolution.

This approach is discussed by Blake, Shepard, and Mouton in their book *Managing Intergroup Conflict in Industry*.[15] They present a framework for viewing intergroup conflict and propose three management orientations toward it. Within each orientation, scaled according to the level of payoff, are alternative conflict resolution strategies. Thus, if conflict is perceived as:

1. Inevitable with agreement impossible, then the strategies in descending order of intensity are (*a*) win-lose power struggle, (*b*) third-party arbitration, (*c*) fate.

2. Not inevitable, yet agreement not possible with strategies of (*a*) withdrawal, (*b*) isolation, (*c*) indifference.

3. Not inevitable, but agreement possible when it does occur, generating strategies of (*a*) problem-solving, (*b*) compromise, (*c*) peaceful coexistence.

Without going into an extensive analysis of the authors' model suffice it to say that they believe that conflict resolution strategies short of "problem solving" produce dysfunctional consequences. Conflicts are not effectively resolved, they think, because of relational inadequacies between groups, or their representatives, at points of tangency in organizations. To Blake and his coauthors the problem-solving strategy is innovative. By unrestrained communication between people who are skilled in effective social behavior, differences between groups may be settled and the grounds for conflict eliminated. But what is most important is that authentic interactions produce creative solutions to conflict which are unobtainable from other strategies. Because these solutions are the product of joint group effort, they become the vehicles for securing intergroup cooperation. All this, provides the climate for an individual's commitment to wider intergroup goals, rather than to the narrow interests of the group with which he immediately identifies.

The method for achieving these ends is the intergroup laboratory, where people develop their relational skills. In this setting, each group through communication and interaction, gets to see the problem from the perspective of the other. Additionally group members develop an appreciation for the motives and the pressures which mold the behavior of participants. Insights into the attitudes of others and themselves are engendered which break down barriers to successful problem solving. Out of these interactions, people in opposing groups begin to realize in the authors' words:

. . . that the problem is in the *relationship between groups*. This is far different from perceiving the difficulty to be in each group *separately*. Thus, if

---

[15] Robert R. Blake, Herbert A. Shepard, and Jane S. Mouton, *Managing Intergroup Conflict in Industry* (Houston: Gulf Publishing Co., 1964).

the problem is in the relationship, then it must be solved by those who have the relationship. Also, if solutions are to be developed, the solutions have to be generated by those who share the responsibility for seeing that the solutions work.[16]

Once this is appreciated, new, creative solutions to conflict situations emerge. All in all, organizational atmosphere improves. It is less dominated by restrictive special interests, and the opportunity for new levels of effectiveness and individual satisfaction is increased. This applies to conflict among organizational command units, and even between two organizations as a union and a management.

THE "WHY" OF TRAINING

We looked at some of the methods for making inputs to create change in individuals and organizations. Now we must consider why we want to make these changes at all. This section gives us a chance to pull together and elaborate upon certain ideas already expressed in other parts of this book.

The reader may ask, "Isn't this an odd place to discuss the goals of change—under a training topic?" It is not so strange if it is recalled that the modern "change agent" has his greatest impact on an organization in the training activity. As we indicated in Chapter 13, interventions may be made through research, consulting, and training. But, by and large, training is the area where those interested in planned change presently find their greatest acceptance.

The values change agents bring to training do not differ from those we talked about earlier in Chapter 13. That is, they are biased against bureaucracy and rational norms of organizational behavior; and they are biased toward democracy and participative leadership. Further, they hope to achieve through training, as part of their total program for organization change, those objectives which were given in detail on page 263.

Given this contemporary perspective, we might consider what the trend in training philosophy is. Are there any differences in the 1960's compared with the 1950's? We can say, with some degree of assurance, that there has been a qualitative shift in emphasis. There has been a movement away from the notion of "human relations skill development" making managers better able to "deal" with people. Presently the focus is on developing the person to realize his potentialities and on the redesign of the organization to fill the social and psychological needs of man. The fountainhead for this twofold change is found in motivational and leadership theories.

---

[16] *Ibid.*, pp. 87–88.

The Hierarchy of Needs Concept

The hierarchy of needs concept cannot be ignored when explaining the changed orientation of training. Such champions of this approach as Maslow and Argyris set the stage in the 1950's. Today the more advanced programs make much of helping the individual achieve a higher order of self-awareness. Certainly lab training is aimed at developing an individual's potential in the realm of social behavior. By effective interaction the individual, through the group, acquires awareness by greater understanding of his own behavior and its effect on others. *Thus, training is seen as a vehicle for enabling people to satisfy a higher order of need—that of self-actualization.*

This highly personal aspect of training was not fully appreciated in the 1950's. Nor, indeed, were the methods and the organizational climate of the times such that this goal had much chance of successful implementation and acceptance. Today, instruments are available to achieve it, as we have seen in the previous section. But what is equally important organizations are readier to accept it as a legitimate goal.

Leadership Patterns

Probably the most influential force shaping training philosophy is the democratic leadership school. It has many variations, but the leading proponents of its basic theme are McGregor,[17] Likert,[18] and Bennis.[19] Their position, while representative of contemporary industrial humanism, grew out of Elton Mayo's neoclassical school, which in turn drew from the work of Kurt Lewin and John Dewey. It is expressed as a reaction to autocracy which seems peculiar to hierarchial, bureaucratic systems.

Persons who are delegated headship roles in formal organizations often are not chosen because of their leadership qualities or group acceptance. Headships are frequently given to the best technician or to the best tactician in organizational power plays. But regardless of why an individual ends up in a headship, he finds that once there it is necessary for him to influence people.

Prescriptions have been offered in management literature for years as to the best ways for motivating subordinates. The scholars working in the areas of bureaucracy and classical organization theory often neglected the human variable. They assumed that a division of work and a rational structuring of an organization along functional and scalar lines would result in a system where people could almost automatically accomplish objectives and derive their personal satisfaction from so doing.

---

[17] Douglas McGregor, *The Human Side of Enterprise* (New York: The McGraw-Hill Book Co., Inc., 1960).

[18] Rensis Likert, *New Patterns of Management* (New York: The McGraw-Hill Book Co., Inc., 1961).

[19] Bennis, *op. cit.*

The neoclassical treatment of organization theory stressed the human variable; and out of this orientation came a unique approach to leadership. The neoclassical doctrine of leadership emphasizes the *consent* of those led. By the same token, it plays down the authoritarian form of leadership based on domination. This approach has a number of labels, including "democratic," "participative," and "nonpressure-oriented" leadership. The most frequently used is "democratic leadership" and this is adopted in the following pages for uniformity.

For many years, and particularly since the end of World War II, democratic leadership has been accepted as the appropriate *and* the most effective pattern of leader behavior for employee motivation. Its doctrine carries force because it has been supported by research findings and it has the additional advantage of moral suasion. How can a leadership pattern be denied if it results in higher productivity, greater human happiness, increased group solidarity, *plus* conformance with the democratic ideals of American society?

Endorsements for democratic leadership are not difficult to find in either management or behavioral science literature. The general theme is that people work better, are happier, and are more apt to accept change in an environment when they are allowed to have some say in matters that affect them directly. The opposite of the democratic philosophy is the autocratic where individuals are permitted little if any chance for self-determination.

The contrasts which Laird and Laird draw between these leadership patterns are shown in Figure 16–1.

FIGURE 16–1
Autocratic versus Democratic Leadership

Autocratic Subclasses of Behavior	Democratic Subclasses of Behavior
Authoritarian	Equalitarian
Dictatorial	Facilitative
Leader centered	Group centered
Production centered	Worker centered
Restrictive	Permissive

Source: Donald A. Laird and Eleanor Laird, *The New Psychology for Leadership* (New York: McGraw-Hill Book Co., Inc., 1956), p. 44.

The essential feature of democratic leadership philosophy is its orientation toward those led, particularly the group. Laird and Laird's choice of descriptive words and phrases is particularly good for highlighting the basic philosophy of democratic leadership. They succinctly illustrate the ideas of group centeredness, the atmosphere of permissiveness, and the consideration which pervade the democratic organizational environment. In short, the philosophy of democratic leadership rests on allowing the expression of the collective will. It disclaims any part of organizational "cults of personality."

Now, of course certain problems arise when democratic leadership is applied to organizations which are authoritarian in concept and structure. Obviously, an organization in which the decision process is democratic from top to bottom is not tenable. Consequently, democratic leadership has to undergo some modifications.

The instrument regarded as the most satisfactory for introducing democratic leadership into an administrative setting is *participation*. In its extreme, participation allows employees to share in all decisions which affect them; that is, they may decide on goals and on methods to reach the goals. In its less extreme form—designed to protect the authority of the designated leader—employee participation applies to sharing in the decisions relating to the *alternatives* open for the accomplishment of the objective. Thus, the objective is given by the boss; employees participate in deciding on the methods to achieve it.

Democratic leadership in an organization involves far more than participation. Democratic leadership implies a "climate" where employees have a chance to grow and develop, where formal supervision is considerate and the application of sanctions is not arbitrary, and where employee attitudes are sincerely respected and solicited. Thus, democratic leadership is a "state of mind" in which the management is committed to the recognition of the dignity of employees as men and not merely as factors of production.

That democratic leadership and the goals of laboratory training go hand in hand is obvious. Individual self-awareness can stem only from a work situation to which an individual feels he has some commitment and involvement. It cannot come from that which, as Argyris says, goes counter to his psychological needs as a mature adult. The democratic climate, therefore, is supportive of and necessary to the development of individual aspirations along higher motivational lines. The realization of greater personal potential stems only from an organizational atmosphere which allows its participants freedom to decide and to act. If this is stifled by restrictive authoritarianism, the individual as well as the organization suffers. Thus, we see the rationale behind the philosophy which has become influential in management development circles.

PART IV-C

Problems and Issues in Administration

17

The Status of First-Line Supervision

LIKE THE LADY who protesteth too much, management feels compelled to reassure itself and the foreman that he is still part of management. Fifty or sixty years ago such protestations would not have made much sense. They are understandable today because the status of the foreman has changed.

Around the turn of the century the foreman knew where he stood; he was part of management. There was no doubt in anyone's mind about it. However, industrial philosophy, organization, and technology have undergone vast transitions since the time the foreman was master of the shop. As a result, the foreman, like many other occupational categories, has ended up in an historical backwash to the mainstream of industrial change.

Since the end of World War II many people have concerned themselves with the plight of the foreman. Businessmen and academicians have combined to commiserate with him and to reaffirm that, indeed, he is still the keystone of management. But in spite of what company presidents say at annual foremen banquets, the status of the foreman has declined. And the factors which have produced this decline are as complex as the industrial evolution which caused it.

Merely saying the foreman is part of management avoids the issues. The foreman's status is complicated by a number of events which are considered in this chapter. Whether or not the foreman is a segment of management is in part a matter of definition, in part a matter of personal identification by the foreman with management, in part a matter of legal mandate, and in part a matter of acceptance of the foreman by higher levels of management. These problems and others are dealt with in detail in this chapter.

For many foremen, the debate about their managerial status has only remote interest. The declining status of the foreman relative to the rest of management is, more or less, an academic issue. But one problem is of practical concern to the foreman; it is that his status is not clear. As a matter of practical, day-to-day significance, the foreman is aware and concerned that he operates in an ambiguous setting. He knows, for example, that his daily activities bring him into contact with others who have diverse expectations of what might be called desirable supervisory behavior. Chief among these groups and individuals are the union, members of the staff, his boss, and his subordinates. These expectations play upon the foreman's position from many directions, making his role difficult to discharge effectively.

The current problems of foreman status are attributable to three basic causes.

1. The declining skill level of the operative employees supervised.
2. The usurpation of functions by the staff.
3. Indifference of higher executives.

It is evident that these causes have not had equal impact in all industrial segments. Consequently, the foreman's role appears to be affected differentially from industry to industry, or for that matter, from company to company. Ample evidence is available to demonstrate that the "problem foremen" are largely concentrated in one particular part of the American business complex. So, before going any farther, it is important to indicate what foremen are being considered and why other first-line supervisors are left out of the discussion.

DEFINITION OF FIRST-LINE SUPERVISION

The foreman's position may be defined descriptively and functionally. From a descriptive point of view, it is said that the foreman:[1]

1. Is a head of a department or section in touch with rank and file workers.
2. Receives policies and directives from higher management and is responsible in varying degrees for their execution.
3. Gives orders and direction.
4. Does little or no work of a manual variety since such work is usually handled by subordinates.
5. Receives compensation usually higher than subordinates.

Descriptively, the main point of distinction between the foreman and higher levels of management is the supervision of operative personnel. In the line organization, *the foreman is the only person who does not supervise other managers.*[2]

---

[1] American Management Association, *The Development of Foremen in Management* (Research Report Number 7 [1945]), p. 14.

[2] This is not entirely accurate. In Chapter 8, "Status and Role," mention was made of the working supervisor and the unique role he has enjoyed in manufacturing. It was noted in this chapter that the working supervisor possesses some limited managerial prerogatives such as training, making work assignments, and acting as lead man on the production line. The working supervisor, however, does manual operations. Further the scope of his supervisory authority is so restricted that he is eligible for union membership and is not included in an exempt status for purposes of the Wage and Hour Law.

Functionally, the foreman performs the activities of planning, organizing, motivating, and controlling, as do all other personnel having executive responsibility in a business organization. But the foreman's position is the lowest level in the management hierarchy where the performance of the basic functions of management can be clearly identified. Thus, the foreman represents the first line of management to rank and file employees at the point of physical production of goods and services.

Manufacturing Classifications

Now that the organizational position of the foreman has been established, it is possible to reintroduce an idea raised earlier. The status of first-line supervision is not universally the same across American business. Indeed, the locus of foreman status problems is seated in one particular part of American industry. It is convenient to follow Howard L. Timms[3] in establishing which foremen are most affected by a declining status situation, and why. Timms' breakdown of manufacturing into three types is useful for pinpointing the problem segment. The three manufacturing classifications are: continuous, job order, and intermittent.

Continuous Manufacturing. Companies falling in this category are commonly in the process industries. Included are petroleum refineries and the producers of chemicals. The makers of highly standardized goods such as tennis balls, flashlight batteries, and some electronic components frequently are also part of this overall category.

Typical of continuous manufacturers is production in anticipation of demand rather than in direct response to customer order. Paralleling anticipatory production is making goods to inventory so that production can be maintained at a fairly constant level over a period of time. The product itself is made uniformly to a standard. The length of the production run is relatively long and the lot sizes manufactured are relatively large.

Continuous manufacturing lends itself quite readily to a high degree of mechanization or, in some cases, automation. The activities involved in the production process are repetitive, and the flow of product through the production cycle is continuous from one stage to the next.

Job-Order Manufacturing. In the broadest sense, job-order manufacturing requires customizing a product for a buyer. The characteristics of this type of manufacturing are almost exactly the opposite of continuous manufacturing. The products are heterogeneous, varying according to different customer specifications. Production is undertaken only as a result of demand—specifically, the receipt of an order. Products are not manufactured to stock. Production runs are relatively short and the lot sizes are small. The nature of the production process is largely nonrepetitive.

---

[3] Howard L. Timms, *Production Management* (Bloomington: Bureau of Research, Indiana Readings in Business, Number 22, 1958), pp. 1–3.

Some examples of companies in job-order manufacturing may be found in the machine-tool industry, the construction industry, and in the electronic industry where a firm might be making, say, miniaturized parts for missiles.

Intermittent Manufacturing. This type of production is a hybrid of job order and continuous. It is the type commonest in American industry. Contrary to popular opinion, mass production assembly industries, like the automotive industry, are the intermittent rather than the continuous variety.

In this form of manufacturing the components of a particular product are made for inventory, although the final product can be made to reflect different component combinations specified by the customer. For example, an automobile dealer can request the colors, body styles, and equipment he needs to meet customer demand. Each dealer order accompanies the car through the assembly process. Thus, the car is "made to order" by putting together a certain combination of components selected from a wide variety of standardized parts and equipment.

Therefore, in intermittent manufacturing parts are usually produced on a continuous, or repetitive, basis to stock. The finished product is not produced to inventory. Typically, then, intermittent production is in part in response to customer demand and in part in anticipation of demand. The finished product is heterogeneous, but it is heterogeneous within a range of standardized variations established by the manufacturer.

All in all, the intermittent manufacturer has quite complex problems to solve, including scheduling, forecasting demand, coordinating production activities, and balancing inventories. Within the intermittent category fall automobile manufacturers, aircraft manufacturers, and radio and television producers.

Manufacturing Types and Foreman Status

The foreman discussed in this chapter is generally not found in continuous or job-order manufacturing. There are several reasons why this is so.

First, purely continuous manufacturing is something of a rarity. The number of foremen employed in process industries is relatively few compared to the total.

Second, in those few cases of continuous manufacturing where the foreman is found, his role often is quite different from the stereotype. Those individuals who might be defined as first-line supervisors are frequently in charge of crews of highly specialized and skilled maintenance workers. This hardly conforms to the common picture of the foreman heading up a gang of semiskilled assembly workers. The status and nature of supervision in continuous manufacturing is not typical for the bulk of American foremen.

Third, the pure job-order shop, while not as rare as the continuous manufacturer, still does not employ foremen on a mass scale. The job-order manufacturer is often small. The foremen on the payroll must be highly qualified and capable of handling the variety of technical problems which often occur with the production of a customer's order. Since each order usually presents a different problem, the foreman must be skilled and flexible enough to meet each effectively.

Fourth, because of the small size of the job-order shop, the technical staff usually is not large. In these cases, of course, the staff has not usurped the foreman's prerogatives. Consequently, the functions of planning, organizing, and controlling still devolve on the foreman to a great extent. Thus, because of the need for considerable skill and the retention of traditional management functions, the foreman's status in job-order manufacturing has remained relatively high.

In summary, the foremen in continuous and job-order manufacturing have managed to maintain their status position while the foremen in intermittent manufacturing have suffered a declining status. In large part, the relatively higher status of the foremen in continuous and job-order manufacturing is attributed to the fact that the skill level of the people they supervise is high. Other factors are at work here, of course, but the level of skill of those supervised appears to be the crucial determinant of the foremen's status in industry. Hence, the higher the skill level supervised the higher will be the foreman's status.

The Foreman in Intermittent Manufacturing. Intermittent manufacturing is by far the most important type in American industry by any measure one wishes to apply, be it the number of people employed or the value added to gross national product. Intermittent manufacturing is found in most of the major industrial classifications, ranging across the automotive, appliance, steel, electronic, farm equipment, and garment industries. Therefore, the foremen in intermittent manufacturing are the main focus of this chapter.

In the sphere of intermittent manufacturing, the determinants which have lowered the foreman's status can be singled out easily. Manufacturers in this category have been diligently engaged in rationalization, which in part involves the specialization of labor. For production jobs specialization means constant simplification, leading to a decrease in the skill level required of operative employees. Lowering operative skill levels naturally affects the amount of skill needed by the foreman. At present the foreman in intermittent manufacturing supervises only a fragment of the total production process and heads a department employing semiskilled or unskilled workers.

As noted before, the problems of intermittent manufacturers tend to be complex. Where companies are large enough and can afford it, a technical staff is usually introduced. Bringing in staffs to facilitate the planning, organizing, and control functions can have just one result from the standpoint of the foreman. It is the dilution of his job. Technical staffs in planning, production control, cost control, quality control, product and process development, and industrial management have all combined to machine tool many decisions that the foreman made previously.

The lowering of skill requirements of foremen and the usurpation of their functions by the staff has had this effect—*any particular foreman, like any particular production worker, is easily replaceable.* This fact of industrial life of course has its impact on higher management's thinking. Managerial attitudes toward the foreman have been characterized by

FIGURE 17–1

Events in Intermittent Manufacturing Which Have Contributed to the Decline in Foreman Status

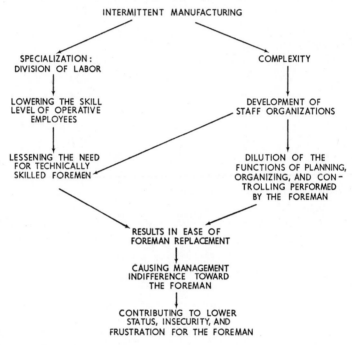

indifference in many instances. The foremen's response to indifference has shown up in attitude surveys as feelings of insecurity; in large part, insecurity played a major role as the motive behind the union organization movement of the foremen in the 1940's.

Figure 17–1 summarizes the factors in intermittent manufacturing which have had direct bearing on the lowering of the foreman's status. The dilemma of the foreman in intermittent manufacturing today is the product of industrial evolution. It could be said that the modern foreman represents an historical anachronism in the process of being phased out. In any event, it is useful to gain a perspective of current foreman problems from the standpoint of history.

HISTORICAL BACKGROUND

In 1920 Sanford E. Thompson related a conclusion he reached when he was a young man. He said that the 19th- and early 20th-century foreman could not be effective unless he possessed a completely sulphurous vocabulary.[4] Another writer observed that the early foreman ". . . was picked . . . for two reasons, he knew his job technically and mechanically better than the others and he was aggressive; he would not spare himself and he could be depended upon that no one of his men lay down on the job."[5] In a description of the early foreman's job, Jones writes:

> The foreman is commonly the sole administrative agency of the shop. He is expected to look after tools and machines, find material and supplies for his men, instruct them in the manner of doing work, arrange tasks so that every one is kept busy, enforce a proper pace, write up the job cards and other records, preserve order, make orders and reports as requested concerning the progress of individual jobs, and give an opinion on which to base promotions and discharges.[6]

The early foreman filled the picture of the autocratic stereotype well. He disciplined and fired with impunity and he was arbitrary in the distribution of favors. The unchallenged authority of the foreman in the shop led John Golden of the United Textile Workers to remark that next to wages, the biggest problem of organized labor was "the autocracy of minor officials, including the foreman."[7]

The composite which emerges from this indicates that the early foreman had uncommon responsibilities of both a technical and human nature. He was required to be a technical specialist, a shop administrator, and an enforcer of harsh labor policy. In respect to the latter responsibility, Sumner H. Slichter notes that the foundation of management's labor policy rested in crudity and the drive system. He points out further that labor policies were designed to overawe the worker with power, and that the foreman was the main instrumentality for accomplishing this end.[8]

But the foreman did not retain his pivotal position long after the turn of the century. It was evident to many writers in the 1920's, including Jones, Clark, and Thompson cited above, that a new type of foreman was emerging as a product of a number of industrial changes which undermined the foreman's power. Key among these were:

1. Management's labor relations philosophy.
2. Functional foremanship.
3. Growth of human relations idealism.

---

[4] Sanford E. Thompson, "The Foreman," *Bulletin of the Taylor Society*, February, 1920, p. 43.

[5] Charles W. Clark, "Field of the Foreman in Industry," *Industrial Management*, January, 1920, p. 18.

[6] Edward D. Jones, *The Administration of Industrial Enterprises* (New York: Longmans, Green and Co., 1926), p. 268.

[7] Quoted in Jones, see *ibid.*, p. 295.

[8] Sumner H. Slichter, "The Management of Labor," *Journal of Political Economy*, December, 1919, pp. 814–16.

Management's Labor Relations Philosophy

Immediately following World War I, the "American Plan" was introduced. The purpose of this plan was to combat the union movement which had grown extensively during the war. The plan's strategy was to give the workers wage, hour, and "fringe" concessions directly which the unions hoped to achieve indirectly through organizing and collective bargaining.

A staff position introduced in industry shortly before 1920 came to act as the administrative agency for the American Plan. This position was best known under the title of "employment manager." It is interesting to note that the first major intrusion by a staff organization on foreman activities was in the area of personnel. Another quotation from Jones shows some of the results that this change was expected to have.

> . . . the foreman is relieved of the importunities to hire the friends of the employees of his department. . . . He can no longer sell jobs, nor hold his favorites in soft assignments. He is deprived of the easy device of covering his own incompetence by firing a man.[9]

The outcomes of the employment manager's efforts were mixed, because so much depended on the effectiveness of the man in the job and the management philosophy under which he had to operate. A well-administered personnel program could beneficially eliminate a good deal of foreman arbitrariness. It must be remembered, however, that one of the chief motivating forces behind the establishment of the employment manager was to offset the gains of organized labor and, for that matter, to destroy the union movement itself.[10] Alone, the American Plan did not constitute a fundamental change in management's attitude toward workers. It was a "soft sell" to convince workers they had nothing to gain by joining unions.

Management's labor relations philosophy is not the primary concern of this chapter. The main point is that the personnel function was the first major foreman activity to be diluted on a large scale by the growth of the

---

[9] Jones, *op. cit.*, p. 392.

[10] Of course, other important factors led to the creation of the personnel staff. The press of World War I focused attention on the ineffective use of human resources. Sources of all labor were drying up. Old wastes could not be tolerated as they were under the prevailing inadequacies of foremanship. Specialists in the form of employment managers were brought in to develop a science of work-force administration. See Paul H. Douglas, "Plant Administration of Labor," *Journal of Political Economy*, July, 1919, pp. 544–60. Another influence which cannot be overlooked is the scientific management movement. The application of scientific management principles to personnel administration was felt, especially by the Gilbreths, to be quite appropriate. These principles could be best applied if their execution was delegated to a specialist in personnel.

staff.[11] Clark nicely characterized the impact of the change on the "old-fashioned" foreman when he said:

This type of man [the autocratic foreman] is the man who at the present time is rubbing his eyes to find out where he stands. . . . He has hired men and fired them at will. The employer now organizes a new department called the "Personnel Department" and the men under the foreman's direction are hired and discharged according to a new-fangled scheme he does not understand![12]

Functional Foremanship

Frederick W. Taylor introduced functional foremanship for the purpose of making intensive use of foreman specialization to render him a more valuable person to the company. The ironic consequence of functional foremanship was the undercutting of the position of the foreman in an unanticipated way. This was the evolution of staff groups with functional authority, a point which we have already covered in some detail in Chapter 5.

The rising significance of the staff and the parallel decline of foreman status cannot, of course, be attributed to a plot of power-mad technocrats. One might conclude that the growth of the staff was inevitable, given the evolution of industry to higher forms of technology and greater degrees of complexity. The typical foreman simply was not equipped to cope adequately with specialized problems of control and engineering.

Industry was forced to accelerate its demands for more effective controls over quality, quantity, and cost. Additionally, manufacturers needed advanced planning and organizing efforts in the areas of product research and development, process engineering, work simplification and work standards. Faced with these needs, it is not surprising that the staff emerged in force, displacing the foreman from many of his traditional activities and imposing new imperatives which the foreman did not understand nor appreciate.

Growth of Human Relations Idealism

Much is made of the point today that the foreman, above and beyond everything else, *must be a leader of men.* The emphasis on leadership responsibilities of foremen is nothing new. Clark in 1920 said, "The former most important qualifications for foremanship . . . are eclipsed by the modern requirement that a foreman must know how to handle men."[13]

---

[11] See Henry Eilbirt, "The Development of Personnel Management in the United States," *Business History Review,* Autumn, 1959, pp. 359–64.

[12] Clark, *op. cit.,* p. 18.

[13] Clark, *op. cit.,* p. 18.

With his other functions reduced or denied him, it is obvious that the foreman is left with only the function of motivating. This is not to underrate the significance of the motivating activity. The foreman, as a competent leader, can go far to create the conditions necessary for an efficient and quality-conscious department. Also, by establishing a satisfactory "work climate" the foreman may be able to reduce labor turnover, gain the confidence of employees in management, sell them on the value and legitimacy of their work, and reduce gripes, complaints, and grievances. In short, the foreman has an interpersonal laboratory to which he goes every day. The way he exercises his skills can contribute immeasurably in the structuring of a cooperative system within the limits of his department.

At first, management was slow to realize the true value of the democratic approach in dealing with operative employees. More than anything else, the Hawthorne studies brought home to management the importance of centering leadership on the satisfaction of human needs as a prerequisite for accomplishing organization goals without sacrifice of an individual's dignity.

After the initial impact of the Hawthorne studies, the philosophy of the movement spread rapidly. First-line supervision was most affected, because it was felt that here the greatest gains could be made. This can be attested to by the number of human relations training programs for foremen undertaken with the blessing of higher levels of management. The outcomes of these programs have not been uniformly satisfactory. However, this is not the place for a discussion of human relations training. Let it suffice to say that the foreman's leadership role based on the principles of human relations loomed very large and management recognized the significance of this role by intensifying training for it.

It is evident that the foreman's job entails daily face-to-face contact with his subordinates. It is possible that the foreman has on the average more contacts with more subordinates than any other person in the management hierarchy. Thus, a certain expertness in interpersonal relationships is essential to his job. Further, this ability or "specialization" in leadership is something which cannot be delegated to a staff to perform. Motivation of subordinates on a face-to-face basis is most likely to remain a function uniquely associated with foremanship.

Yet, from the standpoint of the foreman leadership does not pay off. Precisely what does this mean? First, promotion is not based entirely on leadership potential. The "best" operative employees do not always make good leaders at the foreman level. Selection criteria for promotion purposes rest largely on technical qualifications. Hence, the foreman's position often is not filled by one who represents the best leadership risk. Second, the ability to lead and to motivate as a function relative to the functions of planning, organizing, and controlling, is not sufficiently recognized so that the status of the foreman can be elevated by it alone.

Consequently, while human relations idealism has not actually contributed to the deterioration of the foreman's status, neither has it raised it. The shifting of emphasis to motivation and leadership has not proven to be a substitute in compensating foremanship, statuswise, for its reduced scope in the other spheres of management activities.

THE FOREMAN LOOKS AT HIMSELF AND HIS JOB

The foreman has been the object of a number of research studies. Consequently, considerable data are available on which to base this section concerning foremen attitudes, problems, and self-perceptions.

Foremen's Self-Perceptions Reflect Their Unique Position in the Manufacturing Process

Certain rigidities or role stereotypes are readily apparent in a manufacturing organization of some size. Roethlisberger[14] has summarized these rigidities as follows:

1. *Production workers* are supposed *to conform* to standards and changes that they do not originate.
2. *Foremen* are supposed *to uphold* or enforce standards of performance determined by other groups.
3. *Technical experts,* usually staff, are supposed *to originate* better ways of doing things.
4. *Top management* is supposed *to formulate* policies.

To Roethlisberger, these rigidities have the effect of insulating people into groups according to the role they play. This process of exclusion causes the individuals in a particular group to develop a common perspective regarding their own function, plus a warped view of the functions performed by other groups.

This conclusion is supported by a good deal of research. Porter pointed out that the foreman's self-perception is distinct from upper management and the line operative employee. The self-perceptions of the foremen are those of a different group compared with groups above and below them in the organizational hierarchy. Porter concludes that his study ". . . tends to show that the self-perception of the supervisors reflects their unique position in the structure of the organization. Their self-descriptions show certain differences from those of men they direct, but they also show somewhat the same differences from those of men who direct them.[15]

One feature of the foreman's position is the conflicting role expectations which impinge on him from many directions, in particular from those he

[14] Fritz J. Roethlisberger, "The Foreman's Dilemma," *Planning Supervisory Development* (American Management Association, Personnel Series #96, 1945), p. 7.

[15] Lyman W. Porter, "Self-Perceptions of First-Level Supervisors Compared with Upper-Management Personnel and with Operative Line Workers," *Journal of Applied Psychology,* June, 1959, p. 186.

supervises and from those who supervise him. As a result of these differing expectations, the foreman is forced to tread a fine line. He cannot completely satisfy one set of demands without forsaking another set. The only feasible course of action *is* compromise.[16]

Porter's study shows, quite in line with these observations, that the foreman's self-perceptions reveal him to be an individual acting with restraint and caution. The game he plays requires keeping peace among groups with different opinions of what constitutes effective foreman behavior. The foreman is usually aware of these conflicting expectations and he takes the only acceptable course of action. He compromises.

There are other dimensions to the foreman's unique position. As already noted, the foreman is the only individual in an organization with supervisory responsibility who does not supervise other managers. That the functions of foremanship provide the connecting link between policy levels of management and operative employees at the point of production is, indeed, quite unique. Whether or not this position is a "keystone" is debatable. However, it is certain that effective performance at this level of the organization is a major contribution to a company's success.

It is fair to say that foremen have an awareness of their peculiar role in the organization. Stemming from this role are a number of conditions found by foremen to undermine their morale and effective performance.

Conditions Which Undermine Foreman Performance and Morale

Although not exhaustive, five major deficiencies in management policy and practice are cited by foremen as reducing their effectiveness and morale. These are: poor communication, little participation in management, disagreement regarding job responsibilities, compensation, and using foremanship as a training ground.

Communication. Probably the biggest foreman complaint, next to pay perhaps, is poor communication. Communication pertaining to policy matters seems to be weakest at the foreman level. Obviously, all policy considerations should not be transmitted to foremen. The foreman, however, ought to be appraised fully of policies which affect his job directly, and policies which stimulate him to identify with management.

In the first case, careful indoctrination in labor policy is a matter of crucial importance. The second case is more difficult. A foreman would find it hard to feel associated with management if he were not informed, at least in a general way, of top-level deliberations regarding the future directions of the company and the effect of such directions on supervision. It is unpleasant to work in the dark and not see the significance of one's activities as they relate to the overall goals of the company.

The failure of the foremen's immediate supervisor to keep them ap-

---

[16] William S. Toddie, "When Foremen Feel 'Sacrificed'," *Personnel Journal,* October, 1957, pp. 170–73.

praised of their job performance is another communication deficiency frequently mentioned. Foremen complain they receive little praise for a well-done job; and they do not hear soon enough about their weak points.[17]

Little Voice in Policy Decisions. The second group of foreman complaints is in the area of participation in policymaking. According to Mullen's findings, foremen feel they are given infrequent opportunity to voice their sentiments in labor negotiations.[18] If true, this is indeed a blind spot in management practice.[19] Because the foreman is in a strategic position in the administration of the labor agreement, it seems reasonable that he be provided with channels through which he can express his opinions about the content of the agreement.

In addition to the problem of nonparticipation in labor policy, the foreman would like to extend his authority and increase his voice in decisions relating to the overall administrative aspects of his job. But there appears to be some discrepancy between what the foreman visualizes as the content of his job and what his boss sees as his responsibilities.

Disagreement Regarding Job Responsibilities. In large part the foreman's problems relating to job responsibilities are a matter of role definition. Herbert H. Meyer's study of this issue reveals a fairly high level of disagreement between the foreman's and his boss's conception of the foreman's job responsibility.[20] Interestingly enough, even the most effective foremen in the study disagreed with their general foreman on the content of their job as often as the least effective. Apparently, the level of foreman achievement, as appraised by the general foreman, was not a factor conditioning the degree of disagreement. The best foremen were as much at odds over the content of their jobs with their boss as the worst foremen.

Meyer concludes that:

Some of the disagreement between foremen and general foremen may very well be due to the nature of the foreman's job itself. . . . In almost every area

---

[17] Some steps taken by management to overcome communication difficulties are reported by Wilmar F. Bernthal, "Foremanship: Business' Achilles' Heel?" *Business Horizons,* Spring, 1958, pp. 115–19.

[18] James H. Mullen, "The Supervisor Assesses His Job in Management: Highlights of a Nationwide Survey," *Personnel,* September, 1954, pp. 101–104.

[19] Contrary to Mullen's findings, a *Management Record* report indicates nearly all the firms in their survey solicited information from foremen relative to contract negotiations. Sixty-one of 213 firms allowed foremen to sit in on negotiations. Other firms obtained information in a variety of ways through conferences, questionnaires, and interviews. The conclusions indicated that foremen opinion was especially useful in seniority, wage, and discipline matters. See James J. Bambrick, Jr. and Marie P. Dorbandt, "Role of Foremen in Collective Bargaining," *Management Record,* January, 1957, pp. 2–5.

[20] Herbert H. Meyer, "A Comparison of Foreman and General Foreman Conceptions of the Foreman's Job Responsibility," *Personnel Psychology,* Autumn, 1959, pp. 445–52.

of his job he shares responsibility with functional specialists. "When" jobs are to be performed is often dictated in part by production planning specialists, the "how" is taken care of by methods specialists, to what standards the work is done is determined by quality control specialists, and in the personnel area many of the foreman's responsibilities are shared with employee relations specialists.[21]

Thus, the scope of foremen authority and responsibility is complicated by functional staff groups. Where there is a large number of staff bodies the ambiguity of job definition is so great that the boss himself probably is not clear where his foremen's authority begins and ends. The real issue is not so much *what* the foreman is supposed to do but to what *degree* he possesses authority in a given area.

This issue is raised specifically in another study.[22] The question is: what authority does a foreman have over people who visit his department—for instance, maintenance men or quality-control inspectors. Does he have control over them? Is he responsible for their work? Almost three quarters of the bosses and supervisors in this report feel that the activities of outsiders do fall in the scope of the foreman's jurisdiction. They are, however, uncertain as to the degree of this jurisdiction. For example, can the foreman assign work to the outsider? There seems to be no clear-cut answer to the whole problem of the extent of the foreman's authority over the staff.

The leadership characteristics which make a foreman effective constitute another area of disagreement pertaining to job responsibilities. Kay[23] conducted a study at a company of 600 employees and asked the foremen, their subordinates, and higher management what characteristics in their opinions made the most effective foreman. All three groups agreed on the following characteristics:

1. Ability to develop subordinates.
2. Practice of tact and discretion.
3. Ability to plan.
4. "Proper" behavior.
5. Willingness to assume responsibility.

The differences among the three groups are interesting. In addition to the above, higher management added:

1. Ability to think for himself.
2. Attention to detail.
3. Adherence to company policy.

The foremen added:

---

[21] *Ibid.*, p. 451.

[22] Lee E. Stern, "The Foreman's Job: What Are the Boundaries?" *Supervisory Management*, July, 1958, pp. 15–23.

[23] Brian R. Kay, "What Makes an Effective Foreman?" *Supervisory Management*, May, 1959, pp. 2–12.

1. Ability to communicate.
2. Concern for worker welfare.
3. Ability to distinguish between important and unimportant work.
4. Concern for safety.

The subordinates added:

1. Communication with them.
2. Willingness to support them.
3. Respectful treatment.
4. No show of favoritism.

Kay's results, although different in detail, conform closely to the findings of other studies of "appropriate" foreman behavior. These common elements emerge:

1. The foremen, their subordinates, and executives above the foremen agree that "human skills" are essential for foreman effectiveness.

2. Higher management wants the foremen to police organization policy; in addition, as other studies show, they want the foreman schedule-production oriented.[24] This is especially true for foremen in assembly-type operations. That there is perhaps a discrepancy between the human relations approach and the policing–production-orientation approach is evident here.

3. Subordinates are most attached to foremen who are considerate of them, respect and support them, and communicate with them.

Thus, the foreman and his subordinates see his job as requiring a good deal of expertness in human relations. The foreman's boss does too, but he adds what may be at times the contradictory requirement of schedule and output mindedness. The demands for consideration and production efficiency create a leadership dilemma for the foreman which in the final analysis often is solved by compromise.

Foreman Compensation. One notable deficiency undermines foreman effectiveness and even prevents foreman identification[25] with higher levels of management. That is the problem of compensation. The issue of narrowing pay differentials between first-line supervision and operative employees is keenly felt by foremen.

The problem of wage differentials is complex. There has been an overall national trend for many years to narrow differentials among various skill levels of operative employees. This trend has also been observed between operative employees as a whole and the first line of supervision. Added to this historical trend is the problem of overtime pay. Foremen are exempt from the provisions of the wage and hour law

---

[24] See, for example, Edwin R. Fleishman, "Leadership Climate, Human Relations Training, and Supervisory Behavior," *Personnel Psychology*, Summer, 1953, pp. 205–23.

[25] Mullen makes the point that positive foreman attitudes toward his job and identification with management correlate more highly with level of earnings than with other variables like age, seniority, or education. See Mullen, *op. cit.*, p. 107.

whereas operatives are subject to it. This means that employers must pay operatives overtime while there is no such requirement for foremen.[26] Finally, the gains of organized labor have done much to reduce the pay gap between operative employees and foremen. In addition to achieving higher wage levels for production workers, many economic fringe benefits have been won by unions and introduced into the wage package. These gains include shift premiums, premiums for holidays, and pension and insurance plans.

Several recommendations[27] followed by a number of companies have been offered to attack the wage differential problem. They fall into five categories.

1. Use a higher base rate, with a built-in adjustment factor to compensate for upward movements in the base rates of production employees.

2. Pay overtime.

3. Allow foreman participation in executive compensation plans such as profit sharing, bonuses, and the like.

4. Relate foreman fringe benefits to an executive scale rather than the scale used for production workers.

5. All-in-all management should be concerned with maintaining adequate foreman-operative differentials on a gross annual earnings basis. Week-to-week fluctuations in differentials are not too important.

Foremanship as a Training Ground. The practice of using the foreman's job as a step in executive development can be extremely galling to old-line supervision. Historically, the job of the foreman, despite its frustrations and shortcomings, was looked upon by ambitious production workers as a career opportunity. Once achieved, the individual settled into it without anticipation of further promotion, much like a master sergeant in the Army or a chief petty officer in the Navy.

----

[26] Many employers voluntarily pay foremen overtime. One survey showed that of 345 companies, 201 paid overtime. The reasons given for paying overtime were to maintain differential, to apply overtime policy equally, and to preserve the ability of the company to attract and hold qualified supervisors. Nicholas L. A. Martucci, "Overtime Pay Practices for Exempt Supervisors," *Management Record*, April, 1959, pp. 110–13, 134–38.

[27] Robinson makes the comment that the emphasis on salary differential is misplaced. He says attention is focused on foreman-subordinate differentials, not on foreman-management differentials. Further, he observes, "This type of sustained emphasis and attention to the problem of proper differentials orients the foreman-compensation thinking toward the hourly-rated workers, rather than toward other management personnel. It confuses the foreman's own thinking as to his true status in the organization." See Carl W. Robinson, "A Critical Look at Foreman Compensation," in *Building up the Supervisor's Job* (American Management Association, Manufacturing Series #213, 1953), pp. 19–26.

Whatever merits Robinson's argument might have, it obscures one important fact. *The foreman knows what his subordinates make;* he probably has only a foggy idea of what his boss makes; and he probably has no idea of what "other management personnel" makes. So if the foreman is going to engage in invidious comparisons on the matter of pay they will be between himself and his subordinates where he has data to compare.

The glow of achievement in obtaining this position has been dampened by the practice in some companies of using the supervisory job as a training ground for management recruits. Side by side with foremen who "came up the hard way" are youngsters just out of college enjoying their first "real" job. This fact alone is enough to take the edge off a career foreman's ardor. Certainly the significance of his accomplishment is reduced. To him, management apparently considers his job such that anyone—regardless of tangible experience—can fill it. Added to this, management trainees are a transient lot. They move about to different departments; they move up the promotion ladder; or they quit or are fired. In any event the whole business is rather demoralizing to one who sees his career objective tampered with in such a cavalier fashion.

THE FOREMAN—A MARGINAL MAN

The decline of the foreman's status, his singular role in the organizational hierarchy, and his perception of the problems associated with this role combine to give the picture of a "marginal man," as Donald Wray dubbed him a number of years ago. This appellation has remained associated with first-line supervision ever since.[28]

Marginality in the case of the foreman means that he is on the periphery of the mainstream of industrial events. He is bypassed. Marginal roles in society are common, but they are nonetheless uncomfortable to fill. The foreman is neither fish nor fowl in terms of his industrial status. He is not a worker nor has he had much success with the trappings of unionism so effective for the status of production workers. He is told he is part of management but he has little tangible evidence in the form of acceptance accompanied by the symbols of executive status. It is reasonable to say that the foreman is in a group unto itself, isolated from the technical staff, the higher line executives, and the production workers. It is a group which:

1. Does not enjoy the high status the *staff* derives from technical specializations.
2. Does not participate in the high status of *line executives* based on authority positions in the scalar chain.
3. Does not have the security of *production workers* based on the collective strength of organized labor.

Thus, the gains which any of these groups accomplish in the industrial world stem from their own peculiar characteristics of organizational power and influence and do not necessarily accrue to the foremen. Such is marginality!

---

[28] Donald E. Wray, "Marginal Men of Industry: The Foremen," *American Journal of Sociology*, January, 1949, pp. 298–301.

Implications of Being Marginal

Gains and losses are associated with the individual's decision to participate in any organization. The losses to marginal groups seem to be disproportionately large. Some of these losses are brought out next.

Trait Differentials among Organization Personnel. Ghiselli's study of traits found among individuals at various organization levels shows some interesting differentiating characteristics.[29] Ghiselli divided the organization structure into four categories—top management, middle management, lower (supervisory) management, and production workers. These groups were compared by measuring the traits of intelligence, supervisory ability, initiative, self-assurance, and occupational level. The last trait involved measuring the accuracy of role perception of individuals in the four groups.

Ghiselli found that:

1. Top and middle management score much higher than lower management and production workers and are, therefore, quite distinct from them on the basis of the above traits.

2. The differences in trait-measurement scores between lower management and production workers are negligible.

The findings of this study show that the foremen were quite similar to the people they supervised but quite different from higher management levels, from the standpoint of the traits measured. It is questionable therefore that any differentiation between foremen and production workers can be made on the basis of traits. The major distinguishing feature between these two groups is found in the amount of authority and responsibility accruing to them from their position in the formal organization. This distinction is sufficient in itself to insulate the foremen from production workers.

As expected, the trait differences between higher management and foremen are dramatic. The foremen are insulated, therefore, from middle and top management not only by differences in degrees of formal authority but also by great differences in intelligence, initiative, supervisory ability, and so on.

Although not conclusive, these thoughts at least suggest that the foreman's personality and motives are more closely akin to production workers than to the executives above him. Foremen are, however, separated from production workers by the rigors of the formal structure of authority in organizations. Hence, foremen constitute a separate group founded on personality traits and formal authority. As such, the foreman is prevented from participating with real effectiveness in the affairs of

---

[29] Edwin E. Ghiselli, "Traits Differentiating Management Personnel," *Personnel Psychology*, Winter, 1959, pp. 535–44.

either higher management or production workers. Now, what can be said regarding the uniqueness of the work of the foreman?

The Boundaries of Foremanship. Reducing the foreman's job to a planning, organizing, motivating, and controlling form of analysis is useful for an insight into the nature of his work. Figure 17–2 shows the management functions with specific foremen activities peculiar to them.

FIGURE 17–2
Foreman Activities within the Scope of Management

FUNCTIONAL AREAS			
Planning *Organizing*		*Motivating*	*Controlling*
1. Personnel require- ←—— ments, manpower——→ allocations, work assignments.		1. Induction and orientation. 2. Training.	1. Quality. 2. Cost. 3. Production.
2. Materials, tools, and equipment ←—— needed for current——→ operations, re- placements, and program changes.		3. Rating and classification. 4. Settling gripes, complaints, and grievances.	4. Man hours. 5. Expenditures of materials, tools, and equipment.
3. Methods improve- ←—— ment. ——→		5. Safety. 6. Leadership of subordinates to goal accom- plishment.	

Listing activities is useful but tends to hide the qualitative and quantitative aspects of the foreman's job. It does bring out one point, however. The foreman still performs work in all management functions, in spite of the limitations placed on planning, organizing, and controlling activities. The foreman's work in these latter areas is dominated by routine and detail with most of it involving policing programs and plans passed on to him by staff groups or higher line executives for performance at the operative level.

Figure 17–2 also brings out another point. It is difficult to distinguish between the planning and the organizing functions performed by the foreman. His activities overlap these functions. The nature of foreman planning is short range. The futurity of his considerations seldom extends further than a month ahead and is largely involved with daily and weekly adjustments to meet changing production situations. The quantities of manpower, tools, and equipment that the foreman plans for are intimately associated with the organization of work in his department. Hence, when a foreman thinks ahead about his personnel needs it is difficult to say whether he is engaging in a planning activity or an organizing activity. A "pure" foreman planning activity which constitutes a regular part of his job is difficult to conjure up.

The function of control is the area which involves the foreman in much administrative detail. Control in the various spheres of cost, manpower, quality, and so on requires the foreman to relay quantitative data on performance to functional staff groups as well as his own boss. A good deal of the foreman's time is used in filling out records and reports for interested groups that have established performance standards. While the foreman is required to maintain control systems and to feed back control information, he has very little to say about setting the standards against which his effectiveness is measured. The job of the foreman as a policeman is never more evident than in the control function.

Foreman Morale. It is easy enough to state that the foreman's morale is low. Certainly, the factor of marginality plus the deficiencies observed in management policy and practice would make such a universal statement tempting. Morale, however, is an individual's state of mind; it is not an attribute of a group as amorphous as "the foremen."

The morale level of foremen is at once a question of relativity and a question of individual reactions to his role. In the first instance, if the foreman's morale is high or low, to what other individual or group of individuals is he being compared? It is of scant encouragement to find that foremen's morale on the "average" is higher in a company than the morale of the operative employees. This is particularly true when the same company finds that the morale of the foremen is lower than other levels of management, on the "average." A discovery of this type simply reinforces the case of foreman insulation from management and reduces the possibility of foreman identification with higher-level executives.

In the second instance, no two individuals react exactly the same to the demands of their role. Certain generalized behavioral patterns may indeed develop, but the proof of the relationship between morale and foreman performance must be tested in each and every department. One of the consequences of generalizing about foreman morale is the hasty introduction of poorly conceived panacea. Foreman training in human relations is an example of such a faddish cure-all.

At one time, wide-scale human relations training for foremen was thought to be a solution which would cause the foremen to identify more with management and to improve their human skills simultaneously. The success of foreman training in accomplishing these objectives is questionable. The morale of the foreman probably would be improved universally by more money (perhaps a prorata share of the cost of the training program) and a clarification of the scope of his job.

All in all, it is not surprising to hear talk of low foreman morale. But at the same time it is useful to locate both specific morale trouble spots and specific cases of high foreman morale. In both situations it is more than necessary to find tangible reasons for the level of morale.

Foreman Identification with Management

There is no doubt that the foreman is part of management, at least from the standpoint of the logic of formal organizational theory. The issue is whether or not the foreman "feels" he is part of management. A direct or easy analysis of this issue is impossible.[30] The evidence offered in this chapter points to the conclusion that if the foreman identifies at all, it is with his own group.

Being a distinct group *between* other groups is not abnormal in itself. The foreman's role has its dual aspects. He must lead production workers and empathize with their problems. He must also support management policies and pursue goals set by higher executives. As Walker and his associates point out, the danger is that the foreman does not appreciate this duality. He may "overidentify" with production workers or management.[31] Overidentification in either direction could reduce foreman effectiveness as leader of the operative group on the one hand, or as a member of management charged with managerial responsibilities on the other.

Those who insist on unequivocal foreman identification with management do not realize what a paradoxical situation this creates. It asks the foreman to identify with a group which appears to have personality characteristics quite dissimilar from his own. It asks the foreman to go against the nature of the role he plays as intermediary of two very diverse groups. And it asks the foreman to overlook all those conditions of marginality and deficiencies in practice which have separated him from other executives.

Perhaps, when all is said, it would be better to look on foremen as a distinct group, one of a number of such groups created by industrial change. If the uniqueness of the foreman group is accepted, then it is possible to treat with greater effectiveness the problems of status, communication, authority, compensation, and the leadership and technical needs that are peculiar to this group.

'So much for the current issues. What now can be said for the future of foremanship?

THE FUTURE OF FOREMANSHIP

Massive upward shifts of operative skill levels in intermittent manufacturing are essential to a general upgrading of foreman status. This conclusion has been stated before. Management may treat symptoms of low, meager status, or management can redefine the foreman's job,[32] but the

---

[30] See M. J. Balma, J. C. Maloney, and C. H. Lawshe, "The Role of the Foreman In Modern Industry: III; Some Correlates of Foreman Identification with Management," *Personnel Psychology*, Winter, 1958, pp. 535–44.

[31] Charles R. Walker, Robert H. Guest, and Arthur N. Turner, *The Foreman on the Assembly Line* (Cambridge: Harvard University Press, 1956), pp. 135–38.

[32] See " 'Upgrading' Foremen with an Ax," *Business Week*, February 11, 1961, pp. 110, 112.

only lasting cure for the status problems of the foreman is to provide conditions in which he has the opportunity to make a greater economic contribution to the firm.

Automation is one of the products of changing technology. The effect of automation on upgrading skill levels is not altogether clear. James R. Bright questions the proposal that automation will result in a significant upgrading of the labor force.[33] One consequence of automation will be to displace large quantities of direct labor. The direct labor that does remain in a company after automation is not likely to be any more skilled than the assembly workers who have gone before them. So supervisors of direct labor in an automated factory probably will not enjoy any higher status than the production-line foreman does today; but their number will be reduced substantially.

The hope of higher status for foremanship lies in the supervision of certain categories of *indirect* labor required by automation. It is well to quote Bright on the specific nature of these labor classes.

1. New types of setup work may require extraordinary education-skill increases as in computer or numerically controlled machine tool programming work.

2. Machine design and building skills required are increased significantly.

3. Some classes of maintenance work show severe increases in skill requirement. . . . There is evidence of need for a new kind of "over-all machine repairman" who understands *all* the control technologies and has superior ability at "trouble-shooting."[34]

Obviously the type of foremen who supervise labor in these skill categories needs high technical competence indeed. Foremanship in the future under automation will be different than what is known of it today. The future foreman may be the analogue of his earlier predecessor—the skilled craftsman who was head of the shop. Ironically, just as it was innovation which displaced the foreman who was the master craftsman, so is it also innovation which may restore the status of the foreman by demanding higher degrees of technical competence.

Technological change causes shifts in employment patterns. It should not be anticipated that the foremen now supervising assembly operations will be upgraded, *as individuals,* into higher-status jobs. The function of first-line supervision will remain in automated plants but the activities of this function will be discharged by different people possessing the requisite skills. Therefore, the future of the typical modern foreman in intermittent manufacturing is not bright. The probabilty is high that he will be displaced because his job is eliminated. At the same time, he will find

---

[33] James R. Bright, "Does Automation Raise Skill Requirements?" *Harvard Business Review,* July–August, 1958, pp. 85–98.

[34] James R. Bright, *Automation and Management* (Boston: Graduate School of Business Administration, Harvard University, 1958), p. 187.

difficulty relocating because he does not have the skill necessary to supervise technical indirect labor.

The advent of the new foreman will be just as fast as industrial transition permits. The modern assembly foreman will probably be phased out slowly, but perhaps never completely. However, it may be stated plausibly that as industry introduces new technologies in production the foreman of today will become less common. The problem of modern foreman status may never be solved; it may just cease to exist.

CHAPTER 18

Executive Roles

THE FUNCTIONS OF MANAGEMENT are ubiquitous, and so too are the professional managers who are found in business, government, private nonprofit organizations, and even in labor unions. The professional executive is indeed a key figure in our times. He is strategically placed in crucial decision roles, and his actions have such far-reaching influence that some writers have spoken of a managerial revolution.

This chapter explores some facets of the business executive's behavior and personality as they are manifested in his job. Also considered are the intricacies of the role of the executive and the problems he encounters in his climb up the promotional ladder. The following chapter treats some of the broader implications of management practice within the framework of the corporation.

The manager in the business organization is the central focus of this chapter. A good deal of research has been done on executive groups in industry; this chapter draws on much of this work. Most of these studies have divided the executive segment of the organization into four groups for comparative purposes. Lateral studies have been made of line and staff executives. Vertical comparisons have been drawn between various levels of executives in the managerial hierarchy. Since the problems of line-staff relations are considered in previous chapters, they are not treated in detail here. The main distinctions made among executives in this chapter rest on differentiating personality and role characteristics found in the organization strata.

THE JOB

The first step in this discussion of management is to look at the job. This must be done in a generalized way. It is traditional to state that the job of management is planning, organizing, motivating, and controlling. More recently, some writers have viewed management functions as communicating, decision making, and resolving conflicts. All these activities are part of the management process. They are important, but they reveal little of the people who perform them.

Rather than a process, it is more valuable in the context of this book to look upon the manager's job as a role. By knowing something of the dimensions of the role inferences may be drawn regarding the sorts of personalities in it. Every role has a counterpart in a personality. The individual generally will accept the role that he knows best, believes in, and finds rewarding. In other words, the personality of an individual may modify a role to some degree but it is more likely that people are preselected, drifting into roles to which they are readily adaptable.[1] And so it is with the role of the executive and the kinds of people who play it.

It is difficult, if not impossible, to talk of *an* executive role. Higher levels of management comprise no more a homogeneous body than do the foremen. Take the breakdown between middle and top management, for example. A company does not have to get too large before considerable distinctions appear separating middle managers from those on top. Rifts begin to show along several dimensions of the managerial role. Although these distinctions are indeed matters of degree, the degree itself often is of such a magnitude as to make the role barrier between the two groups quite insurmountable for the bulk of lower-level executives.

Facets of Management Roles

The six role dimensions described below are found in all managerial jobs. They are really forms of role expectations which adhere to a greater or lesser degree to all the levels of the executive hierarchy.

FIGURE 18–1

Comparison of Time Perspectives of Decision Situations at Four Levels of Management

Time	*Works Manager, Percent*	*Division Superintendent, Percent*	*Department Foreman, Percent*	*Shift Foreman, Percent*
Short (0–2 weeks)............	3.3	54.2	68.0	97.7
Moderate (2 weeks to year)....................	46.1	41.4	30.4	2.1
Distant (one year and beyond).................	50.0	4.3	1.5	0.0
Total...............	99.4	99.9	99.9	99.8

SOURCE: Norman H. Martin, "Differential Decisions in the Management of an Industrial Plant," *Journal of Business*, October, 1956, p. 251. Copyright 1956, by the University of Chicago. Used with permission.

The Time Dimension in Decisions. Top management must think in terms of long-run strategies. As one goes down the executive hierarchy the extent of futurity in programs and decisions is shorter. Part of Martin's research, shown in Figure 18–1, gives evidence of this phenomenon.

---

[1] William E. Henry, "The Business Executive: The Psychodynamics of a Social Role," *American Journal of Sociology*, January, 1949, p. 286.

Martin's data reveal that of the total decisions made by managers in the plant studied, the highest percentage of decisions with the greatest futurity is found at upper echelons. From these results one would anticipate that management at levels above the works manager would be involved in even higher percentages of distant decisions.

Besides the span of the time perspective, a qualitative difference is found among the decisions at various organization levels. Speaking of higher management levels, Martin says, "Because the true meaning of an event cannot be ascertained until it is actualized, one of the consequences of being involved in situations of distant time perspective is that the executive is in a difficult position to judge correctly the value and meaning of intervening events."[2] Essentially this means that the longer the time span between the decision and the result the harder it is to appraise the quality or "correctness" of any particular decision. Thus, top management lives in a world clouded by uncertainty. It includes not only uncertainty of the future but also uncertainty of the true success or failure of decisions which are matters of record. This is partially attributed to the complexity of the organizational system, where easy separation of causes and effects is impossible.

As the management scale is descended, the time perspective shortens. It is simpler, consequently, to assign specific results as products of specific decisions. The decisions themselves at lower organizational levels increase in frequency but are more highly structured, dealing with more objective and tangible alternatives.

The decisions made by top management generally are quite subjective. But these decisions will affect the future of the company well beyond the time of an executive's tenure in it. The decisions he makes are fewer but more far-reaching than his subordinates. Down the hierarchy, the tempo of decision making increases. However, the alternatives are more concrete and the results of the decisions are more rapidly forthcoming. Thus, lower management decisions, from the standpoint of the time perspective, do not require the degree of "risk," "vision," or "intuition" demanded of top management.

Sense of Mission. The perception of the proper relation of the company to its environment is fundamental to the role of top management. This facet of the management role requires mature judgment of organizational objectives as they relate reciprocally to social values. Kissinger has underscored the importance of reflective thought and creativity to aid in implementing the perception factor of the management role. Kissinger warns, however, "One of the paradoxes of an increasingly specialized, bureaucratized society is that the qualities rewarded in the rise to eminence are less and less the qualities required once eminence is reached."[3]

---

[2] Norman H. Martin, "Differential Decisions in the Management of an Industrial Plant," *Journal of Business,* October, 1956, pp. 251–52.

[3] Harry A. Kissinger, "The Policy Maker and the Intellectual," *The Reporter,* March 5, 1959, p. 30,

Stress is placed at lower management levels on the so-called technical skills. Such skills are necessary because of the specialized functions prevailing in the lower echelons. The middle manager develops proficiencies in these routines. Technical competence, however, is not necessarily related to the leadership and creative needs required as he moves up.[4]

The Setting of Shorter-Range Goals. Top management sets the targets to make it possible for others below them to interact. Top management stages activities at lower management levels and gives direction to them. Of course, the shorter-range goals are implemented by middle management, and implementation must always be consistent with the overall objectives or mission. Top management, functioning in a control capacity, ensures such consistency.

Stated again, as organizations get bigger it is more difficult for the top manager to preserve consistency between the objectives of programs of different time durations. That is, priority may be given at lower management levels to the accomplishment of short-range goals to the disadvantage of the broader mission. To counteract this possibility, the top executive depends upon subordinates to brief him on policy and performance at lower organizational levels. Out of this situation develops the specialist in briefing, who is frequently given to making biased interpretations. Overreliance on staff advice can undermine the top executive's judgment and perspective. The chief executive has to maintain some independence from the judgment of lower levels in the organization so that he is able dispassionately to integrate and coordinate short-range goals with long-range strategies.

Combining and Utilizing Resources. At any level in an organization, but particularly at the highest levels, coordination is a consuming job. Intimate knowledge of mission and shorter-range objectives is the only route to successful coordination. But this is far from being the whole story. Top management must balance time. It has to weigh the attention given to internal coordination with the demands on it to abstract from the organization and to view the company, in its total context, in relation to its setting. Top management must have the ability to detach itself from the internal imperatives of coordination and to reflect on the general purposes and objectives of the company in its industry and society.

Only top management is required to do this kind of thinking as part of its role. Middle management's scope does not extend greatly beyond the horizons of its activities. So it is expected that middle management attends to internal coordinative problems. As a result, much middle management thinking is circumscribed by the boundaries of the company and for that

---

[4] Leavitt and Whisler see the elimination of routine middle management jobs as a result of breakthroughs in information technology. The consequences of the new technologies will be to reduce the number of middle managers. Those remaining will do more creative work of the type associated with top management. See Harold J. Leavitt and Thomas L. Whisler, "Management in the 1980's," *Harvard Business Review*, November–December, 1958, pp. 41–48.

matter even specific jobs. This consideration constitutes a formidable role barrier between middle and top management.

The Socratic Approach. Top management questioningly evaluates the ideas brought up from below. In this respect, top management is both teacher and judge of subordinates in an ultimate sense. Such a role requires infinite patience and sensitivity to the interactions among people below and the material resources with which they work. Top management, therefore, has the final obligation for training and for structuring an effective staff of executives that will be thoroughly oriented and equipped to carry out the missions and programs assigned to it.

"Aloneness." Top managers, by the nature of their role, are often detached from outside judgment or objective criteria against which they can appraise their approach to problems, their decisions, and their philosophy. The production worker has a skill accompanied by a tangible output which is a source of justification and a criterion of performance. The foreman's role, though ambiguous, has at least one objective measure in terms of department efficiency. The staff has a high degree of specialized training, and, at times, "professional" standards against which performance is judged. Middle and upper-middle management get into the twilight zone, but here managers can look to numerous colleagues for support and appraisal. Top management enjoys few of the advantages just enumerated for subordinates. Partially, its problem of aloneness stems from the long time span of decision and the subjectivity of the job. Additionally, the number of top managers is limited, restricting the extent of support and critical commentary available from colleagues.

All members of management tend to look to their own reference groups and their immediate superiors for backing and critical appraisal. Top management is not unusual in this respect. Where intangibles, intuition, uncertainty, and subjectivity are involved in action, the manager naturally turns to colleagues facing similar circumstances for vindication of his attitudes and behavior. Middle management finds reference groups within the company. Top management, however, frequently has to turn outside to colleagues at similar levels in different companies to "talk out" problems of philosophy, and to participate in mutual admiration cliques.

Aloneness has a number of behavioral by-products. Several of these are the attitudes of optimism, rationality, realism, and practicality which appear to be ingrained in the American business executive's ideology.[5] These attitudes are probably necessary concomitants of a role which requires decisive action in spite of risks and lack of sources for the justification of the legitimacy of decisions. Such attitudinal expressions are not unlike whistling while walking past a graveyard at midnight.

Quite the opposite of the above attitudes is the contrary aspect of

---

[5] See Francis X. Sutton, Seymore E. Harris, Carl Kaysen, and James Tobin, *The American Business Creed* (Cambridge: Harvard University Press, 1956), chap. 5.

aloneness which frequently forces the individual into assuming a conservative posture. There often is more pressure on an individual when he makes a mistake than when he fails to take advantage of an opportunity. Particularly at higher organizational levels, foregone opportunities are debatable as to whether they *were* indeed opportunities in the first place.[6] Top management must be constantly aware of this human tendency lest valuable alternatives pass by it.

Another by-product of aloneness is the committee, which Kissinger says is often more a spiritual necessity than a decision-making device.[7] The committee offers support and a degree of anonymity to individuals. It is something of a defense against individual responsibility when making decisions for action. The motivations to use the committee tool are complex; many companies have adopted it as a problem solving-morale building device. The committee, however, as a bulwark against aloneness must be considered among the motivations.[8]

Accompanying these aspects of management roles are the pressures of strains which are in evidence in the executive's job. Some of these are outlined below.

Pressures in the Management Role[9]

Pressures for Achievement. The modern executive must compete for success—and compete not only with other companies and their managements but also with colleagues in the executive's company. He usually will compete on the basis of his own specialty, particularly if the executive is in the staff or middle management in the line. As a result—and this often is frustrating—the executive's other talents and interests are allowed to atrophy.

The executive's achievements, or lack of them, are measured against those of his associates. This is not to say there is no abstract or generalized success criterion. There is. But usually such a criterion is expressed in quantitative terms such as efficiency, profitability, rate of growth, and so on. More infrequently is success measured qualitatively. Thus, size alone is a success criterion and constitutes a claim for achievement.

Pressures for Change. Change and the quest for novelty are an occupational hazard of managers, with the exception of executives in stagnant organizations. Pressures for change are initiated by competition and by internal demands in the organization. Change is common in a dynamic

---

[6] Kissinger, *op. cit.,* p. 31.

[7] *Ibid.,* pp. 31–32.

[8] Once established as part of operational procedures, committees are infrequently abandoned. For a discussion of why U.S. Rubber Company *eliminated* committee management see "U.S. Rubber Moves Ahead," *Business Week,* October 22, 1960, pp. 101–11.

[9] Unless noted otherwise, the following treatment of strains in executive roles is adapted from Sutton *et al., op. cit.,* chap. 16.

society and managers must accept it as part of their job. Survival demands an initiative and flexibility without which the executive cannot survive.

Executive adaptation to change requires more than a state of mind predisposed in this direction. It requires a life pattern adjusted to the possibility of frequent movement about the country while moving up the promotional ladder. Not only the executive but also his family absorbs the brunt of change, to say nothing of the community in which he lives as something like a migrant worker.

The Pressures of Uncertainty. No greater strain exists than that of the uncertain and hostile environment in which the executive must act. This environment creates situations in which there are discrepancies between the effort expended by the executive and the rewards derived. Therefore, considerable effort is often repaid with only marginal success or often complete failure. The executive, however, is judged on outcomes, not effort.

The presence of uncertainty causes most executives to think in terms of the controllable and uncontrollable factors in his environment. The controllables represent some factors over which he has the power to reduce or eliminate uncertainty. Naturally, the executive attempts to increase the scope of his power over these factors. Ordinarily, the uncontrollables in the environment are thought as consumer sovereignty, the government, community acceptance, price and availability of raw materials, and, of course, competition. But even here the efforts of management in advertising, political action, public relations, reciprocal agreements with suppliers, and mergers act to bring these conventional uncontrollables into the sphere of managerial influence. Consequently, the pressure of uncertainty extends the boundaries of the manager's job well beyond the traditional limits of the firm itself.

The Pressure for Conformity. The vehicle for administrative action is the organization. It is the structure in which executives work. Employment in a company requires the individual to make certain sacrifices largely in terms of his freedom of action and expression. The executive is expected to conform to rules, regulations, and policies. For his sacrifices and contributions to the company the individual receives rewards.

Some writers, like William H. Whyte, Jr., see in the organization a manifestation of all that is evil in the social ethic.[10] He notes that some companies are demanding far more conformity from executives than they have the moral right to expect. The upshot of this evil is the annihilation of the individual's personality.

Whyte and other observers[11] are concerned about the "organization"

---

[10] William H. Whyte, Jr., *The Organization Man* (New York: Simon and Schuster, 1956).

[11] See, for example, Erich Fromm, *The Sane Society* (New York: Rinehart and Co., 1955); David Riesman, *The Lonely Crowd* (New Haven: Yale University Press, 1950); and C. Wright Mills, *White Collar* (New York: Oxford University Press, 1951).

becoming a monster which converts people into automatons. These protests about modern organizations and their conformity pressures are part of a larger pattern of reaction against the individual's absorption by the group or the collectivity generally. Whyte concludes that the individual executive must *fight* the organization when it attempts to make inroads on his privacy. The manager must fight because it is necessary if he is to retain his individuality and his self-awareness.

Pressure for Role-Conflict Resolution. Often the executive is faced with the necessity of making a decision requiring a choice between conflicting expectation generated by different interest groups. The executive, in other words, is confronted with a dilemma. Suppose the executive is presented with two incompatible alternatives. According to Shull and Miller,[12] he can act in the following ways:

1. Conform to alternative *A*.
2. Conform to alternative *B*.
3. Attempt to compromise between the alternatives.
4. Avoid making a decision.

A decision to act along the first two lines would satisfy one group and disappoint another, with the result being organizational disharmony. Since it may be supposed that both groups are pressuring for a favorable decision, the executive is likely to try the path of compromise. If compromise is out of the question, then the issue might be avoided entirely, in the sense that the executive delays making a decision with the hope that the problem will resolve itself.

Too frequently in organizations conflicts of interest arise among subordinates and have to be resolved by the executive. The temptation is great to compromise these interests for the sake of organizational harmony. The executive, however, has to withstand group pressure and make decisions which are compatible to organizational objectives. At times avoidance and compromise are reasonable tactics. But at other times the executive has to be prepared to face the wrath of interest groups which may be inconvenienced by unfavorable decisions.

In spite of the pressures and strains of management, most executives are adjusted to their role. They accept the role's inherent difficulties because they believe in the worthiness of what they are doing. The next section treats the type of personality which seems best equipped to endure the exigencies of the management role.

PERSONALITY AND SELF-PERCEPTIONS OF EXECUTIVES

An hypothesis was forwarded in the last section stating that the role of management is a selection device, attracting people whose personalities are

---

[12] Fremont A. Shull, Jr., and Delbert C. Miller, "Role Conflict Behavior in Administration: A Study in the Validation of a Theory of Role-Conflict Resolution" (an unpublished paper, 1960).

most readily adaptable to it. Some personality modification occurs once the individual occupies the role, but not much because of the preselective qualities of the role itself.

FIGURE 18–2

Executive Characteristics

General

1. Intelligence is higher than population average.
2. Healthier.
3. Has fewer neurotic tendencies.
4. Not introspective—lacks deep awareness of motivations.
5. Essentially a pragmatist.

Values

1. Identifies with company and with immediate superior.
2. Strongly motivated to achieve.
3. Values money and power as symbols of status, not as ends in themselves.
4. Strong reality orientation—revolts against theory.
5. Tends to think about others in black-or-white terms.
6. Highly positive and optimistic attitudes.
7. Apprehensive of failure.
8. Earnestly seeks approbation for his actions.

SOURCE: Adapted from Ephriam Rosen, "The Executive Personality," *Personnel,* January–February, 1959, pp. 8–20; Perrin Stryker, "On the Meaning of Executive Qualities," *Fortune,* June, 1958, pp. 116–19, 186, 189; William E. Henry, "The Business Executive: The Psychodynamics of a Social Role," *American Journal of Sociology,* January, 1949, p. 286.

A vast amount of research has been done in the area of executive personality. The scope of the work covers the qualities of managerial leaders,[13] the average executive personality profile, and the deficiencies in personality which cause executives to fail.[14] A composite or profile of the "average" executive is given in Figure 18–2. Although there are many dangers in drawing up a profile, it does point up one rather important observation. The business executive has characteristics or traits which appear to be fairly commonly distributed throughout the population as a whole. But, as Rosen puts it, "He has them *to a stronger degree.*"[15]

Probably more valuable than the listing of typical executive traits are the perceptions of executives themselves in reference to their functions and roles in an organization. The work of Porter and Ghiselli reveals some interesting contrasts between the self-perceptions of middle management compared to those of top management. See Figure 18–3.

---

[13] Perrin Stryker, "The Rarest Man in Business," *Fortune,* May, 1960, pp. 119–20, 210, 212.

[14] Frederick J. Gaudet and A. Ralph Carli, "Why Executives Fail," *Personnel Psychology,* Spring, 1957, pp. 7–21.

[15] Ephriam Rosen, "The Executive Personality," *Personnel,* January–February, 1959, p. 19.

FIGURE 18–3

Self-Perceptions of Middle and Top Management

Middle Management Sees Itself as:	*Top Management Sees Itself as:*
1. Providing the backbone of the organization.	1. The dynamic brains of the organization.
2. Providing stability through careful analysis and investigation.	2. Not being swayed entirely by objective evidence.
3. Seldom taking rash actions or making hasty, unfounded decisions.	3. Willing to take risks based on personal judgment and faith in its abilities.
4. Not as confident as top management.	4. Confident that its actions will lead to success.
5. Placing reliance on rules and regulations rather than plunging ahead on its own.	5. Action oriented, able to capitalize on opportunities, and self-reliant.
6. Wishing to avoid being controversial and wanting to be thought of as stable and dependable.	6. Confident in social and business relations.

Source: Adapted from Lyman W. Porter and Edwin E. Ghiselli, "The Self-Perceptions of Top and Middle Management Personnel," *Personnel Psychology.* Winter, 1957, pp. 397–406.

The findings of Porter and Ghiselli bear out in terms of the executives' perceptions the descriptions of middle and top management roles given earlier. These authors summarize their findings as follows:

Not only is there a difference in the types of decisions that the different groups see themselves as most capable of undertaking, but there also seems to be a difference in the way in which they arrive at the decisions. The results suggest that top management go more on their own hunches which they think are good, whereas middle management people seem more reluctant to rely on themselves and inclined to rely on an accumulation of available evidence.[16]

Thus, the role of top management requires that executives operate on such subjective factors as vision, intuition, hunches, and judgment. The self-perception study reported here apparently confirms that top managers see themselves behaving this way. The case is similar for middle management. Its role is more highly structured, using concrete factual data as bases for decisions.

Role and personality go hand in hand. The normal person will usually perceive his role with a fair degree of accuracy and play it according to the rules of organizational policy. All this says is that people have attitudes which are consistent with their actions. It does not mean, of course, that the middle management role is necessarily a straitjacket binding a "middle-management personality" to it. Indeed, the achievement and the change pressures found to some degree in most executive positions es-

---

[16] Lyman W. Porter and Edwin E. Ghiselli, "The Self-Perceptions of Top and Middle Management Personnel," *Personnel Psychology*, Winter, 1957, p. 405.

tablish the channels for role changes, enabling the individual to progress in the company.

PROMOTIONS

Much has been written about the many determinants of career success. For Horatio Alger these determinants were "pluck and luck." Nothing was more important in Algerian idealism than honesty, clean living, and hard work. But even these factors were not sufficient for success because fate, in the form of some lucky break, always lurked in the background to give the hero an extra nudge to success. Modern explanations and scientific investigations of success patterns are far more sophisticated (but not as much fun) as the Horatio Alger approach. One form of analysis is to study the backgrounds of successful executives to find commonalities in them.

The Biographic Approach

Probably the most elementary condition in anyone's background is his social origin. Studies of executive origins have shown that most have fathers who were themselves executives, professional people, or self-employed businessmen of a middle- to upper-middle-class status.[17] But writers like Warner have noted that over the years there has been a tendency toward "freer competition" for top jobs in large organizations.[18] People from humbler origins can aspire and can attain major positions in large companies.

This democratic trend is explainable in two ways. First, the large corporation bases its selection of executives on rationalistic policies.[19] The best trained and most competent for a post are selected. This policy is opposed to the more traditional procedure of selection based on family ties, which perpetuates relatives in executive posts regardless of qualifications. The large, impersonal corporation destroys this form of vested interest.

The second cause of greater democracy in competition for top positions is education. Relatively free access to education has made it possible for those of lower origins on the social scale to become equipped with the

---

[17] Statistical studies of executive origins relating to this point are offered by Mabel Newcomer, *The Big Business Executive* (New York: Columbia University Press, 1955), chap. 5; and W. Lloyd Warner and James C. Abegglen, *Big Business Leaders in America* (New York: Harper and Bros., 1955), chap. 2. These authors also present a wealth of data relating to other aspects of executive backgrounds such as nationality, religion, education, and wives.

[18] W. Lloyd Warner, "The Corporation Man," in Edward Mason (ed.), *The Corporation in Modern Society* (Cambridge: Harvard University Press, 1960), pp. 106–21.

[19] Stuart Adams, "Trends in Occupational Origins of Business Leaders," *American Sociological Review*, October, 1954, p. 548. This democratization factor stems largely from the bureaucratic characteristic of selection based on the qualification-for-office criterion discussed in Chapter 12.

knowledge and skills necessary to qualify for managerial jobs. Through the growth of large organizations and widespread educational opportunity, access to the top levels of corporations has become more of a reality for people in all socioeconomic brackets. But *realistically* it must be emphasized that it is still far more probable that the sons of fathers of higher social origins will be future executives than, say, sons of laborers or farmers. So in spite of the democratization process, the probabilities of becoming a top executive still tilt in favor of those born in higher socioeconomic strata.

The biographic approach has turned up other similarities in executive backgrounds. Higher education appears frequently, along with Masonic membership, a favored ethnic composition, membership in "correct" clubs and societies, political affiliation of a conservative nature, judicious consumption and display of material well being, and participation in civic associations and charitable works.[20]

The individual's background helps frame his perspectives. Looking back on the life of successful executives it can be demonstrated how one advancement became their take-off point for further progress through the company. The individual's *level of aspiration* was such that he strove constantly for greater successes. Perhaps the most significant feature of an individual's background is the role it plays in gearing-up a person's aspirational level. All the opportunity a company offers will not get a man to move if he does not aspire beyond a certain point.

Of course, there is more than one way of satisfying aspirations other than vertical mobility in a company. For example, the supervisors in Pellegrin's and Coates' study achieved a small degree of vertical movement up the organization hierarchy. But when they reached the supervisory position they did not appear to aspire further. They were quite content.[21]

This situation is an apparent denial of the psychological theory that achievement at one level of aspiration leads to higher aspirational levels. However, it may well be that the supervisors in this example found satisfactions outside the organization after they reached this management level. Their aspirations probably shifted from a job to a nonjob focus.

Summing up, McClelland's work[22] gives immediacy and significance to the notion that culturally most Americans regard business and financial success as an important value. These norms condition the individual's

---

[20] Charles H. Coates and Roland F. Pellegrin, "Executives and Supervisors: Informal Factors in Differential Bureaucratic Promotion," *Administrative Science Quarterly*, 2 (1957), pp. 204–8; and Melville Dalton, "Informal Factors in Career Achievement," *American Journal of Sociology*, March, 1951, pp. 407–15.

[21] Roland F. Pellegrin and Charles H. Coates, "Executives and Supervisors: Contrasting Definitions of Career Success," *Administrative Science Quarterly*, 1956, pp. 513–14.

[22] David C. McClelland, *The Achieving Society* (New York: D. Van Nostrand Co., 1962), and "Business Drive and National Achievement," *Harvard Business Review*, July–August, 1962, pp. 99–112.

achievement needs and his ascending levels of aspiration for material well being. In a sense, each person is a microcosm of the larger national achievement trait producing a success syndrome. The achievement needs of the individual and the national success challenge are interacting and reinforcing. Of course, for most people the success challenge must be met by mobility within an organization.

Vertical Mobility—Two Points of View

How free is an individual to determine his progress in an employment situation? This is, of course, a relative matter which is reducible to a degree ranging on a continuum of dependence to independence. Naturally, in every organization a person will find he has some latitude to determine his own progress, based upon his abilities and aspirations. He will also discover that he is dependent upon established promotional channels, policies, sponsors, and rituals.

At one end of the dependency continuum is the "American dream"—that a man gets ahead solely on his own merits. In this case, the individual is the primary determinant of his own success. At the other end of the continuum is the notion that in spite of ability, drive, and aggressiveness, the individual is dependent on well-structured organizational channels and methods defined for promotional purposes. One of the main mechanisms in this process is the seniority or tenure-in-job criterion which requires a certain amount of time "in-grade" before moving to the next step. Both these points of view have received a good deal of treatment in management literature.

The Model of Dependence. The concepts associated with status passage are closely allied to this model. The reader should refer to this section in Chapter 8 for a detailed discussion of the subject. But for here we say briefly that progress, vertical mobility, takes place along *established* career lines which have evolved in an organization. The emphasis in this model is upon the individual's compliance with the promotional channels and "timetables." While he has some latitude for self-determination of his career progress, the crucial stategy on his part is discovering the nature of the promotional lines, the sponsorship system, and the rituals associated with climbing the organizational hierarchy.

The Model of Independence. A different emphasis to career progress is given by Dill, Hilton, and Reitman. To them, "Career progress . . . depends greatly on the strategy or heuristics that an individual employs in 'his game' with the organization environment that he encounters at work."[23] The executive's awareness and sensitivity to the environment play an important part in their model.

---

[23] William R. Dill, Thomas L. Hilton, and Walter R. Reitman, "How Aspiring Managers Promote Their Own Careers," *California Management Review,* Summer, 1960, p. 10. For detailed case studies of promotion strategies by the same authors see, *The New Managers* (Englewood Cliffs, N.J.: Prentice-Hall, Inc., 1962).

The large organization, they observe, is indifferent to the advancement of most individuals as personalities. Therefore, it is incumbent on the executive who wants to get ahead to behave with social and political expedience in light of what he finds the tone of his environment to be. He must maintain a detached and objective attitude toward the job situation. The aspiring executive cannot allow himself to be incumbered by alliances with sponsors that might prove fatal in the event of organizational power transitions. He must consider himself as an "active agent" in the promotion of his career. In this respect, the executive should abstract himself as far as possible from the internal machinery of advancement and address himself to the solution of the immediate problems at hand. But always the aspiring executive keeps a wary eye on the subtle human nuances in the job situation and at the crucial time he applies the appropriate tactics which will be effective for his career.

The model posed by Dill and his associates represents the "cold-blooded" maneuvering required if the individual wants to get ahead in an organization which at best is indifferent or at worst hostile to his progress. Such tactics may indeed be appropriate for an executive's struggle to the top of the middle-management jungle. The question might be raised however as to whether these tactics employed by a manager to worm his way through middle management might not produce insurmountable barriers to his progress beyond. Is it the operator and the politician who get to the top?

The two promotional models just discussed are not mutually exclusive. The matter is one of emphasis. The first model emphasizes a certain dependence on procedural and sponsorship elements in progress through a career line. The Dill, Hilton, and Reitman model stresses independence and self-determination in career progress. Both models underscore two key ideas. First, the typical modern executive's future is related to a rather highly structured organizational environment. Second, it is important that the executive maintain vigilance to extract clues as to the career alternative to select and the appropriate form of behavior necessary to secure advancement.

THE TRANSACTIONAL CLIMATE

Up to this point we have looked at some of the static elements in the executive's role such as the job, pressures for performance, self-perceptions, and promotional strategies. Now we must shift focus and discuss another dimension.

Traditional theories of organization and executive behavior have stressed the superior-subordinate aspects of managerial "human relationships." This emphasis may be appropriate for relatively small organizations uncomplicated by advanced technology and numerous groups of staff specialists. However, as organizations grow and begin working with difficult problems of research, manufacturing and distribution, the vertical relationships between superiors and subordinates start giving way, in terms of the time spent on them, to lateral contacts with managers on much the same level. We hinted at the existence of these kinds of inter-personal exchanges for the sake of coordination in our discussion of the functional and matrix organizations in Chapter 6. But nowhere in the literature has the sense of the dynamics of these relationships been caught better than by Leonard Sayles in his book *Managerial Behavior*.[24] We can merely note here some of the dynamics which Sayles develops so elegantly in his book.

Our point of departure is the so-called command unit consisting of an executive with a group of subordinates. Let us assume that this unit is performing an element of work in a sequentially patterned activity. In other words, it takes inputs from preceding units and converts them to outputs for succeeding units. Further, let us suppose that the manager of this unit acts as a representative of his activity's interests to external units which affect the stability and efficiency of his operation. We may ask now, what kinds of relationships does he form with these outside units and the managers of them? Sayles identifies three basic relationships: trading, work flow, and service.

The command unit manager in the trading relationship attempts to establish agreements with "buyers and sellers" within the organization. That is, other managers may be in a position to either supply needed inputs or take the outputs or use surplus resources of a given department. The manager of that department tries to negotiate these transactions to the net advantage of his unit. Such negotiations develop in three phases: (1) the unit managers search for potential suppliers of inputs and users of outputs and resources of his unit in the organization, (2) once found the terms of the agreement are set, and (3) communication between contracting parties determines the precise nature of their needs and capabilities.

The command unit is a part of a work flow. It is a step in a sequence of activities leading to a final output of the organization. In this relationship, the manager has the responsibility of insuring smooth flow of work into and out of his unit. This makes the reduction of uncertainty between adjacent units in a work flow crucial. A great deal of a manager's effort should be spent exchanging information with adjoining unit managers when problems of timing and synchronizing respective inputs and outputs of work are likely to occur or are already occurring.

The unit manager also has external relations with service functions. These groups provide assistance to command unit managers in the work flow. They are similar, of course, to staff functions. These groups possess skills and informational inputs which are organizationally scarce re-

---

[24] Leonard R. Sayles, *Managerial Behavior* (New York: McGraw-Hill Book Company, Inc., 1964), chaps. 3–8.

sources. Frequently command unit managers must bid for them. The trading relationship often emerges between service unit managers and command unit managers where the latter attempt to outbid one another for the resources of the former. This is especially evident when some part of the work in a work flow unit must be performed by a service unit. Naturally the command unit manager is anxious to build up "points" with the service unit so that the vital function is performed expeditiously.

Trading, work flow, and service roles are as Sayles indicates "operating patterns" of executive behavior. He also indicates that there are other external transactions which are designed to resolve some problems of organizational maintenance. These are advisory, auditing, and stabilization relationships. The advisory relationship is typically a conventional kind of staff activity in which work flow managers initiate the requests for assistance. But rather than be content with being on the passive receiving end of requests for help, as is the service manager, the advisory executive constantly tries to enlarge the scope of contributions to his clients. The more "help" he is able to supply enhances his status and power, as well as, legitimatizes his role vis-à-vis the rest of the organization.

The next set of relationships involves the auditing activity. In this role, the audit group acts as a control function, monitoring the work done by work flow managers. It is obvious that being in a position to evaluate the work of others, with a direct communication link to higher levels of management, is a status boost for the executives in this capacity. We have already seen in Chapter 15 how the audit group is used to overcome the problem of filtered communication and how it acts as a device to pressure managers into compliance with organizational procedures and policies.

The stabilization role comprises the remaining set of relationships. Here the manager and his group are in a position to initiate activities, rather than simply monitoring on-going undertakings. Production control or scheduling is often found in this capacity. The focus is on them as initiators. The direction of communication is from them to other managers. They "blow the whistle" to begin work. This, indeed, in status terms, is the most enviable of all the maintenance functions.

Sayles offers as a general proposition that managers, in the quest for status, attempt to increase the "balance of initiations in their favor." That is, they seek a more active role which requires other managers to seek them out, to seek their approval for work. There is a hierarchy in which the four relationships fall. The least favorable is service, then advisory, then audit, and finally stabilization. Sayles observes that executives are motivated to shift their roles through this hierarchy in their search for greater organizational influence and power.

The issue of executive behavior is discussed further in the next chapter.

CHAPTER 19

Executive Incentives and Constraints in the Corporate Setting

TECHNICALLY, the corporation is an engine of finance. It is a device for the aggregation of capital, spawned by the heavy financial demands of a mass-production and mass-distribution economy. But the corporation is more than a legal and financial instrument. The large modern corporation provides a domicile and a way of life for thousands of executives. Also, because of its peculiarities of structure and social role, the corporate environment makes behavioral demands on executives dissimilar to those made by partnerships or single proprietorships. Further, the corporate executive is circumscribed by influences of a profit orientation in markets characterized by varying degrees of competition for customers and resources. Therefore, what is said in this chapter about attitudes and behavior of the executive in a business corporation should not be taken to apply necessarily to administrators in nonprofit organizations.

The corporation is unique, in the sense that it makes possible a combination of human, financial, and material resources which are quite unlike combinations possible under other legal and economic institutions. Woodrow Wilson said many years ago: "A modern corporation is an economic society, a little economic state—and not always little, even as compared to states."[1] To this might be added that the corporation is indeed more than an economic society. It is also a society which offers social and psychological rewards to participants. And it is a society which exerts political power and influence in relation to other institutions in its quest for survival and growth.

The corporation in this chapter is not considered in its legal or economic manifestations primarily. Instead, the concern here is on the motivations and inhibitions to executive action within the boundaries of corporate organization. Additionally, since the corporation has a pervasive

---

[1] Woodrow Wilson, "Annual Address," American Bar Association, Chattanooga, Tenn., 1910. Cited in William Z. Ripley, *Main Street and Wall Street* (Boston: Little, Brown, and Co., 1927), p. 6.

influence in our society issues of power and responsibility are considered in the concluding sections of this chapter.

THE CORPORATE ENVIRONMENT

Corporate enterprise is a means for marshaling and distributing a business' resources. Among the many advantages of the corporate device, the most obvious is the opportunity it affords a business to amass large amounts of capital. This method of capitalization involves the relatively simple expedient of selling stock to private and institutional buyers.

The use of the corporation device is extensive. Not only have many businesses elected this method of financial organization but also the largest companies in America have assumed the corporate form.[2] The corporation is a characteristic landmark in American business.

The corporation is often stereotyped as a large organization engaged in a wide range of production and distribution operations. The modern corporation frequently is depicted as an ever-changing, complex appratus serving the material needs of customers, owners, employees, and the public. These stereotypes are misleading because corporations assume many sizes, shapes, and types, each pursuing objectives with varying degrees of success.

All corporations possess the peculiar legal characteristic which admits the possibility for the separation of ownership from control. That is, the control over a property may be detached from the ownership of the property. Of course in many corporations this possibility is not realized. Such is the case when the stock of a corporation is owned entirely or in large part by one person or a family. However, when the stock of a corporation is widely distributed among a large number of small owners, the occasion for the separation of ownership from control arises.

The issue of separating ownership from control was raised in Chapter 1. This consideration, however, is so pivotal to the main theme of this chapter that it is worth going over again in greater detail.

The nature of property is the basic issue at question in any discussion of corporate ownership and control. Traditionally, the characteristic of property includes the privilege of control over the acquisition and distribution of what is owned. The owner, within limitations, has full power to administer, to gain benefits from, and to dispose of his property in ways he sees fit. Thus, ownership and control are centralized in a single decision source.

The corporation creates the opportunity to change this traditional view of property. The open corporation allows many small investors to gain property rights in it, but at the same time the investor delegates his

---

[2] Roughly 130 manufacturing corporations produce half the manufacturing output in the United States.

control privilege over his property to hired managers. The consequences of this for many American corporations are the centralization of control and the decentralization of ownership.[3]

Conceivably, corporate executives should administer property in the best interests of owners. Regardless of whether or not this is the case in fact, shareholders have precious little chance for satisfaction if they feel their interests are not being served.[4] Their only recourse is to sell their holdings and reinvest in other firms. Therefore, more than anything else the modern investor buys management rather than property.

The management of large, widely held corporations is in a curious position. The common leading symbols of management in these circumstances are associated with the ideas of trusteeship or stewardship. The adequate and dispassionate dispatch of stewardship duties leads directly to the notion of the "professionalization" of management. Like the stewards in the Bible, the modern corporate manager symbolically serves the master—the owner. But these owners, unlike their Biblical counterparts, are not especially powerful or articulate. Further, they are usually small and tend to neutralize each other. Thus, management is left with a fair degree of freedom to do as it likes, within the boundaries of "prudent business practice."

Then, too, it is not an altogether obvious fact that the owners are management's only masters. Indeed, it is questionable whether or not they are the most important among many masters. A case can be made that corporate management treats the owners as one of a number of groups whose interests in the corporation must be balanced. This view is far from the "pure" stewardship notion that management's overwhelming responsibility is to maximize the return on the shareholder's investment. Of course, it may be that in the long run the management which serves the owners best is the management which balances the interests of all clients having claims on the material resources and the human talents of the corporation. But this is getting ahead of the story.

The corporation has presented a number of abiding problems to those

---

[3] The problems posed by this situation are not new. An early treatment of the subject may be found in William Z. Ripley, *Main Street and Wall Street* (Boston: Little, Brown, and Co., 1927). The classic treatment is Adolf A. Berle, Jr., and Gardiner C. Means, *The Modern Corporation and Private Property* (New York: The Macmillan Co., 1933). There are many contemporary studies of the corporation. See, for example, Adolf A. Berle, Jr., *Power Without Property* (New York: Harcourt, Brace and Co., 1959); also Edward S. Mason (ed.), *The Corporation in Modern Society* (Cambridge: Harvard University Press, 1960).

[4] A distinction must be made between *de facto* and *de jure* control rights. Legally (*de jure*) the ownership has control privileges, but in fact these privileges are not operative because of the small amount of ownership interest vested in an individual. Theoretically, many small owners acting in concert could muster sufficient strength to assert their legal control prerogatives if they were dissatisfied with the management of their corporation. Practically, such joint action by the ownership is quite difficult and often impossible.

who are interested in matters of executive behavior, power and influence, and responsibility in our society. These problems, outlined below, are treated in greater depth throughout this chapter.

Executive Incentives

Corporate enterprise shatters the traditional owner-manager image. The owner-manager, typical of an earlier era, had direct proprietary interest in his business. For practical purposes the modern manager does not have much, if any, ownership interest in the firm which employs him. Hence, the goals which motivate him might be expected to be considerably different from the ends sought by the owner-manager. But even if the ends of the "professional" and the owner-manager are not substantially apart, it is certain that the modern corporate manager acts in a far more complex environment. The intricate nature of the corporate world is in itself sufficient to produce a "breed" of executives quite unlike those of the past.

The Corporate "Image"

Under the law, the corporation is a person—a legal entity. Unfortunately, the corporation has assumed the attributes of a human being. Common parlance reflects this by statements such as "The corporation formulates policy," "The corporation has decided to merge," or it "has decided to introduce a new product," and so on. Actually the corporation decides nothing, because it is an abstraction. It is the management of the corporation which acts. If a corporation "is soulful," or "has a conscience," it is because management has decided that these attributes are worthy of the corporation image. Though this may be a mundane point, all too often favorable or unfavorable judgments are rendered by the public toward an inaccessible corporate image rather than toward the praise or condemnation of the management of the corporation.

Legitimacy and Power

The corporate device allows for concentration of power. Our society, however, provides only imperfect sanctions for the misuse of power. This is a rather delicate point since our culture insists that the exercise of power be legitimate in the sense that it is responsible to higher authority. For reasons set forth later, the traditional sources of sanctions—the sovereign consumer, the government acting for the public, competition, and of course the owners—have been neutralized in varying degrees as sources of effective control.

Business Goals and Objectives

The freedom to incorporate has been a major factor in the growth of business and the extension of its influence into many aspects of American life. As businesses grow it is more difficult for them to maintain their monolithic role of profit orientation. Instead, large companies take on the semblance of multipurpose institutions with the function of achieving ends that are not directly related to economic activity. This leads, of course, to the question of the capability of managers to make decisions, render judgments, and use corporate power to promote and obtain goals which lie outside the economic order.

The corporation is a product of industrialization, in spite of the issues, dilemmas, and paradoxes raised by it. Technology requires large capital aggregations, mass employment, and many investors ready and willing to become "people's capitalists;" and this makes for a situation in which corporations with centralized control emerge and thrive.

Although there are many criticisms of corporations, these criticisms are paralleled by statements extolling the virtues of corporate enterprise and professional management. Issues appear which make interesting and stimulating copy. But whether these issues are straw men or real is a matter which cannot be easily determined.

The corporation (and hence corporate management) is a complex affair. The corporation is so thoroughly integrated in American culture that fundamental changes in it would undoubtedly modify the fabric of society. In this respect, it has been said that if by divine decree the corporation is eliminated as a legal fiction, the corporation itself would continue to exist and fulfill its functions with very little change in structure and executive behavior. Nothing short of general catastrophe could persuade society to cast off that which it has deemed so essential to its well-being.

Social need alone, however, is not sufficient justification for power, particularly for those who feel that power in all forms must have restraints. Since corporations are really the creatures of those who run them, it is apparent that management must ultimately become the focus of consideration when matters of responsibility are discussed. The pressure on management and the incentives for action in the corporate environment are really the motivating and constraining forces which eventually cause the managers to shape the "corporate personality." Consequently, it is relevant to present some of the incentives, both positive and negative, which prompt executive action.

EXECUTIVE INCENTIVES

Financial Incentives

Making money is supposedly the cause for going into business. Ideally, profits are the guiding criterion for judging the correctness of business decisions; and they are the incentive necessary to entice people to perform an economic function. The role of profits for the owner-manager of a relatively small concern is clear and unambiguous. They constitute his reward for successful practice.

Like most else in the corporate world, profits and their role are not so forthright. Profits frequently are means rather than ends for the professional manager. As such, they are only loosely correlated with executive incentives. Certainly the management of a corporation cannot disregard profits as a minimum expectation necessary to ensure passive stockholders and directors. But beyond this, it is a moot question whether executives seek every rational economic alternative to enlarge profits. Instead they may pursue other alternatives, such as personal power, organizational stability, organizational growth, consumer respect, social philanthropy, and employee welfare.[5]

Personal Financial Success and Corporate Financial Success. The owner-manager is directly dependent on his own wit in running his business for the income it returns to him for his efforts and on his investment. Ultimately, of course, the financial success or failure of a corporate enterprise will also affect the livelihood of its management. However, in the usual course of events the managements of large, relatively stable corporations are not faced with the extreme circumstances of stupendous successes or dismal failures of the companies which are immediately translated into earning fluctuations.

Instead, corporate executives have relatively stable basic salaries which are fairly detached from corporate earnings. Methods of executive compensation take numerous forms beyond the basic salaries, however. Bonuses, pensions, and stock options are typical of short- and long-range deferred-income plans.

Some parts of executives' total incomes are more sensitive to corporate earning fluctuations than others. For example, bonuses move quite closely with earning changes over short periods. The decisions of executives to exercise stock options are also intimately related to the current earnings of the company. However, salaries are just moderately responsive to earning fluctuations, while pension programs are relatively insensitive to earning movements.[6]

Another important feature of executive compensation is its relative stability compared with other occupational categories. The owner-manager thrives or perishes as a result of short-range conditions which are frequently beyond his control. The operative employee and the foreman are susceptible to layoffs due to seasonal and cyclical business conditions. The executive, however, is fairly immune to serious income difficulties caused

---

[5] Robert Aaron Gordon, *Business Leadership in the Large Corporation* (Washington, D.C.: The Brookings Institution, 1945), p. 327.

[6] One facet of executive compensation plans is that as an executive builds up a substantial interest in profit sharing and retirement programs he becomes less and less inclined to move from his company. If he did leave the loss of participation rights would result in a considerable financial penalty. Thus, executives tend to think twice about moving from their jobs even though attractive opportunities are available elsewhere. See Arthur H. Cole, *Business Enterprise in Its Social Setting* (Cambridge: Harvard University Press, 1959) pp. 92–93.

by short-run economic adjustments.[7] Executives are retained to the bitter end in economic adversity in anticipation of better times to come. A company would be hard put to replace its executive cadre constantly.[8]

From this it may be concluded that executive income exhibits a fair degree of inflexibility when related to corporate earnings.[9] This leads Gordon to observe that, "This system of incentives is far removed from the classical method of remunerating business leadership in a private enterprise economy. The particular reward of business leadership is supposed to be profits which link the businessman's remuneration directly and completely to the success or failure of the firm's operation."[10]

Thus a direct coupling between executive compensation and earnings does not prevail. The question now is what else besides profit provides incentives for executive action. Perhaps a partial answer is found in growth.

Incentives Stemming from Growth

Managers are led to pursue objectives which are attractive to them as managers, not as owners. The interests of owners and managers need not be incompatible, of course, but they may differ as to the scale of size on one hand versus the amount of return on investment on the other. Nevertheless, owners may be content to forgo high returns if they realize an enhancement in the value of their property. Since appreciation is associated with a growth policy, the objective of management to expand finds a desirable mate with the objective of many investors to experience capital gains. This may explain why owners are happy with limited returns in the face of large retained earnings; but it does not get to the core of the issue of why management finds incentives in growth.

Many executives claim "we grow because we have to." In essence, they mean that growth is thrust upon them by the exigencies of their environment. Preservation of the status quo is not the way a progressive management meets the challenges of competition and the insatiable demands of the consumer. There can be no doubt that growth is necessary for

---

[7] For an example see "Top Pay Resists Slump," *Business Week*, May 20, 1961, pp. 63–68.

[8] Knauth observes: "Management looks upon salaries as a means of building up a corps of elite personnel that will carry on its essential policies. Each member acquired specialized knowledge that might be sacrified were he to leave the organization. His value to it is disproportionately large in comparison to his market value. . . . The objective of management is to assure continuous functioning and the amount paid in salaries is a small part of total expense. It is natural, therefore, that salaries should be named for a long period and should be on the liberal side." See Oswald Knauth, *Managerial Enterprise* (New York: W. W. Norton and Co., 1948), p. 156.

[9] Katona says, "It has been found . . . that moderate increases in corporation profits rarely have a direct effect on the executive's remuneration or on the assurance with which they hold their positions." George Katona, *Psychological Analysis of Economic Behavior* (New York: McGraw-Hill, Inc., 1951), p. 197.

[10] Gordon, *op. cit.*, p. 296.

survival for many firms. And there can be even less doubt that conditions external to a company make growth policies the only feasible long-run strategy for management.

Management, however, is not composed simply of passive actors responding to external stimuli. The growth of the firm offers executives forms of material and egoistic satisfactions which are not available through any other corporate incentive. Some of these satisfactions are explored below, running from the simple and obvious to the less obvious and complex.[11]

1. Growth makes more opportunities available for promotion.

2. Salaries are often dependent more on the size of a department or the size of a company as a whole than on profitability. Given the maintenance of a standard of efficiency and profitability, salaries are geared to such considerations as volume of sales, number of people employed, and volume of manufactured output. This is the same as saying salary is linked more to an executive's responsibilities than to profitability. As an organization grows there is no assurance its *rate* of profit will increase, although its absolute dollar profit might. However, increasing size generally carries increasing responsibility which provides a basis for higher compensation.

3. The third growth incentive is called the "instinct of workmanship" (for lack of a better title). Man has cravings for the personal satisfaction connected with a well-done job. This desire is no less evident among managers than among master carpenters, evidence of the mastery drive, no doubt. However, the satisfaction an executive derives from his work is more intangible—although no less real—than the concrete satisfactions produced by the creation of a beautifully carved cabinet.

A growing and efficient organization is both a tribute and a monument to managerial ability. Also, the chance to develop a vital organization is an outlet for the creative mind of an active personality. The fact cannot be discounted that "doing a good job" as reflected in organization growth is an incentive underlying management action. Rewards forthcoming from successful accomplishments along these lines have very few substitutes in the business world.

4. Growth to a respectable size is prestige building in a business setting. Prestige, for reasons peculiar to our society, is associated with magnitudes of influence over large numbers of people and control of considerable quantities of resources. The ancient and often-cited characteristic of materialism is concerned with measuring success quantitatively rather than qualitatively.

It might be argued that a manager derives as much satisfaction from the quality of his operations or products as he does from the net worth, volume of sales, or the number of employees in his company. But size per

---

[11] Most of the satisfactions in this section are adapted from Clare E. Griffin, *Enterprise in a Free Society* (Homewood, Ill.: Richard D. Irwin, Inc., 1949); esp. chaps. 5, 6.

se has a prior claim in support of the legitimacy of a business which quality does not possess. A hint of this is found in advertisements calling the public's attention to the point that this motion picture or this circus is the *biggest* and the best offered yet.

The objection might be raised that a company's growth is predicated on the quality of the goods and services offered, plus adherence to high standards of internal operations. This poses something of a chicken-egg problem which becomes helplessly entangled when the question of executive motivations is considered. Does management pursue quality and service objectives as means which eventually will produce a large and successful company? Or does management seek quality and service objectives as intrinsic values in themselves which may have the happy by-product of giving a firm a commanding position in an industry?

These questions do not admit generalizations. At best, answers to them must consider management's personal goals and the situational character of the corporate setting. But one thing is fairly certain. An executive's affiliation with a large and successful organization is frequently sufficient in itself to reflect considerable prestige on the individual.

Prestige is bestowed from a number of sources which tend to give size a high priority in their value system.

a) Prestige is internally bestowed by fellow employees. The manager of a large department has a high stature because responsibility for a department of considerable magnitude implies a high degree of competency.

b) Prestige is externally bestowed by colleagues in other businesses.

c) Prestige is bestowed by the stockholders upon the management of influential companies.

d) Prestige is bestowed by the public because of awe-inspiring size and contributions to community well-being resulting from corporate influence in community affairs.

e) Prestige is bestowed by customers as a result of the provision of products and services which are available only through large companies.

Thus, size commands the respect and recognition of others. It is natural, therefore, that management should adopt organizational growth policies leading to increased size which will ultimately resolve themselves in the satisfaction of executive's prestige incentives. As expected, organization size goes hand in hand with power. Indeed, power and prestige are quite inseparable.

Power is socially defined. The culture of a society stakes out those institutions which are more favored as sources of power. Then it is up to the individual to affiliate with that institution which he appraises as yielding him the greatest opportunity to achieve personal power (if indeed power is an objective in an individual's life).

Many institutions have power potential—the church, government, the military, education, and business. Those people who are so disposed will gravitate to the institution which offers the greatest opportunity to exert power. In the Middle Ages the church offered careers which provided power incentives sufficient to attract the talented and the ambitious. The military in the Prussian state offered to the impoverished aristocracy the major outlet for their power drives. In our society the corporation of today has a good deal of potential in the power realm. Of course, not all of those who elect a career as a corporate executive will accumulate much personal power. But nevertheless the opportunity is there, and it is more or less democratically available to people from many different backgrounds.

Business yields power in a number of ways of which the most apparent is the production and command over wealth. But in addition, large corporations have other power incentives to offer their executives. Among these are influence over people, control over resources, and control over the machinery of organization. Another important adjunct of corporate power is the opportunity it gives executives to make decisions favorable to themselves as a management group. More is said of this later in the chapter.

Power is useful to perpetuate interests already vested in an organization. An established top management is usually sufficiently in control of proxy machinery that it seldom has to worry about retaining its position in face of discontented minorities or corporate raiders.

The corporation as a device for marshaling resources also makes possible the marshaling of power. As Latham points out, "A mature political conception of the corporation must view it as a rationalized system for the accumulation, control, and administration of power."[12] Management by expanding corporate power also expands the prestige and influence which go with it. Of course, as corporate power is extended the power of the individual executive is comparably expanded. Thus in a growing corporation the executive finds a setting offering sufficient opportunities for the satisfaction of his power drives.[13]

So far two forms of executive incentives have been treated in their various ramifications. These are the financial incentives and the satisfactions obtained from company growth. Other motivations for participation in a corporation are indirectly associated with both the financial and the growth incentives.

Social Approval

Personal power and prestige are derived from occupying high status positions in the management of a large corporation, whereas "social approval" implies society's recognition of the worthiness of the activity

---

[12] Earl Latham, "The Body Politic of the Corporation," in Edward S. Mason, *op. cit.*, p. 220.

[13] The individual advances his power interests two ways: by promotions through the organizational hierarchy and by affiliating with a growing concern. Obviously, it is more to the advantage of the individual with strong power drives to associate with an expanding organization and work his way up than to attempt to work up through a fairly stable company.

itself.[14] Key men in criminal syndicates do not enjoy social approval, but they have considerable power as well as prestige in their immediate circles.

Historically, businessmen did not have a great deal of social approval. There is not much glamor about the self-seeking pursuit of wealth, even though wealth is supposed to be the reward for providing vital goods and services to the community. There has always been a deep-seated sentiment in our culture that the pursuit of wealth is not the noblest of man's endeavors. But the sentiment against business as such is wearing down for reasons enumerated below.

First, as a dominant institution in our society business claims the attention of the public. Size and influence often carry grudging social approval as long as they are not used to transgress loosely defined boundaries of propriety. Further, the owner-manager and the independent farmer are no longer social influentials. The executives of medium-sized and large corporations are now the spokesmen of free enterprise and individual liberty. These modern torchbearers are far differently situated than their predecessors.

As indicated earlier in this chapter, managerial financial incentives are not so rigid that the pursuit of wealth alone necessarily enjoys a singular or even a top-priority position on the index of an executive's work motives. Other objectives become more important—or at least equally important—than the attainment of wealth itself. Thus, the "uncouth" pursuit of profit is tempered by the executive's interest in more socially acceptable objectives.

Second, associated with these transitions in personal goals are changes which have taken place in business objectives.[15] It is frequently pointed out that the corporation is a quasi-public institution in the sense that it has major objectives beyond the economic which make claims on its resources. The corporation, therefore, can be thought of as a multipurpose institution. Such objectives as industrial peace, community development, philanthropic activities, and employee well-being extended into areas which are sensitive to social approval or disapproval.

And third, in recognition of their quasi-public nature and their social visibility, large corporations have intensified public relations activities to sell the community on the idea that they are aware of their social obligations and are discharging them. Public relations programs are frequently directed toward building the image of good corporate citizenship and corporate responsibility.

The large corporation, in general, has succeeded in improving its

---

[14] Griffin, *op. cit.*, p. 81.

[15] Dent observes that, "Not only do larger businesses subscribe to public service more than smaller ones, but growing businesses likewise mention public service more frequently than declining ones. . . ." James K. Dent, "Organizational Correlates of the Goals of Business Managements," *Personnel Psychology*, 1959, p. 389.

position in public esteem.[16] Also, by the process of osmosis the smaller corporation is able to participate in the reflected glories of the larger. Flowing from this, management has grown in stature as an honorable and worthwhile "profession." Both established executives and young executives starting their careers are fairly assured that their choice of occupation will carry with it greater social approval today and in the future than it has in the past. Still, however, the corporate executive does not enjoy the approval usually given to doctors, clergymen, or lawyers. In fact, other less honorific occupations like teaching, social service, and governmental service, carry more approval, at times, than the management of a business. Consequently, the search for social acceptance by corporate management constantly goes on.

The Quest for Approval

There can be no question of the modern corporation's impact on the processes of American society. The extensiveness of corporate influence makes it difficult to talk of the corporation and corporate management as instruments of economic rationality. The corporation is a way of life for its members and for people outside it who come within its orbit of influence.[17]

The executives employed in a corporation carry into their communities the corporate image, either directly as agents of "good corporate works" or indirectly by the mere fact of affiliation with a particular company. It is because of the high degree of visibility of both the corporation and its executives that management is concerned with promoting an acceptable image.

Image slogans—such as the corporate conscience, the soulful corporation, and good corporate citizenship— have become popularized. The fact that such anthropomorphic characterizations are quite absurd does not seem to be a matter of much concern.[18] In reality, what is meant is that the management of a corporation is soulful, has a conscience, and accepts the responsibility of citizenship.

Achieving these heights of managerial nobility as a matter of fact and not as a matter of public relations is a difficult affair, involving built-in paradoxes. For example, a corporate management would be socially conscious and a good citizen if in times of recession it would expand its capital investments, and if in times of prosperity with inflationary overtones it would contract its capital investments. However, most businessmen would

---

[16] Now and then the polished image of the corporation becomes a little tarnished. The antitrust proceedings against large manufacturers of electrical products did not do much to advance the cause of good corporate citizenship.

[17] Carl Kaysen, "The Social Significance of the Modern Corporation," *American Economic Review*, May, 1957, p. 319.

[18] See Earl Latham, "Anthropomorphic Corporations, Elites, and Monopoly Power," *American Economic Review*, May, 1957, pp. 303–10.

say that such decisions do not make sense *from the standpoint of the company*. Probably they are right. The point is that decisions which are beneficial to society as a whole often may be detrimental to the firm in particular.

Management is faced with this same paradox when it moves into the political sphere of activity, when it moves into action on social issues, and when it sees fit to move into the areas of education and aesthetics. The dilemma is always one of organization good as opposed to social good. The nature of private enterprise forces American management to give priority to the company, although management sometimes makes good copy with decisions which simultaneously promote the interests of the firm and the welfare of society.[19]

Executives as chief actors in the economic order are forced to balance the need for social approval with the needs of their company. A management of a corporation does not win social approval by committing anti-social acts even if these acts are in the best interests of the firm. But at the same time, business ideology has it that the primary aim of management is economic rationality, at least in the long run. Also, society is perverse enough to punish those companies which do not live up to the obligations imposed by undertaking a business enterprise.

So management must somehow reconcile the demands of society for socially conscious behavior with the demands of economic rationality also expected by society. This situation would present an impossible dilemma were it not for two circumstances:

1. Social consciousness and economic rationality need not always be antithetical.

2. Social consciousness and economic rationality are not "either-or" alternatives. Between these two alternatives, management has a range of discretion in which the social demands of the moment and the future can be balanced with short- and long-range economic goals.

The difficulties created by the dilemma just considered are on a rather high level of abstraction. The difficult issues of the social good and the individual good do not have wide appeal. Hence, the problem of social consciousness is geared down to a more mundane level. In this respect, some suppose that management dispatches its social obligations by contributions to worthy causes, thereby obtaining social approval.

Corporate giving as a means of gaining social approval is too large to be ignored. Richard Eells, one of the major exponents of corporate giving, states that management must use some funds for philanthropic purposes in order to ensure the survival of the corporation. He points out that corporate philanthropy is not a capricious diversion of assets. Rather, the

---

[19] Recognizing the inherent discrepancies which exist between society's aims and the aims of independent companies within society, the apocryphal statement, "what is good for General Motors is good for the country," makes little sense.

corporation strengthens its positions socially and economically by contributions to deserving beneficiaries.

Philanthropic activities, according to Eells, are related to a company's long-range broadly conceived social objectives. Corporate giving also has a crucial role in business strategy because an intelligent program enhances corporate power, prestige, and influence in a competitive situation. But a philanthropic program must be rationally conceived in a sense that the corporation must give in sufficient amounts to individuals and private organizations who are most influentially placed for granting approval and support to the management of the corporate donor. The recipients of grants should be in a position to respond with favorable opinions of the corporation which will percolate to the greatest extent possible through society. The salutary corporate image created by philanthropy facilitates the accomplishment and acceptance of other corporate goals as profitability and market domination. Thus, the guiding principle of corporate philanthropy is enlightened self-interest.[20]

A program of corporate philanthropy uses a number of channels for giving. Contributions are made to individuals for research and education; grants are bestowed on universities for either unrestricted uses or in support of specific research projects; and private research organizations benefit from corporate donations. In addition, corporations also contribute to charitable fund drives and community cultural and recreational programs.

Eells has an interesting statement pertaining to the philosophy of selecting grant recipients:

A corporation would not only be justified in supporting *research* into the whole problem of corporate survival in varying degrees of restraint on freedom of association; it should go further, and give *active support* to the vital private sectors in its immediate environment that work for the principle of freedom of association and represent that principle in practice. This includes not only economic groups, but also health, recreational, educational, religious, professional, scientific, artistic, and other associational efforts to serve human needs.[21]

Although it might seem ungrateful, corporate philanthropy—and, indeed, the whole matter of corporate social responsibility—has not gone unchallenged. For example, Levitt claims that the major responsibility of business is to perform an economic function for a profit. The issue of social responsibility serves only to confuse the goals of business.[22]

Levitt notes that most advocates of the social responsibility doctrine admit, under close questioning, that they are motivated by cold cash. It is

---

[20] See Richard Eells, *Corporation Giving in a Free Society* (New York: Harper and Bros., 1956), p. 7.

[21] *Ibid.*, p. 103.

[22] Theodore Levitt, "The Dangers of Social Responsibility," *Harvard Business Review*, September–October, 1958, pp. 41–50.

good business to be responsible. But still, there has been considerable talk about the altruistic motives behind corporate giving as a way to meet social obligations. Levitt feels the subtle danger is that executives will begin to believe their public relations image and accept the idea that their philanthropy is out of the pure love of man. Levit concludes by saying, "Business will have a much better chance of surviving if there is no nonsense about its goals—that is, if long-run profit maximization is the one dominant objective in practice as well as in theory."[23]

Levitt's basic point is that management should stick to what it is able to do best—run a business. Management should not dabble in functions where it is on shaky ground—social responsibilities. This argument is extended by the notion that management ultimately makes its greatest social contribution through the operation of an efficient, profitable economic enterprise.

This issue is carried still further by questioning the predisposition and adequacy of management to judge the inherent value, objectives, and performance of nonbusiness undertakings which presumably fall within the scope of management's social responsibility.[24] According to Eells, in his statement quoted above, management should be interested in supporting health, recreational, educational, religious, professional, scientific, and artistic groups as long as they conform to principles of freedom of association.

More is at stake here than freedom of association. Certainly business is concerned with this important aspect of freedom. Educational institutions, and religious, scientific, and artistic groups are predicated on freedom of association but they thrive on freedom of expression as well. There are two dangers connected with corporate giving. The first is that socially valuable undertakings may not receive needed support because they do not ascribe to business ideological standards of philosophy and performance. The second, and more disastrous consequence, is that voluntary associations may modify *their* objectives and temper their freedom of expression to conform to business requirements for the receipt of support.

Eells' enlightened self-interest policy of giving is tricky because it leads

---

[23] *Ibid.*, p. 49.

[24] Thorndike questions the role of businessmen as "keepers of public morality" in a shrewd article from which the following quotation is taken. "The virtues and services the world needs from producers, merchants, owners, and managers are not just the same as those which it needs from priests or teachers. The primary service of the former is to satisfy human wants; the primary service of the latter is to improve them. The cardinal virtues of the former in their capacity as economic agents are to maximize production, minimize waste, and distribute goods and services so they will be used to the maximal advantage of the human species. . . . Many farmers, miners, manufacturers, and merchants who do first-rate work for the world in their present states of mind would probably be confused and misled if they tried to behave as trustees for the public." Edward L. Thorndike, "The Psychology of the Profit Motive," *Harpers*, September, 1936, pp. 431–37.

to satisfying just those social obligations which produce the greatest material and ideological returns to the corporation. Other obligations are ignored. In this philosophy, the altruistic enhancement of social good is not the criterion of giving at all.

If the principle of corporate giving is accepted, then the issue resolves to what is the best means for making allocations for the advancement of social good. There are three other alternatives in addition to direct corporate giving:

1. The Government. Presently the federal government encourages corporate giving by tax advantages. Supposing these advantages were removed, would the government make a better and more impartial agency for the distribution of funds derived from increased tax revenues? Or would anything be gained from retaining tax advantages but permitting the government to designate organizations to which contributions are acceptable or not acceptable for tax purposes?

2. The Stockholders. In the short run, stockholders are deprived of some part of their dividends by a corporate giving policy. Would it be better for the corporation to withhold all contributions and distribute them to stockholders? Then stockholders could use this extra income as they see fit.

3. Trusteeships or Foundations. This alternative centralizes giving but at the same time it does not have the onerous connotation of a government dole. It overcomes at least two objections which can be raised to the other alternatives. Thus, would it be an adequate solution to corporate giving to do so through a private agency, distinctly removed from the influence of the management of the corporation or corporations which have established it?

It is not without a reason that these alternatives have been stated in the form of questions. The whole matter of corporate giving and the motives of management underlying it is highly debatable. Ultimately, the reader must decide for himself the appropriateness of corporate giving in our society. If he decides it is appropriate he must then consider the most effective means for the distribution of funds.

The Profit Incentive

One aspect of the profit incentive has already been touched on in this chapter. It is the relationship between executive income and the profitability of the firm. The conclusion of this discussion it is recalled, is that profit in itself is insufficient as an incentive to explain executive motives in the corporate setting. The question of profit as an incentive factor is reopened now to explore some of its other dimensions.

It is wise to make a distinction, following Drucker, between profitability and the profit motive. Profitability, according to Drucker, is an *objective* principle of social action. It is a measure of economic rationality and a criterion of success of a business enterprise in performing economic functions. The profit motive is a subjective facet of human motivation.[25] People pursue profits in order to gain personal satisfaction.

From the standpoint of the owner-manager, the profit motive and profitability are clearly inseparable. The owner-manager satisfies his personal material needs directly through the profitability of his firm. The case of the hired professional manager is not so simple. The manager's material wants are satisfied through a fairly stable salary and employment situation. As a first approximation, it could be said that the corporate manager is motivated by profit and seeks profitability to satisfy the needs of others having claims on the company.[26]

Perhaps the best place to begin talking about the profit issue is with the various claimants to corporate gross income. Gross income is apportioned among six claimants: suppliers, government, employees, maintenance, depreciation-obsolescence, suppliers of capital, and surplus.[27]

The last two items in this list require further explanation. Suppliers of capital as claimants include bondholders and stockholders. In the latter case, while it is not accepted accounting practice, some corporations have treated stockholder dividends as fixed charges implemented by a level dividend policy. Such a policy allows management to retain a high percentage of earnings in good periods for expansion purposes and to provide a bulwark against poor earning periods. From a strong position of retained earnings management is also able to pay the "usual" dividends regularly, thus keeping stockholders satisfied during times of lower-than-average earnings.[28]

As for the last item, that which is left over after the claimants to the corporation's gross income have been taken care of is called loosely profit or surplus. Now, profit has claimants, too. These claimants are the government (more taxes), employees (fringe benefits and incentive rewards), stockholders (extra dividends), the public (social beneficences), and finally management itself (bonuses and other amenities). Management occupies the unique, and at times uneasy, position of both participant in and dispenser of corporation profits. The allocation by management of gross income, but particularly profit, to claimants underscores management's need to balance the distribution of assets among the several groups having legitimate claims.

The Problem of Retained Earnings. "Plowing back" earnings into a company is a fundamental part of American business ideology. Sutton and his associates observe that, "So enchanted is the business creed with the

---

[25] Peter Drucker, *The Concept of the Corporation* (New York: The John Day Co., 1946), pp. 234–36.

[26] The distinction is not so neat, however, because as indicated earlier there is a relationship between profitability and the gross income of managers.

[27] Knauth, *op. cit.*, pp. 149–50.

[28] *Ibid.*, pp. 145–46; pp. 159–60.

social beneficence of plowing back that in some circumstances it is reluctant to count retained earnings as profits at all."[29]

Probably the roots of the philosophy of plowing earnings back into the business are traceable to the period in history when America was a capital-poor nation. During this time Europe supplied some capital for the development of railroads. In general, however, businessmen came to rely on self-financing as the most reliable source of funds for expansion purposes. Over time the notion of financing growth out of internal capital resources became ingrained in business mentality.

One would expect, however, that as this country moved from a capital-poor to a capital-rich nation the reliance on internally generated funds to support expansion would give way to the use of funds available externally in the capital market. But apparently any vast shift from internal to external financing is not discernible, or not in this century at least. Lintner says:

> The relative shifts in the reliance on internal or external funds as the level of business activity, profits, and total financial requirements change have been remarkably stable over a full half century, and the ratio of internal to external funds has been approximately the same in years of comparable level and rate of change of activity.[30]

The classical rationale behind the decision to retain earnings for self-financing or to pay them as dividends is simple and straightforward. According to the theory, if the directors and management of a corporation are to act in the best interests of the stockholders they must reinvest earnings in the business or pay dividends in conformance with marginal principles governed by the ruling rate of interest. Management should act as if it feels stockholders' potential dividends will earn more if plowed back into the company than these dividends would command by being paid to owners and then employed in other investment channels.[31]

In practice, data to support such marginal calculations are extremely difficult to come by. It is really impossible to say whether a retained-earnings policy best serves the interest of the stockholder and the free enterprise system or results in a misallocation of capital resources.

In spite of this, the use of retained earnings for expansion does have some interesting implications which focus on the profit incentive as a managerial motivation.

First, "the plowing in of earnings on the part of business corporations is

---

[29] Francis X. Sutton, Seymore E. Harris, Carl Kaysen, and James Tobin, *The American Business Creed* (Cambridge: Harvard University Press, 1956), p. 85.

[30] John Lintner, "The Financing of Corporations," in Edward S. Mason (ed.), *op. cit.*, p. 184.

[31] Norman S. Buchanan, "Theory and Practice of Dividend Distribution," *Quarterly Journal of Economics*, 1938, pp. 70–78.

another means of securing predominating influence for the groups in control. . . . Self-financing . . . is an expression of the general tendency of modern business management to work for the business as such and not for the capitalists and creditors."[32] Beckerath's observation points up a key idea often cited in management literature. The typical corporate executive identifies with the company and finds his relevant reference group among other executives. He does not usually identify with others having interest in corporate affairs.[33]

Making profits coupled with the opportunity of keeping a sizable chunk of them allows for a managerial flexibility in the decision area which will strengthen the company and ensure its expansion. Additionally, corporate growth, continuity, and affluence are essential to the perpetuation of incumbent management, affording it an opportunity to enhance power and prestige. Hence, there is a very happy wedding between managerial objectives and retained earnings policies which is not entirely explainable by the marginal logic relative to the "ideal" distribution of corporate profits.

Second, "plowing-back insulates the expansion projects of existing firms from the test of the market . . . plowing-back enables the management to go ahead with its investment projects . . . even if the appraisal of the market is that the funds could be better used elsewhere."[34]

Self-financing frees management from the possible limitations that could be imposed by having investment plans subject to the veto of the capital market. By detaching itself from this constraint management can make investment decisions which may be good for the firm, but without prior endorsement of the affair as a socially useful undertaking. Freedom from the capital market allows management to present corporate "outsiders" with a *fait accompli* in an investment sense.

This discussion should cause the reader to realize that the opportunity to make a profit invokes a very complex set of motives in corporate management. Retained earnings are obviously based on profits. These earnings are used for a variety of purposes, such as expansion, freedom from market tests, securing the future of the corporation and its management, and making possible a continuous and level dividend for stockholders. Also, corporate profits force management to make balancing decisions in terms of distribution to various claimants. In this role management is at once a distributor of profits and a claimant of them. Management then must be cautious of the returns it allocates to itself relative to the other parties.

---

[32] Herbert von Beckerath, *Modern Industrial Organization* (New York: McGraw-Hill Book Co., Inc., 1933), pp. 68–69.

[33] On the point of managerial identification see C. Addison Hickman, "Managerial Motivation and the Theory of the Firm," *American Economic Review*, May, 1955, pp. 549–50; and Katona, *op. cit.*, pp. 196–97.

[34] Sutton, *op. cit.*, p. 88.

All of this should not obscure the fact that there is a profit orientation, pure and simple, to which corporate management subscribes. Whether this orientation is one of maximization or something else is highly debatable. It is certain, however, that management does not seek profits for the sake of directly improving its personal fortunes (although this may be the happy result over a moderately long period of time). Also, there is doubt that management seeks profits for the owners alone.

It is fair to conclude that management seeks profits so that corporate well-being is assured, thereby satisfying those who have stakes in it. A vital corporation is a monument to management. That such a corporation is also profitable is a necessary fact of life. But by no means is profitability the only incentive, or even the main incentive, for management action. It is a means to an end.

The various incentives and their implications provide some insight into the reason for executive action. Limitation on executive behavior is also apparent in the corporate setting and must be treated to round out the discussion. Therefore, constraint on management is the topic that follows.

EXECUTIVE CONSTRAINTS

The constraints on executive action are no less important than the incentives which promote action in the corporate environment. It could be said that even the incentives have built-in limitations. For example, organization growth may bring new people to the organization and result in a dilution of the power and influence of established executives. Profits or market domination might create adverse public reaction and cause antitrust proceedings to be instituted by the federal government. Stockholders may rebel on the issue of management stock options. Thus, the incentives are not absolute in any sense.

This section, however, does not examine the limitations which logically adhere to executive incentives. Rather, it explores some other limitations imposed on executive behavior by sources both internal and external to the corporation.

Internal Sources of Constraints

The constraints treated under this heading flow from limitations to executive action generated by the interpersonal and organizational dynamics found within the firm. The internal constraints are dwelt upon at length. Many of the following considerations have been analyzed in other chapters. Most of the issues appearing below are simply applications in a specific context of ideas covered elsewhere.

Formal Internal Limitations. The limitations in this classification are derived from classic organization theory. It is obvious that in a military, chain-of-command type of organization the behavior of subordinates is circumscribed by the demands of superiors. Authority, responsibility, and accountability are the formal devices which limit executive behavior to a certain extent. Reinforcing the authority structure of the formal organization are policies, procedures, and rules which provide quasi-automatic regulations that the individual accepts by curbing his inclinations and modifying his behavior to accord with formal company requirements. Submission of the individual to these internal controls is prerequisite to his continued participation in a firm.

Formal constraints, of course, do not cover all possible behavior patterns. And they are not always effective in the cases they do cover. Formal constraints set out the ground rules for behavior. Far from being comprehensive these rules allow individuals and groups considerable latitude for unregulated behavior.

Quasi-Formal Constraints.   Many behavioral codes never find their way into written, formal company policy. These constraints are real nonetheless, and they limit an individual's freedom to behave as he likes. These codes range from relatively innocuous prescriptions like the manner of dress, modes of transportation to and from work, and the pecking order in executive dining rooms, to matters of policy vital to the firm. The methods of executive promotion discussed in the last chapter are also included in this area.

The quasi-formal constraints can be described best as customary behavioral forms which have developed historically. They are traditions to which executives better conform in order to avoid embarassment and trouble. They are the how-we-do-it-here codes which are not committed to writing but are generally known and accepted by the executives in a company.

Informal Constraints.   Informal organizations among executives often spell out the power groups influential in directing the destiny of a company. Like most informal organizations they possess the characteristics of social control, sociometric structuring, informal leadership, and the like. In other words, there is a certain universality about the characteristics of the informal organization as it is found throughout all levels of the company. But the stakes of informal association are higher in upper-management levels. The influential informal organization of higher management is perhaps more rigorous in its selection of membership. At the same time, the individual member must be more cautious in his alliances and in the way he behaves once an alliance has been contracted.

The informal groups are often referred to as centers of influence in the organization. Through such groups an individual can gain considerable personal power, if he receives the necessary group support. But if support is withheld or withdrawn an individual's power aspirations may be doomed. An executive must keep one eye on the formal aspects of organization and the other on their sources of internal support for programs. No executive can remain aloof from power alignments, because they provide him with valuable assistance for the implementation of his programs and for support in his position. An executive is constrained in his actions by the expectations of his informal associations in the organization. He must service these expectations or be faced with the consequence of the denial of group support. The seriousness of group denial for an executive is situational. It depends on the degree of independent, personal power, and prestige of an executive; it also depends on the structure and magnitude of group influence.

Committees. It is difficult to categorize the type of constraints that result from committee activities. In a real sense, the constraints they impose are of a form combining all three of the restraints mentioned previously. First of all, the committee is a formally constituted body within the structure of a company. As such it is endowed with power and limitations much as with any other formal activity. These limits to authority circumscribe the behavior of the membership of the committee. Second, committees, particularly standing committees, develop over time folklore and rituals all their own. These traditions delineate acceptable and unacceptable forms of behavior. Third, the element of informal pressure is active in committees. The group decision-making process is a powerful force for bringing into line recalcitrant individuals.

A variation on this same theme is noted by Cyert and March.

> There is a reasonable amount of evidence to support the prediction that an individual with an attitude at variance with his perception of the group's attitude will tend . . . to adjust his "public" position to conform to the position he expects the group to take. Such behavior may be exhibited even in the limiting case where all members hold a position at variance with their common perception of the group standard.[35]

The committee is an excellent spot for the display of interpersonal dynamics. As a body of the formal organization the committee allows for the "legitimate" interplay of personalities. The chances for power maneuvering, discrediting adversaries, and building one's personal prestige are rife in these situations. The committee offers an excellent stage for organizational gamesmanship.

That the group demands conformity is fairly well established. But there is doubt that conformity to a group decision in the committee setting will result in individual conformity to this decision outside the committee room. Whether or not an individual conforms depends on company philosophy[36] and the sanctions he might anticipate from a deviation from a group decision.

Much more can be said of the internal constraints on management. Role theory could be restated along with administrative problems of communication, morale, and balance. But since these matters have received atten-

---

[35] R. M. Cyert and J. G. March, "Organizational Structure and Pricing Behavior in an Oligopolistic Market," *American Economic Review*, March, 1955, p. 133.

[36] See Drucker's concept of the "chief-executive" team which stresses joint deliberation but individual decision. Peter Drucker, *The Practice of Management* (New York: Harper and Bros., 1954) pp. 176 ff.

tion earlier it serves no purpose to go into them again in this section. The reader should be able to list a dozen more internal constraints on executive behavior after a cursory review of the conceptual areas in Part III. The issues associated with the external constraints are treated next.

External Sources of Constraints

Woodrow Wilson said in 1910, "We have witnessed in modern business the submergence of the individual within the organization, and yet the increase to an extraordinary degree of the power of the individual—of the individual who happens to control the organization."[37]

Twenty-two years later Berle and Means observed, "In its new aspect the corporation is a means whereby the wealth of innumerable individuals has been concentrated into huge aggregates and whereby control over this wealth has been surrendered to a unified direction. The power attendant upon such concentration has brought forth princes of industry, whose position in the community is yet to be defined."[38]

Speaking of the corporation in 1960, Rostow asks ". . . has it become a free collectivity, divorced in its business life from significant public or private control, save the will of the small group which happens to have inherited its management?"[39]

These quotations represent abiding problems of the corporation which thoughtful writers have focused upon throughout the century. The first problem is corporate economic, social, and political power. The second problem is the role of management in the exercise of this power. And the third problem is the source of external control over this power. This last provides the theme for this part of the chapter.

Power and Responsibility. Deeply ingrained in American tradition is the notion that power must be responsible. Those who possess power have to give account to others of the way in which it is used. Only because of accountability is power considered legitimate in our society. Thus, power is granted when controls over it are available. Theoretically, corporate power is tolerated in the name of economic necessity; but more importantly power is tolerated because society accepts existing external constraints as sufficient to render management of the corporation responsible. Four traditional constraints on the power of corporate management are reviewed next.

Traditional Constraints. 1. *Property.* Stockholder participation in the affairs of the company is a classic solution to managerial autonomy. But efforts in this direction are doomed. The dispersion of ownership makes effective stockholder participation hopeless.[40]

2. *The Consumer.* The sovereignty of the consumer is another fre-

---

[37] Cited in Ripley, *op. cit.,* p. 1.

[38] Berle and Means, *op. cit.,* p. 2.

[39] Eugene V. Rostow, "To Whom and for What Ends Is Corporate Management Responsible?" in Edward S. Mason, *op. cit.,* p. 50.

[40] For Rostow's position on this point see *ibid.,* pp. 53–56.

quently cited traditional element of control over managerial autonomy. Businessmen are careful to point out that competition for the consumer "votes" in the form of dollars is a real constraining force. Therefore, business must follow the lead of the consumer. That consumer tastes are molded by advertising and sales promotion is somewhat in opposition to the claims of consumer sovereignity. Sutton and his associates make the interesting observation that the more businessmen attempt to condition consumer behavior the more they proclaim the doctrine of consumer autonomy.[41]

3. *The Public.* The public's capability for imposing restraints on management assumes three forms. The first is as a mass capable of violent reaction by force against misdeeds; revolution, in short! The second form is an orderly expression through representatives of sentiments that are eventually manifested as new government regulations or enforcement of existing regulations. The third form is spontaneous public reaction to irresponsibility through various communication media such as the press and the organs of voluntary pressure associations. These methods of expression and others constitute the verbalization of the restraining force of public opinion.

Public sentiment as a means of constraint operates with varying degrees of effectiveness. Discounting revolution as a likely possibility, public opinion and government regulation remain. The efforts of public relations to create a favorable image are at least in apart an attempt to neutralize the sovereignity of public opinion.[42] It has been sagely suggested by a businessman, however, that the harping of public relations departments on corporate social responsibility has raised public expectations of corporate behavior. A misdeed that might have been passed off years ago by the public as, "Well, what more could you expect from businessmen?" now elicits severe critical judgments.

Government regulation has traditionally been negative in that it prescribes what a corporation cannot do in the interest of public well-being. Typically, it has not been positive by encouraging and supporting those groups that have stakes in a company; it has not backed the efforts of those wishing participation in corporate affairs. Chayes points out that regulatory "nay-saying" has proven ill-adapted to answer the question of corporate power.[43]

4. *The Economic System.*[44] The role of the "unseen hand" of compe-

---

[41] Sutton, *op. cit.*, pp. 360–62.

[42] For an interesting commentary on public relations see Bernard D. Nassiter, "Management's Cracked Voice," *Harvard Business Review*, September–October, 1959, pp. 127–33.

[43] Abram Chayes, "The Modern Corporation and the Rule of Law," in Edward S. Mason (ed.), *op. cit.*, p. 45.

[44] The problem of retained earnings discussed earlier may be reread in connection with this section. The propensity of the capital market to supply or withhold funds for business is another aspect of constraints imposed by the economic system.

tition in classical economic theory secured the responsible allocation of resources despite ignoble intentions and actions of individual businessmen. This automatic regulating force was something of a reality for a 19th-century economy which approximated a purely competitive system more closely than the 20th-century market structure.

That this impartial force is potently operative today is generally discounted. However, some writers who speak of uncertainty under oligopolistic conditions and of countervailing power make the case that these situations result in a form of "workable competition" which achieves outcomes not unlike those created in highly competitive economic systems.

The alternative models to the "invisible hand" of competition do not give as tightly reasoned explanations for the allocation of resources as does the model of pure competition. Management has such a wide range of discretion under imperfectly competitive situations that if it does behave responsibly it is not because it is reacting to an impersonal and impartial market force. It is for other reasons which must be sought outside the economic order.[45]

The discussion so far has highlighted the shortcomings of the traditional constraints on management. The preceding should not obscure the fact that these four constraints are still operative with varying degrees of effectiveness. The constraints, however, have been diluted, leaving regions in which management can act without being accountable for its behavior.

The gaps created by the breakdown of classical constraints allow for two forms of management behavior. They are managerial exploitiveness and managerial morality.

Exploitive Behavior

A number of years ago James Burnham's thesis of the managerial revolution caused quite a stir. George Orwell, commenting on Burnham, summarizes his thesis.

> Capitalism is disappearing, but Socialism is not replacing it. What is now arising is a new kind of planned, centralized society which will be neither capitalist nor, in any accepted sense of the word, democratic. The rulers of this new society will be the people who effectively control the means of production: that is, business executives, technicians, bureaucrats, and soldiers lumped together by Burnham under the name of "managers." These people will eliminate the old capitalist class, crush the working class, and so organize society that all power and economic privileges remain in their own hands. Private property rights will be abolished, but common ownership will not be established.[46]

---

[45] See Edward S. Mason, "The Apologetics of 'Managerialism'," *Journal of Business,* January, 1958, pp. 1–11.

[46] George Orwell, *James Burnham and the Managerial Revolution* (London: Socialist Book Centre, 1946), p. 1.

Orwell's interpretation of Burnham is not altogether accurate. The managerial expropriation of the working class is overstated. But the central theme of Burnham's thesis is indeed the idea that neither capitalism nor socialism will survive. These systems will be replaced by "managerialism."

Burnham does say that the managerial economy will be exploitive. However, he carefully qualifies his meaning of "exploitation." Since Marx, exploitation in an economic sense has meant the gouging of classes by a ruling class. Of exploitation, Burnham says it "is . . . simply an economy wherein one group receives a relatively larger share of the products of the economy than another. . . . All class economies are exploiting . . . and the managerial economy will be exploiting."[47] Thus, because of their strategic location in industry managers will be able to get for themselves more than their "rightful" share of the fruits of the economy. However, this does not mean that managers will necessarily be predatory.

While much of Burnham's thesis can be dismissed, one facet of it remains of vital concern. As the power of managers in key decision-making situations increases the question must be raised as to how prone they will to be subordinate their interests, collectively or individually, to the interests of the groups they are supposed to serve. Exploitation is a continuum. At one extreme are rewards which "naturally" accrue to groups because of their position in society; at the other extreme are socially burdensome advantages which favorably situated groups extract because they have the opportunity to do so.

Managerial Morality

The Burnham thesis imputes to management two reasons for being responsible. The first is that managers work for the efficiency of the industrial system as a value in itself. The second reason is that managers stand to lose their exploitive advantages if the system fails to function effectively.

This thesis sounds foreign to American business folkways because nowhere in it is the notion of simple morality as an underlying reason for responsible behavior. Out of the considerable literature dealing with American business ethics and morality one is able to extract the leading idea that, deep down, management is of good and kind disposition.

But it is not even necessary to go to the literature to find support for this point of view. Public sentiment largely reflects the attitude that management is basically responsible. And this attitude has a rather firm foundation in fact. On the whole, management does behave responsibly in the sense that decisions which have moral and social implications are made in accord with prevailing social values and public policy.

---

[47] James Burnham, *The Managerial Revolution* (New York: The John Day Co., 1947), p. 123.

This affirmation of faith in the basic morality of businessmen hardly answers the question of why management is responsible even in situations where society cannot impose direct sanctions. Perhaps part of the answer is found in a notion of positive and negative reasons for morality.

Management has a genuine concern for mass opinion and its latent potential of being felt in government and in the market place. Unfavorable public sentiment can be expressed through more intensive regulation of business. All in all, the public can modify the existing system by legal means. This ability is a deterring force that prevents gross irresponsibility. Management feels it has more to lose than gain from risky acts that might stir up public opinion. It is better to be comfortably assured of what one can get under the status quo rather than risk substantial loss.

There is another negative explanation for managerial responsibility. Many corporations, particularly the large ones, are in oligopolistic industries where firms are uncertain of the decisions of other firms. There is no assurance under these circumstances that all companies in a particular industry will act irresponsibly at the same time; so the management of any particular company hesitates to take the risk of being the first to have the spotlight turned on it. What results is a kind of responsibility vacuum, which each firm's management fears to be the first to fill with irresponsible acts.

A positive type of morality is motivated by a sincere feeling of social responsibility. Positive morality is a product of professionalization and is manifested as the pure notion of managerial stewardship.

Mason's alternatives regarding managerialism are excellent for summarizing the thoughts developed in this section. He says it is possible that:

1. The economy is not so managerial. It is still subject to classical constraints.

2. The economy is managerial, but not enough is known about it to explain why managers act responsibly in the public interest.

3. Managers do not generally behave in a responsible manner.[48]

Of the three alternatives, the second appears to be the most promising for two reasons: it accords with the intuitive feelings of many who are directly or indirectly concerned with corporate enterprise; and it opens up an avenue of research, evaluation, and critical judgment which may either support or prove the error of public opinion.

---

[48] Edward S. Mason, "The Apologetics of Managerialism,'" *op. cit.*, p. 9.

EPILOGUE

The Organization as a System of Government

ADMINISTRATIVE thought in this century has been shaped by scientific management, human relations, and industrial humanism, each movement in its turn. While dissimilar, these movements have in common the fact that they are salvationist creeds. They propose to achieve by relatively simple formulae the integration of man with organization, social harmony (sometimes called cohesiveness or solidarity), and the simultaneous satisfaction of needs both institutional and individual.

The leading figures in these movements often have doctrinaire mentalities. Each has his own idea of the "good organization." These visions are tracings of reality. Nevertheless, true believers think that there is an imperative about their sketch because it conforms in a vital way to the natural order of things. Since it does, the doctrinaire mentality never feels his scheme is coercive.[1] This accounts to some extent for the peculiar ambivalence toward the concept of power in administrative theory. We say more about this point later.

While the three major movements in management thought are divergent in point of view, they are similar to the extent that:

1. They have a clear (and fairly simple), though differing, conception of the nature of man upon which they base,
2. Their interpretation of power, and,
3. Their approach to conflict resolution.

Figure A sets out the ideological sketch of each major movement. Each is elaborated upon in the next section.

THE MOVEMENTS

Our intention in this section is to develop the themes outlined in Figure A. We do not plan to go over much of the territory covered in previous chapters. The premise held here is that the values of a particular system of thought, or philosophy if you will, condition the kinds of recommendations made for organizational reconstitution. It is essential that the concluding chapter place these issues in relief.

---

[1] For a discussion of this point see J. L. Talmon, *The Rise of Totalitarian Democracy* (Boston: The Beacon Press, 1952), pp. 135 ff.

FIGURE A

Sketches of Major Movements

Movement	Starting Point	Nature of Man	Attitude toward Power	Justification for the Use of Power	Means of Resolving Conflict and Reducing the Necessity for Employing Power
1. Scientific management..........	The collective entity (the organization)	Weak and corrupt		Necessary for maintaining order and getting people to act in a way alien to their nature	Mutuality of interests through productivity
2. Human relations...	The collective entity (the organization)	Good, plastic, capable of wide differences among individuals	To keep power submerged as far as possible beneath the surface of interpersonal relations, particularly superior-subordinate relations	Necessary to preserve order and induce organizational solidarity	Integration of interests through manipulation of needs and need satisfactions
3. Industrial humanism..........	Man (reason)	Good, infinitely plastic, and capable of perfectibility		Necessary to hasten the progress of individual perfection and organization harmony	Personal awareness, interpersonal competence, and intergroup problem solving leading to the democratization of organization

Scientific Management

No doubt the starting point of scientific management is the organization. By improving its ability to produce, the dominance of its hierarchy is sustained, indeed, legitimated. Additionally, the natives within the organization are kept subdued. It is also a matter of record that Taylor at least, and perhaps his colleagues and those who followed them also, viewed the "operatives" as a restless and shiftless lot. This dismal perspective resulted from the notion that man is essentially weak and imperfect by nature. This was a not uncommon attitude during this period.[2]

These defects had to be compensated for by organizational change. Hence, the mechanisms of scientific management came into being. But beyond this, the underlying aim of scientific management was, as we have already seen, to create mutuality of interests through ever expanding productivity. This was the instrumentality which would resolve conflict. Because all (employers-employees) sharing in greater economic benefits would have no cause for quarrel. Thus, power in the form of coercion would be unnecessary, or more precisely, it would be submerged so deeply beneath the surface of superior-subordinate relationships that it would hardly be a factor except in extreme cases. However, in circumstances where the use of power was required, it could be justified on the grounds of order, ordained by the rights of property and the delegated rights of management. It would be used to overcome the weakness and corruption natural to man by forcing conformance to a system producing social utilities which demanded honest effort by those engaged in the production.

Human Relations

The sketch of human relations is harder to draw, because of the schizophrenic character of the doctrinaire mentality in this movement. Again the starting point for most human relationists is the organization. There must be little argument that the objective of the founders of this field, and its fervent advocates, is to improve the functioning of organizations by introducing a more rational form of management of men. That is, administrative skill would take into account human idiosyncrasies which were largely assumed away by scientific management. Thus, hopefully, the dominance of hierarchy would be preserved and legitimated by simultaneously producing economic utilities as well as satisfying the complex social and psychological needs of workers.

This latter feature of the human relations movement distinguishes it

---

[2] There is a dichotomy between economic thought and political philosophy. Basically the ideals of democracy conceived man as good and unsullied in his "natural state." Whereas, the assumption of "classic" economic thought looked upon man's nature as fallen and hence defective. There is no question about which line influenced scientific management the most.

sharply from scientific management. Human relationists admit the natural goodness of man; they call it human dignity. But further, they stress that man has a plastic nature, capable of acquiring greater degrees of goodness. Finally, the wide differences in human personality and motivation are not a source of confusing frustration to the human relationists. Rather, they are an opportunity to vary the organization and adjust leadership style to take maximum advantage of individual differences in the quest for the cooperative system. Therefore the aim of human relations is to motivate people to collaborate in a productive enterprise. Its promise is greater economic, social, and psychological well-being.[3]

One need only contrast the assumptions of McGregor's well-known Theory X and Theory Y to appreciate the differences between scientific management and human relations.[4] In fact let us do it now!

Assumptions of Theory X:
[Traditional management, often attributed to scientific management]
1. The average human being has an inherent dislike of work and will avoid it if he can.
2. Because of this human characteristic of dislike of work, most people must be coerced, controlled, directed, threatened with punishment to get them to put forth adequate effort toward the achievement of organizational objectives.
3. The average human being prefers to be directed, wishes to avoid responsibility, has relatively little ambition, wants security above all.

Assumptions of Theory Y:
[Enlightened management, at first associated with the human relations movement, later with industrial humanism]
1. The expenditure of physical and mental effort in work is as natural as play or rest.
2. External control and the threat of punishment are not the only means for bringing about effort toward organizational objectives. Man will exercise self-direction and self-control in the service of objectives to which he is committed.
3. Commitment to objectives is a function of the rewards associated with their achievement.
4. The average human being learns, under proper conditions, not only to accept but to seek responsibility.
5. The capacity to exercise a relatively high degree of imagination, ingenuity, and creativity in the solution of organizational problems is widely, not narrowly, distributed in the population.
6. Under the conditions of modern industrial life, the intellectual potentialities of the average human are only partially utilized.

----

[3] Keith Davis, *Human Relations at Work* (New York: McGraw-Hill Book Co., Inc., 1962), p. 4.

[4] Douglas McGregor, *The Human Side of Enterprise* (New York: McGraw-Hill Book Co., Inc., 1960), pp. 33–34 and 47–48. McGregor, of course, is not a human relationist in the "pure" sense. His work stands between, and is a kind of bridge from human relations to industrial humanism.

The human relationists' sentiment toward power is similar in one respect to the traditional. Power must be reduced as a regulating influence in organizational relationships. It should be supplanted by a system of management which stresses willing collaboration rather than control. But again the application of power, and indeed the justification of its use, is not ruled out when a "crisis" in human relations occurs. Power is justifiable to preserve the order underlying the dominance of hierarchy. This view comes from the traditional element in human relationist thinking taking its starting point from the collective entity. But the use of power is also justifiable to bring about organizational solidarity. In other words social harmony is as much a profitable organization concern as cost analysis, market penetration, or product development expenditures, *and it should be controlled as such*. As Davis unequivocally puts it, "controls, therefore, are necessary to ensure the degree of emphasis on human relations which is desired."[5]

Harmony, being a major goal of human relations, places high priority on satisfaction of social and psychological needs which if unattended might create conflict. As productivity was the instrumentality of harmony for scientific management, so participation, communication, and democratic leadership are the touchstones for human relations. Through these action-oriented devices, managers are supposedly capable of influencing human behavior for results which are satisfying and productive. If used skillfully, organizational conflict potential is reduced and the climate of work made rewarding.

In the psychological dimension, human needs in the organization are shaped (some prefer the word developed); and at the same time the organization itself undergoes a transformation to make it more conducive to want satisfaction of employees. The purpose of all this is to wrap up interpersonal conflict in a cocoon hoping that it does not undergo a metamorphosis and reappear in another hideous form. It is worth repeating that the object of most of these endeavors is the interactional climate existing between superiors and subordinates with special emphasis on workers and first-line supervision.

The manipulative overtones in the human relations movement along the social dimension are even clearer. The small group (informal organization) is, of course, a natural formation. Thus, attempts to eliminate it, and its communication arm—the grapevine—will create all sorts of trouble for the manager. Rather, the human relations strategy is for the manager to work with the small group, win the informal leader to his side, and tune in on the grapevine to find out how things are going. Therefore, the skillful manager can put the small group to work for the cause of formal organizational objectives by operating within the framework of natural human social tendencies rather than against it.[6]

---

[5] Davis, *op. cit.*, p. 67.

[6] *Ibid.*, pp. 255–56.

The critical aim of the human relations movement is the integration of individual goals, social and psychological, with those of the organization. This is the thrust of McGregor's argument, and it is reaffirmed by Davis. The principle as McGregor formulates it is, ". . . we seek that degree of integration in which the individual can achieve his goals *best* by directing his efforts toward the success of the organization."[7]

In this light, it is difficult to see *in principle* any real difference between the ultimate objectives of scientific management and human relations. Naturally scientific management took a simpler view of human motivation in its quest for mutuality of interests on purely the economic level. Whereas human relations, assuming a more complex interpretation of human behavior seeks integration on social and psychological levels as well.

Industrial Humanism

Because industrial humanism has a different starting point, its consequences are quite unlike those of the other movements. Industrial humanism begins with man rather than the collective entity of organization. It affirms that man can find fulfillment more adequately in an egalitarian environment where he has a high degree of self-determination. This kind of setting allows the individual to develop his fundamental goodness, and by his reasoning faculties progressively unfolded by education, he is able to reach higher levels of personal satisfaction.

Charles E. Merriam,[8] writing in the field of political science, states the case for industrial humanism and the application of democratic philosophy to organizations nicely. Paraphrasing him, he says, democracy:

1. Assumes the essential dignity of men plus the need of protecting and cultivating personality on an equal rather than hierarchial basis;
2. Assumes there is a steady trend in the "human condition" toward the perfectibility of man;
3. Assumes that organizational gains are basically the gains of people in them and the benefits (or satisfactions) flowing from these gains should be distributed as rapidly as possible to those responsible for them;
4. Assumes that those who are in organizations should be, in the last analysis, the source of consent for those who make policy and establish controls;
5. Assumes that change in the organization should be the product of full awareness of alternatives and consensus by participants.

Given an organization where these assumptions form a vital part of its operating philosophy, man's progress toward perfection and social harmony is hastened. As a result, is power ruled out as a means of influence

---

[7] McGregor, *op. cit.*, p. 55.

[8] Charles E. Merriam, *The New Democracy and the New Despotism* (New York: McGraw-Hill Book Co., Inc., 1939), pp. 12–38.

and control? The answer is no. But in no other movement is the problem of power more difficult to resolve.

Scientific management and human relations conceived of power as vested in the "establishment," and there is no nonsense about this. These movements, like industrial humanism, want to see power out of the sphere of interpersonal relationships. But their reasons are quite different. To the scientific manager, power is a costly and inefficient means for achieving compliance to productivity objectives. The human relationist would agree with this, and would add that a manager taking advantage of natural social and psychological propensities in man could widen the area of collaboration beyond the economic without recourse to power and coercion.

However, the industrial humanist, following the logic of his premises, must reject the dominance of hierarchy as repressive to man's emergence as a self-actualized human being. Yet power is present in the humanist's thesis all the same, for who is going to structure the climate of organization so that a rational kind of democracy based on individual sensitivity and interpersonal competence will emerge? The solution is those of the elite who are best able to "read" the wishes of the rank and file. Presumably the organizational elite, this new administrative breed, works with the spiritual mandate and the concrete consensus of those led. Hence the power to introduce democratic programs for the good of the people in the organization comes from the people themselves. So what is done by the elite to achieve democracy is done with the approval of the participants in order that they might enjoy a fuller life within the organization.

It has not gone unnoticed that this way of thinking allows a good deal of elbowroom for the elite to do a great deal of mischief. In fact, the need for "an enlightened few" to guide, educate, and remake the unenlightened many is an enduring dilemma in democratic theory. Does not this elite represent simply a different kind of hierarchical dominance? The formal answer to this question is that the elite acts as the consciousness of subordinates until they become fully aware to act in their own behalf.

REMAKING ORGANIZATIONS VERSUS CHANGING MAN

And so we have our sketches! What do they tell us? Let us review the similarity of the points.

1. All agree that organization change is necessary.

2. Each is a salvationist administrative creed which is supposed to settle a wide range of "people problems," including collaboration in a collective undertaking, morale, motivation, and productivity.

3. Because they are salvationist they visualize power, as an instrument of oppressive coercion in achieving collaboration, being proscribed to the extent that it is not a crucial factor in behavioral influence.

4. But while power has no role in the utopia visualized by these sketches, it

does have the interim function of sustaining either the organization in crisis situations when the dominance of herarchy is challenged, or in prodding individuals along the road to self-realization and social harmony.

Although these creeds share common characteristics, as most ideological thinking does, there are sharp differences among them. In fact scientific management and human relations have numerous areas of tangency, while they together differ radically from industrial humanism. The reason is their starting points.

Beginning with the collective entity, the organization, scientific management and human relations are committed to programs of modification in order to make the organization more in tune with assumed behavioral propensities in man *which are taken as givens.* Are not givens man's tendencies to seek economic gain, his self-interest, his desire to form informal groups, his need to communicate, his drive to fulfill psychological motives? And would not the organization be better off if these factors are considered when planning change, setting up incentives, and developing administrative skills? So the questions resolve to how best can the organization be remade and administrative practices modified so as to conform with these hypothesized attributes of "man's nature" without sacrificing the preeminence of the dominant hierarchy.

But these earlier schemes were not wholly satisfactory because they attempted to change institutions to correspond to these assumptions. In both scientific management and human relations man stayed the given and the organization provided the variable. This is true despite the fact that human relations, relying on the behavioral sciences, discovered more dimensions in the nature of man's behavior at work than those figured by scientific management to be relevant.

So then, even while human relations has a complex interpretation of behavior and a more optimistic outlook on the nature of man compared to scientific management, it, nevertheless, remains an instrument of hierarchy. Baritz' book makes this point with biting clarity especially in a chapter called "Human Relations and Power."[9] Baritz touches a sensitive issue here, although his position is overstated with respect to the boundless cynicism and crass motives he ascribes to business executives and behavioral scientists. Summing up his argument, Baritz observes, "many managers have not hesitated to make explicit the point that their use of social scientists and their skills is for the purpose of human control."[10]

The focus shifts suddenly when we pick up the strands of industrial humanism. Because, as we have said several times before, the starting point of this ideology is man. Now make no mistake, organizational change is as crucial a factor in industrial humanism as it is in scientific management and human relations. Indeed, the ways in which organizations should be

---

[9] Loren Baritz, *The Servants of Power* (Middletown, Conn.: Wesleyan University Press, 1960), chap. 10.

[10] *Ibid.,* p. 207.

remade, and the strategies for doing so, occupy the bulk of the writings of the humanists. But there is a critical difference between this ideology and the other two. It is best caught by Schlesinger's statement that, "the reform of institutions becomes an indispensable part of the enterprise of democracy. But the reform of institutions can never be a substitute for the reform of man."[11]

Taking this observation as a cue, let us see where it leads. According to the assumptions of democratic theory, for man to realize his dignity, goodness, and freedom requires the minimization of personal dependence. Put another way, *equality* is the indispensable component for individual happiness and social harmony. Essentially, then, man *is by nature* antiautocratic, antihierarchy, antitotalitarian. That man is "ungood," that he quarrels, and often does violent, antisocial things, results from faulty institutions which have kept him subjugated by hierarchy in an unfulfilled state. This, as democratic theory goes, is opposed to his instincts and his nature.

So, we may ask, if man is democratically inclined why does not he assert himself and cast off autocratic influences? The answer is that man has been kept ignorant and has been misled so long he has neither the moral fortitude nor the material means to do so. The vested interests, the dominant hierarchies, want to maintain the ignorance of their subjects for selfish reasons, rather than to promote the development of a virtuous, enlightened commonwealth.

Therefore, the reconstitution of man, who has been corrupted by evil institutions, has top priority in democratic theory. Reformed man is to be made aware of his dignity and freedom so that he will be able to participate in the democratic heritage of which he has been so long deprived. Thus the remaking of man is a process of democratization using education and dialogue as catalysts.

If we could say nothing else about industrial humanism, we could at least say with certainty that it is democratic to the core of its spirit. It clearly calls for molding man to accept, to vibrate in sympathy with, the ideals of democratic liberalism. Warren Bennis, more than any other writer has caught the thrust of this movement and has stated its premises well in his recent book. Summarizing the impact on management of democratic theory supported by the behavioral sciences he says that it has forced:

1. Reconceptualization of man [along the lines which we have already elaborated];
2. A new concept of power based on collaboration and reason;
3. A reformulation of organizational values reflecting a humanistic bias.

Warning, however, that utopia is not yet at hand Bennis goes on to say—

---

[11] Arthur S. Schlesinger, Jr., *The Vital Center* (Boston: Houghton Mifflin Co., 1949), p. 250.

The last thing I want to do is overstate the case, trapping us all in a false dream. I do not mean that these transformations of man, power, and organizational values are fully accepted, or even understood, to say nothing of implemented in day-to-day organizational affairs. These changes may be light-years away from actual adoption. I do mean that they have gained wide *intellectual* acceptance in enlightened management quarters, that they have caused a terrific amount of rethinking and search behavior on the part of many organizational planners, and that they have been used as a basis for policy formulation by certain large organizations, mainly industrial leviathans, but also by many other nonindustrial institutions.[12]

Bennis rightly emphasizes *intellectual* acceptance of democratic principles. However, that the democratization of organization is the wave of the future is more generally taken for granted by change agents and social consultants, then by practising managers. This ideological posture is in fact a logical necessity to the requisites of industrial humanism. A few examples show why.

1. *The democratic man is an aware man.* One conclusion we must underscore in the work of Maslow[13] and Argyris[14] is that the self-actualization process includes the development of democratic consciousness. As Maslow rhapsodizes:

> We must ultimately assume at the highest theoretical levels of eupsychian theory, a preference or tendency to identify with more and more of the world, moving toward the ultimate of mysticism, a fusion with the world, or peak experience, cosmic consciousness, etc.[15]

Somewhat more mundanely, as man becomes aware of himself and begins to realize his potential, he, at the same time, is sensitized to the feelings of others. But beyond this he learns the content of their interpersonal relations. Such consciousness, such awareness, is the blood and bone of finding consensus, which, in turn, is the essence of the democratic process.

2. *The democratic man is able to solve problems rationally and creatively through groups.* Blake, Shepard, and Mouton tell us that conflicts are not resolved effectively because of relational inadequacies between groups, or their representatives, at points of tangency in organizations.[16] Blake, and his co-authors see creative problem solving as the rational approach to conflict resolution between groups. By unrestrained communication between people who are skilled in effective social behavior, differences between groups may be settled and the grounds for conflict

---

[12] Warren G. Bennis, *Changing Organizations* (New York: McGraw-Hill Book Co., Inc., 1966), p. 188.

[13] Abraham H. Maslow, *Eupsychian Management* (Homewood, Ill.: Richard D. Irwin, Inc., 1965).

[14] Chris Argyris, *Personality and Organization* (New York: Harper and Bros., 1957).

[15] Maslow, *op. cit.*, p. 33.

[16] Robert R. Blake, Herbert A. Shepard, and Jane S. Mouton, *Managing Intergroup Conflict in Industry* (Houston, Tex.: Gulf Publishing Co., 1964).

eliminated. But what is most important is that authentic interactions produce innovative solutions to conflicts. Because these solutions are the product of joint group effort, they become the vehicles for securing intergroup cooperation. All this, provides the climate for an individual's commitment to wider intergroup goals, rather than to the narrow interests of the group with which he immediately identifies. This approach reflects the long-run gains of collaboration through reason. It contrasts with problem solving by win-lose conflict or raw coercion.

3. *Man's democratic inclinations are reinforced, rather than opposed, by organizational values.* Bennis comes through with clarity on this requisite. It boils down to the crucial matter of organizational health. Bennis observes the parallel between the criteria of organizational health and mental health: "to perceive reality, both internal and external, and to examine unflinchingly the positions of these realities in order to act intelligently."[17] These criteria hold equally for individuals and organizations.

From this general observation, Bennis draws three criteria of organization health.

a) *Adaptability*. The ability of an organization to learn and to change programs of action.

b) *Identity*. The ability of an organization to know what it is and what it stands for.

c) *Reality Testing*. The ability of an organization to know its field of relationships, and to appraise its role in it realistically.

It is evident that no organization which is healthy would embrace values and practices which were contrary to the nature and well-being of its participants. Reality testing helps find paths of action. But the problem remains of when reality testing is real and not merely a case of organizational self-delusion.

In his book, Sofer explores the application of psychotherapy in the field of social consultancy.[18] While he does not come to grips directly with the subject of democratic values, Sofer demonstrates a *method* by which organizations can be helped. That is, how they can be aided to identify themselves, adapt to change, and reality test their programs and policies.

There is in the literature much support for the idea that psychotherapeutic methods, primarily but not exclusively in the form of group therapy, are valuable ways of helping people and organizations solve problems of interpersonal and institutional effectiveness. However, this approach is not aimless from an ideological standpoint. As we have seen, social consultants, or change agents, go into organization requesting help

---

[17] Bennis, *op. cit.*, p. 51.

[18] Cyril Sofer, *The Organization from Within* (London: Tavistock Publications Ltd, 1961), esp. chap. 4.

with a predisposition toward democracy as a *desiratum* governing policy-making and administration. The methods suggested by Sofer and others are means to this end.

NOTES ON POWER AND LEGITIMACY

Power, as we have seen, is the ability to influence human action by control of a reward and punishment system. Most participants in society have some power—father over children, a clergyman over the faithful, an officer over soldiers, a gang leader over gang members. But our concern here is with the elites in a society who have sufficient power to influence the destinies of the many by commanding allegiance to their decisions. Of interest is the source of their power and the grounds for its justification. A subject like this could occupy volumes. But we need not engage in a lengthy discourse. We have to observe simply, on the basis of the three previous sketches, how the justification of organizational power has shifted.

It has been said that "sovereignty keeps watch over power." At one and the same time sovereignty grants power to its agents and controls its use. In the past various soverigns have been appealed to as the source of power. From God came the divine right of kings; from ownership of property came the delegated right to manage; from consensus of the people came the right to govern in democratic states and institutions. So then we find three sovereigns: God, property, and the people.

It is fairly clear that in the process of justifying power, elites (the dominant hierarchies) looked outside themselves to a sovereign source of power. At any particular time this source could have been God, property, or the people, or a combination of the three. This legitimating process is no different now than it has ever been. Only the grounds for justification have changed. God as the sovereign has today little relevance except in religious organizations; and so there remains property and the people. Of these two, property provides the traditional basis for justifying power; people provide, the more liberal or modern base of justification from the standpoint of administrative organizations.

We have already observed how scientific management and human relations were ideologies of the traditional establishment, of hierarchies which justified administrative dominance on the basis of derived rights of property. However, with the growth of important hierarchies such as government agencies, unions, and the separation of ownership from control in giant corporations, this means for legitimation of power is losing its persuasiveness. A new sovereign must rise. It has. It is the people. *This is the thrust of industrial humanism which sees in the process of democratization people in organization asserting their rights of sovereignty.*

Autocracy of the Right or Left?

Scientific management and human relations are the handmaidens of conservative autocracy in organizations. Industrial humanism aims to free man from this oppressive burden by substituting the sovereignty of the people. But is it not possible that one form of domination is merely replacing another? The chance that this will happen, and has happened in the past, is discussed by writers in political science. They call it totalitarian democracy. It is useful to quote two authors who address themselves to this point.

Talmon says:

> The very idea of a self-contained system from which all evil and unhappiness have been exorcised is totalitarian. The assumption that such a scheme of things is feasible and indeed inevitable is an invitation to a regime to proclaim that it embodies this perfection, to exact from its citizens recognition and submission and to brand opposition as vice or perversion.

> The greatest danger is in the fact that far from denying freedom and rights to man, far from demanding sacrifice and surrender, this system reaffirms liberty, man's self-interest and rights. It claims to have no other aims than their realization. Such a system is likely to become the more totalitarian precisely because it grants everything in advance, because it accepts all liberal premises a priori. For it claims to be able by definition to satisfy them by a positive enactment as it were, not by leaving them alone and watching over them from the distance. *When a regime is by definition regarded as realizing rights and freedom, the citizen becomes deprived of any right to complain that he is being deprived of his rights and liberties.*[19]

De Jouvenal observes:

> . . . popular sovereignty may give birth to a more formidable despotism than divine sovereignty. For a tyrant, whether he be one or many, who has, by hypothesis, successfully usurped one or the other sovereignty, cannot avail himself of the Divine Will, which shows itself to men under the forms of a Law Eternal, to command whatever he pleases. Whereas the popular will has no natural stability but is changeable; so far from being tied to a law, its voice may be heard in laws which change and succeed each other. So that a usurping Power has, in such a case, more elbow-room; it enjoys more liberty, and its liberty is the name of arbitrary power.[20]

These writers warn of an autocracy of the left whose power is legitimated in the name of the people. In a real sense, according to De Jouvenal, such an autocracy may be even more oppressive than that of the right. Because it is not bound by absolute laws either of God or those governing the use of property. Rather, it is free to interpret, as it sees fit, "the will of the people." And as Talmon says, how can the people complain since this form of domination exists in their name!

Of course, Talmon and De Jouvenal direct their criticisms at the state and the kind of government it embraces. But their points have significance for administrative organizations as well, since they are like political enti-

---

[19] Talmon, *op. cit.,* p. 35. Italics mine.

[20] Bertrand de Jouvenal, *Sovereignty* (Chicago: The University of Chicago Press, 1957), pp. 42–43.

ties with systems of governance. It is crucial, therefore, that we heed these objections to democracy in organizations. We must be aware that it has totalitarian pitfalls of a sort not dissimilar to the kinds which appear most objectionable in traditional systems of organizational government.

Indeed, these tendencies may be all the more dangerous. Remember in these pages we have been discussing the abstract reality sketches of doctrinaire mentalities representing movements whose goals are to alleviate the people problems of management. In the cases of scientific management and human relations, concrete applications of their principles have often resulted in a perversion of the utopian ends sought by these movements. How frequently have the claims of inhuman sweating of workers been aimed at scientific management, or cynical manipulation at human relations? Could not administrators managing in the name of industrial humanism be open to charges of exploiting people in the name of the people?

IS DEMOCRACY *REALLY* INEVITABLE?

In light of the foregoing discussion we must return to Bennis' "democracy is inevitable" proposition. We know from Chapter 13 that Bennis attributed shifting organizational values to both ideological and occupational determinates. He sees the organization of the future governed by values which reflect:

1. Full and free communication, regardless of rank and power.
2. A reliance on consensus, rather than on the more customary forms of coercion or compromise, to manage conflict.
3. The idea that influence is based on technical competence and knowledge rather than on the vagaries of personal whims or prerogatives of power.
4. An atmosphere that permits and even encourages emotional expression as well as task-oriented acts.
5. A basically human bias, one which accepts the inevitability of conflict between the organization and the individual but which is willing to cope with and mediate this conflict on rational grounds.[21]

Whether these are democratic or humanistic values is a matter of interpretation. However, Bennis chooses to call them democratic, so we really cannnot argue because it is a term with a variety of definitions. The question is if the democratic departure attempts to extract from the organizational condition more than there is in it in the first place? Can the will to dominate, the instinct of hierarchy, and the desire for personal power be supplanted in organizational life by free dialogue, rationality in conflict resolution, and consensus in decision making to the extent that

---

[21] Bennis, *op. cit.*, p. 19. For a different view of why democracy is not inevitable, see Otto Kirchheimer, "Private Man and Society," *Political Science Quarterly*, March, 1966, pp. 1–24.

people will have in the organization a vehicle for emotive and rational expression?

The industrial humanist will answer, yes: to a degree unknown in organizations of the past. We can find little to dispute in this position. It is good that organizations are offering a more fulfilling life to their participants whatever the causes are. Neither do we find much to quarrel with in the nature of the values themselves which make changes in administrative practices possible; that is, as long as the consequences lead to the rule of the rights of individuals in organizations rather than a substitute form of autocracy which merely draws its name from the people.

The main objection to "the democracy is inevitable proposition" grows out of its exclusiveness. It tends to close the intellectual door to other alternatives for organizational government except the one directly opposed to it—dominance of hierarchy. One gets the impression from the literature that the lines have been drawn. Choice is crystallized on two ideological alternatives between which there is very little chance for reconciliation. However, is it so clearly the case of either autocracy or democracy? Or is there evolving in organizational government a "third way" which has gone largely unnoticed? It is our feeling that there is another alternative. We call it the constitutionalization of organization and we trace its major aspects in the next section.

THE CONSTITUTIONAL ORGANIZATION

Now that we have criticized other authors' sketches of organizational reality, it is time to present one of our own. It is the movement toward the constitutionalization of the organization and it emphasizes the role of law in administrative relationships. Its purpose is to limit the arbitrary power of administrators with respect to their subordinates. The framework of the constitutional organization is a kind of legalism which emphasizes the rights of organizational participants as spelled out in pacts, covenants, or contracts. In addition to these "statutes" are systems of appeal which allow an individual to seek redress if he feels that his rights under the law of the organization have been transgressed by the actions of an administrator.

The "constitution" of an organization is not a single document. Rather, it is a body of agreements (some externally imposed, some internally generated, some formally explicit, some merely understood) which have arisen to govern administrative practices with respect to the rights of organizational participants. Certain of the forces which have created these laws are outside the organization, others stem from dynamics within. Of the former, we are familiar with, for example, the impact of unionism on management and the effect of public policy on the affairs of business organizations. These external determinants of organizational law are enormously important in understanding the body of individual rights which cover matters ranging from employment security to fair employment practices. Of similar significance are the various arrangements by which individual appeals may be heard through grievance procedures in union contracts or hearing boards in regulating government agencies.

Lesser known, but of almost equal importance, are the system of rights, duties, and obligations of individuals which arise out of the processes of organizational life itself. These intraorganizational laws, and provisions for appeal under them, have received little formal treatment in the past. We restrict our discussion in the remaining pages of this chapter to these latter developments, fully appreciating the role played by extraorganizational forces in molding the character of organizational law.

Assumptions of the Constitutional Organization

A priori assumptions about the inherent goodness or defectiveness of man, and the efficacy or undesirability of a dominant hierarchy are not essential to this sketch. Rather, the operational assumption with which we start is that man is a political animal and the collective entities in which he seeks collaborative goals are governmental systems.[22] In this light, power, in the words of Merriam is ". . . a phenomenon of group cohesion and aggregation, a child of group necessity or utility, a function of the social relations of men."[23] Thus power in interpersonal relations does not have to be swept under the rug or wished away. The justification of its use is in the interest of the aggregate governed, but with due regard for individual rights determined by extra and internal organizational influences. These influences may take many forms; that is, the law may be formulated in many ways; by unilateral formulation of bureaucratic rules, by win-lose struggles between contending parties at interest, by bargaining and compromise, or by rational problem solving. But regardless of how the law comes to be, it is the basis governing interpersonal relationships. We recognize, as well, that a law may be a just one or unjust. And also that equity is a paramount issue.

Administrative Behavior and Constitutionalization

We have argued elsewhere[24] that bureaucratic processes have within them the germs of constitutional practices. In this discussion we relied heavily on an analysis by Howard M. Vollmer. It is useful to review the main dimensions of his approach here, elaborating on it when appropriate.

---

[22] We are not using an analogy here. Any organization, political, economic, social, religious, is a system of government. It is concerned with the legislation and execution of policy and the implementation of justice under the law.

[23] Charles E. Merriam, *Political Power* (Glencoe: The Free Press, 1950), p. 16.

[24] William G. Scott, *The Management of Conflict* (Homewood, Ill.: Richard D. Irwin, Inc., 1965), chaps. 4 and 5.

Vollmer's study, *Employee Rights and the Employment Relationship*[25] is about the impact of the bureaucratic process upon personnel and human relations practices in large organizations. Vollmer is concerned with how organizations try to achieve Chester I. Barnard's imperatives of technical effectiveness and human efficiency. Faced with increasing size and complexity of interdependence, administrators seek both Barnard's aims to improve cooperation. It is well to quote Vollmer regarding what these efforts mean in administrative practices which have bearing on the rights of organizational participants.

[Noting that bureaucratization involves the proliferation of rules, Vollmer points out] . . . the rules which have developed with regard to selection, lay-off and retention, promotion, and discipline and discharge have resulted in significant limitations upon the arbitrary exercise of managerial prerogative and power. These limitations are not simply the result of trade union pressures through collective bargaining; they are more in the nature of self-restraint which managements have imposed upon themselves as a result of organization needs for coordination, specialization, and personnel regulation. Thus, management, motivated by considerations of technical effectiveness in achieving organizational goals, has been impelled to systematize authority relationships, to differentiate functional specialties, and to establish personnel regulations—yet the very system and rules they have established have become commitments which have tended to bind the hands of the rulemakers themselves. What is more, most large businesses have established personnel offices or agencies to maintain and implement these mechanisms of self-restraint. Finally, the nature of the self-restraint imposed as a result of the process of bureaucratization may be expressed most generally in the principle of "equal treatment for all employees."[26]

On the other hand, the need for industrial enterprises to utilize their employees in the manner most *efficient* for the achievement of organizational goals and for the satisfaction of individual needs has resulted in the development of human relations practices. An important aspect of these practices has been the attention given to either changing or manipulating individual employees' needs and interests in directions more amenable to organizational goals, or adapting organizational goals to certain individual needs. In both cases, human relations practices have resulted in the self-imposition of restraints upon management—that is, management has become committed to some degree of flexibility in the application of rules and regulations to individual cases. This flexibility over time has, in turn resulted in common expectations among employees and management officials that individual needs and interests will be respected and retained in the relationship of employment.[27]

It is evident that the first paragraph refers to the efforts of administrators to secure *effectiveness* in personnel practices by the uniform regula-

---

[25] Howard M. Vollmer, *Employee Rights and the Employment Relationship* (Berkeley: University of California Press, 1960).

[26] *Ibid.,* pp. 17–18, used with permission.

[27] *Ibid.,* p. 61, used with permission.

tion of actions affecting the employment status of organizational participants. The second paragraph deals with efforts to promote *efficiency* by allowing decision flexibility in the administration of rules for individual cases.

An idea common to both paragraphs is *managerial self-restraint*. In the first instance restraint comes from the self-imposition of rules. Merriam says in this regard:

> The ruler finds it difficult to escape from the world of law which he himself and his system have invoked. The most errant impostor may thus find himself irrevocably committed to a system which no longer allows him that untrammeled liberty of choice and action, which he may dearly love but which by virtue of his very power escapes him. His sense of power is once more reduced to the dream world from which it came, and its earthly shape eludes him. So it may be said, the price of power is limitation. The ruler is ruled by his own rules.[28]

In the second instance, mutual behavioral expectations, resulting from precedents based upon prior administrative actions, arise between subordinates and superiors. Consistency must be preserved in these relationships otherwise there is no ground for anticipation of behavior which is the interpersonal bulwark of organizational stability. The crucial element for our purpose in this case is the personal knowledge of the organizational participant that even in the face of rules "individual needs and interests will be respected and retained."

Finally, Vollmer sees the personnel department as the agency which maintains the rules of personnel practice and secures consistency of interpersonal relations. In other words, the personnel department polices the system of self-restraints imposed by administrators on themselves or evolved out of the dynamics of human interaction. Figure B is a schematic of the process discussed in this section.

So slowly and hesitantly, different from one organization to another, arises a quasi-legal environment based on rules which crystallize and stabilize organizational government. From the standpoint of the dominant hierarchy, self-limitation of power means turning its back on the sovereignty which permits arbitrary actions toward subordinates. At the same time, accepting rules, both formal and informal, restricts subordinate sovereignty to act outside the framework of the rules in the name of mass consensus. The point, or better, the range where these mutual limitations on their respective sovereignties find tangency is where the substantive aspects of the organizational constitution are found.

Convergence and Divergence of Interests

As we have said, the organizational constitution represents the place or places where the sovereign interests of the dominant hierarchy and organ-

---

[28] Merriam, *Political Power, op. cit.*, pp. 19–20.

izational participants are tangent. This is not to say that the sovereignty of either domain is forsaken. Rather, it is where both sovereignties recognize and agree upon the terms of their relationship. Concretely, they may cover formalistically, for example, organization-wide rules of tenure. Or, informally within a single organizational unit, special rules could evolve regulating a coffee break.

Now, of course, these tangency points are established in many ways. They may appear as the result of trading relationships and transactions of kinds discussed by Sayles.[29] Also they may come from rational problem solving emphasized by Blake, Shepard, and Mouton.[30] They may grow out of stress reduction behavior in conflict situations considered by Kahn et al.[31] Or they may be the product of the bureaucratic process of

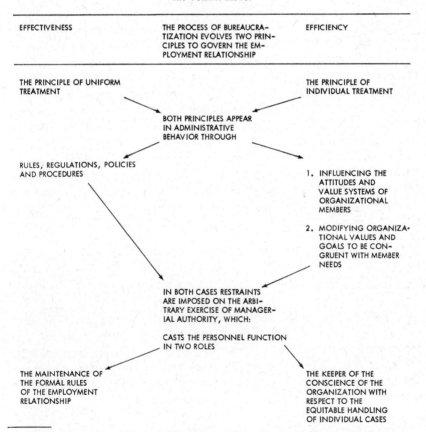

FIGURE B
The Vollmer Model

EFFECTIVENESS

THE PROCESS OF BUREAUCRA-
TIZATION EVOLVES TWO PRIN-
CIPLES TO GOVERN THE EM-
PLOYMENT RELATIONSHIP

EFFICIENCY

THE PRINCIPLE OF UNIFORM
TREATMENT

THE PRINCIPLE OF
INDIVIDUAL TREATMENT

BOTH PRINCIPLES APPEAR
IN ADMINISTRATIVE
BEHAVIOR THROUGH

RULES, REGULATIONS, POLICIES
AND PROCEDURES

1. INFLUENCING THE
ATTITUDES AND
VALUE SYSTEMS OF
ORGANIZATIONAL
MEMBERS

2. MODIFYING ORGANIZA-
TIONAL VALUES AND
GOALS TO BE CON-
GRUENT WITH MEMBER
NEEDS

IN BOTH CASES RESTRAINTS
ARE IMPOSED ON THE ARBI-
TRARY EXERCISE OF MANAGER-
IAL AUTHORITY, WHICH:

CASTS THE PERSONNEL FUNCTION
IN TWO ROLES

THE MAINTENANCE OF
THE FORMAL RULES
OF THE EMPLOYMENT
RELATIONSHIP

THE KEEPER OF THE
CONSCIENCE OF THE
ORGANIZATION WITH
RESPECT TO THE
EQUITABLE HANDLING
OF INDIVIDUAL CASES

[29] Leonard Sayles, *Managerial Behavior* (New York: McGraw-Hill Book Co., Inc., 1964).

[30] Blake, Shepard, and Mouton, *op. cit.*

[31] Robert L. Kahn *et. al.*, *Organizational Stress* (New York: John Wiley and Sons, Inc., 1964).

formalization which this author has investigated.[32] Any one or a combination of these forces contribute to the "writing of the law of organizations." These processes may be thought of as leading to a convergence of interests between the sovereignties in the organization as a whole or localized (departmentalized) segments within it.

Thus, there are three realms of interest between sovereigns: those converging, those diverging, and those emerging. Convergent interests represent the sphere of sovereign relationships which have been constitutionalized. That is the law has been established and the parties live under it. This does not mean that these relationships will not change or that they have been removed from the subject of further negotiation. They are less a source of on-going tension and conflict as the other areas.

The areas of divergent interests are those where the issues are clear but the conflicts unresolved. However, the protocols are established for reconciliation, but the substantive terms of the constitutions are not decided.

Finally, the emerging areas of interest are undefined. Thus their substantive nature and dimensions are ambiguous. But, what is more important, the protocols for resolving conflicts of interest here have not been established. It is in these emerging regions that the most dramatic changes in organizational relationships happen.

The Difficult Matter of Justice and Equity

It takes very little understanding of organizational realities to appreciate that the strengths of sovereignties are not equal. The dominant hierarchy usually outweighs the domain of organizational participants. And, thus, it is able to impose its will on the other in formulating the terms of the constitution. Just a modest acquaintance with the history of labor in this country is needed to know that some compacts in the employment relationship are so one-sided that great inequities are heaped upon one of the sovereignties. To right these wrongs and to find a modicum of justice, recourse to extraorganizational influence had to be made. Therefore, the union and the government entered the picture to support those who lack the strength to establish equitable terms along the economic dimensions of the constitutions.

But it is unduly limiting to speak of constitutional processes solely in terms of the economics of labor-management relations. As we observed earlier in this Epilogue, the thrust of the industrial humanism movement has been to strengthen the sovereignty of organization participants with respect to the dominant hierarchy. This means that other dimensions of satisfaction must be achieved in addition to economic. That these satisfactions will be meaningful outside a constitutional framework is doubtful.

---

[32] Scott, *op. cit.*

Selznick and Vollmer make this point explicit in an important article.[33] In their research they found that most of their subjects want a rule-governed environment. But they want different rules which not only preserve uniformity in employment relationships, but are sufficiently flexible to account for and reward individual differences in interest and achievement.

When we reach the end of the analysis we find that the significance of the modern movement of industrial humanism is the enfranchisement of organizational participants. Not that the dominant hierarchy is superseded by an anarchy. Rather, the spirit of the trend is for something like greater equivalence of power to exist between the sovereigns so that the participants have a real voice in structuring and changing the terms of the constitution under which both parties live. Presumably, through participation in the governmental processes of organizations the balance of power in organizations can be shifted.

---

[33] Philip Selznick and Howard Vollmer, "Rule of Law in Industry," *Industrial Relations*, May, 1962, pp. 97–116.

INDEXES

Name Index

Subject Index

This book has been set in 10 pt. Janson with Caledonia Bold italic and 9 pt. Janson, both leaded 2 pts. Part numbers are 30 pt. Alternate Gothic; part and chapter titles, 24 pt. Alternate Gothic. Chapter numbers are 14 pt. Alternate Gothic. The size of the type page is 27 by 47 picas.